AF680591

Socio-Cybernetic Study of God and the World-System

Masudul Alam Choudhury
Sultan Qaboos University, Muscat, Sultanate of Oman
& Trisakti University, Jakarta, Indonesia

Information Science
REFERENCE
An Imprint of IGI Global

Managing Director: Lindsay Johnston
Production Manager: Jennifer Yoder
Publishing Systems Analyst: Adrienne Freeland
Development Editor: Allyson Gard
Acquisitions Editor: Kayla Wolfe
Typesetter: Christina Barkanic
Cover Design: Jason Mull

Published in the United States of America by
Information Science Reference (an imprint of IGI Global)
701 E. Chocolate Avenue
Hershey PA 17033
Tel: 717-533-8845
Fax: 717-533-8661
E-mail: cust@igi-global.com
Web site: http://www.igi-global.com

Copyright © 2014 by IGI Global. All rights reserved. No part of this publication may be reproduced, stored or distributed in any form or by any means, electronic or mechanical, including photocopying, without written permission from the publisher.
Product or company names used in this set are for identification purposes only. Inclusion of the names of the products or companies does not indicate a claim of ownership by IGI Global of the trademark or registered trademark.

Library of Congress Cataloging-in-Publication Data

Choudhury, Masudul Alam, 1948-
Socio-cybernetic study of God and the world-system / by Masudul Alam Choudhury.
pages cm
Includes bibliographical references and index.
ISBN 978-1-4666-4643-8 (hardcover) -- ISBN (invalid) 978-1-4666-4644-5 (ebook) -- ISBN 978-1-4666-4645-2 (print & perpetual access) 1. Islamic ethics. 2. Ethics--Religious aspects--Islam. 3. Knowledge, Theory of (Islam) I. Title.
BJ1221.C46 2014
297.5--dc23
2013025031

British Cataloguing in Publication Data
A Cataloguing in Publication record for this book is available from the British Library.

All work contributed to this book is new, previously-unpublished material. The views expressed in this book are those of the authors, but not necessarily of the publisher.

The Socio-Cybernetic Entirety

Two things fill the mind with ever new and increasing awe and admiration the more frequently and continuously reflection is occupied with them; the starred heaven above me and the moral law within me. I ought not to seek either outside my field of vision, as though they were either shrouded in obscurity or were visionary. I see them confronting me and link them immediately with the consciousness of my existence (Kant, 1949).

Kant, I. (1949). Critique of Pure Reason. In Friedrich, C. J. (Ed.), *The Philosophy of Kant*. New York, NY: Modern Library.

This book is dedicated to the memory of my dear friend, colleague, and active academic worker to the end of his earthly life in establishing the monotheistic worldview in the worldly functioning of economy, society, and institutions, Professor Dr. Sofyan Syafri Harahap, Professor of Accounting, Dean, Faculty of Economics, Director, Postgraduate Program in Islamic Economics and Finance, Trisakti University, Jakarta, Indonesia.

Table of Contents

Chapter 7

Chapter 8

Foreword

Scarcity of resources, unlimited wants, self-interested individuals, maximization, Darwinian competition, substitution at the margin…these familiar concepts and analytical tools of neoclassical economics led us to a particular understanding of the world as it is, with the rider that it was difficult to improve the situation by regulation or reorientation. Marxism disagreed but failed to improve in any abiding way. Everybody took materiality for granted and failed to connect man with God, the here with the Hereafter.

Masudul Alam Choudhury, a prolific writer who has several times published in critique of modern approaches during the last 30 years, will have none of these. He presents a convincing case for abandoning materialistic, individualistic, competitive approaches to the understanding and bettering of man's economy, pointing out to all the Katrinas, Chernobyls, Enrons, AIGs, the recurring financial crises, and increasing inequality within and between nations. He is especially irritated by some academicians' efforts to convince us that these are prices we must pay for the unprecedented prosperity we are enjoying. He does not recognize the anxiety-increasing prosperity and does not concede it was necessary to pay that price.

Choudhury presents his holistic, integrative, and participatory needs-focused vision of a human society at peace with the environment, because of its reaching out to God and also because of its taking the Hereafter into consideration in calculations done in the context of bettering the living conditions here on earth. The secret lies in abandoning the space-time bound material world for the unlimited possibilities of the three-dimensional world of knowledge-time-space. Knowledge revealed as well as acquired through observation and experimentation plays a key role in our writer-philosopher's system. The failure to realize the potentialities of knowledge in cementing relationships—between man and man, man and the cosmos, and man and God—lies at the root of all the limitations from which current social theories suffer. Economics remains neglectful of the resource creating capability of knowledge.

There could never be scarcity in a knowledge-based world system. The source of knowledge must be brought in to remove these limitations. The first gain will be admittance of ethics and morality in social analysis. A quest for fairness is embedded in human nature, supported by a sense of right and wrong (ethics) and the recognition of the good from the bad (morality). Economics and social sciences in general have been ignoring this reality, led by an unrealistic notion of rationality pervading human behavior.

Choudhury appreciates A. K. Sen's views on development and his critique of the economists' definition of efficiency. Quoting Quran (17:70), Choudhury puts human dignity ahead of material fulfillment and self, though both necessary in themselves. As a pillar of his social system and cybernetic view, the consultative organization of life (Islamic term shura) acts as participation in social decision-making. This organizational arrangement reforms social as well as economic life. Information asymmetry, agency problems and all, are taken care of in his integrated system focused on sustainability rather than accelerating growth.

Before Choudhury's man enters the market, he is a member of a family. It is in the cooperative, integrative, loving, and caring environment of the family (not in the "competitive" market of the economists' imagination) that man's behavioral norms are formed and altruistic values thrive. There is no reason to believe, no evidence to prove, that men and women deliberately suppress these values, giving an upper hand to uncaring maximization of private gains once they enter the marketplace. This applies to all human civilizations.

Particularly in the Islamic civilization, economic philosophers discussed managing the home (tadbir e manzil) before they bothered with international trade. For example, al-Farabi (d.950AD) contended that the way to get ahead of other nations was not the Islamic focus. Rather, it was how to build a prosperous and contented house to hold in a society where people care for one another. That approach would have far-reaching consequences were it to be adopted today for studying the global village.

Unfortunately, having opened this vista, our author failed to focus and explore the far-reaching possibilities this offered. Did Muslim intellectuals of the past study the connection between the family and the market? The same person nursing a newborn or taking care of a parent in terminal illness, what happens to him as he enters into trade negotiations across borders? People taking the risks of maritime trade before the age of insurance, did they involve their kith and kin in the affair? It is not only the spiritual and intellectual possibilities that need to be explored. What does reality say? Are any empirical studies available: If so, to what results?

Shah Waliullah Dehlawi's (d. 1762AD) Hujjat Allah al-Balighah, is, perhaps, the last of the classics on Islamic social sciences discussing family (tadbir e manzil), market behavior, and cooperation as the crux of man's economy, all in the same book. The few writings on early Islamic economic thought making the rounds (including the ones written by the writer of this foreword) hardly follow that line of approach. Alas, our author of the day also failed to do so. One has to keep waiting for "the spark from heaven to come!"[1]

MAN AND MONEY

Our author has a lot to say about money and finance. It would be difficult to summarize it or discuss its potentialities in a few lines. The most important conclusion is the rate of interest's tendency to obstruct the flow of money to the real economy where a productive role awaits it. He sees "interest as impediment to wellbeing and resource mobilization." Guaranteed repayment with a positive return makes money a tool for playing games of chance and exploiting those facing difficulties in life. Projected to international relations, debt-financing with interest has the potential of destroying nations and disrupting world peace. That is exactly what it has been doing throughout history. Remove the institution of interest payment and you have a society in which trade between people results in production of the good things of life and their distribution through needs-focused institutions. There is an inverse relationship between trade in the good things of life and the rate of interest. When people's savings are mobilized through trade-related instruments, they go on to finance real sector development. On the other hand, savings mobilized by conventional banks through rate of interest do not necessarily end up financing real sector development. The author champions the cause of Islamic banks replacing interest with trade-related financial instruments.

Choudhury rightly rejects the idea of money being a means of exchange over time. Neither equivalence nor fairness can be ensured in exchange of money for money over time. Money serves only two basic functions, namely unit of account and measure of value, but "overtime there cannot be valuation of money as medium of exchange or unit of value." "Money is thereby a convenience to value prices, but it does not exist in the absence of goods in exchange in the first place."

In the intertemporal case of resource mobilization, it is difficult to ascertain the state of demand and supply of goods and services at future time-periods. It is also difficult to ascertain the risk-contingencies that exist at future points of time. Also, consumer preferences, systemic risk, and costs of future flows of goods and services, and financial demand in projects are based on subjective factors and are thus undeterminable. Consequently, it is impossible to ascertain the value of goods and services in exchange, and thereby, the value of money that would back up such a real economic value. Therefore, money does not have any market of its own, which otherwise results in interest rates as the price of money and financial instruments.

As regards time, which marks the intertemporal change as in monetary allocation, Choudhury points out: "Time cannot be a factor of change, knowledge can." Time simply records change.

In Choudhury's schema, gold and silver play a pivotal role. He proposes a hundred percent reserve against currency backed by gold/silver kept as reserve in the central bank vaults. Both parts of the scheme, 100 percent reserve and use of gold and silver as reserve, are controversial, with a lot of literature for and against. There is no way these controversies can be resolved in a short note like this foreword. What must be commented on is the sanctity given to the author's gold-centered schema in this book.

As Ibn e Taymiya (d.1328 AD) made clear, money is a matter of convenience, and so is the commodity (or non-commodity?) people find suitable for being used as money. The contrary view, claiming Allah made gold and silver to be used as money, held by Ghazali (d.1111AD) and Ibn e Khaldun (d. 1406 AD) has no basis in the texts of the Quran and Sunnah. A famous narration in Imam Malik's Muwatta substantiates Ibn e Taymiya's stand. It reports the second Caliph, Syedna Umar bin Khattab proposing to deal with shortage in money supply by making money coins out of camel's hide. The idea was soon abandoned when it was pointed out that it would surely result in drying up of camel supply.

Dr. Choudhury is free to support his stand by reason as well as empirical evidence, but he better avoid involving God in this matter. For God has already spoken to man for the last time, and gold standard is not there in what He said! Like the other technological matters, the ways and means of managing money is left for man to decide.[2] That any choice about what to use as money and how to regulate its supply is likely to have ethical/moral implications is nothing unique to this matter. All technological choices share that characteristic.

All in all: thank you, our Philosophe! Though I have yet to meet a person who claims to comprehend you 100 percent, even my meager capacities are sufficient to admire the lofty structure of the edifice, the breadth of your vision, and the abounding self-confidence you exude in these turbulent times. Wish you Godspeed!

Mohammad Nejatullah Siddiqi
Aligarh Muslim University, India

Mohammad Nejatullah Siddiqi is Professor Emeritus, Aligarh Muslim University, Department of Business Administration, 2010, was awarded King Faisal International Prize for Islamic Studies, 1982, the Shah Waliullah Award, Institute of Objective Studies, New Delhi, May 2003, the American Finance House Award, 1993, the Award for Life-Long Contributions to Islamic Insurance and Banking, Takaful Forum, New York. He was a Distinguished University Professor at the International Islamic University, Kuala Lumpur, Malaysia, August-September 2006, Visiting Scholar, Islamic Research and Training Institute, Islamic Development Bank, Jeddah, Saudi Arabia, November 2002 - April 2003, a fellow, Center for Near Eastern Studies, University of California, Los Angeles, Fall 2001, Professor of Economics, King Abdulaziz University, Jeddah, Saudi Arabia, 1978 – 2000, and Professor of Islamic Studies, Aligarh Muslim University, India, 1977 – 1983.

ENDNOTES

1 Although this is my viewpoint, the author of the book contends that in his theory of the family in the system and cybernetic framework he has endeavored to accomplish the general framework of the family in a good society, reconstructing a fallen acquisitive.

2 The author of the book however contends that he has asserted such an alternative choice, holding money circulation in a money-real economy, creating an interactive and integrative socio-cybernetic system in other forms, such as paper, promissory notes, contracts, including asset-backed gold valuation of contracts. The author contends that by including God in his socio-cybernetic system of study, he has focused on the monotheistic law at work in its most efficacious form as determined by analytical wisdom using the episteme of oneness.

Preface

The socio-scientific and cybernetic study of God in the world-system is a scholarly and applied work involving mind-matter interrelations in reference to the role that morality and ethics play in the transformation of "everything" according to the monotheistic law. A system is defined by its internal dynamics of causality as well as the evolutionary dynamics of the continuity of such inner dynamics across continuums of events and change. Such systemic dynamics together lead to the attainment of certain objective criterion. In received socio-scientific theory, causality explaining mind-matter dynamics starts from and ends up in the continuum of space-time. This causes constriction of reasoning to the order of materiality. Yet it is deeply ingrained in received socio-scientific worldview thoroughly. No demand for moral and ethical inquiry along with the embedding of the material socio-scientific order in these values is invoked.

On such a mind-matter phenomenology writes Hawking and Mlodinow (2010, p. 44):

For example, according to the principles of quantum physics, which is an accurate description of nature, a particle has neither a definite position nor a definite velocity unless and until those quantities are measured by an observer. It is therefore not correct to say that a measurement gives a certain result because the quantity being measured had that value at the time of the measurement. In fact, in some cases individual objects don't even have an independent existence but rather exist only as part of an ensemble of many.

On a similar nature of formalism in the social sciences Wallerstein (1998, p. 57) writes:

For social science, the rise of complexity studies represents an epistemological revolution. On the other hand, it undermines totally the basis of the eternal TimeSpace, while at the same time rejecting that of episodic, geopolitical TimeSpace, substituting for it the rules of social processes for as long as these rules are relevant. For the "orders" that are represented by these rules constantly yield place to periods and loci of chaos" out of which new "orders" are constantly generated. This is precisely the concept of structural TimeSpace with cyclico-ideological TimeSpace located within it, coming to moments of transformational TimeSpace.

Much earlier the principal proponent of space-time conception, Einstein (1954, p. 155) wrote: "There is no such thing as an empty space, i.e. a space without field. Space-time does not claim existence on its own, but only as a structural quality of the field."

These viewpoints by leading proponents of western socio-scientific thinkers establish the domain over which its reasoning prevails. Yet, if the space-time domain of continuum is expanded to include the knowledge dimension, then substantive new thoughts and consequences can be attained. Many revolutionary consequences on reasoning, formalism, derivation of thought, and application in the real world can be grappled with. The nature of events (occurrences, experiences, concrescence, and observations), and their explanation in the expanded dimensions of knowledge, time, and space are introduced for intellection and moral reconstruction of a deficient world-system. The quandary of critical examination of socio-scientific doctrines is now engulfed in the following question: Which comes first, knowledge or time to explain socio-scientific entirety (Choudhury, 2009)?

The answer to this quandary is not a simple one. The enforcing of a perspective of knowledge of the rationalistic construct in explaining phenomenon is an unacceptable starting point. The answer to the quandary is not well resolved by the exercise of rationalism as an epistemology followed by its prototypes. Examples of such prototypes are economic rationality, and a meaning of rational conduct in social choices. Just a few examples here will prove the vacuity of such treatments in the construction of the rationalistic world, whose constriction is narrowly bounded by the space-time dimensions. Credence in such explanations is given to the limits of material order alone. The mind then relents to the immanent understanding of reality. Consequently, the mind-matter consciousness of reality begins and ends within this narrow and constricted rationalistic worldview.

Yet the *functional* ontology of such a constricted worldview washes away the substantive consideration of the great threshold of knowledge, the nature of knowledge, and its power to enable organic learning in the open world-system of knowledge, time, and space dimensions. In the emergent learning multiverse, in which particulars form subsets of the generalized or universal worldview, knowledge and the world-system assume a coherent methodology and its *functional* ontological formalisms.

The concept of multiverse presented in this book in the context of the learning universe governed by epistemic unity of knowledge is quite different from the idea given in the literature. Hence, our conception of multiverse is an originality and advancement of the general theory of unity of knowledge and its relationship with the world-system. In the literature, Elis (2008, pp. 59-60) presents the mainstream idea of multiverse in the following words that show that the sub-systems of this conception of multiverse are disjointed from each other:

Then we can reserve Multiverse for a collection of genuinely disconnected cosmological spacetimes – those which are not locally causally related. When the discussion pertains equally well to disjoint collections of universes (multiverses in the strict sense) and to the different domains of a multi-domain universe, I will refer to as Ensemble of Universes, or Ensemble for short.

Hence, such sub-systems cannot be relational, and therefore not of the cybernetic nature. Thereby, the substantive need for learning universes remains in abeyance. The emergent universes of intellection and cognition are incapable of establishing causality and unification between them. The evolution of such separable universes intra- and inter-systems by learning under the universal and unique episteme of unity of knowledge is impossible. The resulting sub-systems of the mainstream conception of multiverse turn out to be differentiated new universes as extensions of the physical and social orders that are newly discovered, but not out of the continuums of learning domains, rather without any systemic continuity existing across continuums.

The following are examples in the two kinds of multiverse conceptions: Incomplete market due to the absence of information exists as disjointed domain in the mainstream conception of the economic multiverse, but then no valuation can be done in this market, no inferences can be drawn, no moral and social choices can be attained, etc. On the other hand, an incomplete market in our conception of multiverse is a concept of incessantly new learning that emerges as continuum of the prevalent market. They are caused by product and technological diversifications, innovation, and discovery. Information is never complete, and the markets learn at different levels reaching out for the ever mores that are constructed out of interactive and integrative learning between participants in respect of the verity of issues and problems pertaining to the intellectual quest.

Another example of a phenomenon in the physical world-system is that of the Black Hole. The Black Hole was once thought to be black due to the disappearance of matter and energy falling into its Ergodic region (Wald, 1992). Hence, no information could be retrieved. Yet the *evaporating* Black Hole can exude information as found in recent studies (Hawking, 1988).

Therefore, where can a primordial epistemic premise of the multiverse, existing in knowledge, time, and space dimensions be discovered? Rationalism as doctrin cannot help us out here, as long as its worldview remains constricted within the limits of space-time alone. Instead, in the pages of this book we have undertaken an analytical search for the primordial cause of knowledge and creation in the world-system entirety. Thereby, this book undertakes a critical examination of prevalent thoughts in the economic, financial, social, and scientific spheres. This ensemble presents our meaning of the world-system. It is also a cosmic entirety involving the total interrelationship between Mind and Matter in every system and cybernetic case by deductive and inductive reasoning. The end result has been to establish that the epistemological premise of rationalism cannot yield the substantive and sustainable worldview for explaining, formalizing, and applying the *functional* ontology (Gruber, 1993) of moral-social construction of the socio-scientific totality. Such a totality gives the meaning of the world-system of moral and ethical wellbeing that embeds by it all of materiality.

The primordial foundation of moral-social construction is discovered in this work in the ineluctable and irreducible foundation of the divine law of unity of knowledge and its induction of the unified (paired as complementary, participatory) world-system. This book searches for the most foundational episteme of discovering the unified world-system of Mind and Matter, of the moral and ethical embedding of the material order, and formalizing upon these a substantive analysis – all to lie in the monotheistic law of unity of knowledge. The permanence of this epistemic law is found to be indelible in the Islamic epistemological worldview of the monotheistic law relating to "everything." Most religions have thought about monotheism as the fundamental law. Hence, the primacy of the monotheistic law as the fundamental episteme of reality is common to all religions and people. A worldview premised on such a unique and universal law of unity of knowledge must therefore be appealing to all peoples with their diverse religious persuasions and cultural appeals.

On such a perspective of the monotheistic law and the world-system, Hallaq (2009, p. 83) writes (edited):

To sum up, the theological-epistemological premises of legal theory (objective and purpose of the Islamic law = maqasid as-shari'ah) set the stage for a legal project that is thoroughly religious in nature: thoroughly, in the sense that there is implied a continuous link between the guiding spirit of the Qur'an and the Prophethood lineage (Sunnah) (which ended with Muhammad).

This book is on *specific* applications taken up within the *generality* of the theory and application of epistemic unity. The elaborate philosophy of science derived from the *Qur'an* and the *Sunnah* in the understanding of the epistemic world-system governed by monotheistic dynamics can also be found in the author's *magnum opus* (Choudhury, 2006). This field of vast inquiry *res extensa* is not expounded in the present work. That is not the objective of this work. Instead, we formulate the essential dynamic and formal nature of the monotheistic law that works on and with the world-system. Thereby, the work applies the formal methodology of unity of knowledge derived in a formal way to specific world-system issues. The objective in the end is to bring out the remiss that has been created in the rationalistic orientation of socio-scientific intellection by leaving out God from the details of issues and problems comprising the world-system. Thereby, all of socio-scientific inquiry has remained devoid of an endogenous embedding of ethical and moral substance in it. Ethics and morality exist either as neutral elements or are exogenous elements in the study of details of the world-system.

A brief discussion, with details left for the ensuing pages of this book, on the concept of "universality," "uniqueness," and consequential prevalence of the episteme of unity of knowledge in "everything," may be highlighted now. At this point, these concepts will be summarized in a holistic form, leaving details for later analysis.

THE CYBERNETIC UNDERSTANDING OF THE PRECEPTS OF UNIVERSALITY, UNIQUENESS, AND "EVERYTHING"

In the cybernetic language of system-interaction and learning, we define universality as the prevalence of a perpetual law for all possible transformation of any sets of variables and their relations defined on anything. This is an acceptable definition of set-theory, which by its mathematical operations, does not differentiate between the nature of entities and their configurations. Thus, in this sense of the overarching mathematical existence of anything that is not restricted by its nature and configuration, we define universality by the crypt relationship: $\mathbf{x}(\theta) \in \Omega$, where $\mathbf{x}(\theta)$) denotes any element that is embedded in values of any kind denoted by θ, and Ω is the universal set. Therefore, *any* transformation (positive or negative) on $\{\mathbf{x}(\theta) \in \Omega\}$, denoted by $S(\{\mathbf{x}(\theta) \in \Omega; \{\theta\} \in \Omega\})$, becomes a candidate of $\{\theta \in \Omega\}$. However, in order to realize such transformations *on* Ω and *from* Ω *to* Ω, there must exist particular mathematical properties of the entire set, including the trifle $\mathbf{x}(\theta)$. That is, $[S(\{\mathbf{x}(\theta) \in \Omega$; with $\{\theta\} \in \Omega\})]$ remains well-defined on any and every set, $S(\{\mathbf{x}(\theta)\})$.

Note in this general definition of universality of Ω super-space, $\{\theta\} \in \Omega$ may represent either unity of knowledge or the rationalism based on multiplicity of episteme. Yet on the contrary, there is no way that rationalism can develop the theory and analytical dynamics of the episteme of unity of knowledge. Hence, the super-space, better noted as mathematical topology (Maddox, 1970; Dewitt, 1992), $[S(\{\mathbf{x}(\theta) \in \Omega$; with $\{\theta\} \in \Omega\})]$, remains unique as it is also universal by its most generalized mathematical property of the *res extensa* of reality.

Finally, by the generality and *res extensa* of functional ontologies generated on and by $[S(\{\mathbf{x}(\theta) \in \Omega$; with $\{\theta\} \in \Omega\})]$, this law overarches across both rationalism and the episteme of unity of knowledge. In other words, the episteme of unity of knowledge formalizes, analyzes, and applies to both the world of ethical and moral embedding by the monotheistic law and the episteme of rationalism. The tripartite circular relationship existing in continuity across continuums of the dimensions of knowledge, time, and space is now integrated into a consistent entirety as follows:

Formalism

$\cap(\Omega\leftrightarrow\Omega)$ decomposes into,

$$[S_1(\{\mathbf{x}_1(\theta_1)\in \Omega;\text{ with } \{\theta_1\} \in \Omega\})]\leftrightarrow[S_2(\{\mathbf{x}_2(\theta_2) \in \Omega;\text{ with } \{\theta_2\} \in \Omega\})] \quad (1)$$

$$[S_u(\{\mathbf{x}_u(\theta_u)\in \Omega;\text{ with } \{\theta_u\} \in \Omega\})]\cap [S_r(\{\mathbf{x}_r(\theta_r) \in \Omega;\text{ with } \{\theta_r\} \in \Omega\})] = \phi \quad (2)$$

u denotes unity of knowledge; r denotes rationalism.

$$[S_u(\{\mathbf{x}_u(\theta_u)\in \Omega;\text{ with } \{\theta_u\} \in \Omega\})]\cup [S_r(\{\mathbf{x}_r(\theta_r) \in \Omega;\text{ with } \{\theta_r\} \in \Omega\})] =$$

$$[S(\{\mathbf{x}(\theta)\in \Omega;\text{ with } \{\theta\} \in \Omega\})] \quad (3)$$

By the distributive law of set-theory,

$$\cup\cap[S(\{\mathbf{x'}(\theta')\in \Omega;\text{ with } \{\theta'\} \in \Omega\})] \quad (4)$$

exists and belongs to the generalized set of "everything,"

$[S(\{\mathbf{x'}(\theta')\in \Omega;\text{ with } \{\theta'\} \in \Omega\})]$ is defined on the universal set of variables and their unconstrained relations, $\{(\theta,x(\theta),S(\theta,x(\theta);\ \{\theta\}\in\Omega\}$. (5)

Finally, there exists a substantive well-defined mapping of the type,

$$[S_u(\{\mathbf{x}_u(\theta_u)\in \Omega;\text{ with } \{\theta_u\} \in \Omega\})]\rightarrow [S_r(\{\mathbf{x}_r(\theta_r) \in \Omega;\text{ with } \{\theta_r\} \in \Omega\})]; \quad (6)$$

But there is no well-defined mapping of the type,

$$[S_r(\{\mathbf{x}_r(\theta_r) \in \Omega;\text{ with } \{\theta_r\} \in \Omega\})]\rightarrow[S_u(\{\mathbf{x}_u(\theta_u)\in \Omega;\text{ with } \{\theta_u\} \in \Omega\})] \quad (7)$$

This is the property of uniqueness.

In the end, in the generalized integrated and system and cybernetic sense of holistic interrelationship, we write the following embedded circular causation relationship between concepts of "universality," "uniqueness," and "everything."

Universality (uniqueness, everything)
Uniqueness (universality, everything)
Such circular causation relations exist in continuity across continuums in the case of the endogenous (embedded) interrelations between (U,U,E) in terms of any simple or complex functions as defined on $\cup\cap[S(\{\mathbf{x'}(\theta')\in\Omega;\text{ with }\{\theta'\}\in\Omega\})]$.

Masudul Alam Choudhury
Sultan Qaboos University, Muscat, Sultanate of Oman
& Trisakti University, Jakarta, Indonesia

REFERENCES

Boland, L. A. (1989). On the methodology of economic model building. In *The Methodology of Economic Model Building*. London, UK: Routledge.

Choudhury, M. A. (2006). *Science and epistemology in the Qur'an*. Lewiston, NY: The Edwin Mellen Press.

Choudhury, M.A. (2009). Which of the two? Knowledge or time. *Philosophical Papers and Review, 2*(4).

Dewitt, B. (1992). *Supermanifolds*. Cambridge, UK: Cambridge University Press.

Einstein, A. (1954). Relativity and problem of space. In Lawson, R. (Ed.), *Relativity: The special and the general theory*. London, UK: Methuen.

Elis, G. F. R. (2008). Multiverses and ultimate causation. In Watts, F. (Ed.), *Creation, law and probability* (pp. 59–80). Minneapolis, MN: Fortress Press.

Gruber, T. R. (1993). A translation approach to portable ontologies. *Knowledge Acquisition, 5*(2), 199–200.

Hallaq, W. B. (2009). Legal theory: Epistemology, language and legal reasoning. In *Shari'a, Theory, Practice, Transformations* (pp. 72–124). Cambridge, UK: Cambridge University Press.

Hawking, S. W. (1988). *A brief history of time: From the big bang to black holes*. New York: Bantam Books, Inc..

Hawking, S. W., & Mlodinow, L. (2010). *The grand design*. London, UK: Transworld Publishers.

Maddox, I. J. (1970). *Elements of functional analysis*. Cambridge, UK: Cambridge University Press.

Wald, R. M. (1992). *Space, time, and gravity: The theory of the big bang and black holes*. Chicago, IL: The University of Chicago Press.

Wallerstein, I. (1998). Spacetime as the basis of knowledge. In Bordo, O. F. (Ed.), *People's participation: Challenges ahead* (pp. 43–62). New York, NY: Apex Press.

Acknowledgment

I acknowledge with thanks the preparation of this research project and book to a list of collegial contributors who enabled its successful completion. The result is a rare scholarly contribution in a slim but intensifying theme in recent times. The book as a research project has brought into the academic forum for the first few scholarly attempts the setting up of monotheistic law in the ontological working of the world-system. Within this research project, it has been possible to introduce the theme of human consciousness centered in a rigorously analytical socio-scientific epistemological enterprise.

Towards my accomplishment, I thank the College of Commerce and Economics at Sultan Qaboos University, which awarded me a book preparation research grant, 2010-2011, for the completion of this project under its Internal Research Grant Program. I thank the Department of Postgraduate Studies and Research at Sultan Qaboos University for approving my Research Leave to carry on the research work.

My thanks are to Professor Jack Quarter, Director of the Social Economy Center at the University of Toronto, for offering me a Summer Visiting Professorship, 2011. I spent this time writing and preparing the book towards its completion. The Social Economy Center and the abundant facilities of the University of Toronto libraries were richly instrumental in helping me realize this project.

My thanks go to IGI Global Publications for awarding me a contract for the publication of this book, considering its system and cybernetic methodological overview. In the field of innovation, epistemic evolutionary learning regarding the functioning of the generality and the specifics of issues and problems of the world-system plays a central role. The theme of the monotheistic law (God) is thereby studied in a systemic way (world-system) that examines and consciously embeds the monotheistic episteme in the study of selected issues of science and society.

Finally, my thanks are to Professor Emeritus Dr. Mohammad Nejatullah Siddiqi of Aligarh University, India for embellishing this book with his erudite Foreword.

I consider the scholarly message that this book reaches out to the informed reader on the ontological functioning of the monotheistic law in the details of the world-system as a singular feat of great rarity. This alone remains my greatest sense of comfort and confidence.

Masudul Alam Choudhury
Sultan Qaboos University, Muscat, Sultanate of Oman
& Trisakti University, Jakarta, Indonesia

Introduction

OVERVIEW

The chapters of this book are intended to convey the study of the impact of the moral law on issues concerning economy, finance, and society, but also invoking the ethical meanings embedded in proper scientific methods. We thereby study the nature and functions of money, finance and real economy with the moral-embedding in a fast changing scenario of economic, financial, policy, business, banking and social order. These areas comprise the study of sub-systems within the grand interactive cybernetic system, which we refer to as the world-system. The totality of the sub-systems including its scientific study is thus referred to in this manuscript as the world-system. Besides, the explanation of such a relationship between morality, ethics, economy, institutions, and the social world-system as the field scientific intellection is of deep import. We refer to the study of the moral-social construction of money, finance, institutions, and social order as the socio-scientific inquiry of the world-system.

From such socio-scientific intellection arise myriads of practical implications in human and institutional experience in our modern and post-modern world. This book is a scholarship in these directions. To examine how God is brought into the study of the world-system is to firstly understand the rigorous role of integrating morality and ethics in the underlying scholarly thought. This is an academic enterprise of massive proportion. But besides this endeavor in this book, there are also deep policy, institutional and applied perspectives acting as the media to bear the impact of the moral-social epistemological order on the experiential world-system. Islamic banking is thereby invoked to study a specific case of God in the institutional system of finance, banking, economy and business.

This book undertakes these two rigorous tasks. It studies them within the core axiom of unity of knowledge and its impact on the unity of the world-system as the relevant domain of application. The search for such an axiomatic core of the entire socio-scientific investigation takes us into the unique and universal epistemology that solely harbors the foundation of epistemic unity of knowledge. Through the intellectual search and discovery the premise of the epistemic core is found in the divine law of monotheism, and none other. We will prevail on a specific example of this case of moral embedding in all of socio-scientific inquiry. But, as pointed out in the Preface of this book, the monotheistic worldview is found in every religious persuasion and diverse cultures. Yet this book is devoted to the functionality of the monotheistic law in moral and ethical embedding of socio-scientific inquiry. Such a functional treatment of the moral law in the moral construction of socio-scientific inquiry and the attenuating world-system is termed as functional ontology (Gruber, 1993), contrary to metaphysical ontology (Heidegger, 1988).

In the history of thought the monotheistic divine law exists in its pure form in the *Qur'an* and the *Sunnah*. Monotheism as the moral law establishes the principal purpose and objective of the *shari'ah*, the Islamic Law, termed as the *maqasid as-shari'ah*. Thus the *Qur'an* and the *Sunnah* together with the discursive medium of human agency establish the purpose and objective of the Islamic Law concerning the socio-scientific intellection on moral-social worldview. The objective foundation of the moral and ethical law in Islam is the premise of the *maqasid as-shari'ah*. Such an approach that we take to the understanding of *maqasid as-shari'ah* encompassing worldly affairs and the scientific intellection is different from the interpretive meaning based on traditions of various schools of thought.

The formalism and application of the moral and ethical law premised on the episteme of unity of knowledge arising from the law of monotheism are used in this book to inquire into outstanding contemporary issues. Among them are the moral-social construction of the new financial architecture; the generalized formalism of monetary, fiscal and real economy inter-relationship in the presence of tradable instruments and phasing out of interest rate; the attainment of wellbeing, within which are achieved great and pressing moral-social objectives. Among them are poverty alleviation, sustainability and stability in basic needs regime of development; and the nature of monetary, fiscal policies, and institutional structures. These are among the several policy-institutional-theoretical issues that we will formalize. But since science of nature cannot be dissociated from that of society, so we also embed both of these worldviews universally and uniquely in everything of both science and society (See Preface to this book). Thus we extend the traditional and narrowly constrained notion of the purpose and objective of the divine law (*maqasid as-shari'ah*) to worldly affairs alone.

It is stark reality that despite the clamor for ethical functioning of the economic, business, banking and social academic enterprise, such an aspiration has staggered behind. Very little progress in this direction has been attained at the intellection and practical levels the world over.

In the Islamic world too, despite referring to the epistemic premise of monotheism that we invoke to bring God into the banking, business, economic, social, and scientific world-system, the failure of governments to mould collective will towards authentic Islamic change failed the Muslim countries and the global expectation to be gained. To this predicament also added the failure of the Islamic scholars in discovering fundamental premises of new thinking based on their epistemological premise, the *Qur'an* and the *Sunnah* to evolve a new worldview that can be fully discoursed among the Islamic learned and the polity and markets at large. On the other hand, progress in these directions necessitates the need for the Islamic discursive society.

Such new origins are carved out in the most methodological and authentically Islamic texture of unity of knowledge of the world-system in the light of the terminology for monotheism, *tawhid*. We extend the meaning of *tawhid*, which refers to the precept of the oneness of God to encompass the unity of the divine law of monotheism and of the unified nature of the world-system -- of 'everything' that emanates from the epistemic premise. The terminology 'everything is a substantive concept of socio-scientific phenomenology (Barrow, 1991; see Preface to this book). It can also be interpreted as the domain of the 'multiverse' or the universal ensemble.[1] The *tawhidi* worldview takes this new vista of thinking away from strict abidance with old *fiqh* (traditional interpretation of the *shari'ah* rules, Islamic Law). It replaces this traditional approach by foundational understanding of the *Qur'an* and the *sunnah* (referred to as *ijtihad*) within discursive social milieu that excites moral and social consciousness (discursive consultation, participation = *shura* and consciousness in everything = *tasbih*).

PRIMARY OBJECTIVE

Thus in the economic, financial and social sphere in all, the primary objective of this book is to lay down the analytically rigorous methodology for the construction of unifying relationships between money, finance, production, output, prices, employment and wellbeing with poverty alleviation in the light of the underlying moral-social construct. At the end, there is lesson on the permanent ethical goal of mankind seeking for a more secure tomorrow in the good things of life concerning the worldly matters and science.

The nature of inquiry in the analytical study that ensues brings together the normative and positive, deductive and inductive reasoning. This recognizes that any modeling of a worldview premised on its own ramifications, axioms and hypothesis may be relevant to its domain of inquiry. On this issue wrote Friedman (1962): ".... The relevant question to ask about the 'assumptions' of a theory is not whether they are descriptively 'realistic', for they never are, but whether they are sufficiently good approximations for the purpose in hand." In the light of this observation in model-building, the moral-social worldview of epistemic unity of knowledge and 'everything' has its infallible roots in the monotheistic law explained and applied by its epistemological origin.

The message learnt out of the chapters in this book is thus on the construction of a moral-social worldview for all and in 'everything'. At the same time, the theme of this book presents the immanent new Islamic revolutionary worldview of rethinking on the topic of moral-social premise introduced by the money-real economy unified relationship as derived from the implication of the monotheistic law of the *Qur'an* and *sunnah* through the human discursive medium. Taken altogether such an epistemological premise is referred to as the *maqasid as-shari'ah*. Towards such an analytical study, the undertaking in this book is rigorous in its technical presentation and analytical formalism.

CONTENTS OF CHAPTERS IN THIS BOOK

The chapters of this book will bring out the theoretical importance and applied consequences along with new methodological intellection in the direction of critical thought on moral-social reconstruction. The methodology relies upon the union of the normative and positivistic reasoning, the deductive and inductive reasoning. The analytical thinking and reasoning developed in this book are not subjected to traditional interpretation of Islamic thought and the cluttered nomenclature that has entered the writings on Islamic economics and finance. All this is termed as fiqh. On the contrary, the methodological foundation of the chapters is based on the singular episteme of unity of knowledge and its epistemological impact on the nature of the unified world-system as the moral-social consequence.

The epistemic approach is applied to the special case-study here, namely the unifying interaction between money, finance, production, output, price, employment and wellbeing. The study is carried out in comparative perspectives in order to bring out the unavoidable power of the monotheistic law, referred to in Islamic terminology as the *tawhidi* methodology in studying various problems examined in this book. The rest of the investigation, instead of hinging on fiqh, and an old way of understanding the *shari'ah* and *shari'ah*-compliance consequences, reverts to the objective and purpose of the Islamic Law, the *maqasid as-shari'ah*, as this emanates from the epistemological foundation of the *Qur'an* and the *sunnah*. Such epistemic derivation is then subjected to the medium of learned discourse. Such a methodological approach is studied by the Islamic intellection in the midst of a discursive society formed by the Islamic consultative institution or process (*shura*), which is fired by moral and social consciousness (*tasbih*). This book examines the emergent analytical approach thoroughly in deriving and developing the new and challenging ideas on the nature of organic unity between money and real economy through the themes of finance, production, output, price stability, factor utilization, and wellbeing aiming at poverty alleviation and sustainability. These are all studied in the light of the foundational methodology of unity of knowledge and the unified world-system – together comprising the analytical domain of *tawhid* as the monotheistic law (Choudhury, 2006).

The objective of the book is spelled out in its various chapters. Some chapters establish the analytical worldview of unity of knowledge and the knowledge-induced unified world-system, in this case of money, finance, economy, banking and business and the moral-social order. Other chapters develop the generalized theory of monetary and fiscal interaction and integration in the direction of newer perspectives. Such emergent perspectives turn out to be contrary to mainstream economic theory while explaining how money and real economy are interactively integrated in the learning model derived from the monotheistic law. Relevant questions of wellbeing, poverty alleviation, socioeconomic development, sustainability and economic stability are discussed thereupon.

The book lays down a generalized theory of interactive, integrative and evolutionary worldview of oneness, understood in terms of its dynamics of organic relationalism. It signifies pairing, meaning complementarities and participation, between the good things of life. Among these blessed choices are money and spending (fiscalism) resulting in the theory of production, consumption, ownership and distribution, and socioeconomic stability and wellbeing, all technically treated. These issues taken altogether in their analytical relationships ought to usher in the moral-social construction of the economy and the social order. Such is the system and cybernetic meaning of God in relationship with the world-system.

Some chapters of this book present the theme of money in Islam in a substantively original way in contrast to its treatment as macroeconomic ethically benign aggregates in mainstream economic theory. The problem of monetary transmission in its comparative perspectives is contrasted with the Islamic alternative in the theory of money in Islam. The theme of monetary transmission is of substantive importance to study prediction of the future course of the real economy in conjunction with monetary and fiscal policies in reference to their micro-foundational moral and ethically induced reconstruction.

In some chapters the pressing positivistic issues of production, efficiency, and social consciousness and responsibility (CSCR), and governance are examined in the light of their normative and positivistic perspectives. Thereby, pertinent empirical exercises are carried out in the light of the method of the central positivistic method that also unravels the normative worldview. This empirical method of interaction and integration by inter-causality between the normative and the positive, the deductive and the inductive sets of variables and their relations is referred to as circular causation. It inheres in the estimation and simulation of money and real economy interrelations and relevant socioeconomic development issues through the functional ontology of specific kinds of analytical formalism arising in the course of this study.

THE PHENOMENOLOGICAL CONSTRUCTION OF THE ISLAMIC WORLDVIEW OF UNITY OF KNOWLEDGE: MONEY, FINANCE, AND REAL ECONOMY COMPLEMENTARY LINKAGES BY EPISTEMIC UNITY OF KNOWLEDGE

At the very outset, in order to bring forth the methodological orientation of the work done in this book, we explain the features of the epistemological, ontological and evidential (ontic) constructs of the total phenomenological model of unity of knowledge in light of the monotheistic worldview. This is a complex and extensive field of inquiry. Details of the emergent *tawhidi* phenomenological model have been studied by Choudhury (2006). Underlying all phenomena in monotheistic intellection is this epistemological invoking of a systemic way of understanding oneness of the divine law at work. The phenomenological model of unity of knowledge is universal in the sense of its extensive explanatory and applicative capability. In the case of money, finance and real economy, the problem of organically unifying interrelations has been explained. By premising the epistemological intellection of *tawhid* in the functional ontology of divine oneness, while establishing a world-system of unity of being and becoming, the entire *Qur'anic* project of oneness in the world-system liberates itself away from open theism (Boyd, 2009). The great difference between the two projects is the unshakable core of oneness around which the entire evolving world-system with its generality and specifics revolves. Contrarily the 'open theism' project rests on a pantheistic conception of God as a corporeal being and often as becoming in the corporeal order by a relativistic growth of knowledge, such as of anthropocentric evolution (King, 2004).

As a general methodology, a tuple denoted by $(\theta, x(\theta))$ (see Figure 1), with θ denoting knowledge-flow; $x(\theta)$ denoting knowledge-induced vector of socio-scientific variables; is studied within the generalized evolutionary equilibrium system that simulates the learning relations between the variables of the vector-tuple. θ-values are measured as learning parameters that induce all the variables endogenously to determine the good things of life. These are generated in reference to the epistemology of unity of knowledge (Choudhury, 1997).

Several kinds of organic unity of the phenomenological system can be noted in Figure 1. These features delineate the intra-process and inter-process dynamics, and can be generalized to multiple systems by extension.

First, we note the precept of unity of derived knowledge from the epistemological core within a discursive process. This experience enables the agents and agencies to come up with the limiting value of knowledge-flow. The emergent learning experience along with everything to follow, represent endogenous relations caused by their induction by the knowledge-flow parameters, the θ-values. In other words, the variables and their relations intrinsic to issues and problems of the world-system in its details are embedded in the knowledge-flows derived from the episteme of unity of knowledge (see also Preface).

In reference to the section in the Preface, only the epistemological core, namely (Ω, S), remains exogenous. In Islamic monotheism, Ω denotes the topological knowledge-space of the *Qur'an*, and marks the completeness of the primal knowledge of the monotheistic law as super-cardinal topological space (Rucker, 1982). S denotes the mapping of 'bits' of Ω into the discursive medium by the Prophetic guidance referred to as the *sunnah*. The actualization of Ω is true both at the beginning and the end of the learning processes shown in Figure 1. Hence, the Beginning is equivalent to the End, and the continuity of such a process over the dimensions of knowledge, time and space causes a topologically closed super-space to form.[2]

Secondly, we note the organic unity of knowledge between the elements of the vector tuple (θ, x(θ)). Their pairing phenomenon is explained by the principle of pervasive complementarities together with the use of the functional ontological model (Gruber, 1993; Maxwell, 1962) of simulating the money, finance and real economy interrelations. Besides, the same kind of construction applies for the organically unified interrelations by learning (discourse) between the central bank, the commercial banks (Islamic banks), and the 100% Reserve Requirement Monetary System (100%RRMS) that needs to exist with the gold standard. The applications of such organic interrelations in money, finance and real economy circular causation relations are legion. Some of these are shown in various contexts in this book.

Thirdly, we note that within any socio-scientific systemic learning process the phasing out of interest rates by trade instruments causes heightened resource mobilization. This brings about increased complementary relationships between resource mobilization and social wellbeing denoted by W(θ, x(θ)). Details are formalized in this book as elsewhere (Choudhury, 2011)

Fourth, learning by simulated complementarities between the elements of the (θ, x(θ))-tuple within any learning process involves reflexive discourse over diverse possibilities. We refer to this experience of learning as Interaction. Interactions lead to limiting value of the learning parameter within a process. This is the limiting knowledge-value, θ*. Attaining of θ* as a limiting learning value on specifics marks the phase of Integration (social consensus). It emanates out of Interaction (discourse). At the end of any learning process there comes about subsequent Evolution into new learning processes. Evolutions arise from the combination of Interactions leading to Integration. They carry on the recursive learning processes in continuity over the knowledge-space-time domains (continuums). Continuity and

Figure 1. The phenomenological model of learning in unity of knowledge

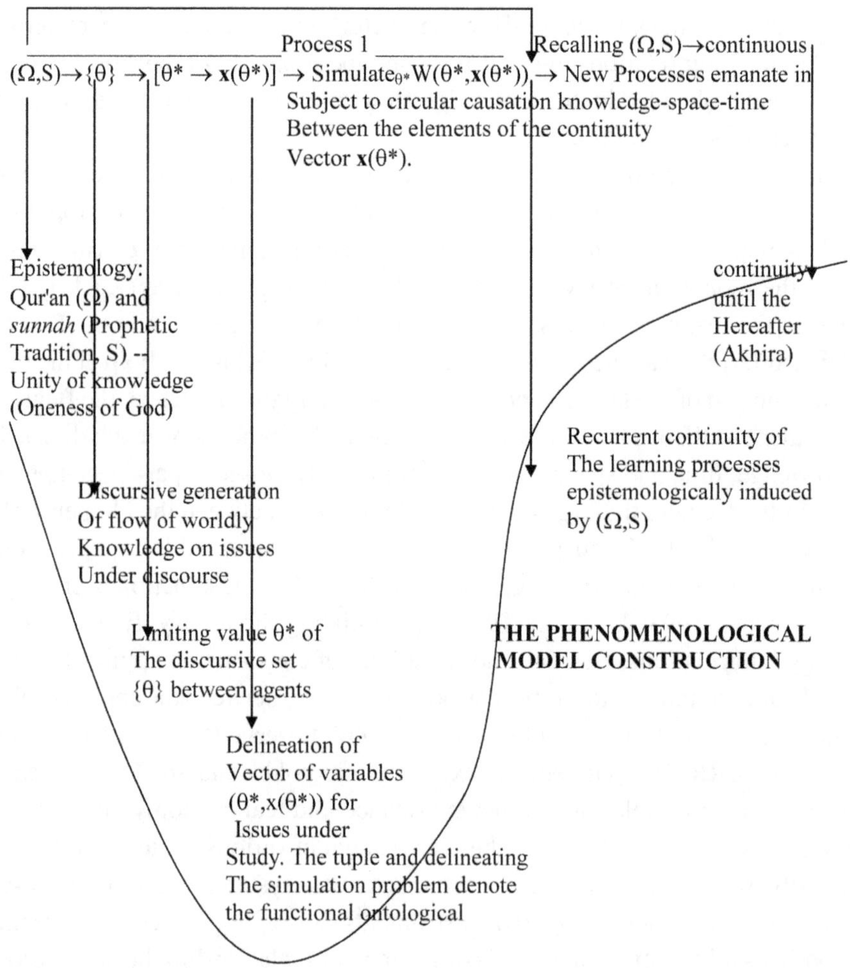

re-origination of the new learning processes are enabled necessarily and sufficiently by the epistemological recalling of (Ω, S) at the start of every evolutionary learning process, as shown, continuously and across continuums of the dimensions of knowledge, time and space.

Fifth, the entire Interactive, Integrative and Evolutionary process, namely the **IIE**-character of the learning process, is universal and continuous by its extensions until the end of all events, referred to as the Hereafter (comprising the nexus of all continuums). The final cumulative knowledge-endowed character of the Hereafter is thus described as the Great Event[3] in the *Qur'an*.

The all-inclusive IIE-model comprises the universal model of unity of knowledge. It describes the phenomenological construction of the epistemological worldview of unity of the monotheistic law in 'everything'. In reference to the Preface, universality is inter-causally related with the simultaneous properties of uniqueness and the circular causation of the learning experience by continuity and evolution of pairing processes in everything.

Figure 1 is a model of organic unitary relationship explained by the method of circular causation in 'everything'. It is particularized in this book by the circular causation model between money, finance and real economy of a general-system framework. In this way, the system and cybernetic worldview of unity of knowledge in respect of the moral-social reconstruction actualized by the objective and purpose of the monotheistic law, and referred to in the Islamic Law as *maqasid as-shari'ah*, is established in 'everything.'

CONCLUSION

The epistemic worldview of unity of knowledge and its induction of systemic unity between the good things of life in the world-system is an analytical undertaking in formalizing a phenomenological model of organic unity in 'everything'. In this permanent epistemic reference, the monotheistic law becomes a dynamic precept, formalism, and application spanning the entirety of 'everything' in its fullest diversity. On this theme of the mind-matter union, conceptualized, and applied under the monotheistic law, writes Hallaq (2009, p. 83, edited): "Knowledge of the law in Islam is what was seen as a happy synthesis between human reason (the world-system) and the divine world (epistemic unity of knowledge)."

The example of such an issue covered in this book is of money, finance, real economy, banking, business, and the interrelated socioeconomic development paradigm, altogether comprising the specific world-system. Much will be dealt with in this book to set up the revolutionary challenges opened up for scholarship and application in the mind-matter issues by the epistemic worldview of unity of knowledge in 'everything'. The monotheistic law is invoked in a rigorously analytical way in all the underlying moral-social construction for realizing a discursive society in the good things of life, barring that which is not for the wellbeing of the world-system; encouraging what remains. Thus the system and cybernetic study of God and the world-system comprises the highly analytical intellection of morality and ethics in terms of the epistemic unity of knowledge and the unified world-system in the details of economic, financial, institutional, banking, business and social order that arises from this epistemic foundation.

The system and cybernetic study of God and the world-system as presented in this book is a socio-scientific study of the monotheistic law in which most religious persuasions believe. Thus such a study is not a parochial study devoted to the Islamic or another monotheistic worldview. The word *tawhid* as the oneness of God and its carriage, the *sunnah*, functioning in constructing the design of unity of the world-system, is a mathematical reality and a moral reality, one connected with the other in a relational continuity. Thus the example of the *tawhidi* methodological worldview is studied in this book as a socio-scientific analytical study at the exclusion of no systemic reality that believes in unity of knowledge, its application in constructing the unity of the world-system, and the precept of wellbeing that will be elaborated in this book. In the end, this book is an analytical study of the socio-scientific worldview of unity of knowledge that is explainable in a system and cybernetic way.

REFERENCES

Barrow, J. D. (1991). *Theories of everything: The quest for ultimate explanation.* Oxford, UK: Oxford University Press.

Boyd, C. A. (2009). The goodness of creation and the openness of god. In Oord, T. J. (Ed.), *Creation made free open theology engaging science* (pp. 111–125). Eugene, OR: Pickwick Publications.

Choudhury, M. A. (1997). *Money in Islam.* London, UK: Routledge.

Choudhury, M. A. (2006). *Science and epistemology in the Qur'an.* Lewiston, NY: Edwin Mellen Press.

Choudhury, M. A. (2011). *Islamic economics and finance: An epistemological inquiry.* Bingley, UK: Emerald.

Friedman, M. (1962). The role of government in a free society. In *Capitalism and freedom* (pp. 22–36). Chicago, IL: University of Chicago Press.

Gruber, T. R. (1993). A translation approach to portable ontologies. *Knowledge Acquisition, 5*(2), 199–200. doi:10.1006/knac.1993.1008.

Hallaq, W. B. (2009). Legal theory: Epistemology, language and legal reasoning. In *Shari'a, theory, practice, transformations* (pp. 72–124). Cambridge, UK: Cambridge University Press. doi:10.1017/CBO9780511815300.004.

Heidegger, M. (1988). The thesis of modern ontology: The basic ways of being are the being of nature (res extensa) and the being of mind (res cogitans). In A. Hofstadter (Ed.), The basic problems of phenomenology, (pp. 122-224). Bloomington, IN: Indiana University Press.

King, C. M. (2004). Model of the invisible realities: The common thread in science and theology. In Ledger, C., & Pickard, S. (Eds.), *Creation and Complexity: Interdisciplinary Issues in Science and Religion* (pp. 17–50). Adelaide, Australia: ATF Press.

Ledger, C., & Pickard, S. (Eds.). (2004). *Creation and complexity: Interdisciplinary issues in science and religion.* Adelaide, Australia: ATF Press.

Maddox, I. J. (1970). *Elements of functional analysis.* Cambridge, UK: Cambridge University Press.

Maxwell, G. (1962). The ontological status of theoretical entities. In H. Feigl & G. Maxwell (Eds.), Minnesota studies in the philosophy of science, vol. II: Scientific explanation, space and time, (pp. 3-27). Minneapolis, MN: University of Minnesota Press.

Rucker, R. (1982). Large cardinals. In *Infinity and the mind* (pp. 273–286). New York, NY: Bantam Books.

ENDNOTES

1 C. Ledger & S. Pickard (eds. (2004). point out: *Introduction* (p.xi-xxiv; xv): "Gunton argues that God is a being-in-relation and that a dynamic or relatedness marks God's creative activity in the world. The network of relations between God and humankind, among humankind and between humankind and the rest of the universe find their basis in the relational nature of God's creative being. The world's unity and diversity are born of God. The complexity of the world and its interrelations, according to a trinitarian understanding of creation, is natural and is manifested in the relations between the smaller physical particles as well as in ecosystems and human social structures."

2 *Qur'an* (92:13): "And verily unto Us (belong) the End and the Beginning".

3 *Qur'an* (78:1-5): "What are they asking (one another) about? -- About the great news, (i.e. Islamic monotheism, the *Qur'an*, and the Day of Resurrection), about which they bare in disagreement. Nay, they will come to know! Nay, again, they will come to know!" Within this great event is embedded the meaning of unity of divine knowledge and its relations with the world-systems in continuity till the end.

Chapter 1
How is God Studied in Relation to Science and the World-System?

ABSTRACT

The chapter discusses the possibility of God in terms of the monotheistic law as the functional ontological way of integrating God with the world-system. Thus, the metaphysical impossibility is replaced by this functional precept. With this groundwork, the epistemology of unity of knowledge is explained, formalized, and the chapter shows how to apply the resulting phenomenological model to the construction of the unified world-system with the monotheistic law. Several physical and social science concepts are thereby explained and revised in light of the phenomenological model. In this way, the early groundwork of the entire work in God, explained by the monotheistic law with the unified socio-cybernetic and system worldview, is established.

INTRODUCTION

God is a metaphysical reality in every religion and philosophical thought. The problems encountered in such an understanding of God in respect of configuring reality in terms of its complex analytical nature pertaining to man, science and society at large with God, are essentially two. Yet we will argue and establish in this book that such a view and the emanating problem out of it in terms of our experiences and existential issues are not necessarily tenable if the understanding of God and human and worldly relationship within this embedded holism is differently viewed from the way that many religions do. Thus the scientific and social question to be examined in this book is the abiding and unshakable nature of the organic relation-

DOI: 10.4018/978-1-4666-4643-8.ch001

Copyright ©2014, IGI Global. Copying or distributing in print or electronic forms without written permission of IGI Global is prohibited.

ship between God, man, and the world-system. The emanating methodology arising out of this inquiry will assume permanence in the realm of intellection, application, and universality that is explainable 'everywhere' and in 'everything'.

Barrow (1991, p. 13) remarked on such a worldview of fundamental unity of the universe and of the laws that govern it in his words: "Different modern cultures have been variously influenced by their religious heritage in coming to a satisfying picture of natural laws. In the Judaeo-Christian West, the influence of the divine lawgiver has been paramount". To this expression I will add the most fundamental truth of unity of the universe and 'everything' in it within the great watershed of the Islamic monotheistic worldview that extends the monotheistic worldview of other religions.

In the latter case are the path-breaking contribution of Norbert Wiener (1966) on the artificial knowledge possibility of learning machines, the discovery of the field of cybernetics as the study of feedback reflexive learning between variables and the relations in fields of complexity. In recent times there is the journal named *Zygon* (see also Ledger & Pickard, 2004) that approaches the study of the interrelations between the divine law and the divine architecture of the universe.

Ledger and Pickard write in the *Introduction* (p. xi-xxiv; xv): "Gunton argues that God is a being-in-relation and that a dynamic or relatedness marks God's creative activity in the world. The network of relations between God and humankind, among humankind and between humankind and the rest of the universe find their basis in the relational nature of God's creative being. The world's unity and diversity are born of God."

Thus, the study of the monotheistic law in relation to the world-system is encompassed in Islam and the Judaeo-Christian religious beliefs. Any book and text in this regard notwithstanding what religion and belief it comes from is worthy of understanding. According to this perspective of the wellbeing of soul, mind, and matter across all world-system of materiality and thought there are these verses of the Qur'an (26:192-196). The verses make no distinction between all God-conscious peoples. "Verily this is a Revelation: From the Lord of the Worlds: With it came down the Spirit of Faith and Truth – to the heart and mind, that thou mayest admonish in the perspicuous Arabic tongue. Without doubt it is (announced) in the mystic Books of former peoples."

THE PROBLEMS OF GOD, MAN, AND WORLD-SYSTEM RELATIONS

1. The Metaphysical Problem

Firstly, God as a purely metaphysical being removed from the world and its detailed artifacts and cognitive relations remains a dysfunctional entity. God then has no explanatory causation of the experiential organic relations. Yet science and the world-system as domains of human experiences, cognition, and utilization of resources for attaining wellbeing for all, are embedded in the study of organic relations with conceptual, empirical, and applied power. If God remains a detached being from such organic relations of the domains of science and the world-system then how can such a being have any meaningful impact on the life of the world, on the formation of human thought, the dynamics of existence, and the delineation of reality?

Thus in such an understanding of God, religion and metaphysics, human experience loses its relevance to God, His Law and the details of the function of God and His Law in the order and scheme of things. The ultimate result of such a metaphysical separation of God from the real world is the separation of science and philosophical thought along with their applications and empirical viability into a detached world of separated cognitive phenomena. God as metaphysical being remains separate in His own dichotomous existence – give to God what is God's; and to Caesar what is Caesar's.

Scientific meaning, cognition, empiricism and application assume a methodology and analytical approach based on self-generated dialectical processes of rationalism. On the other side, God as metaphysical being assumes an absolutist status that cannot be questioned; cannot be explained. Hence no organic causality can be generated with God in such a metaphysical understanding of reality: "Give unto God what is God's; and unto Caesar what is Caesar's."

Science and world-system dichotomously separated between God and organic functional reality was given the intellectual superiority in the Eighteenth Century Enlightenment in the Western World with a deep lament for the prevalence of such a state of thought in Western science and the cognitive world-system. The discontent with such artificial divisiveness is voiced by Dampier (1961) and Dilworth (2008). The problem of conflict that arose between religion, science and the world-system is essentially due to the way that God and religion are understood and take up meaning in our functional lives, and our lives in the midst of a plethora of embedded organic relations. The Eighteenth Century Enlightenment that was followed by the separation of science and religion; with the cognitive world-system declaring its independence from the metaphysical moorings of the Church, marked the lasting impossibility of a metaphysical God and religion in human reality as the discursive socio-scientific order.

In observance of this impossibility of organic interrelationship between God, religion, and the socio-scientific reality, Dawkins (2006) rejects the relevance of God in socio-scientific reality. Likewise, Hawking and Mlodinow (2010) turn their mind to the question of such relevance in respect of a self-regenerating world-system that reproduces automatically under the universal law of gravitation. God becomes irrelevant in such a celestial design of the universe.

The denial of God as a functional being playing out a continuously creative role in the complexity of universal life is a lament regarding the impossibility of the metaphysical God. Such a God is in our imagination, to which for personal solace, man at his individual level assigns imaginative configuration. This is the ultimate subjectivity of the idea, meaning and function of God and religion created simply by individuated human imagination. On such a status of the metaphysical God and religion and the consequential dichotomy between the dysfunctional God and cognitive experience writes Dawkins (2006, p. 141) in the words of his friend, Douglas, who was led to embrace Darwinism in place of religion: "I was extremely doubtful about the idea of god, but I just didn't know enough about anything to have a good working model of any other explanation for, wellbeing, life, the universe, and everything to put in its place."

Likewise, on a similar matter of non-response from metaphysical God and religion to logically explain the evolution of the universal design and patterns of things, Hawking (1988, p. 11) writes: "They would say that God, being omnipotent, could have started the universe off any way he wanted. That may be so, but in that case he also could have made it develop in a completely arbitrary way. Yet it appears that he chose to make it evolve in a very regular way according to certain laws."

Along the same lines of reasoning the social models of being and becoming (Sztompka, 1991; Prigogine, 1980) and the epistemic approach to economic theory (Shackle, 1972; Hayek, 1979) study the rationalistic approach as the ultimate logical foundations of the social sciences. Sztompka (op cit, p. 115) writes in this regard, "God, or Providence, Fate, Immanence or History, even though appealing, do not provide satisfactory solutions for our purposes, because of their basically unempirical, untestable character." On the same theme of consciousness as a rationalistic determined process of an exclusively anthropocentric relevance writes Hayek (op cit, p. 153): "The universal demand for 'conscious' control or direction of social processes is one of the most characteristic features of our generation. It expresses perhaps more clearly than any of the other clichés the peculiar spirit of the age. That anything is not consciously directed as a whole is regarded as itself a blemish, a proof of its irrationality and of the need completely to replace it by a deliberately designed mechanism."

2. The Problem of Understanding Science and the World-System

The second problem of integrating God with the scientific order and world-system worldview in 'everything' is the inability of science to explain the deductive holism. The result is a rift between deductive and inductive reasoning, and between normative and positivistic models of reality. Thus the inability of the socio-scientific methods to extend intellectual inquiry and comprehension, application and empiricism, beyond the narrow anthropocentric horizon remains the permanent nature of modernity, of prevalent science, and the world-system studies. Our perception of such a limited domain searches for an end without possibility. The intellectual process remains forever of the dialectical nature involving the Darwinian conflicting nature between entities. Such conflicts exist both between good and bad, good and good, and bad and bad. The resulting domain of conflicting entities assumes an organic form of polarities devolved out of organic relations in which only the materially strong survive and dominate. This is the idea of Dawkins' (1976) selfish gene. There is no stable meaning and identification of truth. Truth remains relative with Falsehood.

Even the idea of natural selection according to social Darwinism that sifts the good from the bad is determined by the dialectical process of power, strength and superiority. Campbell (1988) notes such an immanent dialectical process of conflict and survival as the emergence of mind. In the social sciences, the same method of dialectical process towards survival of the fittest is noted as the overdetermination problem of competing episteme (Resnick and Wolf, 1987). Einstein prevailed on the same kind of argumentation for establishing the ultimate viability of competing scientific theories (Infeld, 1951) and gave to the realm of ethics a status that was subjected to the methods of material testing, viability and self-assertion, as in the physical sciences.

In this way, at the end, the entire domain of scientific analysis on which we have premised modernity for a long time now, has developed around it an anthropocentric aura. This is a mortal reality from which only a limited view of the open universe of holistic totality and largeness is encapsulated for study, analysis, and use. The picture on completeness and holism, which Capra (1983) refers to as the systems and cybernetic view of entirety, and what Hubner (1985) characterizes as a 'system-ensemble' view of history, encounters the open universes of evolutionary dialectics that remain embedded, but not comprehensive of the universe entire. The resulting intellection concerning such limited, dialectical, emergent, and evolutionary universe arising out of Darwinian type natural selection process and permanently prevailing, forms the encapsulated extant of modernity and socio-scientific reasoning, comprehension and understanding.

Therefore, the question: Is the claim of logical positivism the finest accomplishment of scientific reasoning, its ultimate staying power, and its extant in explaining the universe, as science knows it? The divide between deductive and inductive reasoning known as Popper's (2004) problem of demarcation, stultifies the end-goal of science. Hawking typifies such scientific ultimate goal as the search and discovery of the unified worldview of the physical universe. But this is yet limited by the anthropocentric notion of the physical universe. Hawking's (1988, p. 10) vision of the penultimate reality of the physical universe is inherent in his words: "The eventual goal of science is to provide a single theory that describes the whole universe. However, the approach most scientists actually follow is to separate the problem into two parts."

What truly ought to be the ultimate precept of holism in scientific reasoning is lost on differentiated epistemic grounds. The logical problem of modernity and scientific enterprise manifests itself by its inability to extend substantive methodology and the consequential influence of intellection gap on the world of experience. In fact, the broader implication of the ethical and moral domains of human reality, the embedding of human experience in the holism of science, society, ethics and morality remains partial. The opening of the universe in these directions of inquiry involves the quest for the ultimate explanation of unity and unified organic relationship between the diverse elements of human experience, and with the moral and the material substance of reasoning.

In Einstein's (1954, p. 473) words: "Scientific thought is a development of pre-scientific thought. As the concept of space was already fundamental in the latter, we must begin with the concept of space in pre-scientific thought." It is evident then that the old values do mix with the new ones to establish the continuity in human understanding of the world-system, its future capability, and its sustainability.

An inferential problem of incompleteness and non-explanatory nature arises from the dialectical evolutionary perspective of the universe in the direction of nothingness. Knowledge is neither stable nor meaningful in such a randomly open and non-directional, un-purposive universe. Let us consider the following logical case showing the impossibility of attaining knowledge and meaning according to the received premise of scientific reasoning.

A Formalism Differentiating Truth and Falsehood and Complementing Truth in Itself

Let A_1 and A_2 denote two generalized premises of diverse types in the material domain. Say that A_1 denotes the set denoting poverty. A_2 denotes the set of the rich. Development in human experience is found to show increasing alienation between the rich and the poor (Singer and Ansari, 1988). Thus A_1 and A_2 are differentiated sets within the development domain. Yet when one considers the moral domain of social action, A_1 is mapped onto a set Z_1; and A_2 is mapped onto a set Z_2. The two set become increasingly identical as the poor and the rich coexist in this morally induced set comprising Z_1 and Z_2. Thus, the property of differentiation between A_1 and A_2 is not preserved in Z_1 and Z_2. The underlying social theories, behavior and models of man prevail in the two cases of A_1 plus A_2 and Z_1 plus Z_2 in disparate ways.

On a reverse content, it is possible that A_1 and A_2 share common properties, as in the case of a Darwinian perception of truth and falsehood under the rationalist conception of the emergent mind. But in the moral plane, the resulting Z_1 and Z_2 defining the truth and falsehood premises would be completely disjoint.

Diverse forms of similar relations can be exemplified to show the prevalence of differentiation and discontinuity of the consequences of theories, behavior and models of reality in disparate sets like the ones shown above. The problem of incongruence between the material scientific world-system and the ethical and moral completion of the social world-system is a methodological one. The mappings between the above-mentioned sets represent the dissociative methodologies. The implication now is that science has no precise way of projecting the material reality into an explanation of the moral and ethical reality of human existence and experience. A wide discontinuity explained by such a gap now exists. This gap cannot be reduced by the existing episteme of materiality of science and the world-system.

An Inference on Socio-Scientific Methodology

Thus at the end, from all sides of the scientific and moral-ethical debate for organic and holistic extensions of methods, episteme, and logicalness, it is clear that ours is an age of epistemological contests. Thereby, it is also a paramount time now for the search and discovery of the truth that ultimately describes, explains, and applies the theory of organic and holistic symbiosis between the purposeful and good things of life. The path though is a thorny one, as Kuhn (1970, p. 154) remarked regarding the emergence of scientific revolution beyond normal science and paradigm shift: "... scientific revolutions are here taken to be those non-cumulative developmental episodes in which an older paradigm is replaced in whole or in part by an incompatible new one." In our present times, the birth of a new, more inclusive and extant, meaningful and beneficial way of looking at science and the world-system in terms of an organic and holistic model rests on the emergence of a new epistemology.

Albert Einstein writing to his friend Niels Bohr remarked that there cannot be science without epistemology. Likewise, there cannot be a new science without a new epistemology. Indeed it appears that the intellectual vision of the new millennium is essentially such a search and discovery of the new epistemology. But when any particular discipline is awakened by the touch of a new epistemology, all other disciplines are equally awakened. This was the way that economics was touched by the mathematical novelty of the Eighteenth Century Enlightenment. The independence of metaphysics and religion from scientific inquiry was blazed by the philosophical ideas of Kant and Hume. Thus in all, from the prevalent epistemology governing philosophy of science and the world-system, the basis of space-time remains the predominant epistemological premise (Wallerstein, 1998). The more fundamental problem of moral and ethical law and its consequences, though considered important, belongs to an independent branch of study, exogenous to the socio-scientific episteme. If the moral and ethical law is to be considered at all in scientific analysis, it shares its method with those of analytical science and empiricism.

On this matter Edel (1970, pp. 303-304) wrote: "Thus a question like the existence and properties of God may be considered in terms of the scientific study of the ways in which these ideas function in the ethical process in the lives and thoughts of men." But at the same time Edel (p. 302-303) points out the speculative nature of individual religious beliefs in contradiction to the scientific method: "Questions of the possibility of man knowing the divine takes shape in rational, mystical, authoritarian-revealed and individual-intuitive religious epistemologies, with different imbedded conceptions of the character of the human condition."

THE PROBLEM OF SOCIO-SCIENTIFIC IMPOSSIBILITY OF KNOWLEDGE AS SYMBIOTIC UNITY IN THE OLD PARADIGM

The two-sides of methodological impossibility, firstly between science and God; and secondly, between the metaphysics of God and science, is thus established in the above writings. This dichotomy depicts the nature of incompleteness of the socio-scientific epistemology and its methods in both religion and science today. A new epistemology that brings back God into socio-scientific knowledge and simultaneously unifies science with God according to a symbiotic monotheism of matter and mind is needed. We will devote a good part of this book to this new analytical investigation. One such empowering methodology that we will derive, formulate, and apply to a constructed ontological design of socio-scientific structure with God in it is the extension of the space-time structure of scientific analysis to the problem of the knowledge-time-space structure.

This tripartite monotheistic unification will be our analytical reference. We will refer to the encompassing domain of our study of 'everything' in terms of the dimensions of knowledge, time and space. This methodology we will claim and prove in respect of the extension and unification between God and the socio-scientific order will be carried out in the framework of the dimensions of knowledge, time and space. Much is to follow on this theme.

The dimensions of knowledge, time and space of our epistemological inquiry that enables symbiotic unity, and the organic, equivalently cybernetic holism between God, science and the world-system, is not a straightforward embedding of the space-time dimension through physical and material projections. As an example, in economics it is non-substantive to state that, the intertemporal market system of exchange between goods and services is a phenomenon of space-time occurrence. Our existence, which is ethicized by its extension through including ethical laws and behavior into such market exchange, would be missed out in the sheer space-time structure of analysis. That would be simply a case of exogenous injection of values, which in the first place, remain extraneous to the self-interest and competition-by-scarcity nature of resources reflected in consumer preferences, social choice, and market exchange. Indeed, the *exogenous* inducement of ethics into market exchange is the prevalent way of characterizing ethics and economics in the literature (Boulding, 1971; Zsolnai, 2002).

There have been attempts in economic theory to induce ethics into behavior by dynamic consumer preferences (Sen, 1990; Hammond, 1989). But such deontological approaches do not explain the process by which the preferences of agents, either as individuals or the social collective, get transformed into conscious ones. Indeed, economics and finance are not disciplines for a robust study of learning processes as simulacra of endogenous relations and change. This is despite attempts made by Krugman (1996), Collard (1978), and the rational expectation school (Lucas, 1975) to introduce the ideas of punctuated equilibriums (Thurow, 1983) and self-governing organization of preferences, social choices, and markets.

In the sociology of political economy, Holton (1992), Wallerstein (1998, op cit) and Fukuyama (1992) show that, the bifurcated emergence of Darwinian type competing and conflicting organisms to attain hegemony, mark the permanent nature of the modern world-system. The concept of timespace is made of three kinds of its genre. Firstly, there is the structural timespace that remains unchangeable. Secondly, the cyclico-timespace comprises components of the structural timespace. Transformational timespace comprises bifurcations into revolutionary new ideas. Likewise, the Hegelian dialectics of civilization change are found to terminate in the temporal life of a creative order of democratic rationalism.

In all such timespace of replications of the social Darwinian type, no reference is made to the dynamics of endogenous relations that define transformation not merely over time, but also by interactions compounded by change over time. Indeed, such a compounded idea of being and becoming gives rise to the complex formalism of process as the *functional* ontological symbolism of the constructed world-system of forms and meanings. Such symbolism represents the functional ontology, or the engineering ontology (Gruber, 1993) of the constructed world-system. Society is then seen as a complex system of interactive and integrative, dynamic and creatively evolutionary (IIE) body of languages expressed through the medium of simulacra of learning processes. This is also the meaning of semiosis (Heiskala, 2003) and the language game (Glock on Wittgenstein, 2001). In the epistemological sense of the microforms of knowledge and language generative processes, the symbolism of constructed ontology assumes also a complex of mathematical relations in the order of interaction, integration and creative evolution (Choudhury, 2006).

Indeed, the understanding of meaningfulness, objectivity and purpose of relations formed by actions and responses in the ontologically constructed world are coterminous precepts. They underlie the mathematical semiosis that reveals the extensive explanatory power of socio-scientific reality. The order of social actions and responses and the individual and group location in this symbiotic space over the transcendence of time are circular causes and effects of the organic process of knowledge and learning in unity of knowledge. Such circular causation is continuously active across continuums of artifacts that synergize in the dimensions of knowledge, time, and space.

Yet another significance to note is the occurrence of events in the dimensional framework of knowledge, time and space. This topic is to be advanced in greater length later on in the course of bringing God into the world-system. It relates to the category of actions and responses between events acting simultaneously with the occurrence of organic interrelations. In this structure, knowledge, time and space are convoluted according to the conscious deriving, explaining, and establishing symbiotic unity of knowledge as a meaningful evolutionary learning process.

That is to say, in the meaning of process, as opposed to a deterministic and terminal way of describing the occurrence of events and their representative variables and entities, knowledge-flows remain as the interfaced bundle of the epistemic unity emerging out of the ontological knowledge in its originality (Ω,S). The derivations of the total learning process of knowing in the world-system are then governed by the praxis of unity of knowledge. Knowledge is the primal governing power of the entire epistemic system of knowing that is led towards creative evolution through the medium of interactive becoming into integrative being of the discursive variables and entities moving through the systemic learning processes. Thus any learning process is initiated by knowledge-flows derived from the ontology of unity of knowledge, out of the process of convolution of functionals in the dimensions of knowledge, time and space.

The resulting processual phase occurs simultaneously with the knowledge-depiction of the world-system and its details over time. This kind of knowledge-induced reaction causes the formation of the tuple comprising knowledge-flow, as derived from the epistemic origin of unity of knowledge, and the time variable. Time is logically for the sake of socio-scientific analysis, but coterminous with spatial entities and variables and their relations. This is the case because the continuity of occurrence of events must be explained in terms of the time coordinate.

Such is also the nature of the principle of simultaneity between time and event in General Relativity Theory (Einstein, 1954). But the occurrence of time is explained in the dimensions of knowledge, time, and space by the primal existence of knowledge as episteme followed by knowledge-flows as part of the functional ontology at work in the knowledge-induced world-system. Knowledge enables comprehension of events in time and space.

A Brief Note on the Nature of Time in Relation to Knowledge and Events

There are two concepts of time in reference to the two stages of knowledge – primal ontology of unity of knowledge; and the derived knowledge-flows from this primal knowledge as premise. Firstly, time is the absolute topological entity, which is then identical with primal knowledge in the topological sense of completeness and closure of the complete topological space. Secondly, time-flow like knowledge-flow is derived from the topological super-space of primal knowledge and primal time. But to eliminate any confusion regarding suspected simultaneity between knowledge-flow and time-flow in respect of events that are made up of worldly entities, we put the explanation like this: Events, defined as bundles of cause-effects occurring at a particular point of time, or continuously taking shape and form in the dynamic case, happen in reference to time. So Event is an occurrence combining entities represented by variables and agencies with time. Such a combined variable can only be formed, noticed, understood, and interpreted with the prior occurrence of knowledge. Thus, knowledge is primal to the determination of time and event (world-system).

Yet as mentioned earlier, knowledge, time and space get convoluted by their interaction, integration and co-evolution along the path of historical change in individual and social consciousness taken up in a broad sense of social transformation, in which individuals and institutions are embedded. According to such evolutionary complexity of convoluted forms, events determined by the primal influence of knowledge-flows result in new knowledge-flows along the learning process by continued reference to the primal episteme of unity of knowledge (Ω,S). Thereby, the determination of Event as the occurrence of cognitive forms at given points of time (discrete or continuous) under the impact of prior knowledge-flows evolve into new knowledge-flows, and thereby new learning processes. History is thus determined by such interactive and integrative forms of co-evolution (IIE) under consciousness, which means referencing to the primal episteme of unity of knowledge and the emergence of consequential unified knowledge-induced world-system. This deduction is true of science and society; their elementary constituents (specifics and particulars), and the generalized universal formalism in the system and cybernetic form of the knowledge-induced world-system.

A FORMAL DERIVATION

In the end therefore, the anomaly between knowledge, time and space in their convoluted evolutionary complexity is resolved by their simple depiction but underlying complex organism: Primal Ontology of Unity of Knowledge (Ω) mapped on to knowledge-flows (θ) by a well-defined continuous and complete mapping (S) determining the simultaneity of knowledge-induced event in unity of knowledge (consciousness) as the combination of occurrence of entity ($\mathbf{x}(t)$) and time (t). Thus, jointly in the dimensions of knowledge, time and space, the convoluted symbolization is $(t,\mathbf{x}(t))[\theta]$, meaning all the variables are primordially affected by knowledge-flows, $\{\theta\}\in(\Omega,S)$.

Figure 1 presents the convoluted symbolization in the dynamic form of history unfolding itself in consciousness over knowledge, time and space in time-continuity and across systemic knowledge-induced continuums.

AN INTEGRATIVE WORLDVIEW OF ORGANIC UNITY IN THE SOCIO-SCIENTIFIC MODEL: GOD AND SCIENCE

Figure 1 now makes us conceptualize an integrative methodological worldview combining in an endogenously continuous way the metaphysical and the natural scientific approach to the treatment of God in the socio-scientific world-system.

Figure 1. Systemic co-evolution in knowledge-time-space dimension

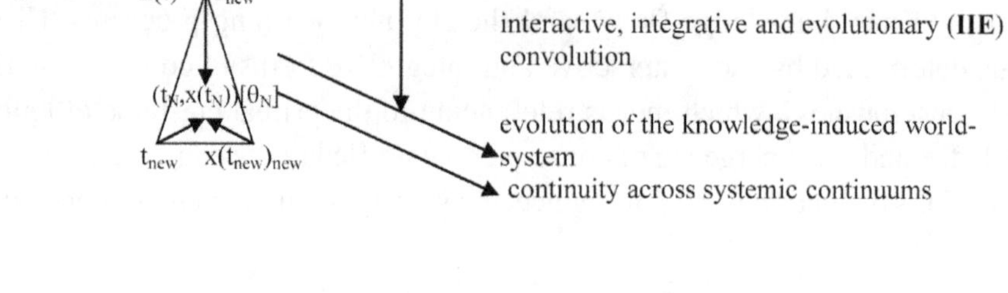

We bring back our simple logicalness of argument presented earlier in terms of the inter-mapped sets, A_1, A_2, Z_1, Z_2. In our present case of the discursively (interactive) actualized integrated (unified) worldview under unity of knowledge, Figure 1 points out that there exists an unique and universal law at the primal topology (Ω,S) that is mapped on to the real world-system. Also conversely, the actualized world-system pertaining to specific problems that form the generic whole, evolves into conscious reassertion of knowledge induction by recalling the primal topology (Ω,S) each and every time an evolutionary learning process resumes. We note then that the world-system that discursively integrates and evolves the historical path of consciousness is fully and pervasively endogenized by knowledge-flows in unity of knowledge. The primal topology (Ω,S) remains permanently exogenous to regenerate and guide the entire logical system across continuity and systemic continuums in epistemic unity of knowledge. Without such a unique and universal exogeneity of (Ω,S) the permanent effect of this primal premise will not exist, and the system will be diluted by a confusion of axioms and social consequences. The contrary is the case of rationalism having the opposite epistemic worldview of reality.

With the unitary perspective in view according to the implication of Figure 1, there must exist the unique and universal law and its properties governing all of A_1, A_2, Z_1, Z_2. As an example, if such a law means gaining overall participation and social justice for the rich and poor on equitable socioeconomic scale at the metaphysical level, the same law is also applied in its discursive form at the worldly level.

The result towards attaining poverty alleviation in this example is abandonment of the usual economic axioms of scarcity of resources, competition, methodological individualism, and postulate of marginal substitution between competing factors of production, consumers, agents, and alternatives. All such axioms are changed for abundance by knowledge acquisition, participation, sharing and social justice to attain equitable distribution of resources, ownership, empowerment and entitlement. The law for ameliorating the poor and the rich are jointly enhanced. There are complementarities gained by organically unified relationship between these groups; which otherwise in economic theory appear as irreconcilable groups. Indeed, knowledge regenerates without diminishing.

Indeed, the ethical goals of poverty alleviation by the discursive, organic and learning processes of coexistence between the poor and the rich are universally acclaimed by a just and enlightened society. The result is a corresponding enlargement of the commonness between the sets A_1 (poor) and A_2 (rich) by the advancing learning process in response to the ideal law of unity of knowledge characterizing the unified sets Z_1 and Z_2. On the reverse causality there is heightened actualization of Z_1 and Z_2 (the ideal law) by the actions and responses in A_1 and A_2 together co-evolving towards the episteme of unity of knowledge. In Figure 1, the implication of such isomorphic mappings between the mentioned sets is to generate actions and responses from the primal ontology of (Ω,S) and return back to this through the learning processes of the world-system governed by the episteme of unity of knowledge. The dimensional analysis throughout in such framework of analysis of organic relationship enhancing consciousness of unity of knowledge is in terms of topological mappings and relations. Such is the consequence of the mathematical semiosis of God, science and society that we referred to.

The preservation of the order of unique and universal relationship that is maintained between the mentioned sets of complements in the dimensions of knowledge, time and space is accomplished by the mapping S of Ω on to the actions and responses of the world-system. Thereafter, the reverse convoluted relations from the world-system accumulates and returns to (Ω,S) in the very large universe of knowledge and learning, continuously and across continuums of systems.

Formalizing the Interactive, Integrative, and Evolutionary Nature of Learning Processes

Let the knowledge-induced unified socio-scientific world-system be denoted by $\mathrm{WS}(\boldsymbol{\theta},\mathbf{x}(\mathbf{t}, \boldsymbol{\theta}))$ as a subset of the total world-system of matter, mind and spiritual capabilities. The epistemic beginning as metaphysical ontology through its semiotic ontological construction of the world-system, and finally accumulating and realizing the total knowledge-induced reality in the primal epistemic end once again, taken altogether, is written as,

$$\{\Omega \rightarrow_{S} \{\theta\} \rightarrow_{g} x(t)[\theta] \rightarrow_{f1} \mathrm{WS}(\theta, x(t, \theta))\} \equiv P_1\} \rightarrow_{f1} P_2 \rightarrow_{f2} P_3 \rightarrow \ldots \rightarrow_{S} \Omega \qquad (1)$$

Taken up in the complexity of systemic continuums in continuous dimensions of knowledge, time and space, expression (1) represents the logicalness of endogenous connection of WS(.) to the exogenous existence of the primal episteme. In this representation, the string relationship as shown is logically closed in the very large universe, which comprises the general system of 'everything'. This string has its analytical properties, which we will examine later on. The properties establish profound analytical results, such as the existence of evolutionary learning equilibriums, the topological continuity of functions like $g, f_1, f_2, \ldots$ describing functional ontologies or the mathematical semiosis of the discursively evolved and constructed states of the learning and unified world-system denoted by $\mathrm{WS}(\theta, x(t, \theta))$. The functional mapping 'g' represents the primal derivation of secondary rules and laws derived from the primal epistemic premise. This is done through human discourse in reference to the fundamental epistemic law and given states of the world-system. The moral-social transformation by consciousness that, attains along the evolutionary path shown in expression (1) and Figure (1), marks the states of the world-system and its specific problems and issues under investigation in the socio-scientific state 'as-is'. This state is followed by its social, ethical, and moral reconstructions as the state of 'ought-to-be'.

The problem of dichotomy and differentiation between the metaphysical realm and the physical world has thus been resolved by bringing the two together in the model of unity of knowledge with evolutionary learning behavior and the discursive process enabling such learning to be attained in epistemic unity of knowledge. The problem of non-uniqueness, hence non-universality of mappings[1] between the sets A_1, A_2, Z_1, Z_2 that we found to exist in the case of their differentiated nature between science, morality and ethics, has been resolved in the second case by the logical continuity and completeness[2,3] of their inter-mappings in the very large universe, while growing towards this completeness from the realms of the small-scale universes denoted by processes P_i, i =1,2,... to the large-scale universe, and up to the largest one, which we referred to as the Hereafter..

One would like to envision what would be the consequences if there were only bifurcations by dialectical negations (Adorno, 2007) and no convergence to a continuous and complete form in knowledge-time-space dimension. In such a case, both the large-scale universe and its specific components as the small-scale universes would remain open without closure. No limiting point would exist. Hence the much-needed properties of continuity of particular convoluted sets and their completeness would not exist. Bifurcations would lead to differentiations between evolutionary chains of entities. Such is the case of social and biological Darwinism along the tree of natural selection (Darwin, 1936). Such is also the abiding mark of all of western theories of the sciences, society, economics and finance, business, governments and institutions.

On the other hand, punctuated evolutionary equilibriums that we referred to earlier would not exist between bifurcations due to the displacement of entities along such bifurcated tree. Consequently, the resulting evolutionary equilibriums would not be contained in continuous sets. Any such equilibrium would thus not arise by causation from its parents. In the end, the path of history that marks consciousness by organic linkages between the past, present and the future through positivistic and normative reasoning, will cease to take well-defined meaning. The idea of meaning and meaningfulness of actions and responses in the convoluted socio-scientific space will fall off from the path of history. The open world-system without evolutionary convergence, continuity and completeness, evolving to the large-scale universe in totality, becomes an uncharted domain of differentiated forms and thoughts.

FROM THE THEME OF GOD AND THE SOCIO-SCIENTIFIC WORLD-SYSTEM TO THE CASE OF GOD AND THE FINANCIAL SYSTEM

The world of economics, finance and banking is an interactive subset of the socio-scientific world-system. In the pervasively complementary world-system in the light of epistemic unity of knowledge the scientific and financial systems, as any other ones, do not exist independently of each other. For instance, the realm of technology shares its meaning, growth and profitability, adaptation to human utilization and wellbeing through the coterminous processes of knowing the appropriate construct, development, and use of technology for the good purposes of existence. Yet technology can be an extensively destructive and differentiating artifact of human acquisition, if it does not serve the reachable meaningfulness, objective of wellbeing, accessibility and capability for development in cost-effective and benefit-intensive ways. Indeed, much of the debt problem of the developing world has been due to reliance on expensive technology imports and expatriates to run such technology. Yet, the local users in technology importing countries experience slow and delayed adaptation to imported technology. In the end, over such delayed adaptation time the technologies undergo obsolescence, overhaul, replacement and change. Under-development continues (Millelman, 1988, pp. 159-186).

Technology and its overarching sustainability is deeply a socio-cultural artifact. On this issue Holton (1992, p. 184, slightly edited) writes: "One major implication of this (economic sociology) is that culture enters into all social activities including economic and political life. We may therefore speak of economic culture or political culture, by which is meant those aspects of economic or political life that involve issues of meaning and values. And the practices in which they are embodied" In the modern treatment of technological evolution the traditional way of the neoclassical school is to treat technology as an exogenous knowledge stock. Its advent influences society and human preferences, markets, development design and bank financing in substantive ways. But the profit-motives of the technology provider, the seller, acquirer, and the financier, continue on to exist as long as alternative better paths of the technological change and profit-motive are not found. Likewise, when technological change reinforced by financing and the technological continuity lasts on our choices, buyer preferences remain one-directionally, influenced by such socio-cultural relations. In all such cases, the supply side of technological relations influences the demand side. With the entrance of technology in the scene of economic, social and political forces, cultural factors cannot be ignored either at the level of formulating postulates of behavior, which is deeply differentiated by modes of thoughts; or by way of the systemic interaction between diversity of forces.

Contrarily, the long durability of technological effect on human preferences following the reign of economic, financial and political power under the acquisition of given technologies, does not cause endogenous technological change. Except in the long while, technological change is not brought about by consumer preferences. Consumer preferences remain datum and fail to have the impact of change. In this case, demand does not determine technological change in the same way that demand can continuously interact with the supply of technology. Technological change fails to be of the endogenous type in traditional mainstream economic and financial thoughts.

For such reasons, classical and neoclassical economic theories of consumer behavior and production and cost assume postulates of marginal utility, diminishing marginal utility, marginal productivity, diminishing marginal productivity, and marginal rates of commodity substitution and technical substitution. Such postulates are necessary for convenience in solving the optimization problems of economic and financial theory, as if these problems had identity with the distribution of nutrients and the determination of the optimal path of a projectile in space. But in the endogenous processes of consumer behavior, preference formation, production, input-use, technological change and their financing, the one-dimensional ultimate objective of profit-maximization and cost-effectiveness do not answer the coterminous interactive objective criterion of organic relations and their recursive circular effects in the total system.

Endogenous growth theory, which does not accept the postulate of diminishing returns of the neoclassical economic school, can be applied to the case of financing, and hence, banking in relation to technological induction of consumer preferences, production functions and resource allocation. In this case, we can assume a circular relationship of feedback and replenishment of resources between the goods and services sectors on the one hand, and the financial sector on the other hand, with technology as a feedback connector between the interactive sectors. The result then will be like this: The determination of the prospective future of financing development and production at the level of the firm is based on a participatory discourse between the representations of the various intersecting sectors and institutions.

The economic and social appropriateness of the project to be financed in regards to the shared profit-motive and social meaningfulness of achieving common wellbeing enters the feasibility report for financing the project. The banking system houses such social discourse in its special departments (institutes) to bring about interactively generated integrative and dynamic evolution of participatory decision-making. The multiplicity and expansion of socioeconomic possibilities proceed on, on the basis of the evolutionary knowledge. The evolutionary possibilities are causally linked with production and risk diversifications under the impact of unity of knowledge causing unity of decision-making and the systemic convolutions, as we explained earlier. Such interaction, integration, and evolutionary (IIE) dynamics form the circular cause and effect of the endogenous phenomenon of development.

Parsons and Smelser (1956) provide their AGIL model of such interactive socio-cultural development and political economy. We will refine this model by introducing in it the role of the banking sector in bringing about the convoluted systemic unity between interactive, integrative, and learning sectors toward codetermining the sustainable wellbeing of self and all. We will also compare and contrast the resulting perspective of organic systemic unity from that of social choice theory of welfare economics (Arrow, 1951; Hammond, 1989).

Parsons taxonomy involving A (adaptation), G (goal attainment), I (integration), and L (pattern maintenance) is embedded in a differentiated way of examining systemic separations and specializations. For instance, AGIL has been further disaggregated into $A^aA^gA^iA^l$, $G^aG^gG^iG^l$, $I^aI^gI^iI^l$, $L^aL^gL^iL^l$ to represent specific differentiations by specializations within the categories of AGIL. An example of such differentiation in AGIL-sense is the business and banking system involving the interrelations between money, finance, political economy, and technology by means of cultural dynamics. But while we examine this here we extend the AGIL framework of social determinations into a participatory form. We adopt the role of the business and banking system in forming and sustaining the participatory dynamics of its social determination in respect of the episteme of unity of knowledge – the endogenous moral and ethical dimensions instead of cultural and technological exogenous force.

In Parsons, the business and banking system represented by A in AGIL-model has a specialized function of its own, which is to circulate a quantity of money by using financial instruments to attain G of maximizing bank-shareholders' wealth. The integrative function of the relationship between monetary flow and shareholders' wealth maximization is realized by financial instruments. Such instruments may be regulatory interest rates, share capital, central bank monetary policies, and commercial bank multiple credit creation. L can be denoted by continuity of the fractional reserve requirement monetary system according to which the central bank and commercial banks establish their monetary relations, and the economy responds to such relationship.

Furthermore, the various disaggregation within AGIL categorization of the business/banking specialization can represent similar AGIL-functions for projects financed by banks by a disaggregate bundle of intra-systemic approaches within the banking system. These micro-AGIL categories are used to maximize shareholders' wealth through the process of diverse specializations for deepening economic competition and acquisition. The elements of differentiation by specialization by and within the business/banking system, causing thereby competition and methodological individualism everywhere in society and economy, abound.

There is no place for studying unity of knowledge and unity of the business/banking and economy and social systems by means of a straightforward adoption of AGIL-model. Likewise, technology and culture as intra-system social neurons do not act as endogenous inter-systemic forces to transcend across different socioeconomic sectors. The methodology underlying interactive, integrative, and evolutionary (IIE) dynamics characterizing learning processes in reference to the episteme of unity of knowledge cannot be used or derived directly in the AGIL-model.

AGIL Adoption to Show Banking Role in Unity of Knowledge

An input-output type relationship between the various categories of inter-sectoral flows of goods, services and resources explaining such linkages is a powerful criterion of systemic unity of knowledge. This episteme is simultaneously translated into the real unity between artifacts comprising variables, their institutional agencies, policies, programs and relations. The evolutionary construction of learning process further transforms the coefficients of inter-variables and inter-systemic unifying relations as manifestations of continuous unification across continuums. In this way, the learning effects of knowledge-flows and emergent knowledge-induced artifacts bring about dynamic forms of input-output coefficients. This is at once also the logical result of the inherent interactive, integrative, and evolutionary (IIE) properties of continuous learning processes across continuums of systemic diversities in reference to the episteme of unity of knowledge.

In the case of the banking system, 'A' can be denoted for the conceptualization and establishment of banks as a financial intermediary charged principally with the goal of mobilizing monetary and financial resources to unite productively with the real economy. Thereby, 'G' will denote the goal of money and real economy linkages in social possibilities. 'I' will denote the choices of appropriate financial instruments to match up with the goals of 'A' and 'G'. 'L' will denote the dynamics of continuum, as in the evolutionary case of continuing the simulation of wellbeing gained out of unity of relationships between the banking system and all others.

The above characterization of AGIL in the banking case can disaggregate into AGIL-components, such as ($A^aA^gA^iA^l$)-components will comprise efforts in establishing such banks that promote ethical and moral objectives as complements with economic and financial benefits. Such banks thereby function on the foundation of socioeconomic participation and participatory organizational form and behavior.

A great deal of human resource induction is required to entrench the above-mentioned cognitive values of such banks in society at large. The approach in such direction can take the form of financing of appropriate projects. The goal of mobilizing monetary resource through financial instruments applies now to feasible projects. The integrative function of 100 per cent reserve requirements monetary system, whose features are established by central bank and commercial bank interrelations, is strengthened. The microeconomic financing of appropriate projects extends the interactive, integrative, and evolutionary (IIE) dynamics of project financing to higher levels of unified organic relations between bank and business, economic, financial, social, moral and ethical continuums.

($G^aG^gG^iG^l$)-components denote the disaggregating of the goal of attaining social wellbeing by means of the specific project financing and in terms of mobilizing monetary resources to meet the organic complementarities between money and the real economy. Such an attainment of social wellbeing denotes the unifying complementarities between the interacting goals.

($I^aI^gI^iI^l$)-components denote the choice of appropriate financial instruments for the specific projects with good complementarities between such financing instruments. The idea of inter-financial instrument complementarities extends to all other elements of the money-real economy unifying relations. An example of such regulatory relationship is the monitoring of the 100 per cent reserve requirements monetary system at the project-level and extending this to the overarching banking/business system marked by AGIL-aggregation. The passage for gaining such systemic unification is actualized in all of the project-specific unifying organic relations between 'AGIL'-components at the project-level 'I'.

($L^aL^gL^iL^l$)-components denote the project-specific level of attainment of the continued interactive, integrative, and evolutionary (IIE) dynamics of the learning processes extending over 'AGIL'-components, and extending this to the overarching AGIL-level for the whole business/banking system. In this way, the continuity of the learning processes that extend over continuums of organic diversities of projects mark the nature of microeconomic aggregation by a complex of organically complementing learning processes to the higher echelons of organization and extension of unifying relations.

In the end, the dynamic interrelations between the disaggregate levels within AGIL-model pertain to micro-aggregation culminating to the overarching social level. Monetary aggregate now assumes the form of micro-money in respect of monetary mobilization into the compendium of real-economy ethical projects. In bringing about such mobilization and money-real economy linkages, appropriate financial instruments are used that generate the free flow of monetary and financial resources into the real economy and in ethically targeted possibilities. An overall complementary (participatory) network of synergistic interrelations is generated between various systemic interacting, integrating, and evolutionary points. The episteme of unity of knowledge and its cognitive function as functional ontology is used pervasively by continuity across systemic continuums.

The concept of money and its relationship with the real economy from the microeconomic level of projects to their relational complex aggregation at higher echelons of relations is established as an intellectual idea. The banking/business system establishes the ontological functions of money, finance. and real economy social relations by its configuration of institutional forms. The social contract on ethical grounds of the epistemic unity of knowledge worldview applied to money and real economy ethico-economic choices is implemented in the banking/business sector by establishing a national and specific institutional discourse bodies on the theme of money-finance-real economic relational dynamics. The financial choice of instruments and the overall developmental effects are realized via the social wellbeing objective criterion premised on unity of knowledge as the episteme.

The bringing together of money, finance and real economic ethical possibilities and evaluating their unifying interrelationships is all together encapsulated in the social wellbeing objective criterion. The institutional mechanism of the learning process in the social contract of the banking/business system establishing unity of knowledge and its cognitive effect through the money, finance and real economy interrelations, goes through repetitions of the interactive, integrative, and evolutionary (IIE) dynamics rising from the small to the large scale socio-scientific systems.

The totality of such institutional phases in conjunction with the intellectual idea on the application of the epistemic unity of knowledge to the interlinked money-finance-real sector ethico-economic relations forms a compendium of quantitative-policy-theoretic undertaking. The banking system, through its institution that undertakes such intellectual and applied discourses and pursuits, becomes charged with the goal of human resource development. The entire intellectual and applied learning experience enhances deepening consciousness of the social political economy of an ethico-economic nature. Amartya Sen (1990) refers to such individual, institutional, and market driven ethical change as the way to formation of deontological social preferences.

THE TECHNOLOGY AND CULTURAL IMPACT ON THE ENDOGENOUS LEARNING RELATIONSHIP IN MONEY-FINANCE-BANKING AND REAL ECONOMY ETHICO-ECONOMIC SYNERGY

How does the epistemic inquiry of the banking/business system in unity of knowledge and the complementary money-finance-banking and real economy synergistic relations treat the issues of technology and cultural forces?

Cultural Differentiation Effect on Social and Economic Forces

Conventionally, under the rubric of economic and social thought, culture is seen as a pluralistic force. Contrarily, the science of culture that Ibn Khaldun for example, studied in his philosophy of history (Mahdi, 1964), and what is referred to as global ethics by the World Commission on Global Governance (1995), have not entered cultural dynamics. Consequently, cultural pluralism following the same kind of methodological individualism (separation), as in the case of individual and group behavior of self-centered entities in market exchange. Such is a deeply differentiating social and economic practice. It leads into segmented trajectories of change and cultural assertion between different peoples. In the end, such an effect causes the rise of cultural hegemony and self-assertion over other ones. A vivid example of such a consequence is the historical practice of Eurocentricity (Tisdell, 1989; Amin, 1977) and Orientalism (Said, 1978). It also falls within the power of world-system studies of capitalism over other politico-economic arrangements. The topic has been studied by Wallerstein (1974).

The words of Robert Holton were given earlier to point out that once the social and economic systems remain differentiated, the impact of cultural pluralism will simply accentuate such differentiation. At the end, the ethical power of matters like social discourse and the universal role of moral and ethical values to prevail in society at large, fails to dawn by the cultural route in the midst of economic and social differentiation.

Technological Differentiating Effect on Social and Economic Forces

Likewise, technology can have differentiating impact on society and economy. For long now there have been studies on endogenous and indigenous technology that generates capability rather than alienation among the technology users. The differentiating and unfriendly nature of labor-market adaptation of technology is one of the clearest causes of the economic and financial resource distributional gaps between the rich and poor countries.

The global debt burden expressed as the ratio of total debt stock to exports caused by dependency on western technology by the developing countries stood at 104.7 per cent in 2003. The debt-servicing burden as a percentage of exports caused by interest charges on debt of the developing countries stood at 17.2 in 2003. These ratios point out that, a substantive part of developing countries' exports are directed towards debt repayment, and then too, additional resources are required to pay off debt burden. The higher percentage over and above the 100 per cent ceiling of use of exports to pay off debt marks the sign of deepening indebtedness. Thus for example, a figure of 147.9 per cent for debt/export ratio for low income countries mark the place of highly indebted poor countries in this 47.9 per cent excess demand for resources to pay off debt burden[4].

The differentiating nature of technology and culture caused by the systemic nature of prevalent social and economic forces are endogenously regenerative of their demeaning effects within their own categories of competition and methodological individualism. Policies and programs that perpetuate these demeaning effects, and thereby, the structure of institutions that establish social contracts, all these are ingredients of the differentiating spectrum of entities in the resulting world-systems. The protraction of such self-reinforcing forces over the *longue durée* of history has marked the fallen consciousness of the great moral and ethical values of equality, justice and freedom. The positivist picture of history is by and large this kind of a deepened organic development of regenerative methodological individualism, contest and conflict.

But unlike the Marxist materialistic interpretation of history, such a trend was not universally true of all civilizations. It is also something that can be reconstructed by normative possibilities. Indeed, the learning process premised on the episteme of unity of knowledge and the consequential unified world-systems with their diverse entities, issues and problems, creates new social reconstructions. The nature of an emergent good society is indeed based on new possibilities of moral, ethical and social reconstruction.

ENDOGENOUS MORAL, ETHICAL, AND SOCIAL RECONSTRUCTION WITH CULTURAL AND TECHNOLOGICAL FORCES BASED ON THE NORMATIVE EPISTEMIC WORLDVIEW OF UNITY OF KNOWLEDGE: THE BUSINESS/BANKING MEDIUM

So when we think of such interactive, integrative, and evolutionary (IIE) socio-scientific relationships between multiple systems, the business/banking system becomes an endogenous development-financing intermediary. The bank promotes continuous circular cause and effect relations by using the mechanism of monetary regulation. In doing so, the business/banking system uses means of appropriate financial instruments to mobilize money and finance toward simulating the social wellbeing objective of the complementing systems that engage in the social construction. All such circular causation relations arising from the method of interactive, integrative, and evolutionary (IIE) dynamics are of the endogenous type. The positive consequences of endogenous relations bear grounds and enhance sustainable advancement of the socio-scientific system and problem under study.

The limitations caused by the traditionally prescribed set of postulates of economic theory are replaced by the capability for advancement in knowledge and knowledge-induced possibilities. Policies, programs, technology and appropriate guidance by way of moral suasion color the business/banking role in concert with other interacting systems. Johannessen (2006) refers to such kinds of organizational behavior as an example in social cybernetic. In such learning processes of organizational change a combination of positivistic and normative reasoning is used to sustain the social system with simulated progress in social wellbeing.

Along these reconstructed paths of moral, ethical, and social change the forces of culture and technology enter as endogenous artifacts based on the episteme of unity of knowledge. Discourse and participation reflected in the individual and collective decision-making for the social good in the light of the epistemic law, guidance, policies and programs, become the drivers of social change. Thus, businesses/banks that play a key role in economic development, and are now equipped with the discursive learning elements of institutional organization think tank of money, finance and real economy interrelations in the framework of the epistemic unity as the driving forces of laws, guidance and practice.

Now in as far as cultural unity and technological meaningfulness play substantive roles in realizing the endogenous nature of moral, ethical, and social reconstruction along with the economic and financial gains, the unifying science of culture *a la* Ibn Khaldun and the appropriateness of technology play their instrumental importance in creative business/banking functions. An important study in this regard that proposes and studies the implementation of cooperative mechanisms (participatory and innovative) of business culture, which would make competition and methodological individualism irrelevant, is by Kim and Mauborgne (2005). Another one is by Daly (1992) in regards to the idea of pervasive complementarities in environmental possibilities contrary to marginal substitution. The same contrasting idea can be conceptualized and applied to the business venue.

A CONFIGURATION OF CULTURAL AND TECHNOLOGICAL ENDOGENEITY IN GENERATING SOCIO-SCIENTIFIC UNIFICATION

Figure 2 shows how technology and culture interact in circular causation ways with complementarities between the diverse ingredients of the disaggregate AGIL-model along with the endogenous effects of technology and culture in the circular causation dynamics. The two-way arrows denote circular causation as the sign of unity between diversities according to the episteme of unity of knowledge. This is also a manifestation of endogenous organic relations between the different parts

Figure 2. Configuring interaction, integration, and evolution in the

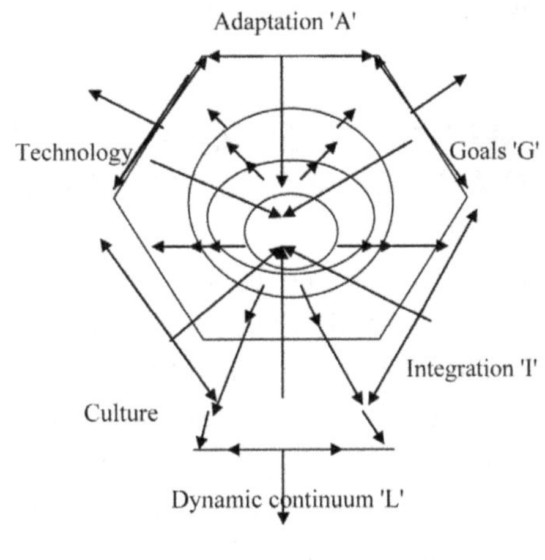

of the AGIL-model, which is now converted into its relational perspectives. The one directional arrow of the circles denotes that, creative evolution as learning by interaction, integration, leading to creative evolution, proceeds on.

AGIL-Model with Interdependency

The same figure can be repeated for any kind of interactive, integrative, and evolutionary (IIE) phenomenon. Thus business/banking is a specific example. The central core of the evolutionary circles by circular causation across learning processes that enables and follows from evolutionary dynamics of epistemic unity of knowledge, marks the primal epistemic basis shown in expression (1). This primal source is the unitary episteme. It continuously and across continuums, generates knowledge-flows and their induced artifacts in the AGIL-model according to the epistemic unity of knowledge.

The deconstruction of technology and culture along with the finer levels of the AGIL-model carries along moral and ethical issues. Consequently, the systemic organic interrelations between all the different levels of disaggregations apply the learning process continuously everywhere. In this way, to bring forth God into the world-system as the holistic socio-scientific system, the moral and ethical nature of social choices must prevail over all interactive diversities. This experience itself is the result of conscious learning processes that are uniquely and universally premised on the episteme of unity of knowledge and unity of the world-system and its diverse artifacts. The implications of extending the prevalence of moral and ethical values to their socio-scientific consequences in increasing details by means of laws and material choices, responses and actions of their interrelations, extends the boundaries of socio-scientific analysis. The metaphysical and material values and artifacts are explained by a unified theory of 'everything'.

CONCLUSION: TOWARDS INTEGRATING GOD WITH THE SOCIO-SCIENTIFIC AND CYBERNETIC WORLD-SYSTEM

From our various viewpoints expressed in this chapter, we have noted that the relevance of God in the socio-scientific and cybernetic world-system is based on the unison that is methodologically established between the ontological nature of belief and the credence of scientific thought and analysis. One without the other ruptures our unified way of understanding of the ontologically functioning of the world-system. The question is how God can be integrated with the world-system with the purpose and benefit in 'everything', as we understand this term in socio-scientific context integrating the philosophy of science and society.

The issue and problem of bringing God into the socio-scientific world-system is therefore a deeply methodological one. This methodology assumes an epistemic form. Because of the unity of knowledge as the epistemic premise that unifies the laws of God with the world-system and 'everything' in it existing in systemic unification, referred to as complementarities and participation between them, there exist perpetual diversity of artifacts. These are seen as possibilities of the good things of life in their organic unity of relations. The details of such an epistemic methodology were pointed out. They will be developed in greater extent in the subsequent chapters.

Along with the epistemic unity of knowledge as the moral, ethical and socio-scientific law of unification in 'everything', the meaning of God and the socio-scientific world-system, assumes the dynamics of such laws, guidance, intellection and applications on the basis of the universal foundation of the oneness of God as belief (metaphysics) and law (world-system). God is thus brought into the socio-scientific and cybernetic world-system by the divine law (monotheistic law) at work in reality. We will dwell on this topic at length in the subsequent chapters (see Table 1).

Table 1. The domain of socio-scientific inquiry

Conventional Approach	Monotheistic Worldview
Rationalism as episteme: materiality, rational premise of methodological individualism in "everything".	Extension to the domain of religion and science episteme of unity of knowledge as by monotheism to explain "everything".
A limited understanding of science as worldview.	Extended understanding of religion and science as socio-scientific worldview.
Limited methodology to explain total reality.	Extensive methodology to explain total reality.
Comparative methods and applications.	Comparative methods and applications.

This chapter concludes by alerting the socio-scientific mind that examining the generality and specifics of the world-system according to the episteme of unity of knowledge as the monotheistic law annuls the separation between science and religion. See Hahne (2012) for an informed awakening on the contemplative mind to understand the two as being uniformly explainable by the deepest empirical and analytical way under the unitary methodological worldview.

REFERENCES

Adorno, T. W. (2007). *Negative dialectics (introduction)*. New York, NY: Continuum International Publishing Group.

Amin, S. (1977). *Imperialism and unequal development*. New York, NY: Monthly Review Press.

Arrow, K. J. (1951). *Social choice and individual values*. New York, NY: John Wiley & Sons.

Barrow, J. D. (1991). *Theories of everything, the quest for ultimate explanation*. Oxford, UK: Oxford University Press.

Boulding, K. E. (1971). Economics as a moral science. In Glass, J. F., & Staude, J. R. (Eds.), *Humanistic Society*. Pacific Palisades, CA: Goodyear Publishing Co. Inc..

Campbell, D. T. (1988). *Evolutionary epistemology*. Evolutionary Epistemology.

Capra, F. (1983). The systems view of life. In *The Turning Point*. London, UK: Flamingo.

Choudhury, M. A. (2006). *Circular causation model in the Koran*. Lewiston, NY: The Edwin Mellen Press.

Collard, D. (1978). *Altruism and economy: A study in non-selfish economics*. New York: Oxford University Press.

Commission on Global Governance. (1995). Global civic ethic. In *Our Global Neighbourhood: A Report of the Commission on Global Governance*. New York, NY: Oxford University Press.

Daly, H. (1992). From empty-world to full-world economics: Recognizing an historical turning point in economic development. In Goodland, R., Daly, H., El-Serafy, S., & von Drost, B. (Eds.), *Environmentally Sustainable Economic Development: Building on Brundtland*. Malta: Center for Development Studies.

Dampier, W. C. (1961). Scientific philosophy and its outlook. In *A History of Science and Its relations with Philosophy and Religion*. Cambridge, UK: Cambridge at the University Press.

Darwin, C. (1936). *Descent of man*. New York, NY: Modern Library.

Dawkins, R. (1976). *The selfish gene*. New York: Oxford University Press.

Dawkins, R. (2006). The roots of morality: why are we good? In *The God Delusion*. London, UK: Transworld Publishers.

Dilworth, D. (2008). *Scientific progress: A study concerning the nature of the relation between successive scientific theories, studies in epistemology, logic, methodology, and philosophy of science*. Berlin: Springer Science.

Edel, A. (1970). Science and the structure of ethics. In Neurath, O., Carnap, R., & Morris, C. (Eds.), *Foundations of the Unity of Science*. Chicago, IL: University of Chicago Press.

Einstein, A. (1954a). The problem of space, ether, and the field in physics. In Commins, C., & Linscott, R. N. (Eds.), *Man and the Universe: The Philosophers of Science*. New York: The Pocket Books, Inc..

Einstein, A. (1954b). Considerations on the universe as a whole. In *Relativity, the Special and the General Theory* (Lawson, R. W., Trans.). London: Methuen.

Fukuyama, F. (1992). *The end of history and the last man*. New York, NY: The Free Press.

Glock, H.-J. (2001). The development of Wittgenstein's philosophy. In *Wittgenstein: A Critical Reader*. Oxford, UK: Blackwell.

Gruber, T. R. (1993). A translation approach to portable ontologies. *Knowledge Acquisition*, *5*(2), 199–200. doi:10.1006/knac.1993.1008.

Hahne, J. (2012). Science and religion: Reality toolkit, *Yale Scientific*. Retrieved from http://www.yalescientific.org/2012/05/science-and-religion-realitys-toolkit/

Hammond, P. J. (1989). On reconciling Arrow's theory of social choice with Harsanyi's fundamental utilitarianism. In Feiwel, G. R. (Ed.), *Arrow and the Foundation of the Theory of Economic Policy* (pp. 179–221). London, UK: Macmillan.

Hawking, S. W. (1988). *A brief history of time: From the big bang to black holes*. New York: Bantam Books, Inc..

Hawking, S. W., & Mlodinow, L. (2010). *The grand design*. London, UK: Transworld Publishers.

Hayek, F. (1979). *The counter-revolution of science*. Indianapolis, IN: Liberty Fund Inc.

Heiskala, R. (2003). *Society as semiosis*. New York, NY: Peter Lang.

Holton, R. (1992). Economic sociology: An evaluation of a culture-inclusive theory of economy and society. In *Economy and Society*. London, UK: Routledge.

Hubner, K. Dixon, P.R., Jr., & Dixon, H.M. (1985). Foundations of a universal historistic theory of the empirical sciences. In Critique of Scientific Reason, (pp.105-122). Chicago, IL: The University of Chicago Press.

Infeld, L. (1951). General relativity and the structure of our universe. In Schilpp, P. A. (Ed.), *Albert Einstein: Philosopher-Scientist*. New York, NY: Tudor Publications.

Johannessen, J.-A. (2006). Organizations as social systems: The search for a systemic theory of organizational innovation processes. *Kybernetes: International Journal of Systems and Cybernetics*, *27*(4), 359–387. doi:10.1108/03684929810219404.

Kim, W. C., & Mauborgne, R. (2005). Creating blue oceans. In *Blue Ocean Strategy* (pp. 3–22). Boston, MA: Harvard Business School Press.

Krugman, P. (1996). *The self-organizing economy*. Cambridge, MA: Blackwell Publishers.

Kuhn, T. S. (1970). *The structure of scientific revolution*. Chicago, IL: University of Chicago Press.

Ledger, C., & Pickard, S. (Eds.). (2004). *Creation and complexity: Interdisciplinary issues in science and religion*. Adelaide, Australia: ATF Press.

Lucas, R. E. Jr. (1975). An equilibrium model of the business cycle. *The Journal of Political Economy*, *83*, 1113–1144. doi:10.1086/260386.

Mahdi, M. (1964). *Ibn Khaldun's philosophy of history*. Chicago, IL: The University of Chicago Press.

Mittelman, J. H. (1988). What works in the third world? In Out From Underdevelopment, (pp. 159-186). Baskingstroke, UK: Houndmills.

Parsons, T., & Smelser, N. (1956). *Economy and society*. London: Routledge & Kegan Paul.

Popper, K. (2004). *The logic of scientific discovery*. London, UK: Routledge.

Prigogine, I. (1980). *From being to becoming*. San Francisco, CA: W.H. Freeman.

Resnick, S. A., & Wolff, R. D. (1987). A Marxian theory. In *Knowledge and Class*. Chicago, IL: University of Chicago Press.

Rosenlicht, M. (1968). *Introduction to analysis*. New York, NY: Dover Publications, Inc..

Said, E. (1978). *Orientalism*. New York, NY: Random House.

Sen, A. (1990). Freedom and consequences. In *On Ethics and Economics* (pp. 58–89). London, UK: Basil Blackwell.

Shackle, G. L. S. (1972). *Epistemics & economics: A critique of economic theory*. Cambridge, UK: Cambridge University Press.

Singe, H. W., & Ansari, J. A. (1988). Forty years of changing thought on development problems. In *Rich and Poor Countries*. London, UK: Unwin Hyman Inc..

Smullyan, R. M. (1992). *Godel's incompleteness theorems*. New York: Oxford University Press.

Sztompka, P. (1991). *Society in action: The theory of social becoming*. Chicago, IL: The University of Chicago Press.

Thurow, L. (1983). *Dangerous currents: The state of economics*. New York, NY: Random House.

Tisdell, C. (1989). Imperialism, economic dependence and development: A brief review of aspects of economic thought and theory. *Humanomics*, *5*(2). doi:10.1108/eb006093.

Wallerstein, I. (1974). *The modern world systems*. New York, NY: Academic Press.

Wallerstein, I. (1998). Spacetime as the basis of knowledge. In Borda, O. F. (Ed.), *People's Participation, Challenges Ahead* (pp. 43–62). New York: The APEX Press.

Wiener, N. (1966). *God & golem, Inc.: A comment on certain points where cybernetics impinges on religion*. Boston, MA: The MIT Press.

Zsolnai. (2002). New agenda for business ethics. In L. Zsolnai (Ed.), *Ethics in the Economy, Handbook of Business Ethics*. New York, NY: Peter Lang.

ENDNOTES

1 Uniqueness means that a unique, well-defined mapping and its reverse mapping up to a scalardifferentiation exist between *every* point contained in A_1, A_2, Z_1, Z_2. Such mappings, differentiated by scalar measure, are compounded with a differentiation only up to a scalar multiple of the identity map, to the extent that learning remains dynamic in reference to the epistemic premise of unity of knowledge. Universality means that uniqueness exists both in the small-scale and the large-scale universes of 'everything'. Alternatively, the property of universality is signified by mathematical self-referencing (see Godel's incompleteness theorem of arithmetic, Smullyan, 1992).

2 The continuity property here is meant in terms of the continuously learning, actions and responses of entities, variables and their relations in the knowledge-time-space dimension. Thus the limiting values of given variables in the interactive, integrative, and evolutionary convolutions of the knowledge-time-space dimension are compounded in the joint limiting variables in the convoluted set.

3 Completeness of the convoluted set in the knowledge-time-space dimension is shown by the limiting convergence to a limiting value of $(\theta,\mathbf{x}(\theta))$ in this convolution that is attained, and thereafter evolved along evolutionary convolutions. For details on the mathematical concepts of continuity and completeness see Rosenlicht (1968).

4 World Bank debtor reporting system: *Complex Challenges in Developing Countries Debt.*

Chapter 2
The Idea of God in Relation to the Social System:
Banking as a Social System

ABSTRACT

The chapter continues from the groundwork of the socio-cybernetic perspective of the monotheistic law and its functioning in the moral and social construction of the unified world-system. The especial case of the financial and banking system is introduced to bring forth the functional meaning of God as the monotheistic law that is activated in the moral and ethical uplift of the world-system with its specific details. Here, the business model marks the particular case of a unified world-system guided by the epistemology of unity of knowledge. A rigorous formalism underlies this extensive worldview. The phenomenological model of unity of knowledge is further formalized to give it a functional explanation for later explanations in this book.

INTRODUCTION

The previous chapter dwelled on the possibility of extending the scientific model of world-system by integrating God into it as the Supreme Being who creates, governs, and sustains the universe by the divine law. The essential nature of the enabling divine law in the world-system was premised on the episteme of oneness of God and His law at work in the details of the world-system. Our claim in that chapter was that the quest for universality and extension of the socio-scientific model to 'everything' rests on the episteme of oneness, the unity of knowledge, and by it the

DOI: 10.4018/978-1-4666-4643-8.ch002

Copyright ©2014, IGI Global. Copying or distributing in print or electronic forms without written permission of IGI Global is prohibited.

unity of the world-system in every specific detail and generalization of the socio-scientific worldview and the particular issues within the generalization.

In this chapter, our objective is to establish the irreducibility and universality properties of monotheism taken up in its meaning of unity of divine knowledge, and how this episteme bestows *functional* ontological forms in respect of the epistemic unity. The essential focus of our inquiry in this chapter is that monotheism cannot be left aside as a sheer metaphysical way of understanding reality. Monotheism as law must have its well-definable, well-explainable, and well-applicable dimensions that carry with them the social discursive machinery and substantive crystallization of the emergent scientific ideas.

The financial system is then taken up to substantiate the holistic nature of the monotheistic law at work in its entirety in the socio-scientific order generating and evaluating a well-defined wellbeing criterion. The example of the financial system is a particular one within the general-system architecture of the universe examined in the dimensions of knowledge, time, and space. The similitude is to man as the meaningful individual who is capable of the divine breeze within the massive storm of the creative entirety. To realize such an inextricably meaningful relationship between self God and other, the world-system with its generalized and embedded particular systems and issues and designs must be a reflection of the functions of the divine law and its unraveling potentiality. The individual self-actualization within the unified and organically related universe is the ultimate meaning of the generalized universal design and of the embedded particulars within the generalized system of the epistemic unity formed, explained and re-generated in the continuums spanning the dimensions of knowledge, time, and space.

Some great philosophers of science have written in regard to such a union between God, self, and the unfolding, meaningful, deciphered universe and its details. The great Islamic philosopher, Abdul-Hameed Imam Ghazzali wrote (Karim, undated, p. 247): "… He (God) is the First in comparison with the things created as all things come from Him in seriatim one after another. He is the Last in comparison with the things that will remain, as they will return from stage to stage till they return to God. That is the end of their journey. So He is the first of the past things and He is the last of the future things."

Gulen (2006, pp. 148-149) puts the meaningful holistic experience wonderfully:

We use 'the horizon of hope' to mean traveling beyond the visible dimension of existence, and considering existence as an interrelated whole in the absence of which things and events cannot be perceived as they really are. Nor can its essence and relation with the Creator as well as the relation between them and humanity be grasped. Scientific disciplines that conduct their own discourse largely in isolation from one another and the prevailing materialistic nature of science that has compartmentalized existence and life cannot discover the reality of things, existence, or life.

Indeed, despite my total disagreement with Bruteau's (1997) pantheistic depiction of unity between God and the universe, the following passage is nonetheless illuminating in depicting the meaning of the divine in our worldly experience:

If you can see the God you love present in, even as, this world, then feel that union and rejoice in that. And be active in it, contribute to it, participate in the building, in the artwork, in the healing, in the understanding. This is where Reality is. You yourself are both a member of the Finite and a member of the Infinite….

Agius (1990, pp. 82-83) summarizes Professor Whitehead's idea of the ontological principle in reference to the functional meaning of forms and relations that organically explain our universe and the details of its world-systems:

Whitehead's philosophical understanding of the universe as an interconnected Web of relations, as well as the ontological nature of the relational self offer a new paradigm of human society. In contrast to the individualism of the liberal tradition, process philosophy defines human society as a relational structure of experience. ... "The present holds within itself the complete sum of existence, backwards and forwards".

We can continue on in this way inquiring into the minds of the galaxy of great thinkers to assert the indispensability of the monotheistic law at work in the grand design of the universe. The question though remains: What must be the elements of the particular monotheistic law that can serve our need of it being the *functional* ontology premised on the unique and universal episteme of unity of knowledge? This ultimate quest for the specific understanding of the monotheistic law must at once also establish the nature of its uniqueness and universality in 'everything'. We now commence our investigation in this direction.

INQUIRY INTO THE UNIQUENESS AND UNIVERSALITY OF THE MONOTHEISTIC LAW

In conjunction with expression (1) of Chapter 1 [recalled here] we write down the entire organic grand design with God, self, and the world in the following expression:

The repeated expression (1) of Chapter 1 is this:

$$\{\Omega \rightarrow_S \{\theta\} \rightarrow_g x(t)[\theta] \rightarrow_{f1} WS(\theta, x(t, \theta))\} \equiv P_1\} \rightarrow_{f1} P_2 \rightarrow_{f2} P_3 \rightarrow \ldots \rightarrow_S \Omega$$

(Chapter 1, expression 1)

The holistic expression of God, self and the world-system (W-S) spanning 'everything' is written down as follows:

$$\Omega \rightarrow_S: (\Omega,S) \rightarrow \text{W-S } (\theta\in\Omega,S) \rightarrow \text{continuums over knowledge, time and space} \ldots\rightarrow (\Omega,S) \quad (1)$$

By a further multi-dimensional extension of expression (1) we obtain the expression (2) now written with simplification:

The problem of uniqueness and universality rests on the resolution of the closed universe emerging out of the learning universe of unity of knowledge. This investigation rests on the understanding of expression (2) (Figure 1) and its critical assessment.

Expression (2) must be explained and understood in the light of the scientific context of the model of God, self, and the world-system. The following steps lead to the proof of uniqueness and universality of the epistemic claim of monotheistic oneness and its organic representation in the unity of the world-system. See also the section on Preface.

Step 1: Epistemic Axiom and Knowledge Formation on the Basis of Unity of Knowledge

The primal axiom is taken as the super-topological space of the divine law of oneness understood in the relational sense of the law to the world and human reason to intellectualize the relational precept of organic oneness (also pairing). It is well-known fact that, without a primal axiom(s) there cannot stand scientific understanding, theory

Figure 1. Expression 2

(This is shown as expression, nit as figure in the text)

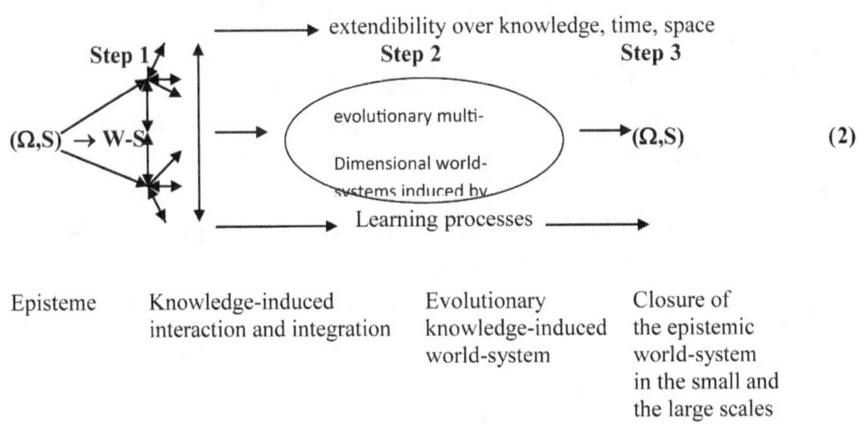

and meaning. Einstein once remarked to his friend Niels Bohr (1985) that, there is no science without epistemology; which is a foundational theory of knowledge.

But as axiom, the monotheistic law is the single most exogenous premise influencing 'everything'. The overarching influence is a topological mapping that carries the axiom into the explanatory domain of action. Without this kind of a relational mapping, the ontological oneness although acknowledged by self, is incapable of externalization and meaning in experiential reality. In such a case, the axiom of oneness remains a metaphysical niche, not an active agency. Expression (2) takes the epistemic origin as axiom represented in the absoluteness of the irreducible premise, namely the law of monotheism understood as the super-topological entity denoted by Ω. The mapping of this foundational episteme onto human experience in its entirety and beyond is denoted by the explanatory power of the super-cardinal mapping 'S' in the sense of its capability of unraveling the meaning of Ω into human comprehension and over historical consciousness. This totality comprises the evolutionary expanse of unification between possibilities according to the law of oneness prevailing across knowledge-induced continuums over time.

Some concepts need clarification here. Firstly, the content of Ω as the domain of super-topology comprises non-corporeal elements. There is only the law that creates, explains, and reaffirms the manifestation of a unified reality arising out of the consciousness, understanding, and application of monotheism into the general and particular embedded issues and problems of material and abstract existences. The functional law is now the foundational axiom Ω along with the mapping S; hence $[(\Omega,S): \Omega \rightarrow_{S}]$.

An example of such relational experience premised on and representing oneness is this: What is the ultimate goal of science? On this question, Hawking like Leibniz, says that the ultimate goal is to explain the universe with the minimum of axioms. This means also leading human inquiry into the limits of its possibility, and its capability for consciousness. Thus there arises the principle of irreducibility in the epistemic search and discovery for the ultimate truth. It is also not possible to understand the relationship of oneness by a segmented view of oneness in a part of the whole only. Thereby, it is meaningless oneness as relational and organic understanding of unity and oneness to have the generalized picture premised on an ensemble of systems unified together by a numinous cosmic oneness or by additive aggregation of independent entities. The Confucius philosophy adheres to such a numinous idea of oneness (Capra, 1982). And still a proper sub-set of the general, that is the particular, is left out of the universal overarching law.

Social consciousness, the human comprehension of organic symbiosis between the artifacts small and large and in between each of these by their relational embedding, must be an interdisciplinary intellectual venture. Yet, modernity is by and large a one-directional view of reality premised solely on specialization, and thereby, perception. On this point Wallerstein (1998, p. 46) writes: "Thus was consummated in the late eighteenth century in what has been termed the divorce between philosophy and science, a divorce that was institutionalized in the reviving university system by establishing separate faculties for the humanities.... And for the (natural) sciences, a segregation that remains to this day the form of most university structures throughout the world. This was the split between what we call today the two cultures, and the divorce was not at all amicable."

The importance of interdisciplinarity as substantive knowing of the world in its ever-growing and increasingly overarching expanse links up economic issues with scientific, technological and philosophical issues. Not to be able to deduce the normative from the positivistic view, and vice-a-verse test the normative model of reality by the simulacra of human possibilities, is a fiasco in socio-scientific inquiry.

Economic activity as an example increases the productivity of its inputs for attaining higher levels of output at stable prices, higher and more distributive entitlement to income, wealth and property ownership at all rungs of society. The end objective is to attain higher levels of social wellbeing for all. In the improvement of such input productivity, technological advancement is required by way of generating feedback relations between technology and economic change. Such feedback relations are endogenous in nature and are well explained by the new growth theory (Romer, 1986; Mankiw, 2003). Continuous technological change over production and risk diversifications require a continuous burst of scientific knowledge spanning over such diversities. The commercial world of markets, businesses and institutions has its own technological growth that adapts to the general socio-scientific milieu to extend the endogenous knowledge-sharing process. In the end, a conscious and wise decision-making in the economic world does not limit its pursuits within a narrow vision.

Kim and Mauborgne (2005) point out that in the blue ocean strategy which they promote for businesses against the traditional red ocean strategy of competition and largeness that suffer from diseconomies of large scale, then the productive scope enlarges tremendously. North American Industrial Classification (NAIC) was the result of the great outburst of industrial sectors in the wake of the new and vaster vision of the business world in the direction of strategic alliances, cooperation, and innovation. The one-sided picture of profit-maximization, which we continue to teach in hard core economics, is being abandoned.

Returning to (Ω,S) in respect of the interdisciplinary view, the law of oneness encapsulated by Ω establishes the worldview of the interdisciplinary unity according to the monotheistic law. The example here is of the moral law of social justice, fairness, and distributive equity that unites with the economic law of productivity, development and growth. The rational process of economics would render such a relationship between the social and economic forces to its fundamental axiom of scarcity of resources. The consequence of this axiom is competition, conflict, self-interest, individualism, and marginal rate of substitution between competing alternatives. In fact, in the multivariate system of resource allocation between various alternatives there are no pervasive complementarities. The postulate of marginal rate of substitution between alternatives reappears with the alternatives now taken up in competing groups.

For more than two competing alternatives denoted by their quantity-variables, one of the variables can be complement of at least one of the remaining two; or it can be complement of both variables. But since the quantity-variables are substitutes of each other, therefore the augmenting other variable will be siding with one of the substitutes to create a joint variable for substitution. Take the case of sugar divided between the tea-sugar and coffee-sugar markets and treated as substitutes for both tea and coffee. But since tea and coffee are substitutes, therefore, the sugar used up in the market for tea say, will substitute the sugar used for drinking coffee in the market place. Thereby, sugar for tea consumption sides with tea; sugar for coffee consumption sides with coffee. Sugar for tea and sugar for coffee in this differentiated sense are thus substitutes in terms of its aligning with either of the substitutes, namely tea or coffee. This condition annuls the result of pervasive complementarities of sugar with tea and coffee, thus allowing only temporary complementarities to exist. Such complementarities revert to marginal rates of substitution just as differentiation soon takes over and scarcity returns.

In the end we note that, despite the clamor for togetherness between social justice and economic efficiency in national development planning and market-institution relations, the existing methodological basis of economic theory does not allow such a scenario to be obtained through an endogenous process of learning and self-consciousness and social-consciousness. At the best, to realize a semblance of complementarities between the social and economic ends of socio-scientific life, exogenous altruistic attributes, government resource, exogenous technology and regulations are required. The self-organizational, conscious nature of endogenous response to change is lessened. A dire example here is of the developing countries, which instead of adopting indigenous technology in national development, turn to foreign technology for borrowed western designs of development. The result is high levels of indebtedness and unequal and inequitable distribution of the fruits of development to all rungs of society. The ethical, moral, social and economic, and technological contexts of development break apart.

Henderson (1999) remarks on such demeaning consequences of the rush to modernity, globalization, and economic growth: "Today's task is, therefore, to shape our mental, moral and decision-making skills to meet the challenges to our very survival that our misguided technological innovations have created. This requires a flowering of social innovation, rethinking of our paradigms, re-engineering and redesigning of our physical and social architectures."

Economic theory has increasingly imitated the color of positivism (Friedman, 1953) and abandoned normative vision, until recently, yet without a proper methodology and a change in human will. Myrdal (1987) writes in this regard:

Hundreds of books and articles are produced every year on "welfare economics", reasoning in terms of individual or social 'utility' or some substitute of that term. But if the approach is not entirely meaningless, it has a meaning only in terms of a forlorn hedonistic psychology, and a utilitarian moral philosophy built upon that psychology. I have always wondered why the psychologists and philosophers have left the economists alone and undisturbed in their futile exercise.

Economic theory is not a study of process. It studies the consequences of end-points of optimization theory, giving the individual and groups the rational capability to maximize without inquiring about the interactive social spirit to share in the simulation process towards attaining collective wellbeing within which the self coexists. On this nature of economic theory writes Shackle (1971, p. 90): "The notion of a wholly foreseen and wholly constrained biography-to-come is nightmarish, let alone the inconceivable complexity of the task of pre-reconciliation and the general implausibility of the logical existence of a solution. A general solution, or general equilibrium, has accordingly to be conceived as a state of affairs and not a course of affairs."

From the above arguments against the possibility of mainstream socio-scientific worldview, which is exemplified by the specific example of economic theory taken within the general model of economic rationality, we reach a firm analytical conclusion. That is, only in the space-time structure of social consciousness, which is an episteme of rationalism and its derived worldview of rationality, scarcity and limitation of knowledge, information, and all forms of resources acquire a specified aspect of thinking. There is no place in this system for the dimension of knowledge to become endogenously integrated with the time-space structure, and thereby endow all things with the attribute of resource abundance by way of continuous knowledge induction.

As an example, a loving mother is considered to have only a stipulated length of time within 24 hours daily to be devoted to her child. Such an allocation of time in loving possessiveness is a notion that is based on the scarcity of time as resource measured in its space time structure, that is as a material artifacts limited by its material utilitarian value.

But consider the same problem in an altogether different way. Think about the limitless value that the loving mother attaches to the time given to her child. This value is extendable to the extent that love and affection make her literally fly with her child. The child and the mother together mutually enjoy each other's love and caring. The two have entered the kind of bond as of God and man in the context of the divine law with which we dance, think, and advance in knowledge. In this way, the endogenous—meaning the organically interrelated integration out of learning– between knowledge, time, and space—establishes the horizons of our valued capability.

On a similar principle of value, preached the great philosopher of the Islamic enlightenment, Imam Ghazzali He said: Self-actualize by the scarcity of resources to attain the love of God (Mehmet, 1997). Another great philosopher of Islam, Imam Shatibi (Masud, 1995) recommended the consumptions comprising necessaries in dynamic basic-needs regimes of social development. The same sublime message of historical consciousness in the advancement of civilization is voiced profoundly by the philosopher of the Islamic enlightenment, Shah Waliullah (undated). Above all, the *Qur'an*[1] declares in many ways the simple enjoyment of life and resources to reach the love of God as the highest edict of value.

The Prophet Muhammad said on charity, simplicity, and moral development as the basis of the expendable resource that is never spent but is always spending (Kandalvi, n.d., p. 198): The Prophet said to Asma, daughter of the later-on first pious caliph of Islam, Abu Bakr, "O Asma, do not put by and be calculating; spend in the path of Allah liberally." After this, Asma started to spend generously. She would say to her daughters and housemaids: "Don't wait for any surplus or excess of requirements before spending in the path of Allah. As the requirements go on increasing in the chances of having something, excess will become more and more remote, and the time for spending in the path of Allah will never come. Remember that you will not lose by spending in charity."

Thus the resources at human disposable are reproducible by the function of knowledge that is premised on divine oneness, for the primal axiom abides: Divine oneness denotes the completeness and absoluteness of knowledge upon which the ontological function rests in the light of the episteme. The reproducibility of the good things of life means circular causation caused by pervasive complementarities between the good things of life. Of these are the necessaries of life, which Rawls calls 'primaries' (see Sen, 1989). In this sense therefore, resources like wellbeing are reproducible benefits in the dimensions of knowledge, time, and space. Consequently, the ever-expanding value of resources and wellbeing by their attributes of reproduction under the impact of knowledge formation taking place continuously in continuums of knowledge, time, and space dimensions annuls the core axiom of resource scarcity found in all of mainstream socio-scientific intellection.

Step 1 of expression (2) has now been established as a socio-scientific primal episteme in the concept of super-topology bestowing meaning and *functional* ontology in the form of organic relations of unity of knowledge and the artifacts of the issues and problems under study. The following features of the epistemic origin and its scientific credibility are shown in Step 1 of expression (2):

1. The functional ontology of the primal premise of unity of knowledge in the divine law can be understood as super-topology[2] in scientific concept. Thus Ω is a meta-scientific reality.
2. The mapping 'S' is well defined, continuous and complete in mapping the divine law of Ω concerning various issues and problems onto the experiential world-system.
3. The mapping 'S' unraveling Ω to the experiential domain takes place via the route of knowledge-formation on the basis of the episteme of unity of knowledge premised on Ω.
4. The space of knowledge formation by social discourse is shown by its extendibility via circular causation (two-way arrow relations) confirming the strongly endogenous unity of relations by pervasive complementarities between the good things of life as determined by the (Ω,S)-law.

The interactive phase caused by the pre-existence of diversity in system complexity is followed by the unitary consequence of integration, that is unification by knowledge sharing in the good things of life according to the (Ω,S)-law.

Step 2: The Evolutionary Dynamics of Continuity across Continuums of Knowledge, Time, Space Dimensions

The idea of evolution must be first understood in the context of continuity of the interactive and integrative knowledge-induced process of change and reinforcement along the episteme of unity of knowledge. The idea of evolution meant here is completely non-Darwinian, and in fact is anti-Darwinian in essence. This is because the dynamics of evolution in the case of the divine law of organic unity of knowledge and life (monotheism) is modeled on interaction leading into integration or organic unity, not into differentiation, conflict, competition and methodological individualism. As an example, the emergence of the mind vouched by the eminent epistemologist Donald Campbell whose works have been compiled by Overman (1988) is based on causality responding to the Darwinian physical and biological organisms.

Contrarily, in our socio-scientific model of unity of divine knowledge (monotheism) the emergence of the mind is not a rationalistic process limited by the material cognitive phenomenon. Instead, the mind is a function of knowledge simulated through the worldly discursive medium by its original and continuous emergence in the midst of the meta-scientific precincts of the divine law.

The implication of the continuity process of knowledge simulation across continuums of verities has a profound meaning. Fundamentally, this process points out that, its evolutionary continuity is inextricably premised on the continuous re-emergence of (Ω,S) followed by Step 1 explained above, 'everywhere' and in 'everything'. The idea of 'everywhere' is conveyed by the continuity, completeness and knowledge-induced pervasiveness across organically interrelated systemic extendibility. The idea of 'everything' is conveyed by the character of universality of the super-cardinal (meaning not limited by dimensionality) and super-topological property of the epistemic oneness premised in (Ω,S). Thus we say that, (Ω,S) is continuously 'recalled' for the commencement of every new learning process both along specific and interdependent emergent systems of complementary forms. These organically share and increase in knowledge-flows generated between each other. And in and through doing so, enhances their reproductive power in terms of resources, artifact and wellbeing to all in the systemic sense of 'everything'.

One can envision how the evolutionary dynamics takes its shape and form, its unitary explanatory power, and its unifying applications by learning processes in the general and the particular perspectives of investigated domains of thought. Figure 2 presents an explanation of the evolutionary systemic dynamics of emergence, and continuity across knowledge-induced continuums in time and space.

The important characteristic of such systemic and symbiotic evolutionary character of learning processes is the embedded systemic emergence out of the continuity of learning and its epistemic formation and re-formation 'everywhere' and in 'everything' as depicted in Step 1. We have explained earlier that, science, technology, the economic and financial system, and society at large are mutually embedded social subsystems. Embedding occurs by way of their organic and mutual sharing of knowledge arising from the epistemic origin, then leading to the formation of the world-system by the discursive learning medium; and this process recursively regenerates the world-system by the dynamics as shown in expression (2).

Along the ever-extendible trajectory of learning and advancing in knowledge of unity of law and functional organisms by the processes of interaction, integration, and creative evolution, as signified by Step 2 of expression (2), all the systemic dynamics of Step 1 re-emerge and continue on for ever. What the systemic characteristic of interaction, integration, and evolution experience are simulacra of possibilities in the dimensions of knowledge, time, and space. About such kinds of endless simulacra Fitzpatrick (2003, p. 128) writes: "Ours, then, is an age of simulations that endlessly refer only to other simulations. The infinite circularity of these self-references is what Braudrillard calls the *simulacra*: everything is a reproduction of other reproductions. Society explodes in on itself and we cannot liberate ourselves from the *simulacra*…"

Figure 2. Step 1 and step 2 of the nexus of interactive, integrative, and evolutionary (IIE) learning experience

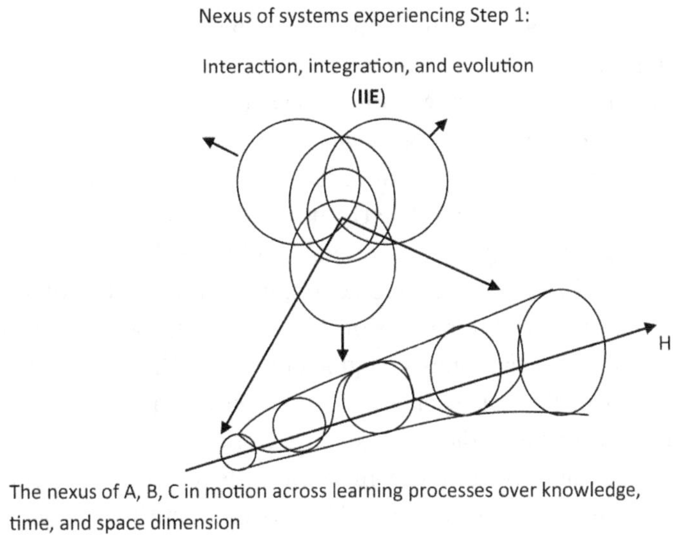

Only a discontinuity of knowledge-formation is the cause and effect of the progressive halt in human consciousness. The longer, deeper, and more extensively this discontinuity lingers, the system suffers from its failure to sustain itself. In Darwinian processes, exemplified further by Popper, the institutions of modernity, and many ideas propounded by the rationalist philosophers reappear and assert themselves in the midst of a de-learning world-system. We will turn to such a de-learning model later on.

The nexus of simulacra of organically unifying relations between cause and effect of evolutionary bundles of complementary forms and relations embody in them all the dynamics of Step 1, and now of Step 2. In other words, the expression (2) represents the interactive, integrative, and evolutionary (IIE) behavior of an organism within itself. An example is of one unit of money changing hands so many times, as in quantity theory of money and prices. Then simulacra in Step 2 denote repetition of the interactive, integrative, and evolutionary (IIE) dynamics in unity of knowledge over nexus of monetary, financial, and real economy systems.

Step 3: Closure of the Very Large Universe in the Knowledge, Time, and Space Dimension

Expression (2) continues on recursively generating, repeating and referring back and forth to the continuity of the chain relations onwards. This is the path of historical reproduction of events as they ought to be and can be evaluated at progressive points in the historical evolution of events. The picture of intra-systemic interaction, integration, and evolution of knowledge-flows at every such momentary event produces the time-space dynamics fired by new and evolutionary events onwards, as depicted in Figure 2. Thus, there is continuous evolution of intra-systemic dynamics of events caused by intra-systemic interaction, integration, and evolution (IIE) into inter-systemic relations and dynamics of the same type. Every event so generated in the progressive intra- and inter- systemic character of the historical evolution is a juncture of social evaluation, social reconstruction, and new knowledge formation along with the emergence of the mind and the world-system along with it.

Thus with every such evolutionary movement the response and action involving interaction, integration, and evolution by intra-systemic and inter-systemic dynamics there arises a new juncture of social transformation, new mind, new visions, and new consequences. Yet all of these and everywhere the events so occurring are the cause and event of circular causality between complementing diversity. This natural consequence is caused by, and by process, returns to the epistemic premise of divine oneness, which is the premise of unity of knowledge.

In such an understanding of the system-ensemble (Hubner, 1985; Sztompka, 1991) characterization of learning processes, the historical creativity of events in the dimensions of knowledge, time, and space is represented by the topological mapping, $H(\theta, t, X(\theta);\theta\in(\Omega,S), t = t(\theta))$. The evolution of H shown in Figure 2 as the system-ensemble of complex events immersed, emerging, compounding, and re-originating in the dimensions of knowledge, time, and space is the characterization of a learning path of certainty. Yet such a path is stochastically driven by the simulacra of knowledge and its induced artifacts. Time in this dynamics is simply a recorder of events. Time is not even a forecaster of events beyond a notion of forecasting at the 'nearness' (proximate region) of an event point, meaning a proximity point to the occurrence of events-bundle. Time is a created artifact of knowledge-flows. For consider our time in sleep[3]; consider simultaneity of event and time[4]; consider neoclassical economic theory in which time remains datum, associated only with events and technology to identify the occurrence of such events at points in space but exogenously.[5] Also, it is well-known that time and knowledge is coterminous entities in the sense of their consciousness explanation by the human presence. Quantum Mechanics refers to such a phenomenon of knowledge and human intelligence as the anthropic principle[6]. In all such cases, time is either non-experienced or is determined simultaneously with the occurrence of event, which is a knowledge induced artifact.

A further example here is of discounting of cash flow over time. Time does not cause and determine the cash flows. In time it is possible to read the value of cash-flows, provided there is an event that causes such values to be attained in the probabilistic sense 'nearest' to the point of occurrence of the event determining the values of the cash-flows. Such an occurrence of event is determined by knowledge. Hence, time reads the occurrence of knowledge, as knowledge *a priori* induces the occurrence of the given event. In the same way, as a socio-scientific variable is induced by knowledge, so also time is induced by the *a priori* occurrence of knowledge. We explain this below.

Furthermore, knowledge and time as the dual representation of consciousness are derived from the epistemic oneness for worldly explanation. How does this statement enter our cold calculation of worldly matters? The initial determination of knowledge derived from the epistemic premise of unity of knowledge normalizes a social construction milieu in the framework of unity of knowledge and its induction of the unified world-system. Thus, the determination of knowledge in this way establishes a structure of the socio-scientific system as an event according to which unity of knowledge induced in the world-system takes place in respect of any specific problem.

The existence of such an event determines the state of the concrescent variable. Say that this variable is cash-flow, determined on the basis of the event of a good contingent state of the economy. The cash-flow is now determined at a time that reads the variable subject to the probability of occurrence of the good economic contingency and the pre-existence of knowledge derived from the epistemic core. In this way, the cash-flow as an expected variable is determined by knowledge-induction at a point of time. This point of time records the occurrence of the cash-flow, the economic contingency, and the level of knowledge attained as consciousness in the problem under study. Time has thus been preceded by the occurrence of knowledge, and equivalently set by the occurrence of knowledge-induced events.

UNIVERSALITY AND UNIQUENESS PROPERTIES IN THE MODEL OF EPISTEMIC UNITY OF KNOWLEDGE

Universality

The connected circles inside the region H in Figure 2 signifies the continuity of the interactive, integrative, and evolutionary (IIE) characteristics of the learning process 'everywhere' and in 'everything'. The domain of 'everywhere' comprises the dimensions of knowledge, time, and space. This makes up the ultimate dimensions that reality can bestow. Any and every event that can be explained within this dimensional super-space conveys the substantive meaning of 'everything'.

The concepts of 'everywhere' and 'everything' also relate to the meanings of universality and uniqueness of the theory explained by H in Figure 2. The continuity and invariability of the interconnection between the normative perspective that is set by the deductive premise of epistemic unity of knowledge and the formalism and *functional* ontology of the positivistic perspective set by the empirical and inferential viability of H establishes the self-referencing result in reference to the monotheistic law, that is the fundamental episteme of unity of knowledge.

Choudhury and Zaman (2009) write: "By self-referencing here we mean the closure of socio-scientific reasoning on the basis of an irreducible episteme that can assign a set of immutable laws and guidance and mind-matter complementary relations. From such relations further deductions can be made pertaining to specific issues and problems. Note that we make a distinction here between laws, guidance and rules of details. By rules we mean the explanation of mind-matter issues derived from the enactment of divine guidance and laws for the conduct of details of life and thought in view of the particular problems that need to be addressed by the instrumentation of the guidance and laws. In such a domain, a vast synergy of human interventions arises for understanding and applying divine guidance and the monotheistic law through their instrumentation into the details of life and thought."

Uniqueness

Uniqueness of the worldview and model underlying the explanation of expression 2 and Figure 2 is based on their singularity of all alternative ways of formalizing unity of knowledge and the induced unity of the socio-scientific world-system. This challenging problem of discerning the uniqueness of logical formalism of the monotheistic law in the world-system out of all existing attempts for explaining the same worldview is an intellection in the history of thought spanning religion, culture, science and the world-system.

The answer to this query is grounded on the search and discovery of that particular scientific revolution, which answers fully the *problematique* of unification. Can such a worldview with logical formalism and universal application to 'everything' and 'everywhere' be found in any other way than the strictly monotheistic law of epistemic oneness? Here is a non-mathematical version of Choudhury and Zaman's paper (op cit) that establishes such a uniqueness property premised on, and whose logical formalism is explanatory and applicative in 'everything' and 'everywhere'. Contrarily, the received socio-scientific theories and formalism do not accept such a formalism of self-referencing and the monotheistic law in preference to the open universe conjecture and socio-scientific pluralism of the rationalist genre (Popper, 1998). We explain below the argument in this regard.

Yet another point to note in terms of the non-uniqueness of science is based on the idea of pluralism. This now grounds much of the process view of science (Hull, 1988, pp. 251-55) and is utterly divorced from the monotheistic possibility of unified thought between the metaphysical and mind-matter connection. Popper's pluralism takes its roots in the world 1 of physical things. It then proceeds on to world 2 of mental states; and finally to world 3 of the products of the human mind and action. Such is the continual prevalence of the problematique of the scientific worldview. A comprehensive worldview and socio-scientific inquiry and a holistic answering are not possible. Uniqueness of the worldview of morality, ethics, mind and matter is thus returned exclusively to the model and formalism of the epistemic unity of knowledge.

Russell (2001, p. 59) claims that all *a priori* knowledge, as in Kant's *a priori* domain of the problem of heteronomy, is universal knowledge. Then all *a posteriori* knowledge is particular knowledge. Indeed, on this same point of a critique of Kant wrote Seidel (1986) on grounds of the divide between *a priori* and *a posteriori* reasoning. What we derive from these argumentations in the mind and scientific constructs of all of received socio-scientific thought is a discontinuous and partitioned view of universality. Thereby also, there is no unique theory of pluralistic scientific permissibility.

An example of this case is also found in Marx's theory of pluralism in epistemologies that is critiqued by Resnick and Wolff (1987, pp 6-7) in terms of the Marxian problem of epistemological over-determinism leading to indeterminateness and non-uniqueness of socio-scientific reasoning: "Reality for Marxian theory is a totality comprising contradictions in theory interacting with contradictions within all the other processes that constitute that totality. Marxian theory specifies that interaction as over-determination."

From the side of religion and culture as well, as modes of thinking, there has also been pervasiveness of the pluralistic demarcation. The effect has been in the demise of the law of monotheistic unification between religion and science. The argumentation goes as follows:

Rationalism that, premises on the non-monotheistic idea of science and religion, may hold up the existence of God as truism. Thereby, any pluralistic understanding of such science and religion also holds up the idea of God's existence. Yet there is no provability of such existence either in mainstream religion or its pluralistic prototypes in non-monotheistic religions. Thereby, the belief in the existence of God remains a belief without evidential proof (Heidegger's ontic phenomenon, trans, Hofstadter, 1988). On the other hand, rationalism also announces the non-substantiation of God. Thereby, all pluralistic transformations of the non-existence of God as argument belong to this category of rationalistic thought and belief. Yet we find that, the postulate of non-existence of God can lead into scientific truths. The conclusion from such a contradiction is that God exists on an individual basis of belief, but not necessarily having either proof of existence in the worldly reality or in scientific explanations of the epistemic oneness. This kind of ruptured relationship between science and religion is a fact of rationalistic epistemology.

Strict monotheistic law proves the belief of the oneness of God in the form of relational unity of being and becoming in the real world. Science along with its various manifestations, such as philosophy of science and the socio-scientific order, also believes on the oneness criterion as the axiom of its systemic worldview. They prove this belief by facts of the experiential order—that is by self-referencing. The uniqueness of the monotheistic epistemological worldview over the rationalistic and spiritualistic pluralism to explain the overarching unity between 'everything' and 'everywhere' is thus established.

Lastly, it needs to be pointed out here, awaiting an extensive treatment of these topics that, the universality and uniqueness properties of the monotheistic epistemic worldview apply to both truth and falsehood. That is, the formal model of unity of knowledge applies to the moral, ethical and social construction of the unified worldview of the socio-scientific and cybernetic world-system; as well as to the explanation by the same methodology of the behavior, attribute and consequences of methodological individualism and differentiation of the Darwinian type world-system. The universal and unique worldview applies to both the explanation and reconstruction of an ethically decadent world-system; and to the furtherance of the moral and ethical system to higher echelons of knowledge and wellbeing.

THE LARGE-SCALE CLOSURE OF THE UNIVERSE IN THE DIMENSIONS OF KNOWLEDGE, TIME, AND SPACE

The properties of strict monotheism explained by the primacy and continuity of the epistemic oneness as organic unity of knowledge occurring continuously in 'everything' and 'everywhere', and the formalism as explained in expression (2) and by Figure 2, establish the completeness of the religion-science blending over a large-scale learning universe. Such a universe and its explanatory power by monotheism are of the universal, unique, and proven category by the property of self-referencing in the formal construction of its argumentative capability.

Thus the large-scale universe attains itself, but in infinite scale of knowledge, time, and space. It attains itself by the process of self-referencing going from levels of knowledge to subsequent levels of knowledge; and by the emergent degrees of knowing epistemic unity between knowledge and the world-system. Since the large-scale universe is a super-space, and a super-cardinal topology, therefore, it is complete. Mathematical completeness and continuity of the super-space categories establish evolutionary equilibriums as the consequence of learning phenomenon in epistemic unity of knowledge.[7]

The nature of the large-scale universe is thus a representation in its completeness by the existence and attainment of equilibriums of the evolutionary learning type, all premised in epistemic unity. Hence the universe through its expanse across multiverses (multi-universes) becomes an explanatory entity. This idea is quite the opposite of Karl Popper's open universe of conjectures or of George Soros' (2000) in the uncharted financial world. Behavioral and normative social reconstruction in linkage with the positivistic worldview and vice-versa happening recursively out of simulacra of possibilities are not the features of rationalistic world-system either in terms of its epistemological groundwork or its constructs.

BRINGING GOD BACK INTO THE FINANCIAL AND BANKING SYSTEM

The Threshold of Good Society

We are writing now on the conceptualizing and application of the above-mentioned epistemological discourse *back* into the financial and banking system, as if the ethical attributes were already there once. We mean by this return to moral and ethical origins, the return of the system to its true place in moral-social meaning. If we have adequately accepted the epistemic premise of strict monotheism in socio-scientific thought, its formalism and application and quantitative policy-theoretic and institutional organizations, then we accept the fact that the moral basis is the natural quality of the business institutions. If the concept and practice of the financial and banking system have departed from their natural position in our lives, to reconstruct them along the ethical and moral lines, is to give back these institutions their due and original lives, their purposive meaning.

In the history of money, the moral aspect of money was embedded in the use of gold and silver as standards for the valuation of money value of assets. It was surmised that over the very long time period the price of gold remained stable. Hence the valuation of assets in terms of gold as the standard of money remained stable and conveyed the true price and value of assets. This idea of measuring the value of assets against the bullion concept of money is understood as the valuation by asset-backed money. What is true of the gold-denomination of monetary aggregates for asset valuation is equally true of using an alternative way of denominating the value of bullions in certificates, and let such certificates be exchanged for the value of gold-backing of assets (Vadilo, 2002). Thus there would be no need for coins and currency to be exchanged in market transactions in terms of these being gold and silver. Yet the *numeraire* standard of the price and valuation of exchangeables will be against gold bullion backing that is quoted in certificates now understood as a financial contract.

Gold and silver held their sway as asset-backing value of money for a long period in history until the monetary manipulation for fractional reserves by the Bank of England and the gold-scarce Fort Knox in the United States led to the demise of the Bretton Woods Arrangement around the nineteen-sixties. In the truly monotheistic money-finance-real economy linkages with the gold standard, bullions were held up as standards of justice and fairness, correctness of value, and stability of prices and production (Allouche, 1994). Gold and silver served as yardsticks of both rendering true value by their stable measure of currency in a time-trend. Besides, a quantity of money matched well with the market value of exchanged things. Over and above this natural effect through market exchange the moral exhortation to consume and produce the good things of life prevailed. Such good things were the ethical goods of a dynamic basic-needs regime of development. Only at the present time, development planners respectful of sustainability promote such ideas (Schumacher, 1973; Rawls, 1971; Streeten, 1981).

On the side of quantity theory of money, a version of this was given by the philosopher David Hume much before Irving Fisher and Milton Friedman (Ekelund Jr. & Hebert, 1990). Hume argued that apart from the case of drastic variations in the quantity of money, prices would remain stable. He wrote (Hume, trans. Rotwein, 2007, p. 33): "… The greater or less plenty of money is of no consequence; since the prices of commodities are always proportionate to the plenty of money … It is a maxim almost self-evident, that the prices of everything depend on the proportion between commodities and money, and that any *considerable* alteration on either has the effect, either of heightening or lowering the prices."

Much earlier still we find the Islamic thought on money and markets in terms of social justice and fairness. The works of Ghazzali on this theme prevail as moral guide (Karim, undated). One such countervailing point is the illegitimacy of using counterfeit currency in market exchange. I would like to expand the meaning of counterfeit here to the printing of excess quantities of money and the earning of interest rate in the modern fractional monetary system as ways and means of raising earnings by speculation and coercion despite what the measure of interest rate may be. The idea in this is that a small rate of interest on a large capital amount can be at least as much as a large interest rate on a small capital amount. This situation exists profusely in the case of funding a large project with soft-loan as by the World Bank, or writing off risk by large interest rate financial collateral on small loans made out to microenterprises by conventional commercial banking.

Thus if counterfeit currency include interest and excess or deficit amount of monetary aggregate then the following rule of fairness abides: Imam Ghazzali said (translated), that the first man who uses counterfeit currency will get the sins of every person who subsequently transfers it to other persons. Furthermore, the importance of gold and silver in preserving the value of money in exchange is pointed out. Gold and silver are capital stocks, whereas their valuation takes place in terms of money. Hence money through finance is the way of assigning the correct valuation of stock of goods that are in market circulation. Such a valuation must be precise. Such precision can be conveyed by the correct nature and measure of money in the valuation of real goods in circulation (McGrath & Barney, 2012). In the absence of this possibility currency as monetary unit becomes counterfeit. A counterfeit currency is considered to be one that does not contain gold and silver in it. Thus paper money and its system called the fractional reserve requirement monetary system can be understood as counterfeit backing monetary system by virtue of their independence from the gold standard, and consequently, the dependence of money creation on price instability and interest rate.

From the above discussion we note that social justice, fairness and the productive link with development sustainability for wellbeing are deeply rooted in the matter of money, finance, and real economy complementary relations. Participative dynamics in this domain are essential for establishing a good society. Consequently, the monotheistic law with its worldly reflection of organic unity is strongly embedded in money, finance, and the real economy interrelations. The *Qur'an* (35:8) declares, "Do not exceed limits in weights and measures; and establish just balance; and do not reduce the measure."

Social Justice

What is meant by social justice, and by social injustice in relation to the function of money, finance, and real economy in the wellbeing function? The answer to this question though being of mammoth proportion needs to be firstly attempted in order to place the *functional* ontology of the monotheistic law in the actualization of a good society with its money, finance, and real economy interactive and integrated, and evolutionary dynamic environments.

Rawls considers social justice and the becoming of good society in terms of his Difference Principle. This can be stated as the acts of the social order, the organization of resource, production, ownership, and distribution in the goods things, the enjoyment of which increases the wellbeing of the most underprivileged. The actualization of such a social order depends firstly, upon the intrinsic nature of the moral law, which Rawls thinks is inherent in all individuals. Such a moral attribute is like Kant's categorical imperative.

Justice and injustice are not mere concepts, as in Rawls' difference principle or in Kant's moral imperative. The precept of social justice is inextricably combined with enforcement, a social order constructed on the principles of social justice, altogether leading to social application of the tenets of justice. The glaring example of such a combination between precept, form, application, and enforcement of social justice, is found in the case of poverty alleviation, equality, and overcoming of social malaise. Here the reformation of institution is preceded by the deontological transformation of human preferences. Upon the complex, as opposed to the linear aggregation of such dynamic preferences, follows the moral-social reconstruction of knowledge and institutions, and policies and programs for the crystallization of the precept of social justice. A multidimensional approach is thus inherent in both the precept and the implementation of social justice in its experiential form.

When we apply this overarching and functional theory of knowledge to the theme of social justice inherent in the use of money, finance, and real economy, the function of business/banking emerges as an institutional one that enforces the complementary linkages between the functions of money and real economy. Money will then carry on its moral and ethical function—thus bringing God into the banking system—if firstly, the participatory function of money and real economy through the function of finance and financial instruments, monetary arrangements and fiscalism (spending) is realized. Secondly, the emergent participation functions on the social choices of the good things of life. That is the money, finance, and real economy complementary linkages are made to spread across the market-institutional complementarities in the good things of life, and as enabled by the appropriate policies, programs, instruments, and choices.

In light of the theory of unity of knowledge and its unifying influence in the money, finance, and real economy linkages along with the dynamics of transformation in social choices, preferences, policies, programs and the market-institution relationship, social justice as precept is understood as follows: That the epistemic reference is to the divine law of monotheism that establishes and applies the law of unity in belief and artifacts. In the financial world-system a principal artifact of the monotheistic law is the avoidance of every impediment to the free flow of financial and productive resources in the good things of life, as these are determined by the monotheistic law. The way towards such well-determination is the transmission of the law into the world-system combined with the discourse medium.

The totality of these situations progressively enables understanding of the precept of goodness and serenity of the law and moral-social choices. A critical artifact for the realization of the spending action through the underlying principle of oneness between the law and the real world for attaining wellbeing is avoidance of the rate of interest in all financial dealings. The result of the avoidance of the rate of interest is the freeing of financial and productive resources in the recommended possibilities that generate higher levels of wellbeing. In turn, the principle of wellbeing is premised on the realization of complementarities and participation as the sign of balance in accordance with the monotheistic law of unity acting upon the financial and real economy. In order to establish the congeries of the balance of unity between the good things of life for wellbeing, the principle of complementarities as balance of wellbeing, must be both consciously embraced and enforced. This is done by the force of worldly laws and institutions, such as the meaningful relationship between the central bank and commercial banks, the monetary and fiscal policies, and the development of interlinked financial and real markets.

Two criteria of the comprehensive meaning of social justice emerge from the above delineation of its *functional* ontology of critically high value. First is the precept of justice and its affirmed enforcement. Second is the example of enacting justice in the financial and social world-systems.

In regards to the first criterion, the *Qur'an* declares (4:135): "O you who believe! Stand out firmly for justice as witnesses to God, even as against yourselves, or your parents, or your kin, and whether it be (against) rich or poor: for God can best protect both. Follow not the lusts (of your hearts), lest you swerve, and if you distort (justice) or decline to do justice, verily God is well-acquainted with all that you do." All the essential elements of a substantive foundation of understanding the precept of social justice emanate from the above-mentioned verse of the *Qur'an*. In the light of this comprehensive picture of the principle of justice a definition of social justice can be propounded.

Social justice extended to human and non-human, animate and inanimate existences is conveyed by the principle of balance between the good things of life. This invokes the episteme of unity of knowledge, which in its universal and unique sense of the foundations of morality and the emerging ethics linked with the moral law, establishes unity between the variables representing agency, preferences, artifacts for the specific issues, and totality of the world-system under investigation. Social justice is a cardinal attribute of the human heart resting on monotheistic belief as the universal way and code of life. It is social capital based on the wellbeing criterion of a unified world-system in the general and particular systems that articulates the epistemic unity in its organic form.

On the specific issue of social justice and fairness in the financial and economic theme of avoidance of interest and the promotion of trade as a productive venture for wellbeing, the *Qur'an* declares (2:274-275): "Those who (in charity) spend of their goods by night and by day, in secret and in public, have their reward with their Lord: on them shall be no fear, nor shall they grieve. Those who devour interest (*riba*) will not stand except as stands one whom the Evil One by his touch has driven to madness. That is because they say: 'Trade is like interest (*riba*)', but God has permitted trade and forbidden *riba*....." The inverse relationship between trade and riba is pointed out in this verse. Upon the transmission of this principle into the discursive socio-financial order, our further understanding, application, and continuity of the principle of trade versus *riba* for the wellbeing of all is simulated (Choudhury, 2010).

Social Injustice

Social injustice is not simply an opposite replacement of social justice; or equivalently stated, social justice is not simply an opposite replacement of social injustice. Contrarily, every gain in the attainment of social justice heightens knowledge of the participatory order by leaps and bounds. Thereby, society experiences a much larger gain in social wellbeing by the replacement of even smaller increments in its reformation towards fairness, equality, consciousness, and justice. A heightened increase in social wellbeing is realized by incremental replacement of social injustice by a society moving towards moral-social transformation.

Just as we have defined the principle of social justice as balance by growing unification as participation between the variables representing agencies and artifacts of complementary possibilities, so also in the case of defining social injustice, increasing injustice is caused by differentiation between these. The result is halting the flow of resources for ownership, production, empowerment and entitlement realized otherwise by market-institutional linkages, as enunciated by epistemic unity and its creative evolution by interaction and integration across learning-type worldly situations realized by human consciousness.

The above-mentioned idea between the opposing relation between social justice and social injustice in the unitary learning model of moral-social reformation (participative model) is exemplified in the case of the money, finance, and real economy complementary model of social embedding of economics and finance with a scientific perspective. So in the case of monetary activation with its free flow into trade and development in the real economy the income multiplier works along with the multiplier in the classical form of the quantity theory equation, the multiplier returns are far more than the quantity of money that flows into trade and development. Financial choices of appropriate instruments to promote such free flow of monetary resources in the absence of interest (*riba*) greatly accentuate the income multiplier effect of enhanced factors in spending in the good things of life. It is possible that such enhanced income multipliers can lead to explosive fission-fusion type results. Fission would be caused by the internal circular causation dynamics between money, finance, and real economy in any given phase of their linkages in socioeconomic development. Fusion will be caused by the enhanced contribution of such strengthened fission-factors as income multipliers (Choudhury & Malik, 1992).[8]

In the above explanation of heightened contribution of a decreasing interest rate on the income multiplier caused by money, finance, and real economy linkages, the multiplier is shown to work by reducing injustice (*riba*). This dynamics progressively causes exploding gains in income multiplier. The result of so reducing social injustice progressively results in the fission-fusion type income multiplier. Underlying this dynamics lie the greatly enhanced gains in social justice. This is shown by the circular causation consequences that take place between equality, empowerment and entitlement, ownership and distribution in the progressively formative participatory framework.

The complementary relationship between money, finance (financial instruments), and the real economy (development) is a sign of the organic unity of knowledge and its effect on specific problems of the world-system that emanate when the epistemic unity of knowledge is referred to in the learning process of social organization. Social perspectives of organization most importantly include learning behavior premised on interaction, integration, and evolution. The organization is then embedded in economic, financial and social dynamics involving human consciousness and the deepening effect of morality and ethics in this. Such complementary perspectives between the variables representing monetary authority, business/banking organization and markets, convey the epistemic organic unity of knowledge and market-institution interrelationship.

Another example that brings out the large socioeconomic multipliers, which ensue even from small decrements in social injustice is the reduction of relative poverty. Reduction of relative poverty is not a policy target. Abolition of abject, absolute and hardcore poverty is definitely a central focus of social policy. But through social discourse in the interactive, integrative, and evolutionary (IIE) model of organic unity of knowledge it is possible to restructure institutions, technology and distribution so as to generate new dimensions in property rights. The result then is a large impact of such change on the income multiplier. The extant of circular causation dynamics in such large multiplier effects arises from the endogenous consequences of participatory market-institution relations, self-organization behavior, and social policies that together carry the assimilative effect of human consciousness. Such effects are implied in Amartya Sen's deontological preferences in social decision-making.

Such are the consequences of the way of deriving the mind-matter outlook of the monotheistic episteme at work in system and cybernetic experience. God is thus brought into the financial system through the *functional* ontology of the monotheistic episteme into the world-system. The result is a correct understanding of the extent of justice, equality, poverty alleviation, ownership, distribution and the like, that can be assigned to all under the principle of a natural justice as a market process combined with institutional synergy between markets and society as endogenous dynamics of the socioeconomic system intensify. Such a synergistic system learns its charted way in society at large through the *functional* ontology of the monotheistic law and the learning process of epistemic organic unity on all socially embedded, hence social-cybernetic issues.

A CRITICAL COMPARATIVE REVIEW OF THE ISSUES OF SOCIAL JUSTICE AND SOCIAL INJUSTICE

The endogenous nature of social transformation caused by participative complementarities between the variables of social wellbeing function representing appropriate social choices in the good things of life is a way towards social justice and its conformable goals. These approaches are different from many ideas presented in the literature. Here we examine a few of these differing views.

The views of Robert Nozick (1974) on entitlement bundles relegate property rights to the pure function of market process. Any public intervention to redistribute property rights such as by taxation and regulation for achieving social equality and social justice is considered by Nozick as morally abhorring. Nozick is thereby resounding the usual neoclassical rule of self-interest regarding property rights by a fullest impact of market forces. There is no robust theory of social policy in neoclassicism, and now also in Nozick's view on social justice and the market-institution synergistic process on such matters.

Rawls' views on social justice are contrary to Nozick's. Rawls engages government/institutional intervention to make a socially unequal society into an equalitarian one by the institutional force at the Original Position of moral-social reconstruction. Rawls' Original Position is the critical point of Kantian heteronomy. At any such social juncture along the path of social change, the *a priori* force of the moral law that would raise human consciousness in connection with a good society does not connect with the unequal state of the emergent society at the *a posteriori* point of the inherited world. Social differentiation between mind and matter at the expense of endogenous learning in a complementary world-system that can be formed by participatory dynamics of the epistemic law with various issues, remains absent in Rawls. The same consequence arises out of Nozick's theory of entitlement on the other extreme of a neoclassical type reliance of uninterrupted market process.

Similar ideas are expressed by Temkin (1995) in his criticism of David Gauthier's theory of social justice. That is social justice by mutual consent, which in our case is determined by the continuous and continuum perspectives of the interactive, integrative, and evolutionary (IIE) model of epistemic unity and the world-system, is a functional theme for the overlapping generation. The overlapping generations comprise not those that are far removed from the domain of discourse – by participation and complementarities. They comprise not only human agents, but also elements between the human world and the animate and inanimate world-systems. This kind of a systemic outlook makes up a cybernetic viewpoint of organic interrelationship. Examples here are human consciousness on the environment and sustainability; and justice that is meted out to the inanimate world-system as well as to the rest. This type of extended justice across experiential existence cannot be meted out to the future non-interactive and non-overlapping generation. Such intertemporal idea of justice for the far future cannot be acceptable in the interactive, integrative, and evolutionary (IIE) model of epistemic unity.

Such a model in our case is different from Nozick, Rawls, and Gauthier's theories. In the other theories there is no evident valuation method for sharing resources between the overlapping generation members in ways that will be fair and just, participatory and sustainable of wellbeing for all. The idea of social and spiritual capital thereby arises in connection with the valuation of the morally and ethically induced resources and assets at probabilistically 'near' points of the occurrence of given events.

The writings of Temkin (1995) and Pogge (1995) also bring out similar problematic concepts on the topic of intergenerational social justice and equality. In our model these two precepts are not perfectly equivalent. Temkin treats equality as the other exact side of social justice. Our epistemic model of unity of knowledge in social justice focuses on equitable as opposed to equal distribution and productive ownership of resources by means of a participatory socioeconomic, market-institution endogenous interrelationship. There is no denial or suppression of natural endowments that can cause inequality between agents according to their diverse situations as in the interactive, integrative and evolutionary (IIE) model. Such interactive diversities continuously spans across continuums of possibilities in the IIE-learning model of unity of knowledge. Likewise, the role of institution in the parceling of social justice is seen as an independent activity by government authority. The endogenous nature of consciousness and deontological preferences in our learning model remains foreign concept to Pogge.

In the specific case of the money, financial and real money synergistic model of epistemic unity the return of moral values into the economic, financial and banking activities is brought about by the endogenous nature of consciousness in the moral-social construction of production menus, social choices, and social preferences. In the above-mentioned references, an understanding of justice and its opposite view of injustice in the sense of social reformation in the learning model cannot be realized. The fundamental caveat in this debility of the mentioned theories of justice is the missing method of social valuation. Such approaches are silent on the method of pricing the future, except by a silent acceptance of discounting the future to the present by a time-preference rate. But a discounting method of cash-flows is neither quantitatively precise nor objective, or safe from the shadow-rate of interest in the capitalization of cash-flows. The very existence of shadow-rate of interest in capitalization cash-flows accepts the system of de-linkage between the money, spending (finance), and real economy activities in the good things of life. The unitary principle is thus annulled both at the epistemic level and at the applied and learning levels. The presence of interest rate in asset capitalization impedes resource linkage with the development of the real economy in the good things of life (e.g. productivity).

CONCLUSION

The financial world is an embedded sub-system of the moral-social order, which comprises the synergy between money, finance, and the real economy. Only the prevalence of the *a priori* episteme of oneness followed by its monotheistic guidance of unity of the world-system can establish the necessary systemic synergy. This is an ontological function that is realized if and only if the episteme is upheld as the crystallization of the monotheistic worldview of unity of knowledge in the world-system.

The specific study of a problem with the unified worldview in this case is the role of business/banking as a system that activates and sustains the money, finance, and real economy relations. The fundamental basis of such a moral and ethical possibility of the business/banking system ought to be to replace every shade of the interest (*riba*) function by the productive trade relations and instruments involving the good things of life. The universality and uniqueness properties of monotheistic oneness and its operation in the unified world-system with its diverse problems, present themselves as the ultimate possibility for realizing the moral and ethical values. Such values exist as endogenous, and hence sustainable, phenomenon of epistemic unity 'everywhere' and in 'everything' having their extensive cybernetic relational meaning.

A good deal of comparative study of key social, moral, and ethical issues that are common to all of mankind, importantly the issue of social justice in its wider meaning of balance and participatory complementarities between the good things of life, has been carried out. This study points out the common perspectives found in the essence of the monotheistic law at work in the domain of unity of knowledge and its impact on the design of the unified world-system. This precept of unity is common to all peoples irrespective of cultural diversity. This was made to implicate the ultimate expanse of the monotheistic law in all of the socio-scientific order and beyond. Such a wider field of valuation cannot be found and studied in the rationalist sciences of nature and society (Bavinck, 2013). The field of economics, finance, and banking was pointed out as a case study, which will be pursued further.

THE FUTURE PROSPECTS

The future prospects of the epistemological and socio-scientific thought presented in this book is expected to be bright and deeply scholar and applied in nature. This is particularly noted in the area of heterodox economic, financial, and social thought that invokes the areas of questioning by the emergent new ways of epistemological scholarship and new institutional applications.

During these times of global financial volatility and non-predicable nature of the traditional economic and financial models, the global economy is provided in this book by the groundwork of thinking in the direction of a new economic and financial architecture. Besides, in the area of high scholarship, the socio-scientific inclusion of the law of unity of knowledge and its indued unified world-system conveys the *res extensa* of such all-inclusive study of socio-scientific reality. The matter is picking up today with the advent of Islamic economics, financing, and world-system thinking in theory and practice. This book has coverered this substantive interdisciplinary area in an extensively comparative study.

The net result of such an extension of epistemological thinking is rightly served by the treatment of theory and issues by complexly networked methodology. This methodological approach of unity of knowledge and the world-system belongs to the innovative area of socio-cybernetic and complex systems. This is a theme not taken up so much in the traditional and current literature. Thus this book is an original contribution in its area of intellection (see Table 1).

Table 1. The domain of socio-scientific inquiry

Conventional	Monotheistic
Worldview	Worldview
The complementary	The complementary
And participatory	and participatory
Worldview remains	worldview remains
Absent	absent
Marginalism prevails	marginalism is
In resource allocation	annulled in resource
And every system	allocation and in
Relations	every systemic relation
Comparative views	comparative study of
On social issues	social justice and issues
Examined	examined and extended
	To the monotheistic law

REFERENCES

Agius, I. (1990). Towards a relational theory of intergenerational ethics. In S. Busuttil, E. Agius, P.S. Inglott, & T. Macelli (Eds.), Our Responsibilities Towards Future Generations. Malta: The Foundation for International Studies in cooperation with UNESCO.

Allouche, A. (1994). *Mamluk economics: A study and translation of Al-Maqrizi's Ighatah*. Salt Lake City, UT: University of Utah Press.

Bavinck, H. (2013). *Essays on religion, science, and society* (Bolt, J., Ed.). Grand Rapids, MI: Baker Academic.

Bohr, N. (1985). Discussions with Einstein on epistemological issues. In Folse, H. (Ed.), *The Philosophy of Niels Bohr: The Framework of Complementarity*. Amsterdam, The Netherlands: North Holland Physics Publishing.

Breuer, R. (1991). *The anthropic principle: Man as the focal point of the universe*. Boston, MA: Birkhauser.

Bruteau, B. (1997). *God's ecstasy*. New York, NY: The Crossroad Publishing Co..

Capra, F. (1982). The systems view of life. In *The Turning Point*. London, UK: Flamingo.

Choudhury, M. A. (2010). The Islamic panacea to global financial predicament: A new financial architecture. *Journal Hadari*, *2*(2), 41–72.

Choudhury, M. A., & Malik, U. A. (1992). *Foundations of Islamic political economy*. London, UK: Macmillan Press Ltd..

Choudhury, M. A., & Zaman, S. I. (2009). Self-referencing as socio-scientific methodology in contrasting paradigms. *Kybernetes: The International Journal of Systems & Cybernetics*, *38*(6), 994–1008.

Dasupta, A. K. (1987). Marginalist challenge. In *Epochs of Economic Theory*. Oxford, UK: Basil Blackwell.

Einstein, A. (1954). *Relativity, the special and the general theory* (Lawson, R. W., Trans.). London, UK: Methuen University Paperbacks.

Ekelund, Jr., & Hebert. (1990). *A history of economic theory and method*. New York, NY: McGraw-Hill Publishing Co.

Fitzpatrick. (2003). Postmodernism and new directions. In P. Alcock, A. Erskine, & M. May (Eds.), *Social Policy*, (pp. 125-133). Oxford, UK: Blackwell.

Friedman, M. (1953). The methodology of positive economics. In *Essays in Positive Economics*. Chicago: University of Chicago Press.

Gulen, M. F. (2006). *Toward global civilization of love & tolerance*. Somerset, NJ: The Light, Inc..

Heidegger, M. (1988). The thesis of modern ontology: the basic ways of being are the being of nature (res extensa) and the being of mind (res cogitans). (A. Hofstadter, Trans.). In *The Basic Problems of Phenomenology*, (pp. 122-224). Bloomington, IN: Indiana University Press.

Henderson, H. (1999). *Beyond globalization: Shaping a sustainable global economy*. West Hartcourt, CT: Kumarian Press.

Hubner, K. Dixon, P.R., Jr., & Dixon, H.M. (1985). Foundations of a universal historistic theory of the empirical sciences. In Critique of Scientific Reason, (pp.105-122). Chicago, IL: The University of Chicago Press.

Hull, D. L. (1988). *Science as a process: An evolutionary account of the social and conceptual development of science*. Chicago, IL: University of Chicago Press. doi:10.7208/chicago/9780226360492.001.0001.

Hume, D. (2007). *Writings on economics* (Rotwein, E., Ed.). New Brunswick, NJ: Transaction Publishers.

Kandalvi, M. Z. (n.d.). *Faza'il-e-a'amal*. Karachi, Pakistan. *Urdu Bazar.*.

Karim, F. (n.d.). *Imam Ghazali's ihya ulum-id-din*. Lahore, Pakistan: Sh. *Muhammad Ashraf.*.

Kim, W. C., & Mauborgne, R. (2005). *Blue ocean strategy*. Boston, MA: Harvard Business Press.

Maddox, I. J. (1970). *Elements of functional analysis*. Cambridge, UK: Cambridge University Press.

Mankiw, G. (2003). *Macroeconomics* (5th ed.). New York, NY: Worth Publishers.

Masud, M. K. (1995). Shatibi's life and works. In *Shatibi's Philosophy of Islamic law*. Kuala Lumpur, Malaysia: Islamic Book Trust.

McGrath & Barney. D. (2012). Capital as money. New York: Kindle Books.

Mehmet, O. (1997). Al-Ghazali on social justice: Guidelines for a new world order from an early medieval scholar. *International Journal of Social Economics*, *24*(11), 1203–1218. doi:10.1108/03068299710193570.

Myrdal, G. (1987). Utilitarianism and modern economics. In Feiwel, G. R. (Ed.), *Arrow and the Foundations of the Theory of Economic Policy* (pp. 273–278). London, UK: Macmillan.

Nozick, R. (1974). Distributive justice. *Philosophy & Public Affairs*, 3.

Overman, E. S. (1988). *Methodology and epistemology for social science: Selected papers of Donald T. Campbell*. Chicago, IL: The University of Chicago Press.

Pogge, T. W. (1995). Three problems with contractarian-consequentialist ways of assessing social institutions. In Paul, E. F., Miller, F. D. Jr, & Paul, J. (Eds.), *The Just Society* (pp. 221–242). Cambridge, UK: Cambridge University Press.

Popper, K. (1998). *Conjectures and refutations: The growth of scientific knowledge*. London, UK: Routledge & Kegan Paul.

Rawls, J. (1971). *A theory of justice*. Cambridge, MA: Harvard University Press.

Resnick, S. A., & Wolff, R. D. (1987). *Knowledge and class: A Marxian critique of political economy*. Chicago, IL: The University of Chicago Press.

Romer, P. M. (1986). Increasing returns and long-run growth. *The Journal of Political Economy, 94*, 1002–1037. doi:10.1086/261420.

Rucker, R. (1982). Large cardinals. In *Infinity and the Mind* (pp. 273–286). New York, NY: Bantam Books.

Russell, B. (2001). *The problems of philosophy*. Oxford, UK: Oxford University Press.

Schumacher, E. F. (1973). *Small is beautiful, economics as if people mattered*. London, UK: ABACUS.

Seidel, V. J. (1986). *Kant, respect and injustice: The limits of liberal moral theory*. London, UK: Routledge & Kegan Paul.

Sen, A. (1989). Justice. In Eatwell, J., Milgate, M., & Newman, P. (Eds.), *New Palgrave: Social Economics*. New York, NY: W.W. Norton.

Shackle, G. L. S. (1971). *Epistemics & economics*. Cambridge, UK: Cambridge University Press.

Soros, G. (2000). Reflexivity in financial markets, reflexivity in history. In *Open Society* (pp. 59–90). New York: Public Affairs.

Streeten, P. (1981). From growth to basic needs. In Streeten, P. (Ed.), *Development Perspectives*. New York: St. Martin's Press.

Sztompka, P. (1991). *Society in action: The theory of social becoming*. Chicago, IL: The University of Chicago Press.

Temkin, L. S. (1995). Justice and equality: Some questions about scope. In Paul, E. F., Miller, F. D. Jr, & Paul, J. (Eds.), *The Just Society* (pp. 72–104). Cambridge, UK: Cambridge University Press. doi:10.1017/S0265052500004684.

Vadilo, U. T. (2002). The architecture of the gold dinar economy: An academic perspective. In *Viability of the Islamic Dinar* (pp. 335–360). Kuala Lumpur, Malaysia: International Islamic University Malaysia, Research Center.

Waliullah, S. (n.d.). *Hujjat allah al-baligah*. Beirut, Lebanon. *Dar Al-Marifat.*.

Wallerstein, I. (1998). Spacetime as the basis of knowledge. In Bordo, O. F. (Ed.), *People's Participation, Challenges Ahead* (pp. 43–62). New York, NY: Apex Press.

ENDNOTES

1 *Qur'an* (2:168): O ye people! Eat of what is on earth, lawful and good; and do not follow the footsteps of the Evil One; for he is to you an avowed enemy. *Qur'an* (4:90-91): O ye who believe! Make not unlawful the good things which God has made lawful for you; but commit not excess: For God loves not those given to excess.

2 Topology (Maddox, 1970) denoted by (T,X) is a class of subsets of X whose union and intersection can be well defined in the class of subset T; and whereby, the null set and the universal set are also properly contained in the whole set T. All such sets are open subsets. Furthermore, any continuous function as relations defined on the sets forms a topology. Topology is a proper mathematical characterization of the relationship between God, self, and the world-system and all related cognitive elements as configurative and non-configurative. That is because by topology it is capable of studying the non-configurative being (divine law) and the cognitive elements (worldly effects). Thus God in respect of the divine law remains non-configurative in the context of the particular aspects of the divine law that are taken up in specific problems, that is in the specific topological space and its mappings (relations).
Super-topology (Rucker, 1982) is the term assigned to the largest dimensional topology with all the above-mentioned properties remaining in tact. Dimensionality here is defined as the endless system of relations concerning the divine law, self, and the world-system. Yet the endless system is not an infinite one; the dimensionality measure is not infinite. Super-cardinality and

super-space or super-topology are non-denumerable concepts enabling the *functional* ontology of formal relations in 'everything' by the universality of its model of unity of knowledge and the functionality of this unitary law in all of experience.

3 *Qur'an* (6:60): It is He who takes your souls by night (when you are asleep) and has knowledge of all that you have done by day, then He raises (wakes) you up again that a term appointed (your life period) be fulfilled, then (in the end) unto Him will be your return. Then He will inform you of that which you used to do.

4 see Einstein (1954).

5 Dasgupta (1987) in his marginalist challenge.

6 Quantum mechanics; see Breuer (1991).

7 *Qur'an* (92:13): "And verily unto Us (belong) the End and the Beginning."

8 By the income multiplier relation, $dY = k.(dSp)$, where Y denotes income; Sp denotes spending; dSp denotes the change in spending; $k = 1/(1\text{-}mpc)$, mpc denotes marginal propensity to consume. As $mpc \rightarrow 1.0$ with the enhancing effect of factors in the utilization of money in the real economy (trade), the resulting effect on dY increases by indefinitely large value.

Chapter 3
The Moral Content of Monetary History

ABSTRACT

The previous chapters are carried forth with a greater emphasis on money and the real economy with the financial bridge between these systems. The argument of the gold-backed monetary system is explained from both the historical and contemporary viewpoints. The phenomenological model of unity of knowledge is applied to the case of monetary and real economy systems with the financial connection. The open economy case of trade in the absence of interest rate is examined. The analytical method of circular causation in this regard is pointed out as a functional approach that is taken up profusely throughout this work.

INTRODUCTION

The evolution of money and along with it the understanding, functioning and policing of monetary aggregates in the real economy form a variegated history. Money and market exchange of goods and services took up certain distinct forms. There was the regime of barter or counter-trade between fungibles either on the spot, or as promissory future transactions. The critical issue is to examine the ethical and economic consequences of exchanging money for money.

BARTER (COUNTERTRADE)

The history of barter is a long one (Davies, 2002). It was always possible for markets to be flooded by diversity of goods in exchange. Yet such goods were mostly of the nature of basic needs that were acquired in the pure state of nature. The returns

DOI: 10.4018/978-1-4666-4643-8.ch003

Copyright ©2014, IGI Global. Copying or distributing in print or electronic forms without written permission of IGI Global is prohibited.

to factors of production, and thereby the price of goods and services, had to be in terms of the agreed upon quantities of goods in exchange. A slave worked for his master in acquiring food and livelihood as a primitive farmer. The master acquired in exchange land and animals as his wealth and social status. International trade too was based on diversity of tradable goods that gave trading partners their individual privileged and geo-political status in terms of power and wealth.

On the disutility of barter as medium of exchange for goods and services in a primitive moneyless world Davies writes (op cit, p. 10): ".... about barter in those long, dark, moneyless ages of prehistory, and thus we tend to derive our knowledge of barter from the remaining shrinking moneyless communities of more modern times." Such shrinking communities in the moneyless, barter worlds of exchange came about by the petrifying effects of disappearing innovation, enterprises and incentive, diversity and possibilities, as the natural consequences of the limited need for goods in exchange. There was also high cost associated with storages and trade in bulky goods. On the other hand, services could not be stored. Along with this limitation, there came about the sterility in human resource development, institutional development, and backwardness of technology. The ever-advancing meaning of organization, creativity and enterprise that arise from learning processes could not be conceptualized, for there was no exchange commodity value for learning as a process of exchanging knowledge. On this problem of barter writes Davies (op cit, p. 17): "Services by their nature cannot be stored, so that bartering for future services, necessarily involving an agreement to pay specific commodities or other specific services in exchange, weakens even the supposed normal superiority of current barter, namely its ability to enable direct and exactly measurable comparisons to be made between the items being exchanged."

PRESENT DAYS' SEMBLANCES OF BARTER

In some sense the idea of barter remains until today in the context of factor price equalization. The theorem on factor price equalization states (Samuelson, 1949): If there was free trade in goods and services between countries, free technology transfer and no transaction costs (transportation as example) in perfectly competitive world markets for goods and services, then the relative factor prices between the trading countries will equalize completely. So also the relative prices of the goods and services will equalize. Production paths will change from a state of autarky to trade, and finally into autarky again after equilibrium between two countries erodes competitive advantage.

A simple problem will prove that the world is still in some sense in the grips of barter or deeply in the problems of inequality of value and distribution of due property rights to all engaged in the partnership of growth and development. This happens when barter or something like barter impedes correct valuation of prices and assets, and thus due ownership.

The conceptual caveat of the barter-type problem arises when in the pure theory of international trade (Kenen, 1985) the trade triangle points out the equality of volumes of exports to imports. That is, the volume of export of a particular good by a country equals the volume of import of the same for the trading partner. The reverse trade of another good in the same way between the two countries is the barter return in the total world trade with two trading partners. That is, $X_{11} = M_{12}$; $X_{22} = M_{21}$; Thus total world trade of the two countries combined together is $X_{11} + X_{22} = M_{12} + M_{21}$ identically. Here X_{ij} denotes the export of good i by country j. M_{ij} denotes the import of good i by country j; i,j = 1,2; i ≠ j. Trade-flows here are measured in volumes of commodity units according to the specific commodities traded.

Although the value of trade enters the terms-of-trade equation, yet trade appears as barter in the above sense of country-specific commodity specification of trade-flows. The conceptual problem arising out of this nature of barter in international trade is this: marginal rate of substitution between exports and imports in commodity specializing countries equates to relative prices, the value of which is a ratio, not price as absolute value of the specific traded commodities. The result here is a strangely uncomfortable one combining our explanation of the factor-price equalization and commodity price-equalization theorems, and the trade equations in perfectly competitive free trade situation. In such a case of autarky to trade reverting to autarky situation as mentioned above, prices equate between trading countries. Thereby, even in value terms, the equality of export and import between trading partners and for world trade as mentioned above remains valid.

The barter situation in international trade in respect of special theorems of free trade prevails. The underlying problem that reveals itself in all of this theoretical formalism is that prices are not necessarily monetized in neoclassical economic theory. Price arises simply as indicator of value, which is denoted by the marginal utility of consumption of a good. Or on the production side, the price of a good is proportional to the marginal production of that good, which is a physical measure. Such are the implications of neoclassical economic theory. Neoclassical economic theory pervades much of economic theory of international trade.

In all of neoclassical economics, which has pervaded economic reasoning in every respect by its principle of marginalism and axiom of economic rationalist (Dasgupta, 1987), there is no robust theory of value. Yet, the theory of value has demanded the most intricate reasoning in economic and social theory. I must say that such a demand for a comprehensive theory of value extends as well to the domain of modeling socio-scientific synergy in various fields beyond economics (Choudhury, 2011). Indeed, there is a definite empirical and scientific way of treating morality and ethics in socio-scientific theory. The claim on morality and ethics studied in the most scientific way with analyticity, measurement, quantitative implication, and world-system applications in specific and generalized ways has been voiced by Einstein (undated) and Edel (1970). The author of this book is a strong protagonist of this claim of empiricism with ethicality and with substantive proof of such validity (Choudhury, 2011).

So how does economic theory define value? Value is defined by the following equation: Value of a good or service in exchange = Price (good or service) = MU (marginal utility of the good or service chosen). Marginal utility concept is a *ceteris paribus* idea of computing with substitute goods and their relative prices (as ratios). Thereby, moral and ethical values are thought to be unmeasured feelings without market representations. They are forgotten in any economic explanation and computation. Price as value is shown on the market demand curve identically as in the consumer demand curve.

The concept of value also takes a more extended form in economic reasoning, for if MU as a concept arises from the background of utility function, and on a social case from social utility function (welfare function), then value also signifies the maximum value of the utility or welfare criteria. In the end we note that a proper definition of the value concept, even if it is limited to price and welfare, must be based on the correspondingly appropriate representation of such cognitive valuations. This is where there ought to be extension of a theory based on convergence between inductive and deductive reasoning in everything of socio-scientific reality.

In moral-social construction of value, we will discuss later on at length that the market price and the market exchange as activity, truly represent the effects of moral and ethical induction of the market process. Price as valuation cannot be determined in the midst of Adam Smith's Invisible Hand Principle of market exchange. Learning as the engine of moral and ethical consciousness in social choices of market goods and services replaces the claimed automatic nature of market process in which this remains benign of moral and ethical values. This entire formalism of learning in unity of knowledge as the episteme and the relevant place of morality and ethics in it are ignored. Yet these bases of moral-social actions form a substantively scientific methodology. We will examine this technical problem later on in this book.

CONCLUDING REMARKS ON BARTER AND THE CONCEPT OF VALUE

We end up now with the topic of barter and its present-days semblance found in neoclassical economics and its entire economic lineage. Barter in every form of its representation is value-less. The study of value then becomes devoid of its substantive epistemological groundwork. Barter fails to establish and explain the long processes of change that economy and society undergo over history. After all, value as a meaning comprising the cognitive, material and the substantive moral and ethical significance in market exchange is a civilizing process and must be studied in its comprehensive sense. But beyond as well, price, market exchange, and the valuation process underlying these engage not simply human emotions toward culture, religion and traditions. Rather, the meaning and significance of the precept of value is at the same time a deeply explanatory worldview of transformation. Barter on the other hand in any form, including its present semblances in economic theory, cannot play a due role in the history of evolutionary moral-social reconstruction. The theory of value must overarch such a comprehensive meaning.

In the domain of money, finance, and banking, the present-days prevalence of the equivalent sign of barter, as in neoclassicism, means that the definition of such artifacts as price, market exchange and its moral and ethical benign stand on the moral-social issue cannot convey the civilizing process of intertemporal change by means of a comprehensive concept of value. This missing synergy between moral, ethical, and cognitive worldview in a comprehensive theory of value is much needed otherwise.

Global currency exchange is an example of the ethical value-benign valuation of market exchange. Currency exchange conveys a ratio that determines the comparative strength of some currencies against other ones. Such a ratio can equally be expressed as the paper-money value comparisons between the GDP of the currency trading countries proportional to their productive capacities. But paper-money is a doubtful definition of money. It can be taken as vouchers, promissory notes, or simply financial contracts. Such ways of holding paper-money are equivalent to bartering in assets and trade. In the absence of a proper definition of money – between barter, gold (bullions), paper and hybrid – the important issues of the nature, use, and wellbeing contributed by money, its instrumentation by finance, and the institution of banking in the relative development of trading countries with trading as an ethically empowering medium, remains a nominal explanation. Such an explanation that is limited to the accounting flows is thereby used to explain, measure, and implement the working of money through the banking system to enhance such accounting flows, for measurement of the comparative strength of paper-money backed traded currencies.

Money and its processes, namely finance, banking and currency measurement remain value-less in the substantive sense of intrinsic wellbeing and development. These have failed to reflect the intrinsic asset-backed valuation in the present-days manifestations of paper-money across everything. To bring back the relevance of money, finance, real economy and the banking medium into a better connection with the global civilizing functions of such artifacts an intrinsic-value idea of money is necessary.

Yet another implication of barter and barter-like related failure of the concept and measurement of value can be found in the growth of return or the cost of capital. Barter cannot assign monetary values to such measures. Consequently, if merchandise were to be exchanged with surplus value, the problems of unmeasured productivity, ownership, distribution, equality and fairness appear. On this point writes Davies (op cit, p. 11): "An amount of a particular commodity would be left in a convenient spot frequented by the other party to the exchange, who would take the goods proffered and leave what they considered a fair equivalent in exchange. If, however, after obvious examination, these were not considered sufficient they would remain untaken until the amount originally offered had been increased."

In modern banking practice, a wasteful levy on money flows through finance for productive and good purposes of increasing social wellbeing is interest rate. Eugene von Bawerk (1890) and the Austrian School of Economics under its Thomist persuasion considered interest rate as the sum of profit rate and interpersonal time-preference rate. But these two components are impossible to dissociate. Interpersonal time-preference rate was always a speculative rate, and constituted surcharge on loanable funds. Consequently, this differential surcharge of a speculative rate as interest charge almost always constitutes a price for non-exchanged goods and services. Consequently, there occurs an exchange in goods and services without a due transaction cost and price. Such an invisible exchange is tantamount to barter. This argument takes us back to the failure of establishing a precise definition, measurement, and application of money in market exchange in the real goods and services comprising the good things of life.

THE GOLD STANDARD WITH ASSET-BACKED DEFINITION OF MONEY

We turn now to examine the moral consequences of an understanding and application of money. We inquire once again the religious, traditional, cultural, ethical and moral, and modern evolutionary representations of money in real exchange using appropriate financial instruments. Our explanation regarding how God enters such an organic interrelationship of the socio-scientific categories revolves around the capability of money to engender justice and fairness, participation and empowerment, ownership and entitlement, productive transformation and sustainable change over the dimensions of knowledge, time, and space in moral-social construction. The theme of poverty alleviation and its effect on ameliorating the grassroots is the natural consequence of attaining wellbeing by way of the sustainability precept (Jackson & Kassam, 1998).

Barter gave way to the medium of exchange by means of bullions. Such bullions, as gold and silver, were held as the assets for valuation and fixation of the value of money. In such cases, if money was equivalent to currency then bullion in the exchange mechanism was treated as commodity. It was circulated as coinage. But it was equivalent to money to be exchanged in the market place for goods and services via the medium of tradable contracts. Such financial contracts could be promissory notes, vouchers, and paper. But their valuation must be fixed against the bullion standard to preserve the value of money backed by assets and circulated by a contractual instrument of exchange. Money in exchange via the tradable contracts does not make money as commodity. Rather, the valuation of money is done by the bullion backing (gold and silver); but the circulation of money carrying with it the bullion-backed valuation is done in alternative forms for easy circulation of money. Among these can be 'notes', financial contracts, tradable vouchers, debit cards and the like. Tradable vouchers are redeemable through hire and purchase. That is installment payments made out toward retiring the financial contract can be made against the voucher value over time (e.g. rents). The voucher can be proportionately used to purchase goods and services over time (e.g. stocks and shares).

The moral and ethical substance underlying such bullion-backed exchange of money for goods and services, thereby leading to the valuation of money in this way, enters money and markets via the unitary linkage between the monetary and financial artifacts and productive continuation in the good things of life. Such linkages are expected to generate *dynamic* basic-needs regimes of development; and the resulting derived demand for labor, investment and government spending. The consequential institutions to generate such ethical consequences arise for sustaining the money, finance and real economy linkages. The relations between money, price, employment and real growth, and all implements of *dynamic* basic-needs regimes of development abide.

The order of consciousness and enforcement of the necessary structure of social transformation must thereby arise from the epistemological foundations of moral-social change. In the moral and ethical order such an epistemic origin is established on the premise of unity of knowledge and its unitary relationship with the generalized and particular structure of the world-system. Money, markets, goods and services, technology, resources, and the whole gamut of social choices now enter the wellbeing function to determine the simulacra of complementary states between the good and productive things of life.

The history and modeling of unitary development and wellbeing is intrinsic to the Islamic explanation of the oneness of God in relation to the divine law and its impact on the learning organic unity of the world-system. The *Qur'an* provides the sustainable model of ecology and balance, in which the paired nature of the *Qur'anic* universe reigns supreme. A particular subset of this model is of the ecological and agricultural order. But this form is a particularity out of the generalized model of organic unity between 'everything' and 'everywhere' in the good things of life.[1] The central message is that unitary balance as pairs between the good things of life causing abundance to arise out of these organically unified artifacts is the foundation of heightened wellbeing for all. The dynamic model of sustainability as learning in the form of such socio-scientific symbiosis and social choices carries moral and ethical consequences. Within such a sustainability model of organic unity attained by learning in complementarities between artifacts and participation between the representing agents, is situated the enabling power of money and resource mobilization in the good things of life for the purpose of generating wellbeing.

When dealing with money, finance, economy and the business/banking system in the model of organic unity of knowledge creating *functional* ontological forms and their interrelations, the issue of sustainable development is addressed by the role that these artifacts play in unifying the domains of economy and society for attaining social wellbeing. The quantitative model for studying the emergent system of simulacra of Interacting, Integrating, and Evolutionary (IIE) relations is premised on the methodology of circular causation. It thereby assumes a scientific meaning and analysis. As artifacts of establishing the organic unity between money, finance, and the real economy with the social choices of the good things of life, the business/banking system now becomes a conscious determinant and actor in the sustainable development process. The moral and ethical law of unity of knowledge and its impact on the construction of the unified world-system is carried through by the function of the business/banking system by means of interrelating money, finance, and the real economy in the good things of life that comprise the *dynamic* basic-needs regime of development.

On the assignment of value to money and goods (services) in terms of the unifying (complementary) interrelations between money, finance, and real economy specific points need to be kept in mind. Firstly, there is the question on how money induces values in real things of exchange. That is, what is the true function of money in the intertemporal sense among the usual kinds of functions that mainstream economic conveys? These are namely, money as medium of exchange between goods and services; money as store of value; money as unit of exchange in the market exchange mechanism. Secondly, we need to understand how the moral perception on the function of money enters the pricing of goods, and thereby the relationship between the concept of value of money and capital accumulation and price determination. Thirdly, we need to determine how the moral and ethical valuation of money in concert with the valuation of goods and services reveals the valuation of social choice.

In regards to all of the above questions there arise deep social derivations connecting all the functions and artifacts mentioned above. The saying of the Prophet Muhammad as a principle coming down from the historical, moral, and ethical high ground is this (Ismail, 1989, p. 374):

Exchange of gold with gold, silver with silver, wheat with wheat, oats with oats, dates with dates, and salt with salt must be on the spot and in equal quantities, but when the two species differ exchange them as you like, but the exchange must be completed on the spot and no credit must be involved.

There is also the famous saying of the Prophet Muhammad on the matter of exchange of different qualities of dates by his beloved companion Belal: The beloved companion of the Prophet, Belal, once brought some superior dates to the Prophet. When the Prophet asked as to how he had acquired the superior dates, Belal replied that he had some inferior dates, which he exchanged in amount of two units of inferior dates to one of the superior kind. The Prophet said such an exchange of dates of the different kinds was like interest transaction (*riba*). He forbade its practice. The Prophet Muhammad recommended that Belal ought to have sold the inferior dates and used the proceeds to buy an equivalent quantity of the superior dates. This would be fair exchange and true valuation establishing equivalence in the values of the two qualities of dates.

The moral, ethical and social implications of the above-mentioned prophetic advice on exchange, and the use of money to value exchange, are a most important one. We imply from the saying of the Prophet Muhammad that although barter is not disapproved as an economic practice, yet it is recommended that money should be the medium of the valuation of things in exchange. This practice of money-value of exchange assigns a just and appropriate weight and value to tradable things. This is the idea of equivalence between the values of goods and services in exchange. It is also implied that the true value of money is measured in terms of its intrinsic value. The intrinsic value is based on bullions (gold and silver). The intrinsic value of money represents its store of value. Spot selling, and thereby valuation of goods in exchange, implies that the market exchange must be well determined in terms of actual things to be valued over time. Thus, there cannot be well-determined price-valuation (even expected prices) of things that are exchanged in the future, say by the present-valuation method. Prices of things can be attached only by the occurrence of given events comprising the goods in exchange and their contingencies realized as probabilistic events 'nearest' to the occurrence of such events at specific points of time. Money thus loses its function of exchange *over time*. The exchange function of money applies only upon the realization of market exchange at specific points of time.

Finally, the exchange of money for money is forbidden unless such exchange takes place on spot; that is by way of currency exchange without a speculative value in a futuristic sense. The price of money for money in the intertemporal sense is interest (*riba*). Such an identical exchange in money is forbidden because of the failure to establish equivalence between the monetary flows and its valuation effect on goods and services in exchange at different points of time. Upon the failure to establish such equivalence, this effect is transmitted into unjust ownership and distribution of resources. The existence of interest (*riba*) due to such consequences is the most inequitable and unjust practice of the financial system. The moral law and the inherent just social contract are thereby annulled. On the other hand, the abandoning of such practices, and their replacement by a well-determination of spot-valuation of exchange and the use of money to price such exchange, assigns equivalences between the intrinsic value of goods and services and their money-valuation as they occur in market exchange at specific points of time across the valuation time-horizon. Such valuation points denote the 'near' points of all resource flows that form into pairs by the epistemic law.

In the end, the function of money is restricted to its store of value. This is the intrinsic value of money in terms of bullions whose value has remained stable in the *longue durée* of economic history. Such monetary standards are found to be gold and silver (Choudhury & Hoque, 2004). Money with such an exclusive attribute performing its function of valuation on realized exchange of goods and services forms a valuation bridge. This establishes the organic connection between money and real economy via appropriate trade-based opposing interest-based financing instruments.

The value of money is thereby measured by equating its intrinsic value (bullions) to the market value of the exchange. The common price of the two valuations—of money and exchange—is the price of the goods in exchange and the intrinsic value of money to support that real exchange.[2] In this context, the quantity of money required to support exchange is determined by the expansion or contraction of money. In turn, the new stock of money as accumulated capital generated by the expansion of market process over the good things of life, as in dynamic basic-needs regimes, forms a cause-effect cycle with the real economy. We refer to such circulatory money as endogenous money. It is also the kind of money that can be construed to arise in the Money-Commodity-Money (MCM) circular causation interrelations (Heilbroner, 1986). Such interrelations are driven by appropriate financial instruments that enable trade in the good things of life, which comprise the dynamic basic-needs regimes of development. They shun interest-based mediums, which are causes of blockages of the resource flows.

The end result of combining various attributes of money, values, artifacts, social values and prices is the objective criterion of wellbeing. Thereby, it is implied from the Prophet's saying that the true wellbeing value of consumption arises from its compounding of consumptions and their social valuations. The wellbeing function is the criterion of the degree of unity of knowledge attained by the moral law and its action upon a unifying world-system by organic unity of being and becoming. Consequently, in the end we derive the price of goods as the value of money in terms of its intrinsic standards (bullions of gold and silver) and in terms of the percentage change in wellbeing index per unit of goods in the complementary vector of the good things of life.[3]

To bring God into the financial system in reference to the moral and ethical precepts that we have studied above is to organize the complementary (participatory) interrelationship between money, finance, and real economy within the framework of price and valuation. The moral signature is established here by the application of epistemic unity of knowledge to the problem at hand.

Figure 1 gives a systemic understanding of the money-finance-real economy interrelationship as an application of the embedded moral law in the epistemology of unity of knowledge. Figure 1 is developed in reference to the definitions of symbols given in Figure 1 from Chapter 1.

Next, we return to the importance of bullions (gold and silver) in the just, stable, and fair valuation of the money-finance-real economy interrelationship. This kind of complementary interrelationship by circular causation between (M,F,R) indicated in Figure 1, represents the organic unity of knowledge of the financial system. In such a holistic interrelationship is embedded the epistemic law that brings moral-

Figure 1. (M.F.R)-system in the epistemic relations of unity of knowledge

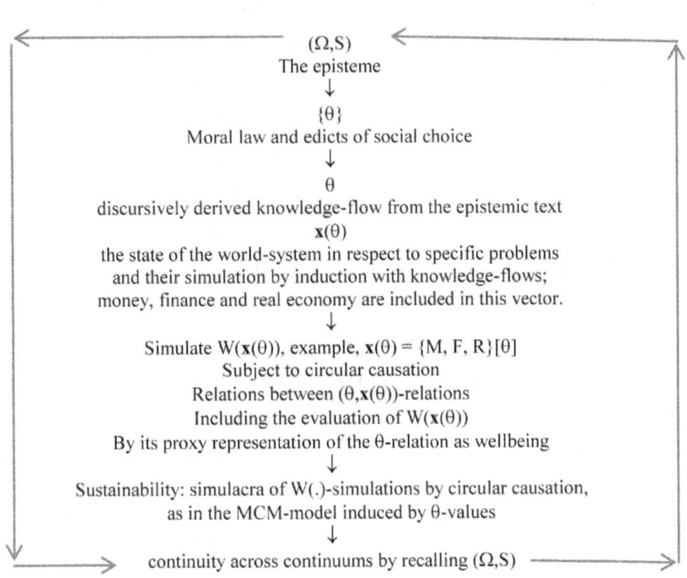

ity and ethics. The presence of these values marks the place of God in the financial system as a subset of the world-system.

Two questions are raised in this formation of the just, stable and fair (M,F,R), organically unified interrelationship by means of the bullion standard. Firstly, we ask: What is the nature of the bullion relationship in the circular causation between M, F, R? Secondly, the question is whether there is any other viable alternative to establish the same attributes in the (M,F,R)[θ] structure of relationships by the induction of the moral and ethical knowledge of epistemic unity denoted by θ-value.

Over a *longue durée* of monetary history gold remained fairly stable in price, thus proving itself as a reliable monetary standard (Hayek, 1999). Stable prices of both goods and services and inputs of production are necessary for both the consumer and the producers in their various categories for total wellbeing. Fairness and justice ensue from the real productive and spending capability that follows on the heels of participatory ventures. In this kind of productive relationship the ever-broadening domain of possibilities evolve embracing together the rich and poor, large and small businesses, communities and nations, and finally, nations and the global membership (Choucri, 1995). Besides, sustainability of the dynamic basic-needs regime of development requires continuity over continuums of diverse systems of the attributes of participation yielding balance, fairness, just order, and stability via the mediums of productivity, spending, diversity, and accessibility in the good things of life. This entire spectrum of attributes in the generalized sense of organic interrelations is the idea of sustainability. Its continuity across continuums of diverse systems is the idea of learning in the epistemic unity of knowledge, and its making of the particulars and the general order constructs of world-systems. Figure 1 from Chapter 1 and Figure1 in this chapter have unraveled such attributes.

Contrary to the bullion standard of monetary aggregates, the barter medium of exchange remains unacceptable on grounds of its failure to establish fair trade and valuation of money and exchange in terms of prices, as shown in the foregoing footnotes. But in terms of spot-buying and spot-selling, barter can be accepted but is not encouraged. This exception is because of the equality of the value of exports to finance the value of imports between trading partners in the pure theory of trade. In such a case with equality in fair trade, the terms-of-trade for each of the trading partners in specific trade equals unity.[4]

Indeed, there is a suggestion now going in Malaysia (Billington, 2002) that gold should be used as commodity to back up international trade between Muslim countries. The implication is that instead of monetary units for valuation of merchandise and capital flows in such international trade, parcels of gold would be used. The argument made is that a small parcel of gold bullion could support a large volume of trade. Besides, the argument is furthered that exchange rate under such gold backing of trade would remain equal to 1 for all trading countries under the gold-backed trading arrangement. This result relates with the result given in the endnote (4); for by definition, terms-of-trade, $t = p_x/p_m = (1 + e - e') = 1$, with exchange rates $e = e' = 1$ under the gold-backed trading arrangement, except for some transaction cost remaining.

The argument made in this chapter is that for reasons of convenience it is acceptable to adopt 'notes' as a medium of monetary circulation but backed by the bullion standard. Thereby, as explained earlier, such a promissory note or voucher becomes redeemable in terms of its value backed up by a proportionate amount of gold. This idea of 'notes' carrying value in transaction in terms of the bullion standard is unlike the other two understanding of the gold standard. The first of this kind of the gold standard is to hold a stock of gold in the central bank to be used as backing to support currency in circulation. Thereby, a large demand for money following economic expansion will require an equivalent expanded amount of gold for currency backing.

International merchandise trade and currency trading took place in return for gold that had to be convertible or simply exist as bullion redemption against merchandise. Central banks required a large sum of gold as the volume of trade in goods, services, and capital increased during the heydays of the Bretton Woods Institutions (1870-1914) (Brown & Hogendorn, 2000, Chapter 17). This state continued on to exist until the breakdown of the Bretton Woods Institution arrangement in 1971. Exchange of gold for merchandise was carried out either by minted coins, which required a large circulation of gold and stockpiling in the central banks of trading countries. Alternatively, fiduciary bills could denominate their values according to stipulated price of gold, which can then be redeemed against merchandise trade.

As long as the circulation of money is in terms of bullion coinage central banks would require a large stock of gold. Without this the increasing trade and economic expansion that would require gold backing would come to have only limited amount of gold. Thereby, the price of gold to shore the merchandise value in terms of prices of exchange would be required to increase. Along with such increase in gold price the exchange prices of goods and services would increase. Inflation would be the natural cause of such gold shortage and excess demand for gold during times of economic expansion. Fiduciary bills should therefore be considered as the alternative way of redeeming gold against merchandise exchange by a new and innovative structural relationship between central banks, commercial banks and the real economy functions using appropriate financial instruments to mobilize money into the real economy. We will later on treat such a monetary system as the 100% Reserve Requirements Monetary System (100%RRMS) with the Gold Standard.

The growth in the quantity of money in relation to the growth of real economy and the stabilization effect of the gold standard on money and real economy relationship generates endogenous monetary flows. The monetary policy and the nature of relationship between the central bank and the commercial bank in this case becomes of the endogenous type. It can then be shown that the full force of action of commercial bank is felt on the mobilization of savings as spending into the real economy in the goods things of life (dynamic basic-needs regime of development).

Consequently, as far as prices equivalently value money in circulation supporting goods in exchange, the trend towards a fuller market economy is based on such endogenous relationship that emulates the interactive, integrative, and evolutionary (IIE) model of wellbeing and sustainability in the (M,F,R)-circular causation model. The 100% Reserve Requirement Monetary System with the Gold Standard is the institutional arrangement within which (M,F,R)-model of endogenous money and markets takes its functional form for the closed and open economy cases. This is a theme for deeper investigation in a later chapter.

EARLY HISTORY OF THE GOLD STANDARD AND ENDOGENOUS MONEY

The Prophetic Tradition and After

On the matter of using the gold standard as the intrinsic asset-backing of money in terms of real exchange in the good things of life, Allouche (1994) points out that the Prophet Muhammad prayed for all those communities who abided by the gold standard in their monetary transaction to support the value of exchange in merchandise. The bullion coin as currency—dinar and dirham during the time of the Prophet—was assigned smaller denominations. The Prophet took part in assigning such denominations. In weight fixation for smaller denominations of coins an example is the assigning of half the amount of wealth tax (*zakah*) for every twenty dinars held. One smaller denomination called *danaq* was equal to 8.4 unshelled barleys during the Prophet's time. The important point to note here is the endogenous relationship between monetary valuation and real market exchange in terms of bullion standard and goods.

Endogenous money as currency in circulation under the gold standard has a rich history in Islamic classical times. Such a system of money and its institutions, namely banking, cannot logically function on the basis of interest rates as a financial instrument. Yet the latter is permanently ingrained in Western economic and social system. It is accepted ethics – human behavior – in Western culture and belief, although it was discouraged in early Christian scholasticism (Schumpeter, 1968).

The history of western banking started in Italy with some very rich families establishing such financial institutions to take care of financial deposits at a cost.

Money in such a barter system was always understood as a commodity that could be the medium for valuation of dissimilar exchange, such as wheat for potatoes, with different periods of preservation. Thereby, money as commodity originated with the idea of holding goods; and later on, money was valued against money in the absence of a clearance mechanism for goods.

This kind of self-valuation resulted in the monetary valuation of debt. Money as commodity in monetary history is thereby intrinsically linked with debt and thereby with interest rate on debt. Modern banking as merchant bank and as financial intermediary has benefited from the lucrative benefit of financing debt at high rates of interest. Interest-based transactions were thereby permitted in modern banking as financial intermediary.

Yet such a modern conception of money, finance, and the real economy is contrary to the Islamic understanding. Some of the Islamic historical heritage on this theme can be mentioned here after noting its significance in the prophetic teachings. The principal conclusion we reach from all such historical lessons is the focus on trade in the good things of life, and shunning interest in every form, as the great enemy of wellbeing of all – human and inanimate entities, such as the economy and society. Interest theory is weak on scientific grounds as well both in conventional and Islamic financial understanding today.

The caveats appear in modern theory of money is that interest rates hold back the flow of resources and thereby the participation needed to establish a productive and equitable society. The cost of loans and the privileges of the rich over the poor caused by debt financing and interest rates stand on the way of an equitable wellbeing of sharing the societal resources. Loss of participation also reduces the possibility of empowerment and ownership by all.

The prevailing thinking in Islamic parlance regarding the commodification of money is a mistake. The monetary theory based on the M-C-M model that we have referred to earlier and will study it further, points out that in the modern conception of holding money and its liquid kind, the commodity of M-C-M is simply a form of money (e.g. bonds). Consequently, the medium that breeds money from money is commodified money (bonds). Such a financial intermediary of money gains its return from valuation of liquid assets, bonds, and bank-savings. These carry semblances of interest rates as return on money and finance. There is no linkage between money, finance, and the real economy in such a case. On this point the *Qur'an* declares (2:275): "Those who devour usury will not stand except as stands one whom the Evil One by his touch has driven to madness. That is because they say: 'Trade is like usury,' but God has permitted trade and forbidden usury."

Abu Hamid Muhammad (Imam) Ghazzali

Dwelling on this universal principle, Imam Ghazzali wrote on the moral function of exchange and its correct valuation by the gold standard of currency in circulation in the absence of debasement and counterfeiting (Ghazzali trans. Karim, undated). By inducing the moral and ethical values of just and fair exchange and its stability of valuation in terms of prices valued by the bullion standard, Ghazzali dispensed the idea of steady-state market equilibrium.

Ghazali never believed on the law of demand. There is no 'invisible hands' principle working in the market process. God is not absent from the market process, the world-system due to the permanent presence of the divine law of oneness. Indeed, prices, Ghazzali held, rise and fall not by the law of demand; rather by the commands of the moral law, God's will. Scarcity is the cause and result occurring in rounds of immiserising resource generation in the face of failure of learning by pairing between the good things of life that generate synergy, and thereby, opportunities continuously across continuums of possibilities. The resulting principle of abundance replacing the postulate of scarcity in economic rationality postulate is the logical consequence of circular causation by evolutionary learning.

Instead of either the steady-state idea of market equilibrium or the Darwinian idea of uncharted market evolution marked by punctuated equilibriums (Grandmont, 1989), there are now simply market contracts in Ghazzali's case. Such contracts are cleared by honesty, trust, transparency and commitment among agents in all kinds of markets between transacting agents. The combination of the attributes of market process such as the honoring of contracts of sale and purchase in a visible way along with the moral values and consciousness underlying such contract clearance, transforms the steady-state concept of equilibrium into learning points of evolutionary equilibriums by the precept of epistemic unity.

Consequently, the entire intellection, modeling, implications and applications of the evolutionary concept of learning equilibriums, change our understanding of economic theory and its synergy with institutional structures, preferences, menus and policies. Within such new dimensions of understanding the economic and social process with the force of scientific analysis rests the treatment of money as medium of valuation (store of value conveyed by the real assets to money) in close connection with real exchange in the goods things of life (social contracts).

Taqiuddin Ahmed (Imam) Ibn Taimiyyah

Ibn Taimiyyah was a great exponent of the bullion theory of money, price and exchange. During the reign of the Mamluks in Egypt when Ibn Taimiyyah lived, the introduction of copper coins increased prices many hundred fold. This caused hyperinflation. Thus was proved Gresham's Law in early history of money: Bad money drives out good money.

But Ibn Taimiyyah vehemently supported the pure market process. Government would levy lowest level of taxes. Market process would respond readily to the natural consequence of heightened consciousness in moral values among consumers, producers, and governments. Such moral attributes are the basis of economic and social stability in which the valuation of money in relation to real exchange survives the best. Gold backing, which is a significant source of monetary stability, conveys stability in all desired variables in the economic and social system. But none of these attributes can be attained without the moral-social endogeneity in the values and functioning of agents and entities.

Ibn Taimiyyah wrote (Islahi, 1988): "*Athman* (price or money) are meant to be measurements of objects of value (*mi'yar al-amwal*), through which the quantities of objects of value (*maqadir al-amwal*) are known; and they are never meant to be consumed." The permanence of gold in terms of value of money, price, and exchange is the universal basis of a stable and progressive economy, wellbeing, and moral consciousness. Money is thereby endogenous in nature (Choudhury, 1997). The permanence of a stable economy in this form implies that the *dynamic* basic-needs regime of development describes the progressive transformation of the economic and social system and the preferences, menus, and evolutionary learning that must go on continuously on the moral-social plane of transformation. Furthermore, because of the inherently intertemporal regime of the *dynamic* basic-needs regime of development, and the functioning of the (M,F,R)-interrelations in this development regime, the strict function of money is limited to that of store of value. Over time there cannot be valuation of money as medium of exchange or unit of value as long as a shadow price, and not market-determined price (or 'nearest' price value), is assigned for the intertemporal valuation of exchange.

Ibn Qayyim al-Jawziyya

Ibn Qayyim as student of Ibn Taimiyyah carried the arguments against interest rates to a high level of sophistication. There are two kinds of financial interest according to Ibn Qayyim. *Riba al-fadl* is the interest-like surcharge in items of exchange. This is the kind of interest conveyed by the Prophet Muhammad's saying regarding equivalence in value between exchangeables. *Riba al-nasiah* is the intertemporal subjective valuation of exchange in the expected, though not actual occurrence of an event. The example hers is that of 'nearest-to-a-point' valuation, such as spot-selling, contrary to estimating uncertain probabilistic futures that cannot be read off, even in terms of their expected values.

A combination of many factors determines the true valuation, pricing and equivalence of exchange and money at distributed points of time. Firstly, there is spot-selling and buying. Such a case is equivalent to the physical presence of things in exchange at a point of time and space. While the occurrence of such an event cannot be deterministic in the absence of perfect knowledge in agents and things of complementary nature, therefore, a probabilistic evaluation of the occurrence of the event of exchange yields always an expected value. This is the idea of the 'nearest' point of occurrence of an event over time and space.

Riba al-nasiah is reduced to the pricing of an (M,F,R)-event 'nearest' to the point of its occurrence. But the determination of the 'nearest' point subject to the contingencies of its occurrence as a probabilistic event requires institutional discourse. Likewise, there is also institutional connection with the discursive elements in order to determine a fair price of exchange at a point of time over the intertemporal horizon. Over and above, there is the effect of moral and ethical factors on the occurrence of the event. In this way, the determination of a 'nearest' point is subject to perturbations that cause evolutionary learning in concert with conjoint market-institutional determinations and moral-social forces. Consequently, events occur at 'nearest' valuation points in the knowledge, time, and space dimensions. Pre-set future pricing at the present time for a projected estimated values at intertemporal points, either as *riba al-fadl* or *riba al-nasiah*, is impossible. Ibn Qayyim's theory of interest and money thus provides a forceful confirmation of the concept of endogenous money in Islam as being solely a store of value (of valued real assets) and not a medium of exchange or a unit of value of intertemporal exchange with money as commodity in the totality of the (M,F,R)-vector.

Taqi al-Din Ahmad Ibn Aki al-Maqrizi

During the times of the Egyptian Mamluks, Taqi al-Din Ahmad Ibn Aki Al-Maqrizi wrote on the function of money for the wellbeing of the Muslim world-nations (*ummah*) in his famous book entitled, *Ighathah al Ummah bi-Kasf al-Gummah* (*Helping the Islamic Community by Examining the Causes of Its Economic Distress*). The ideas of Ibn Taimiyyah and Ibn Qayyim prevailed on Al-Maqrizi's ideas fully.

Al-Maqrizi points out that historically the gold and silver standards had maintained their imputed values in the form of currencies in circulation and as denominated in these bullion-values as these are standardized by measures of basic-needs. Such currencies remained remarkably stable over long time-periods. Allouche (1994) writes on Al Maqrizi's idea: "According to all reports, either valid or invalid, no nation or group of people is ever known to have paid for goods or remunerated for works in ancient or recent times in a currency other than that of gold and silver. In fact, it is said that the first to mint the dinar and the dirham was Adam, who said that life is not enjoyable without these two currencies."

Al-Maqrizi's intellection on the enjoyment gained from material ownership can be explained with the help of Figure 1 as follows: The wellbeing function as criterion of evaluation of the vector $(\theta,\mathbf{x}(\theta)) = (M,F,R)[\theta]$ is now denoted by simulated values of $W(M,F,R)[\theta]$, subject to the circular causation relations between the vector elements according to their respective formal relations. Earlier we have made such a model selection as a product function to signify complementarities between the $(M,F,R)[\theta]$-variables in the light of the moral catalysis of the θ-effect as the principal driving force of social reconstruction and its sustainability over time. This total evolutionary change out of continuity of the inherent interactive and integrative processes is caused by diversity of processes in the knowledge, time, and space dimensions propelled by learning feedback and evolutionary progression summarized as follows:

$$(\Omega,S) \rightarrow \theta \rightarrow \text{Money (Gold and silver as numeraire)} \rightarrow F \rightarrow R \equiv (M \leftrightarrow F \leftrightarrow R)[\theta] \rightarrow \theta' \in (\Omega,S) \rightarrow [M \rightarrow F \rightarrow R \equiv (M \leftrightarrow F \leftrightarrow R)[\theta']_{new} \rightarrow \text{continuity.} \quad (1)$$

Thus there is logical reason to understand what is meant by the statement — "that the first to mint the dinar and the dirham was Adam, who said that life is not enjoyable without these two currencies."

Imam Shatibi

The idea of wellbeing caused by the moral induction of material artifacts in the dynamic basic-needs regime of development was propounded distinctly by Imam Shatibi, as in his *Muwafaqat fil-Usul al Shari'ah*, in the theory of *maslaha wa-al-istihsan. Maslaha* as wellbeing for the objective purpose of worship in the framework of unity of knowledge and unity of the world-system; and *istihsan* as the determination of the public purpose of the wellbeing criterion of *maslaha*, lay down the foundation of the Islamic law (*shari'ah*). This foundation of morality in the epistemological meaning of the objective and purpose of the *shari'ah* is referred to as the *maqasid as-shari'ah*.

In reference to Figure 1 and the Al-Maqrizi's devolution of formalism as shown above, the *maslaha* function now enters as the evaluative criterion. It is now connected with the especial case of complementarities and participation between the elements of $(M,F,R)[\theta]$ and the representative agents of these. θ-value is embedded in the primal expression that drives wellbeing. It denotes a monotonic functional proxy for wellbeing.

Over intertemporal evolution of events and transformation in the knowledge, time and space dimensions every 'nearest' point of simulation of wellbeing subject to the list of circular causation relations is a learning point of complexes of synergies between variables, their relations, and the representative entities. Thereby, Shatibi's economy and the institutions embedded in the moral economy, such as a commercial bank and its relationships along the learning processes with the central bank in the 100 percent reserve requirements monetary system is a matter not only of finance but also of social choices. Such social choices are determined, evolved and sustained within a discursive society. It is a society that is moved by the episteme of unity of knowledge and its constructive ontology of logical formalism, model, rules and applications.

Imam Shatibi linked money to *dynamic* basic-needs regime of wellbeing and development. His prescribed basket of goods and services for human wellbeing comprised necessaries, comforts, and refinements of life. None of these kinds belonged to the luxury basket. Shatibi's basket of such goods comprises graduated basic needs at the three levels of advancement of goods within that category. Consequently, the Shatibi-basket comprised a graduated (*dynamic*) basic-needs category of goods for simulation of wellbeing. This met the goodness of consumers, producers, government and the environment. The graduation of the simulacra of possibilities makes up the sustainable criteria of the ever-increasing wellbeing.

The dynamic basic-needs regime of wellbeing and development after it arose from the conscious directions of the precept of epistemic unity carried on to satisfy the needs environment, the present and future generations, health, income maintenance, price stability, and steady economic growth, production diversity and innovation, enterprise, employment and ownership. In this way, abundance replaces scarcity of resources for life-fulfillment. All these functions establish causality between consciousness, life-fulfillment, wellbeing and continuity across diversity of possibilities. This is the meaning of sustainability. It is also derived from our learning model of the Interactive, Integrative, and Evolutionary (IIE) type.

The fullest effect of the Shatibi model of life-fulfillment is realized by the extension of Figure 1 as simulacra of learning processes in heightened levels of knowledge emanating from the axiom of epistemic oneness, and proceeding on through the world-system to the Great Event of the Hereafter. The Hereafter is thus understood as the End and ultimate realization of the purpose of the moral law and of its impact on the creative order of 'everything'.[5]

Although it is a matter of religious belief, yet one can logically prove the existence of the Hereafter in reference to its axiomatic precept of sole and final optimal point of knowledge that is embodied in 'everything' by conscious recognition of epistemic oneness. We use the concept of systemic limiting points that are interrelated by virtue of domains of organic functions intra-system and inter- systems. In such a case, if we repeated Figure 1 for all such systems, firstly over one process, and then across sequences of learning processes, we would come up with repeated limiting points in expanding domains of limiting points (Maddox, 1970). By the theorem of convergence of these limiting points the ultimate limiting point of all systemic limiting points in the knowledge, time, and space dimensions there would be the end-points for each of the diverse cases under study. Such a limiting end-point is optimal and the end of indefinitely long sequences of evolutionary learning equilibrium. Hence the end point denotes the convergent point of all limiting points of this kind. The Hereafter as the Great Event of continuous learning and evolution of $\{\theta,\mathbf{x}(\theta)\}$ across processes of learning for continuums of 'everything' indefinitely, is the final convergent point of all learning in the knowledge, time, and space dimensions.

Shatibi's *maslaha* function as the wellbeing criterion is a derivative of the *Qur'anic* precept of the Supreme Felicity. This is the wellbeing of the Hereafter. The *maslaha* is the worldly mapping of Supreme Felicity in terms of its usefulness for the public purpose (*istihsan*) according to the purpose and objective of the *shari'ah* (*maqasid as-shari'ah*). See Masud (1995). The *maslaha* is thereby the derivation and evaluation function of the moral law that is embedded in worldly matters (*muamalat*).

The end result is that θ as cumulative knowledge-flow tends to Ω at the Great Event. Yet the dimension of Ω as the absolute episteme of the moral law is not infinite in value. It has a value of large cardinality (super-cardinal) (Rucker, 1983) in respect of the optimality of knowledge. Hence, $\mathbf{x}(\theta)$ tending toward the Great Event of accumulated knowledge does not acquire an infinite value. Rather, the optimal value corresponding to the moral law and the moral worth of things reaches the ultimate limiting point.[6]

When the above ideas are applied to the theme of (M,F,R)[θ]-relationship using the IIE-formalism, money M equals the finest category of money in terms of its intrinsic value in the complete and perfect absence of interest rate. F denotes the finest transformation of business into its perfect relationship with wellbeing. Wellbeing is then attained in terms of the union of money and finance in their perfect states with the world-system.[7] None of these categories of artifacts is infinite in value at the Great Event. They are simply optimal and purest in the light of the ultimate perfection of the epistemic oneness in the order of things. A cognitive transformation to eternal bliss has thus taken place.

CONTEMPORARY THOUGHT ON THE GOLD DINAR AND ISLAMIC MONEY, FINANCE, AND TRADE RELATIONS

The gold dinar and Islamic money are being thought of in terms of circulation of gold coins as currency, rather than gold as asset-backing for money circulating in any acceptable form. An alternative way of circulating gold-backed currency is by 'notes'. These can be redeemed by prices of the real exchange. Gold would play simply a stabilization role in sustaining stable prices and economic expansion. The attributes of the *dynamic* basic-needs regime of development backed by the gold standard will apply. The banking arrangement to establish the inverse relationship between the demand for gold and the circulation of a quantity of money into the real economy with stable prices and economic expansion in a dynamic basic-needs regime of development, is a theme for a later chapter. It can merely be brushed upon here.[8]

Among those who promote the idea of bullions in circulation but do not prescribe the organizational structure of 100 percent reserve requirement monetary system in gold-backed money are Mydin and Larbani (2004), Vadillo (2002), and the previous Prime Minister Dr. Mahathir Muhammad of Malaysia (Islam Policy, 2011). Mydin and Larbani recognize the importance of *maqasid as-shari'ah* that money ought to serve. Yet in international trade, though Mydin and Larbani argue that a small amount of gold can support a large volume of trade, this kind of transaction is treated solely as barter. Thereby, the relationship of the central bank and the commercial bank in respect of the function of money and its gold-denominated storage at the central bank is not explained. There is a complete absence of the organizational function interrelating gold and money stocks in reference to the quantity of money that remains circulatory across real goods.

Mydin and Larbani show that fiat money appears in the form of debt. Such debt is measured by paper circulation in the presence of interest on debt outstanding. Consequently, the higher the debt the more the interest payment on debt and the higher is the amount of money required for financing the debt. Although the authors associate debt and interest with fractional reserve requirement system, there is no treatment of the way to get out of debt and interest, and generate a high volume of trade with small quantities of gold, even as money becomes increasingly circulatory. The organizational relations between the central bank, the commercial and the business community are not explained.

Vadillo (2002) is an all-out supporter of the circulating gold dinar as commodity money having the intrinsic value created in true market exchange of goods and services in the light of their moral and ethical acceptability. In his words (p. 340): "The Dinar is not a financial tool, it is a commodity." In that respect it is of the same nature as a kilo of potatoes. It has a price determined intrinsically by the market. It is not a promise of payment."

While many of the arguments forwarded by Vadillo in support of gold dinar in support of trade and the flourishing of the real economy are valid, what is missing is the connector between the gold dinar and the real economy by means of financial instruments that heighten the flow of monetary and financial resources into the real economy. This is a matter of substantive importance for consideration and policy-institutional enactment by the monetary authority, such as central bank and commercial banks. Gold-backed system generates such financial instruments that can be held for trading and exchange in terms of redeemable valuation of 'notes.'

Instead, the monetary system promoted by Vadillo and others in this category jumps the financial medium of mobilization of money in the form of gold or 'notes' into the real economy. Consequently, the barter concept of monetary units re-enters the money-gold-trade valuation equation. While it is true that gold as bullion will remain unchanged in price and value when parceled proportionately to the needs of trade across nations, yet the value of trade, and thereby of the financial instruments, will vary. Consequently, the quantity of gold and its reverse relationship with the quantity of money held back from mobilization at the central bank will vary.

The quantity of money created at the central bank and mobilized into the real economy through commercial banks has a reverse functional relationship with the quantity of gold minted at the central bank. The financial instruments enter such a money and real economy relationship through the reverse relationship between resource mobilization and the quantity of gold. Gold as commodity money loses its relevance in the presence of the financial medium of the money-finance-real economy relationship backed by gold (bullion). There is no need for gold dinar to circulate in the economy as currency, as long as the gold backing is rendered to money having a store of value only, backed by assets.

This is a substantive matter. It underlies the valuation equation given earlier in a footnote. Recognizing this substantive difference from the concept of money as commodity in the form of gold dinar in circulation, establishes the specific banking system rather than the exchange value of gold as barter. This is the idea of the 100 percent reserve requirements monetary system. The money-finance-real economy dynamics involved in this type of banking system show how the moral-social reconstruction of the banking system can be done away from the vagaries of the fractional reserve monetary system. We will substantially explain the innovative nature of the 100 percent reserve requirements monetary system, which is different from the gold standard construed in mainstream economics and from the other proposition of the gold dinar.

Dr. Mahathir Mohammad's idea of the gold dinar as a monetary unit is similar to the above-mentioned ones. The gold dinar being treated as a coinage is simply a barter. For that reason we find that rich Arab countries have been able to invest in gold dinar as an capital asset. Yet there has not been any active discussion and attempt towards change of the monetary system in the Muslim World. The Muslim World still clings on to, and Dr. Mahathir Mohammad supports the idea that, the gold dinar can works effectively within the fractional monetary system. There is no claim in such thinking of implementing the gold standard in its systemic sense connected with the 100 percent reserve requirement monetary system.

As a result of this kind of silence and ambivalence to a new monetary system with the 100 percent reserve requirement monetary system the monetary policy of the Muslim World has remained unchanged into the new dimensions required for complementing the money, finance and real economy with the prospect of generating wellbeing for all through the moral role of money in such an (M,F,R)[θ]-complementary and learning interrelationship. Along with this failure to think new along the truly Islamic epistemic lines applied to (M,F,R)[θ]-complementary circular causation interrelations, no new intellectual contributions along the epistemic lines have been made. Islamic development organizations have not been successful in formulating the cooperative will in development, and the use of money in this direction.

A starkly failed attempt for monetary union is the Gulf Cooperation Council region (GCC). Here the absence of political will among members, external intervention, self-interest of member countries, and absence of robust thinking along lines of monetary integration, and thereby of markets, institutions and common policies and programs altogether contributed to the overall structural weakness of the GCC.

Even in the case of Malaysia, inter-regional trade and economic integration in the South-East Muslim countries is a disappointing show (Choudhury, 2003). The matrix of trade-flows in capital goods between Malaysia, Indonesia and Malaysia is almost a null matrix. Inter-country trade in the Muslim community has remained unchanged at a level between 9-10 percent of her total world trade (Islamic Development Bank Annual Reports). This implies that 90 percent of the Muslim countries' total trade leaks out to the trading world outside the Muslim community. In the end, no importance has been placed on the development of a custom union leading to common market in the Muslim World. Monetary policies that have galvanized the establishment of the European Monetary Union (Masson, Krueger, and Turtleboom, 1997) have not appeared to the Muslim World. Hence no maturity is gained by the monetary theory that otherwise ought to move the epistemic worldview of the moral foundation of a socio-scientific monetary understanding and its organization.

In the sense of the moral foundation of (M,F,R)[θ]-model Islamic banks have replaced the universal principle of the *maqasid as-shari'ah* by the narrow meaning of *shari'ah*-compliance. This latter perspective is tied down to the selection of certain financial instruments approved by a legal interpretation (*fiqh*) of the *shari'ah* rules. Among such financial instruments is the barter of gold dinar coinage. It neither establishes the concept of value nor the measurement of value in terms of price, unit of money supported by gold standard, and the mobilization of resources for real economy development. Beyond this limitation as well, is the absence of both the theory of wellbeing and hence of Shatibi's theory of *maslaha* as the functional model of the (M,F,R)[θ]-interrelations in the light of the epistemology of unity of knowledge. In Malaysia we have noted, as in most other parts of the world where

Islamic banks exist that, even as the *maslaha* as the wellbeing concept remains absent, so also the precept of the *maqasid-as-shari'ah* is forgotten. This phenomenon is well noted in the case of Malaysia, where the blind pursuit of *shari'ah*-compliance overwhelms the key principle of *maqasid as-shari'ah* in 'everything'.

ABANDONMENT OF GOD IN THE PAPER MONEY BANKING SYSTEM: FRACTIONAL RESERVE REQUIREMENT MONETARY SYSTEM

In Western economies, the gold standard is understood as piling up a stock of gold in the central bank to shore the currency value of gold coins or equivalent fiduciary notes certified by the central bank against gold. This kind of a currency pegging to gold has a problematic history. The main difference between the Islamic and Western traditions of money in bullion history in relation to gold as endogenous money relates to exchange. In the classical Islamic case, exchange takes place in the absence of interest rates (*riba*) and exogenous money related to interest rate. In the Western economic system, the prevalence of interest is complete. In recent times, Muslim countries' monetary system, monetary aggregates and policy have converged with the Western mainstream type. Consequently, money in both and all cases has lost its stability, predictability of monetary policy, and thereby productive relationship with the real economy.

The reasoning and modeling underlying and extending out of the Muslim World's blind acceptance of the mainstream trends submerge all of these together in the problem that Patterson (2010, p. 292) writes about: "That was a problem. The Ph.D's might know their *sines* from *cosines*, but they often had little idea how to distinguish the fundamental realities behind why the market behaved as it did. They got bogged down in the fine-grained details of their whiz-bang models. Worse, they believed their models were perfect reflections of how the market works. To them, their models *were* the truth. Such blind faith, he warned, was extremely dangerous." We will examine the general trend in monetary and real economy theory in economic reasoning and modeling in the light of Patterson's criticism.

The Early History of Monetarism

Monetarism is the study of quantity of money that should remain in circulation. Early monetary history (Bordo, 1989), in fact goes as far back as David Hume's theory of measuring the quantity of money in circulation in response to the quantity of gold that supports the stock of money in circulation. The argument made by Hume was that the mercantilist argument on 'buying cheap and selling expensive in international trade' was basically flawed. This kind of thought meant that gold would be exported outside Britain along with the production of expensive goods. Consequently, less gold will remain available to support the production of nationally provisioned goods. Thus at the end, more gold is needed to support a high revenue-yielding trade regime. Export would be an expensive economic venture with gold.

The total balance of payments (Current Accounts + Capital Accounts) would worsen with higher outflow of bullion-value of trade net of capital inflow (Blaug, 1968). In such a specie-theory of international trade the belief that increasing volume of gold is necessary to support higher volumes of international trade prevailed. This is a theory that is opposite to that of a small amount of gold being necessary to support high volume of trade, as in the 100 percent reserve requirements monetary system with the gold standard.

From the humble but flawed arguments of Hume's specie-theory of money and international trade came about Irving Fisher's quantity theory of money in its simple form. The classical school believed on the idea of intrinsic relations between money and the real economy. But the velocity of money circulation was conditioned by the lower than full mobilization of money into the real economy. Thereby, the definition of money fell short of its sole purpose, which is to measure the value of real exchange. The shortfall in resource mobilization conveyed the fact that, there always must be a gap between the monetary sector and the real economy due to the intervening interest rate functioning in bank-savings. Such impediments stopped the circulation of money, and thereby the growth and development of the economy slowed down. The monetary and financial system could not attain an aspired for level of relationship with wellbeing, price stability, employment, and social choices of goods and services that altogether induce development.

Later History of Monetarism: Friedman's Quantity Theory of Money and Prices

Later on when the quantity theory of money was taken over by Milton Friedman, the nature of resources broke up into two fragmented categories. The first function of money marked its circulation in goods and services. The second function of money was its circulation in financial papers. These two markets compete between them for the direction of a given quantity of money as resource. A less-than unit value of the velocity of money circulation means that the financial sector in the above sense of diverting money from the competing real sector falls short of its usage in the real economy.

Milton Friedman's (1989) more recent paper in regard to the division of money between the competing real and financial sectors appears in his quantity theory equation.[9] The two sectors in this equation are interlinked by the rate of interest, not by prices of commodities in the real sector that would respond to the consequences of money, finance and real economy unified interrelations. For this reason, the velocity of money supply remains less than unity.

Now what does it mean for the velocity of money circulation to equal unity? The equation of exchange then assumes the form, M = Py, where M denotes the quantity of money in circulation. P denotes price level. y denotes real output (RGDP). The implication of this equation is that the quantity of money equals the spending in the real economy. This value of spending equals nominal output (GDP). Now with velocity of money, v = 1, this means that a quantity of money is spend altogether, which is the case of matching money with projects. But if there are many projects then a fraction of the total money will match up with such given projects specifically and wholly.

In strict abidance with monetarist school and the Austrian theory of money the implication of v = 1 exists. The monetarist school (Cagan, 1989, pp. 195-205) like the Keynesian school argued that the maximum income multiplier effect would be attained at the full-employment output state of the economy. Such a state attains full utilization of all forms of resources including money, income, capital and labor. Consequently, the rate of growth in total spending including private and public sector spending must equal the rate of growth of resources. If separately we write total resource flow (R) in monetary (M, m as real money), physical resource (K), and human resource (L) forms, it can then be proved that the rate of growth of real money equals the weighted average of the rates of growth of (K/M, L/M). This vector can be written as (k/m = ((K/P)/(M/P), n/m = (L/P)/(M/P)).[10] This result further implies that the fullest social, and thereby, ethical use of money in relation to the real economy is unexplained in the case of the usual equation of exchange.

But the reason for the existence of the velocity of money circulation 'v' as either constant or variable parameter in the equation of exchange is to accommodate the imperfect state of the money and real economy circular causation relationship. This is a reasonable explanation for the prevalent form of the equation of exchange. It shows that, in the circular causation (M,F,R)-relationship the imperfect state of this relationship can be simulated to attain better states of the complementary relationship. This is an exercise involving simulacra of re-estimations for attaining learning regimes of moral-social reconstructions, as it was explained in the interactive, integrative, and evolutionary model (IIE-model). The moral and ethical elements of monetary policy in the light of the (M,F,R)[θ]-model thus provide the dynamics towards social transformations by simulation using the circular causation model of learning and creative evolution.

Convergence between Keynes and Friedman Theories of Money, Fiscalism, and Output

The Keynesian version of monetary theory in its otherwise fiscal focus converges to the quantity theory of money in its recent Friedman's version that gets deeply affected by the prevalence of interest rates of all vintages in the financial markets. This point was argued above in terms of the full-employment context with price stabilization. In as far as convergence to the pure form of the (M,F,R)[θ]-circular causation relationship is maintained by the combination of monetary relationship in the full-employment context, the convergence between the monetarist and fiscal consequences is attained.

Such a problem of convergence is not popularly recognized because of the nature of economic theory that bases all its arguments on the postulate of marginalist trade-off. In this particular case, the trade-off is shown by the contest between monetary and fiscal policies. The consequences are felt in the macroeconomic frameworks of trade-off between monetary and fiscal policies (Blaug, 1980). The consequences are also felt by the highly volatile effects of short-term interest rates in the equation of exchange. This is particularly true of the type proposed by Friedman lately, where debt, bonds, and securities abound in the creation of monetary paper as opposed to bullion-based wealth (Cagan, 1989, pp. 197-198).

The ethical nature of Keynesian macroeconomics is found on the permanent argument raised: The income multiplier is optimal in its effect at the lowest possible rate of interest, i.e. the low-level liquidity trap. Also at this level of a lowest interest rate the quantity of money remains optimal. The missing point though in these models is the conflicting nature of the (M,F,R)[θ] relationship in the presence of interest rates. Thereby, a whole set of trade-off relations is caused. This occurs between the private and public sectors, between the function of banks and financial institutions as savers and mobilisers of liquid funds and real assets. The moral and ethical elements of the complementarities between monetary and fiscal sides of an otherwise unified economy, is lost. Thereby, resource mobilization as of money, capital, employment, and other forms of resources that is indispensable for establishing a participatory socioeconomic system and theory and application in this direction, is lost.

Money in Austrian School

The formation of participatory economic system, and within it of the moral and ethical elements of development, requires the formalism of a robust microeconomic theory of money-finance-real economy macroeconomics. This attempt has been in the literature for some time now. The failure to transform the theories and concepts into application to realize a non-inflationary and stable economic growth with the focus being on the attainment of the wellbeing criterion is due to that central factor, which acts as impediment to the free flow of resources between complementary sectors and in the good things of life. This key impediment has been argued earlier to be the rate of interest. The structural problem and permanent inability to establish a movement, if not an optimal actualization of a participatory socioeconomic system, is the moral and ethical failure of the prevalent financial system.

In the history of money and monetary policy the Austrian School contributed to formalism in this direction. The famous works of Black (1970), Fama (1980), and Hall (1997), and its re-assessment by Greenfeld and Yaeger (1963) relegate money to the *laissez faire* monetary idea. Yaeger writes in this regard (1997, p. 412): "Government would be banished from any role in the monetary system other than that of defining a unit of account or *numeraire*. We envisage a unit defined by a bundle of goods and services comprehensive enough for the general level of prices quoted in it to be practically steady. Merely by conducting its own accounting and transactions in this Unit—we tentatively so name it, with a capital U—the government would give private parties a strong incentive to adopt the same." Furthermore, Yeager goes on (p. 413): "The Unit would be defined by goods and services having supplies and demand of an entirely non*monetary* character."

These perspectives of money and monetary theory point out the close relationship between the moral and ethical elements of the (M,F,R)[θ]-relations and the Austrian School ideas, especially those concerning the *laissez faire* theory of money and the micro-foundations of money and macroeconomics.

CONCLUSION: CONVERGENCE AND DEPARTURE

The moral and ethical potential convergence between so many theories of the (M,F,R)[θ]-relations can be depicted in Figure 2. This figure reveals the contrasting features of the worldview of epistemic unity, now applied to the theme of endogenous monetary history and the contrary theory of rationalistic positivism in the macroeconomic differentiation of micro-foundations of macroeconomic monetary theory.

Consequently, none of the following macroeconomic theories works out in establishing the micro-foundation of aggregation, which is required to bring forth the function of money in the real economy participation through the medium of participatory financing instruments: The monetarist form of the aggregate monetary equation of exchange; the Keynesian monetary and General Equilibrium theory; and Tobin's Liquidity Preference Theory (Tobin, 1958). Thereby, the microeconomic nature of ethical preference formation as a carrier of moral and social choice cannot be formed by such aggregate monetary and financial conceptualizations.

Figure 2. Contrasting the gold-backed participatory monetary system and the paper-backed monetary system

Main points in a table

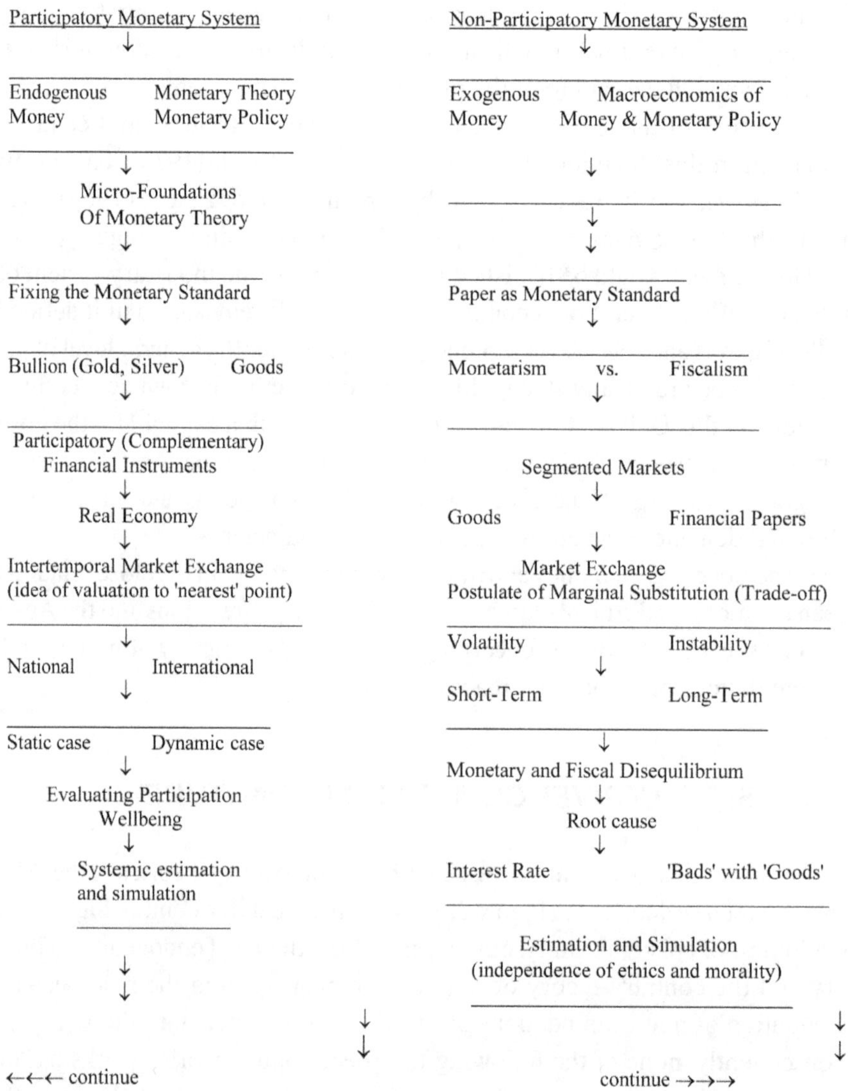

The financial system in such a case cannot come to have a principal-agent model that can explain the ethical choices in the preference function.

Contrarily, the micro-foundations of ethical theory and its carriage through ethical preference from the micro to the aggregate level (so-called macro-level) get infused in the choice and evaluation of assets for bank funding. The two factors are thereby brought together as transparent indicators of ethical choice. Firstly, the selectivity of the direction of monetary spending is determined. Such a choice is caused by epistemic text and institutional discourse centering on such sensitivity of epistemic unity. Secondly, the choice of the financial instruments that mobilize monetary and real resources in the real economy must be other than the interest-based instruments. These latter ones are the root causes of the impediment in resource-flows and distributive equity in the social structure.

The two sides of the conceptual and institutional evolutions are perfectly opposite to each other and follow their independent evolutionary paths of simulation. The example of the epistemic-centered banking system with zero rate of interest in financing, replaced by trade-related financial instruments, is the Islamic one. It is prominently prevalent in the world today in Islamic banks. This idea is also vouched by certain exponents of conventional monetary thought (Wood, 1998).

REFERENCES

Allouche, A. (1994). *Mamluk economics: A study and translation of Al-Maqrizi's Ighatah*. Salt Lake City, UT: University of Utah Press.

Billington, M. O. (2002, November 15). Gold dinar: An economic and strategic response to chaos. *Executive Intelligence Review*.

Black, F. (1970, Autumn). Banking and interest rates in a world without money. *Journal of Banking Research*, 8-20.

Blaug, M. (1968). *Economic theory in retrospect*. Homewood, IL: Richard D. Irwin.

Blaug, M. (1980). *The methodology of economics*. Cambridge, UK: Cambridge University Press.

Bordo, M. D. (1989). The contribution of a monetary history of the United States, 1867-1960 to monetary history. In *Money, History, and International Finance: Essays in Honor of Anna J. Schwartz* (pp. 15–78). Chicago, IL: The University of Chicago Press. doi:10.7208/chicago/9780226066899.001.0001.

Brown, W. B., & Hogendorn, J. S. (2000). *International economics in the age of globalization*. Toronto, Canada: Broadview Press.

Cagan, P. (1989). Monetarism. In Eatwell, J., Milgate, M., & Newman, P. (Eds.), *Money, the New Palgrave* (pp. 195–205). New York, NY: W.W. Norton.

Choucri, N. (1995). Introduction: Theoretical, empirical, and policy perspectives. In *Global Accord* (pp. 1–40). Cambridge, MA: The MIT Press.

Choudhury, M. A. (1997). *Money in Islam*. London, UK: Routledge.

Choudhury, M. A. (2003). *Dynamic analysis of trade and development in the Islamic world: Selected case studies*. Dhaka, Bangladesh: Bangladesh Institute of Islamic Thought.

Choudhury, M. A. (2011). *Islamic economics and finance: An epistemological inquiry*. Bingley, UK: Emerald Publishers.

Choudhury, M. A., & Hoque, M. Z. (2004). *An advanced exposition of Islamic economics and finance*. Lewiston, NY: The Edwin Mellen Press.

Dasgupta, A. K. (1987). Marginalist challenge. In *Epochs of Economic Theory* (pp. 74–98). Oxford, UK: Basil Blackwell.

Davies, G. (2002). *A history of money*. Cardiff, UK: University of Wales Press.

Edel, A. (1970). Science and the structure of ethics. In Neurath, O., Carnap, R., & Morris, C. (Eds.), *Foundations of the Unity of Science*. Chicago, IL: University of Chicago Press.

Einstein, A. (n.d.). The laws of science and the laws of ethics. In *Lectures in Physics*. New York, NY: Philosophical Library.

Fama, E. (1980). Banking in the theory of finance. *Journal of Monetary Economics*, *6*, 39–57. doi:10.1016/0304-3932(80)90017-3.

Friedman, M. (1989). The quantity theory of money. In Eatwell, J., Milgate, M., & Newman, P. (Eds.), *New Palgrave: Money* (pp. 1–40). New York, NY: W.W. Norton.

Ghazzali. (n.d.). *Ihya ulum-id-din*. (M.F. Karim, Trans.). Lahore, Pakistan: Sh. Muhammad Ashraf.

Grandmont, J.-M. (1989). Temporary equilibrium. In Eatwell, J., Milgate, M., & Newman, P. (Eds.), *New Palgrave: General Equilibrium*. New York: W.W. Norton.

Greenfeld, R. L., & Yaeger, L. B. (1963). A laissez-fare approach to monetary stability. *Journal of Money, Credit and Banking*, *15*, 302–315. doi:10.2307/1992481.

Hall, R. E. (1997). The Government and the monetary unit. In Yaeger, L. B. (Ed.), *The Fluttering Veil, Essays on Monetary Disequilibrium* (pp. 383–391). Indianapolis, IN: Liberty Fund.

Hayek, F. A. (1999). Intertemporal price equilibrium and movements in the value of money. In *Good Money, Part One: The New World* (pp. 186–227). Chicago, IL: University of Chicago Press.

Heilbroner, R. L. (1986). The ideology of capital. In *The Nature and Logic of Capitalism*. New York, NY: W.W. Norton.

Islahi, A. A. (1988). Ibn Taimiyah's concept of money and monetary policy. In *Economic Concepts of Ibn Taimiyah* (pp. 139–143). Leicester, UK: The Islamic Foundation.

Islam Policy. (2011, January 7). *Use gold dinar for trade urges Dr. Mahathir bin Muhammad*. Retrieved from http://www.islampolicy.com/2011/01/use-gold-dinar-for-trade-urges-dr.html

Ismail, S. M. (1989). *Critical analysis of capitalism, socialism and Islamic economic order*. Lahore, Pakistan: Oriental Publications.

Jackson, E. T., & Kassam, Y. (Eds.). (1998). *Knowledge shared, participatory evaluation in development cooperation*. West Hartford, CT: Kumarian Press.

Kenen, P. (1985). *The international economy*. Englewood Cliffs, NJ: Prentice-Hall, Inc..

Maddox, I. J. (1970). *Elements of functional analysis*. Cambridge, UK: Cambridge University Press.

Masson, P. R., Krueger, T. H., & Turtleboom, B. G. (Eds.). (1997). *EMU and the international monetary system*. Washington, DC: International Monetary Fund.

Masud, M. K. (1995). Shatibi's life and works. In *Shatibi's Philosophy of Islamic law*. Kuala Lumpur, Malaysia: Islamic Book Trust.

Mydin, A. K., & Larbani, M. (2004). The gold dinar: The next component in Islamic economics, banking and finance. *Review of Islamic Economics*, *8*(1), 5–34.

Patterson, S. (2010). *The quants*. London, UK: Random House Business Books.

Rucker, R. (1983). *Infinity and the mind*. New York, NY: Bantam New Books.

Samuelson, P. A. (1949). International factor-price equalization once again. *The Economic Journal*, 59.

Schumpeter, J. S. (1968). The scholastic doctors and the philosophers of natural law. In *History of Economic Analysis*. New York: Oxford University Press.

Tobin, J. (1958). Liquidity preference as behavior towards risk. *The Review of Economic Studies*, *26*(1), 65–86. doi:10.2307/2296205.

Vadilo, U. T. (2002). The architecture of the gold dinar economy: An academic perspective. In *Viability of the Islamic Dinar* (pp. 335–360). Kuala Lumpur, Malaysia: International Islamic University Malaysia, Research Center.

von Bohm-Bawerk, E. (1890). *Capital and interest.* London, UK: William Smart.

Wood, G. (Ed.). (1998). *Money, prices and the real economy.* Cheltenham, UK: Edward Elgar.

Yaeger, L. B. (1997). *The fluttering veil, essays on monetary disequilibrium.* Indianapolis, IN: The Liberty Press.

ENDNOTES

1 Only a few of the *Qur'anic* verses on the ecological model of the *Qur'an*, exemplified by the organic unitary model of agriculture and consumption and production of the good things of life are mentioned here: *Qur'an* (2:168; 172-173; 7: 56-57; 10: 31-54; 13:1-5; 16: 3-18; 48-50; 66-69; 114-115; and many more).

2 $p_i = (M/G)_i*(1/x_i)$; meaning, $p_i.x_i = (M/G)_i$. We re-write this equation as, $p_i = M_{Gi}/x_i$ = bullion-denominated money per unit of specific goods. This can be repeated for all quantities of goods and services of the vector $\mathbf{x}_i(\theta)$, where θ denotes knowledge-flow based on epistemic unity of knowledge.
Likewise, we denote the wellbeing criterion by $W(\mathbf{x}(\theta)) = \Pi_{i=1}^{n}[x_i^{\alpha i}]$, where the vector of ethically induced goods is denoted by $\mathbf{x}(\theta)$, with the moral/ethical knowledge flow denoted by θ-induction of $\mathbf{x}(\theta)$. The product form of W(.) implies complementarities between the variables.α_i are elasticity coefficients of W(.) with respect to x_i, i = 1,2,..n.
It can be shown that, $\partial W(.)/\partial x_i = \alpha_i*(W/x_i) = \alpha_i*(W/M_{Gi}).(M_{Gi}/x_i) = \alpha_i*p_i$; M_{Gi} is one of the variables of the vector $\mathbf{x}(\theta)$. This implies the moral and ethical induction of both the traded things and money.
We further write by simplification of terms, $\{[\partial W(.)/W]/\partial x_i/x_i\}*(1/x_i)$ = [% change W(.)]/$x_i = \alpha_i*p_i$; meaning that percentage change in wellbeing per unit of x_i is proportional to the price, when money has its intrinsic value in terms of bullions (gold and silver).

3 Thus we derive, $p_i = M_{Gi}/x_i$ = [% change W(.)]/x_i; i = 1,2,..,n.

4 Define terms-of-trade for country 1 as, $t_1 = p_{X1}/p_{M1}$; terms-of-trade for country 2, $t_2 = p_{X2}/p_{M2}$. Then, $(p_{X1}/p_{M1}) \div (p_{X2}/p_{M2}) = (p_{X1}*p_{M2})/(p_{M1}*p_{X2}) = t_1/t_2$. Now by equating $p_{X1} = p_{M2}$; $p_{M1} = p_{X2}$ we obtain, $t_1*t_2 = 1$. When trade is perfectly fair then $t_1 = t_2$. Hence, $t_1 = 1 = t_2$.

5 *Qur'an* 78:1-5 establishes the foundation of belief on the absolute truth of the Hereafter as the Great Event. The Great Event is so, because of its sole and final optimality of endowed knowledge through the learning process of the axiomatic foundation of epistemic oneness and its concrescence in the univer-

sal unraveling of schemes of things. In money, finance and real economy this double causal interrelationship is explained by the (M,F,R)-model of learning according to the IIE-formalism. Even as money is a primal innate creation of man, so also is its continuity until the Great Event. Markets and exchange, and thereby the role of money in it, will exist all the way to the final end.

6 *Qur'an*: description of heavenly attributes in the Chapter 55, *Ar-Rahman*, The Most Gracious.

7 *Qur'an* (24:1): The verse can be specified to the case of money and real economy in the manifestation of unity in the wellbeing function.

8 Consider the equation of exchange of quantity theory of money: M = k.p.y, where M is the stock of money in circulation; k denotes inverse of velocity of money in circulation and can be taken as constant. P denotes price level. Y denotes real income. By our previous results, p = M_G/x, denoting the gold-money backing of production x. y is real economic output. Now, M = k. (M_G/x).y. As x increases (M_G/x) decreases. That is gold-money backing for unit of x decreases. Now less stock of gold and money as savings is required in the banks as much of money is circulated in productive spending. The only other positive effect on monetary stock comes about by the excess demand to fuel increase in output y.

9 M^D = P. f(y, w; R_M*, R_B*, R_E*; u), where M^D denotes demand for money as quantity. y denotes real income. w denotes wealth held in physical assets. R_M* denotes the expected nominal rate of interest. R_B* denotes the yield on bonds and securities. R_E* denotes the nominal rate of return on assets held as wealth. u denotes the statistical residual. P denotes price level. f(.) is a definite function representing the equation of supply (P.f(.)) of goods and services in the form as they are held on the right-hand side with the money demand. The problem arises in this equation due to the causality that can be generated between (R_M*, R_B*) as interest rates and all the other variables. The impediment on resource mobilization comes out of the roots of interest rates that divert money resources into the financial sector, which competes with the real economy.

Consequently, there exist two different velocities of money circulation, one revolving in the real sector (v) and the other in the financial sector (v'). But although money and financial instruments should be the inter-connector in respect of the real sector in this regard, yet the presence of interest rates does not allow this to happen. The equation of exchange then takes the form: M.v + M'.v' = P.y.

10 Write the equation of exchange as, M.v = P.f(R=(k,n)) or as, m.v = f(k,n). Assuming v is near constant, the rate of change of v (denoted by v°) is near zero. Thereby it can be shown by working out that, the growth rate of real money, m° = weighted average of rates of growth (g_m,g_n).

Chapter 4
Bringing God into the Banking System:
Contrasting Meaning of Ethics in Socio-Scientific Reasoning

ABSTRACT

The contrasting meaning of ethics as exogenous factor in mainstream socio-scientific theory and as endogenous factor in the evolutionary learning universe of our praxis in this book is developed at length. In this regard, the contrast between the possibility of the epistemic multiverse of unity of knowledge in the monotheistic worldview and the impossibility of rationalism in this regard is laid bare. Several contrasting works in the review of the literature further establish the basis of these two dividing worldviews in respect to several applied themes in science, society, economics, finance, money, and banking. Thus, the universality and uniqueness of the monotheistic law in the construction of the unified, that is pervasively complementary and thus participatory, world-system is further established.

BACKGROUND

The place of ethics and morality in economic, financial, social, and scientific reasoning is a burning issue of the time. As I see it, this importance is placed in our mainstream intellection because of the failure of many of the theoretical, applied, policy and institutional practices – all that have gone awry in the light of their traditional ways of conceptualizing and applying socio-scientific reasoning. Yet this failure presents a good possibility to look at the world-system in newer epistemological perspectives in regards to 'everything', as we have defined this concept earlier.

DOI: 10.4018/978-1-4666-4643-8.ch004

Copyright ©2014, IGI Global. Copying or distributing in print or electronic forms without written permission of IGI Global is prohibited.

The world is presently experiencing sea change from end to end of the global order. One of the fresh visions of the global future is the dismantling of the old despotic guards of the Arab World. This of course does not mean a necessary transition to liberal democracy in the Arab World. But there is a clamor for change towards participatory democracy. Such a change is inevitable in the near future, though with a massive spread of violent unrest. The economic and financial matters of the rich Arab World is untenable in equating human reality with the Arab elitist desire for wealth against the teeming masses clamoring for freedom and participation in the reconstruction of their own self-reliant destiny. The socioeconomic development is thus playing itself in opposition to the postulates of the wealth maximization agenda and objectives that economics and finance in both mainstream and Islamic intellection, which claimed a fresh outlook beyond mainstream thinking, has played out emptily. Thus there arose a challenge to the drawing boards of new epistemological thinking (Choudhury, 2011a).

Likewise, the reasoning underlying the social and scientific intellection is demanding revision of the steady-state and chaotic world-system of socio-scientific thinking by a new epistemological discursive venue of scientific thought as the dynamic process of the social being and becoming (Sztompka, 1991) in sea change. For instance, the participatory model of reality disengages social thinking from the Darwinian pattern of mind (*res cogitans*)-matter (*res extensa*) dichotomy that is premised on competition, increasing independence between entities and self-interest, no matter how much altruism may be endeared as a human resource. In this terrain of sociological thinking a consequentialist and contractarian approach to ethics and morality and human wellbeing remains methodologically dysfunctional in the old order. An objective way of understanding our place in the universe, our human consciousness and responsibility, have not given adequate shape to a new epistemological capability away from methodological individualism and self-centered independence of causal relations, as these are borne by rationalism and rational choice (Etzioni, 1988).

Much more is required to redefine the human deontological domain of belief, consciousness, understanding and application. In this new social construct abides the intrinsic realization of truth and goodness. The institutions and the social contracts then follow in the midst of a discursive society to implement the moral and ethical learning process that remains intrinsic to the human fold. Society is sustained by such a deontological process of moral consciousness, in which the anthropic actor remains endogenously embedded. That is the actor is also the systemic observer.

In the hard-core natural sciences, the reconstruction of a total cosmic reality requires the extension of our universe and its event-based occurrences in the framework of the knowledge, time, and space dimensions. Such is the domain of new epistemology, which the prevalent structure of scientific thought does not embrace.

The space-time structure of the universe presents a material-based cosmic picture in which there is no empty space. Matter must exist for the universe to be substantive. It signifies that there is no space without matter (Einstein, 1954). The place of epistemic unity of knowledge, which is ephemeral to scientific reasoning, remains an exogenous element of consciousness, understanding, and behavior. Though Einstein wrote on the scientific configuration of ethical consequences, yet such an idea, important though, arose from a material conceptualation of space-time structure.

As an example, consider the question: What is love? The space-time structure of the cosmic totality will interpret love as interactively generated relationship between entities that are subjected to neural responses (artificial morality). Such responses can be consequentialist results that can be cognitively measured. Otherwise, the responses can exist as configured representations. In either case, the epistemic premise of love as interactive relationship for gaining association is the domain of rational behavior and Darwinian natural selection of pairs.

In 'everything' of the mind-matter cognition located in the space-time generality of all of science, rationalism determines deontology, consequentialism, and social contractarianism. Contrary to such a materialistic perception of the socio-scientific world-system, and cosmic behavior in it, something that we can refer to as the morally sensitive anthropic presence, the place of knowledge remains primal in the cosmic psyche. Without this kind of the essence of reality, there would never be the capability of the universe to respond morally and ethically. Competition, self-interest, methodological individualism, self-centered independence, and rendering to cognition only within the limited space-time domain, will prevail.

Contrarily, the essence of the divine capacity of the universe to be merciful, sentient, caring and participatory, something in which we are both the observer and the observed, prevails in the knowledge, time, and space dimensions. As a partial learning segment, we critically study space-time behavior as an extract of the over-arching relational domain of knowledge, time, and space dimensions in 'everything'.

Such a divine breeze of knowledge, presence, and action that activates life is emphatically put down by Bruteau (1997): "If you can see the God you love present in, even as, this world, then feel that union and rejoice in that. And be active in it, contribute to it, participate in the building, in the artwork, in the healing, in the understanding. This is where Reality is. You yourself are both a member of the Finite and a member of the Infinite…."

OBJECTIVE

The objective of this chapter is to review selected works in the literature on moral and ethical reasoning in socio-scientific thought. A cross-section of such works is examined to unravel how ethics and morality have been viewed epistemologically. Bringing God into the socio-scientific system with cybernetic approach implicates invoking moral and ethical values in the treatment of the circular causal *inter*relationship between economic, financial, social and scientific domains in specific problems and issues. Beyond this critical examination, the inquiry of the moral and ethical domain invoking the treatment of issues and problems encompassed by the epistemology of the knowledge, time, and space dimensions is carried out. The socio-scientific system understood as a systemic premise of investigating the interactive, integrative, and evolutionary (IIE) learning relations with the entire gamut of economic, financial, social, and scientific domains, is studied in the positivistic and normative perspectives, and deductive and inductive reasoning of socio-scientific system modeling.

THE GODLESS UNIVERSE

Larry Witham, Marketplace of the Gods

Larry Witham in his book expounds his idea on how mainstream economic theory explains religious behavior, the spiritual capital, and the institutions of religious establishment. This erudite piece of work is nonetheless a tacit acceptance of economic theory without critical questioning in explaining a fuzzy good such as religious behavior and the concomitant religio-economic decision-making in markets, family, and institutions that are enwrapped in complexity, and which optimal economic theorizing and steady-state equilibrium analysis cannot explain. If mainstream economics is enforced to explain religious behavior and consequences in the presence of their fuzzy environment, then the entire meaning of learning dynamics relating to religious consciousness, motivation, cognition, and consequences is missed out. No further demand is made on socio-scientific theory beyond simply an axiomatic and some observational considerations. Here too the judgment reached is questionable and feebly slim or misunderstood by the mentioned author.

Let me dwell on the fundamental premise of the referred to book. That is rational choice taken as the foundational legitimacy of argumentation relating to the author's claim on the power of economics to explain religious behavior. The author does not use the rigorous definition of rationality and rationalism in characterizing rational preferences of reasoned individuals. Thereby, the rigorous characterization of rationality and rationalism does not flow into social preferences, social choices, and institutional behavior. Instead, the idea of rationality is used to mean predictive and reasoned choices by the decision-maker. Rational choice is meant to denote the result of reasoned decision-making based on consistent and predictive choices out of standard reasoning of the many.

Yet in rigorous economic theory, rationality is explained by the law of transitivity: If A, B, C are three possible choices in market exchange, thus having value assigned to them in the state of nature, and if A is preferred to B, B is preferred to C, then A is preferred to C. This is the kind of predictive belief that Sen (1977) refers to as the attribute of the rational fool. Furthermore, the law of transitivity also implies that, value as utility function (U(.)) of the choices in the transitive preordering of preferences means that the state (A preferred to B preferred to C) is causally implicative of $U(A) > U(B) > U(C)$.

Rational choice or the postulate of economic rationality technically means that the assumption of predictive behavior, scarcity of resources, consistency of decision-making, optimization as the goal of agents, and perfect information foresight exist in market exchange. Both market and social prices are known with perfect foresight, on the basis of which predictive consequences are assumed to occur. In a more subtle sense, the notion of uncertainty is associated with an old, traditional and mundane concept of measured frequency-related probability and probability distribution. It takes the form of normal distribution of large samples in a population of variables. On the other hand, the substantive idea of subjective probability distribution of events, the kinds that were conceptualized by Keynes (O'Donnell, 1989), and the kinds that appear in Heisenberg's Principle of Uncertainty to mark hard-core reasoning in the philosophy of science, are not in the author's consideration. Yet religion is a spiritual good. In it the intrinsic factors, such as belief, emotion, action and development resources influence behavior in culturally different ways, not simply diverse and thereby pluralistic ways. Witham believes on the configuration of the marketplace influencing religious decision-making by assuming such intrinsic factors as exogenous elements of behavior and decisions.

In the real world markets, it is impossible to predict beyond the 'nearest' time of occurrence of an event, as the market place and our decisions regarding market choices become intrigued by disturbances large and small. The small ones soon multiply to assume gigantic proportions. Such is the well-known butterfly effect in chaos theory (Gleick, 1987) and outlier event effect in Black Swan Theory (Taleb, 2007). What would change as a result of incorporating such eventualities, which according to today's volatile capital and financial markets, are a generality rather than exception? By ignoring such substantive issues in explaining the direction of effects from economic theory to market place consequences, Witham overlooks the real effects of economic reality. Economic rationality cannot abide in the presence of such perturbations when complex probabilities are present. In fact, as Klein writes: "An economy is rarely, if ever, in equilibrium, therefore the method is based on the assumption that the economy's numerical properties are in equilibrium."

Let us take some examples from Witham. Quoting from Kuran (2004), a most questionable scholar, who is never accepted in the Muslim World for the author's argumentative weakness and lack of understanding Islam, Witham writes (pp. 171-172): "What is needed, in the modern economic view, is a moral system for families and close communities in Islam, a market system that is impersonal and operates on rules of fairness, open and honest business exchange, and the incentive of making a profit. In many cases, Islamic Law has worked against such incentives. The symbol of this mismatch, according to Kuran, is the rise of 'Islamic banking', which purports to follow the *Qur'an's* ban on charging interest." Let us closely examine this kind of argument by the authors.

The objective criterion of an Islamic bank is not singularly profit-maximization motive. Instead, it is the objective and purpose of the *shari'ah* as the moral bridge, to bring God in a purposeful and methodological way into the economic, social, and scientific principles. These bring about the usefulness of the Islamic Law into the common good, including in this the domain of wide interaction that span human and other systems. Such is the wellbeing concept of Islamic socio-scientific order with moral and ethical values being centered in its functions.

Discourse and trade instruments replace interest rate, spending replaces the narrow idea of bank-savings in interest rates, and financial efficiency is defined in an expanded learning objectivity by mobilizing money into the real economy through the function of trading, that is, resource-mobilizing instruments. Innovation, enterprise, and profits are derived results of simulation-by-learning of the wellbeing criterion. They are not the primal goals. The relevance of the wellbeing function as the objective criterion can be well noted by considering the arguments of the opponents of the growth and globalization syndromes (Korten, 1995).

In another case of religion and markets, Witham gives the example of institutional objective of the church as that of maximizing profits and competition between churches. This kind of behavior is seen as the natural result of the economic profit-maximizing objective. Yet the same reasons that should place religion as a powerful agency of social change in a wider perspective of its normative, human sentient, and positivistic roles, ought to be considered as the potential factors in religious institutions as agents of social and global change. Has this not proved itself in the face of the rise of religions as massive social movements everywhere in the world? They range from the Islamic movements in every geo-political situation globally, including its political considerations within the European Union in regards to the much denied membership of Turkey into the EU? Then there is the powerful Christian movement of the rightist genre in South America and Southern United States. The powerful example in South America is of Liberation Theology and in Southern United States there is the Jehova's Witness. While they aspire to gain popularity among the populace, there is a deeply rooted value parameter in each of these movements, which can be identified as the spiritual capital of religious movements. Zohar and Marshall (2004) point out that the motivational and cultural factors that induce spiritual capital, make it impossible to maximize such quantities of goods and capital, as economic theory would otherwise promote by its maximization goal.

Witham is equally mistaken in the economic treatment of the Hereafter in which all revealed religions believe. Yet the Hereafter generates a strongly causal form of relationship between itself and the material and spiritual worlds. This behavioral fact cannot be studied by the rational picture of economic theory that the author paints in respect of an economic theory of religion. Why is this?

The rationality axiom of economic theory relies on measured facts only. When preferences are implicated in decision-making at the individual, institutional and social levels, they become additive in generating utilitarian forms of individual and institutional utility functions or social wellbeing. Such objective functions being additive in nature imply that, a cooperative status of a discursive society, which examines interaction between a vast variety of variables, entities, and their causal relations, does not exist. In other words, any social state and the individuals and institutions in its midst, have become optimal entities by a series of calculations. The end result occurs in a fully informed state of each of such optimal entities. No further interaction can take place. The novelty of learning, as in a discursive society with interaction and conceding (integration), and there from evolving decision-making, has ceased. Such social and individual and institutional states with attained equilibrium and optimal resource allocation cause the objective function to be maximized for each of the agents. The final utilitarian objective criterion is then the sum total of all such optimal utility or social welfare indexes. Yet this is not the case in a perpetually interactive decision-making milieu.

The treatment of the Hereafter in economic, social, cultural, and thereby religion's interface with the rest, is a complex intermix of motivations, beliefs, cognitions, and relevance that cannot be dissociated simply to yield measured utilitarian evidence. Consequently, all the axioms of optimality and steady-state equilibrium of the utilitarian kind cannot exist. A perpetual perturbation caused by endogenous and exogenous factors continues on to disturb the optimality and equilibrium states. On such a perpetual perturbation state remarked Myrdal (1957, p. 9): "Stable equilibrium is one such unrealistic assumption. In its uncomplicated form it implies the notions that every disturbance provokes a reaction within the system, directed toward restoring a new state of equilibrium, and that action and reaction will meet in one and the same time space."

The very assumption of preferences as datum that is inherent in rational choice and in the resulting axioms of scarcity of resources, the *attained* equilibriums and optimal allocation of resources are static cases of economic theory. When intertemporal resource allocation is taken as the time-dependent case a time-dynamic version of the static problem is conducted. Yet in such a case, time as independent variable is shown as the causation of change in the form of interaction between the intertemporal variables. But we know that time cannot be a factor of change. Only knowledge that is endogenous in the behavioral composition of dynamic learning preferences and its induced variables can cause change. Time simply records such change.

Consequently, optimal control theory as a method of optimization for intertemporal forms of objective economic criteria becomes simply a tool of optimization. It carries no epistemological meaning. It is equally dysfunctional in this method to use knowledge as exogenous variable. For then knowledge-flows are simply measured variables taken as independent variables as in utilitarian analysis. Time still identifies the causation of knowledge-flows on the relations of the world-system. Yet only when knowledge is endogenous in the objective criterion function, and induces all the variables, then the complexity of the episteme established by the treatment of the Hereafter enters as the substantive change and explanatory variable. The notion of economic rationality and rational choice is then annulled.

I usually give a teasing question to my intermediate microeconomics students after teaching them everything of rational choice (Pindyck & Rubinfeld, 2001, p. 99, edited): Consumer preferences for various commodities do not change during the allocation and consumption of certain goods. Yet in some situations, preferences do change as consumption occurs. Discuss why and how preferences might change continuously over time during the period of consumption of such other goods. To answer this question we consider the case with and without risk and uncertainty. Such kinds of possibilities appearing in the financial sector, and which can be stabilized by the action of endogenous inputs of knowledge in behavior, are issues left out of Witham's postulate of religious behavior on economic stabilization.

Many of the unexplained nature of effects of economic equilibrium and optimality now fail to exist. Here are some examples: the axiom of resource scarcity, competition signifying methodological individualism, marginal rates of substitution, opportunity cost between substitutes, marginal productivity of inputs, and constriction of the economic space in the absence of a greater scope of socio-scientific embedding. In the end, even the utility and social welfare functionals cease to be methodical, acceptable criteria. These are methodological limitations. Witham's book fails to recognize such essential elements of human reality in explaining the widening scope of economics and religion..

Witham's intellectual horizon does not reach out to answer to the Shakespearean sage in *Hamlet, the Prince of Denmark*: "There are more things in heaven and earth than what is known in your philosophy." Witham's mistakes the meaning of rational choice for reasonable choice. Consequently, a critical examination of economic theory on the theme of God and the marketplace cannot be accomplished in the narrow domain of explanation. No religion doubts reason as the higher faculty of the mind. Yet human perception born of rationality, rationalism and rational choice has its substantively different meanings in mainstream socio-scientific analysis. A constricted worldview is introduced by the analytical constriction of concepts and axioms. The resulting mind-matter picture is as Bergson mentioned – a mind without memory.

A greater reason remains for expanding the scope of the mind-matter modeling to the expansive domain of 'everything', including in it the embedding relationship of religion and the world-system. A substantive topic to deal with is the relationship of the precept of the Hereafter on the nature of human existence, consciousness, goodness and socio-scientific worldview. All these themes cannot be explained by the constricted axioms of self-centeredness and competition idea of methodological individualism upon which the postulates of economic rationality and rational choice rest.

In the end, Witham's claim of independence between the demand and supply constructs of market exchange results in contradiction between these two ends. He writes (p. 191): "The economic approach to religion has emphasized the supply side of the human marketplace." In this claim, the demand side is held constant though existing. Witham then continues on (p. 191): "With the consumer demand constant, it is the supply of religion that will become the key to understanding changes in human religious behavior…."

What does such supply-side religion model give? It yields the possibility for studying faith and belief for reconstruction; security and appeasement in moments of trials and tribulations; and the good choices for attaining human wellbeing. Church, synagogue, mosque, temple and the like, offer these attributes of human wellbeing at a price. But such a price is not the market price. Consequently, the market equilibrium remains indeterminate. Equilibrium is perpetually perturbed. They are punctuated and evolutionary in nature. Therefore, demand and supply of the religious good shift restlessly. Neither the demand nor the supply curves can remain constant. And now if we consider the whole domain of such movements of equilibrium points caused by perpetual shifts in demand and supply, there occurs the specification and identification problem of econometrics. Besides, the multivariate nature of demand and supply curves would not cause constancy in the demand and supply surfaces of religious goods.

The end result is a visage of unpredictability, in which Witham's hypothesis of the supply side with demand remaining constant is untenable. The results of such unpredictability remain un-readable, un-estimable, inconclusive and erroneous in an uncertain world-system. Take for instance, the high shift in the demand curve of Al-Qaida caused by its attributing religious meaning. Take the case of a high demand for religion caused by the precept of Promised Land of Judea by the orthodox Jews. The orthodox Christians and Muslims also share in this highly charged element of belief on their sides. In the Middle East Conflict such issues occupy a high scale of embedded reality on all sides (Shipler, 1986). In all of this turmoil, the religious institutions, and both the Judaea-Christian law and the Islamic law supply their dynamics. This is reality. Witham's postulate ignores this reality. Thereby his supply-side with a weak demand-side postulate of thinly explained economics of the religious marketplace remains problematic in the wider and more real sense of embedded socio-scientific worldview.

Richard Dawkins in God Delusion

A similar kind of argument as of Witham's has been launched by Dawkins (2006). Religion in respect of its individual and social effects has been subjected to cost-benefit analysis by Dawkins.

While discussing pro-life against abortion in the eyes of a secular investigation, Dawkins writes (p. 331): "A consequentialist or utilitarian is likely to approach the abortion question in a very different way, by trying to weigh up suffering. Does the embryo suffer? … Does the pregnant woman, or her family, suffer if she does not have an abortion? Very possibly so; and, in any case, given that the embryo lacks a nervous system, shouldn't the mother's well-developed nervous system have the choice?"

This is a cost-benefit balancing idea to rationalize abortion based on whether the pains from abortion, the cost in resources there from, outweigh the gains otherwise to legitimate abortion, and vice-versa. This abhorring cost-benefit specter of decision-making on abortion overlooks the love, affection and religious consciousness inculcated by the moral human and wellbeing dimensions. The whole idea of cost-benefit analysis is null and void in the absence of well-determined measures of future rewards and costs on the matter of abortion of sanctified life. Now there is no ground for discounting the future material flows for the case of murder (pro-choice) against life (pro-life). How then is it possible to discount to the present-time the gains or pains to mother-child affection in terms of her wellbeing that appears throughout life-experience on the matter of pro-life and pro-choice, respectively? Like Witham's analysis of the religious marketplace under the gaze of rational choice loosely defined, and without the presence of human consciousness, wellbeing and knowledge induction of the interacting variables in life-experience, Dawkins too ignores the richness of knowledge induction of the interacting variables that life-choice engenders.

Dawkins extends the same terrain of argumentation to the themes of permissiveness by homosexuality (pp. 326-329), overwhelmingly hated by all religions, and yet another—a theatrical depiction of all violence against women. The emptiness underlying such laments is either a journalistic reporting or a distorted equation between liberty of women and their automobile-driving rights and going out of home alone in Muslim societies. It is easy to infer that, if such were the symptoms of women's loss of freedom, there would not be the independent dower banking outlets for women, who receive such dower gifts from their husbands at the time of marriage. Women have full custody and control over such dowers. If women's loss of freedom was equated to veils, how could veiled women rise against the ruler in Yemen in their outcry for greater political freedom?

In brief, the question of women's rights, like pro-life against pro-choice, is a value-determined perspective. In Muslim societies these are revered as social sustainability. By such values of consciousness, the moral, ethical, social and individual lives are sustained in Islamic society. In societies that ignore such high values of self and society, competition between men and women is the natural consequence. It has proved to be the cause of dissolution of families. Gender competition against gender cooperation is the hallmark of an individualistic and self-centered society. If trust is the result of a cooperative gender-based social order, then the methodological individualism generated by gender competition, is not a secure perspective of freedom.

Thus like Witham's religious marketplace, Dawkins' idea of cost-benefit calculation of life, freedom, and social security, ignores the learning processes by which religious laws and practices preserve the values of life, freedom and social security. Participation, cooperation, and social security originate in the family. The family becomes a social miniscule and determines the knowledge-induced dynamic preferences in every social choice (Choudhury, 2011b). In this way, the organization of economic life arising out of cooperative self-reliance between men and women in the family, spanning over the gender communities, and the growing consciousness in enlightened preference formation, induces the interactive variables of future learning processes. Indeed, by the social miniscule model of the family (Choudhury, 2000), the social picture of the women assumes that of the sustainer of the family—indeed, thereby of society—"The hand that rocks the cradle rules the world!" Sustainability of the social order by such a gender-relationship, preferences and values, is continued inter-generationally. Mother becomes the revered and crowning attribute of the woman in Islam.[1]

Such values are summarily left out by Dawkins as by Witham in their critical social analysis, particularly of Muslim societies. Thus the same problems arising from the misconstrued postulates of economic rationality and reasoning used by Witham also come to plague Dawkins' conflict universe. Moral consciousness and material competition remain in conflict under the postulates of rationalism and economic rationality. They are not the product of the broad moral and ethical precept of reasoning. The latter attribute embraces the widest field of mind-matter complementary possibilities. They are not competing substitutes in moral-social consciousness. In this case, the economic notion of rationality, and the philosophical meaning of rationalism, lose grounds. They are supplanted by the higher meaning of reason.

Consequently as well, Dawkins makes a blunder in his claimed scientific opposition to the relevance of God in human life. Let us consider his postulate regarding Godlessness and the Anthropic Principle of Theoretical Physics (Breuer, 1991). The philosophy underlying the Anthropic Principle is that the universe was created for observation by and benefit of human beings. The universe and its laws would not be created if man was not created.

Dawkins combines biological Darwinism with Anthropic Principle to accord the following postulate: If creation is caused for human observation and explanation then its diversity and on-going biological evolution have been caused by the multiverses that Darwinism explains. Consequently, observation and symmetry, explanatory power and logical positivism combine to apply Darwin's theory of natural selection and biodiversity. Yet the vastness of the space-time structure of the cosmological order and the biodiversity in it can only produce a finitely evolutionary universe or multiverse, as resources forever diminish. Very beautifully, Sir James Jeans remarked on such a finitely limited phenomenon in an expanding universe and multiverse: We strut our narrow hour in this narrow globe with the knowledge of its final extinction.

So the dimension of reality cannot be limited by the finiteness of an expanding universe. The models of reality therefore, must embody the incessant quest for the reality that stretches out beyond the anthropic finiteness. That extensive multiverse in which our finite universe is embedded, we explained in reference to the dimensions of knowledge, time and space. Such indeed is the cybernetic multiverse of 'everything'. Anthropic principle and Darwinism ignore this primal objective of creation. All of science and materiality remains a race simply within the merry-go-round of the finite universe and multiverse. These are all examined under the constricted lens of finite and constrained space-time structure alone.

If now the multiverse is an embedded, interactive, and evolutionary space-time total reality, then the human order comprising economy, society, and science must be an integral whole of that multiverse. The properties shared by the Darwinian and anthropic multiverse must also reflect similar properties to the theory of the social sciences. We refer to this totality of the intellection domain as the socio-scientific order.

In this cosmic particularity its functions, despite integral interrelations, are bounded with the space-time structure, but finitely functioning. Rationalism breeding rationality and rational choices in the socio-scientific multiverse, equivalently lead to axioms of resource scarcity, an optimal universe, competition, and conflicting and differentiating, rather than participatory domains of interacting, integrating and evolutionary learning processes. A great difference in theory, conception, application and understanding of the multiverse is invoked in the resulting knowledge, time, and space dimensions from those of the material bound space-time structure of these entities.

Thus, there are two parallel constructions of reality in the socio-scientific multiverse. Space-time structure describes it in the framework of mind-matter dichotomy. The knowledge-time-space structure explains the universe in reference to an incessant learning universe with pervasive complementarities and systemic participation. Such a state reflects unity of knowledge and unified nature of the world-system. Dichotomy is eschewed by unity of being and becoming. Truth and falsehood as the most utterly opposed beliefs, as of God and Godlessness, respectively, abide as opposite realities.

Dawkins examines Godlessness and religion on the scale of psychological treatment, as imperfect as cognition remains to date in the science of human perceptual fuzziness. Such perceptual indeterminacy is caused by the split between the school of dualism, which believes on the separation between mind (*res cogitans*) and matter (*res extensa*); and the monists who believe on the representation of matter as a state of mental construct. This kind of vagary in perceptions proves the fickle domain of psychological construction according to different shades of corporeal beliefs.

In the midst of such human perceptions as 'mind without memory', socioeconomic behavior such as rationalism, rationality, competition and conflict, self-interest and methodological individualism, resource scarcity, optimization of objectives, and the empty assumption of perfect information—all these militate against reasonableness. Yet they remain the underlying properties and consequences of economic rationality. Perceptions arise from rationalism. Since economic rationality and rationalism both lead into perceptual indeterminacy of reality, therefore, both of them are incompatible with reasonableness.

Truth and falsehood as mathematical opposites are disjoint universal realities. Truth evolves by knowledge-flows as endogenous force and comprehends the evolutionary learning multiverse. Falsehood evolves by conflict and dualism caused by competition, substitution, self-centeredness, differentiation, and the fear and limit of scarcity. The convergence of Godless theories of creation rests on the falsehood premise. Contrarily, the truth premise explains both itself and its mathematical opposite, falsehood, by the unique epistemic methodology of oneness in the dimensions of knowledge, time, and space.

SOCIAL JUSTICE IN THE CONTEXT OF DIVINE LAW AND RATIONALISM

John Rawls on Social Justice

John Rawls (1971) treats justice as fairness. He divides the realm of justice into natural justice and institutionally established justice. Social justice is inseparably linked with social relations. It can thereby be seen as the macroeconomic precept of justice. Justice as fairness is a microeconomic precept. The transformation of fairness into social justice can be a discursive process; or such an aggregation can be understood as the utilitarian version of additive preferences and related utility indexes. Such are the cases of the Benthamite and Harsanyi types of welfare functions, adding individual preferences and utilities to form social choice and social welfare. Yet for all the depiction of the principles of justice in these two forms, there is no clarification on the definition and concept of justice as it should become a cardinal virtue of moral worth. This is a problem that we will argue here, persists in all of the known works on the epistemology of justice in its comprehensive meaning. We argue therefore that, a substantive meaning of justice is lacking in all epistemological studies of law and society, including the place of economics, finance, and society in it and a scientific treatment of the principles of justice.

Rawls as the modern days' Immanuel Kant looks at justice from the rationalistic epistemological vantage point. His construction of social relationship starting from the Original Position holds that individuals are basically endowed by natural goodness. Hence, if the individuals are to be started off in isolated cells of their own, the individual minds and thoughts will act individually and separately in their original states of goodness. The original virtue endows every individual in the state of nature with pure goodness, which rests on a concept of human value, a concept of moral worth, and a concept of rights and privileges. All these attributes together overarch the social domain as well. Rawls remains silent as to how individual precept of value, moral worth, and rights and privileges are transformed into social attributes based on the individual attributes of goodness. Also Rawls is silent on the origins of such attributes of goodness that induce the individual psyche, and thereby, institutions and society at large.

Indeed, this kind of incompleteness of knowledge in rationalism was a *problematique* in western philosophy of science. It was troubling to Keynes as ethicist and philosopher. The inhering issue of irresolution of knowledge and information in the world of economics was a special case of the general scientific irresolution of the epistemic origins of knowledge and the world-system. The economic world thereby remains overwhelmingly uncertain, and hence imperfectly known for prediction and measurement. Keynes and now Rawls and earlier Moore (1962) all subsumed to the principle of rationalism and rationality to mark the origin of moral-social reconstruction.

It was mentioned before in this book that rationalism has a Kantian epistemological premise (Kant, 1949, p. 25):

This, then, is a question which at least calls for closer examination, and does not permit any off-hand answer: whether there is any knowledge that is thus independent of experience and even of all impressions of the senses. Such knowledge is entitled a priori, and is distinguished from the empirical, which has its sources a posteriori, that is, in experience.

Kantian metaphysics gives rise to a substantive meaning of rationalism. This divides reason, and thereby the capacity to reason, into dichotomous compartments of *a priori* reasoning and *a posteriori* reasoning. The *a priori* reasoning comprises the metaphysics of God and His law concerning creation but not the world-system. The *a posteriori* reasoning comprises the worldly reality of mind and matter as observed and logically reasoned out by right-thinking individuals. Such a dichotomy divides the two reasoning processes into disparate categories that cannot interact and unify. The mind-matter dichotomy fails to inter-relate the greater expanse of the human mind. This overarching domain comprises God, religion, and the law of monotheistic unity and its induction of the world-system. This totality comprises the cybernetic whole of reality.

On the other hand, the dichotomy that separates *noumena* from *phenomena* is the essential characteristic of rationalism. Rationalism thereby expresses the nature of dichotomy between *a priori* and *a posteriori* reasoning. Rationalism marks Kant's problem of heteronomy as the essence of a differentiated total reality. In it the epistemic law of unity of knowledge cannot abide as methodology. Thereby, despite how much is the clamor for a theory of unified world-system and cybernetic embedding the fields of economy, society, and science, the episteme of unity of knowledge as an endogenous force does not exist in rationalism. Morality and ethics thereby exist exogenously in social relations. Consequently, rationalism is the mark of a divided, dichotomous, and differentiated mind-set and its constructed world-system. The episteme of unity of knowledge, hence religion and its wider world of total reality, cannot exist in such a dichotomous world-system on purely methodological grounds. Yet the epistemology of unity of knowledge can uniquely explain both the world-system of unification and differentiation as polar opposites.

The application of the problem of heteronomy marking the intrinsic separation between the *a priori* law and the *a posteriori* law by the middle dark region of mental autonomy, presents the problem of lack of synthesis in reasoning. Rawls' theory of justice in its ultimate devolution to the rationalist domain to define reasoning and the origin of a theory of justice, is a category of the Kantian type. Rawls then draws out of the *a priori* exogenous episteme of rationalism his law of construction of a just and fair individual, a just and fair institution, and a just social order. Rawls shows that inside this kind of social construction a certain initial structure of moral order is needed. This comprises efficiency and justice as attributes of actions. But such attributes remain in opposition to each other in the sense of marketplace objectives, such as utility maximization (individual), profit-maximization (institution, firm), and welfare (society). In the end, Rawls' wellbeing criterion for a just society is defined by what he refers to as the acquiring and practice of primaries – goodness and beauty in the mind and matter edicts by the moral and ethical law.

In his construction of the wellbeing criterion Rawls upholds the principle of equality, except when the sacrifice of some people increases the wellbeing of the underprivileged. By such a social construction, Rawls starts off a just society from its Original Position of perfect equality in the state of isolated individuals who are instilled by the intrinsic nature of the moral and ethical law in separation of each other. Such a law is assumed to be derived from the epistemic premise of rationalism. Yet Rawls holds that social justice is inextricably linked with a discursive social order. In such an evolved social state, the perfection of the Original Position cannot be maintained. The just law and the various institutions affected by the social choice between efficiency (profit-maximization) and social justice (moral worth, social welfare) and enforcing the same, inevitably face inequality. In a state of social evolution Rawls' Difference Principle on accepting inequality of the privileged, and thereby accepting loss of efficiency required to further the wellbeing of the underprivileged, becomes effective by enforcement and conscience.

Rawls claims his theory of justice to be a non-utilitarian approach to the distribution of equality and efficiency between target groups. It comprises firstly, the underprivileged whose wellbeing must be improved; and secondly, the efficient ones whose wellbeing must be reduced by sacrifice out of conscience and enforcement in the Difference Principle. Such social arrangements require social cooperation; that is a discursive mechanism, which is sustained by the moral law and consciousness.

On the contrary side in the economic and sociological agenda, competition remains abound. The technical concept of competition means existence of full-information. It grants firms and groups free entry and free exit from the marketplace, as long as resources enable the firms to earn economic-to-normal profits, and to remain in business. This state of economic adjustment works from the short-run to the long-run for perfectly competitive and monopolistic competitive firms. In other forms of imperfect competition, monopolies and collusive groups always earn economic profits by strategically barring free market entry in the area of production and marketing the product. Such firms characterize the majority of the business world as corporations, cartels, syndicates, and mergers and acquisitions. Competition in favor of such large networks results in unfair competition, for which competition laws and anti-trust laws are enacted. The conclusion is that competition can be a severely harmful situation for small and medium size firms in dominant-firm production and marketing operations.

Rawls like Witham and many others like him make this mistake of inconsistency between etymology and fact when invoking their claim on behalf of competition and yet also upholding social cooperation. These are two distinct and opposed practices. Rawls states in this regard (1971, p. 7): "Our topic, however, is that of social justice. For us the primary subject of justice is the basic structure of society, or more exactly, the way in which the major social institutions distribute fundamental rights and duties and determine the division of advantages from social cooperation. By major institutions I understand the political constitution and the principal economic and social arrangements. Thus the legal protection of freedom of thought and liberty of conscience, competitive markets, private property in the means of production, and the monogamous family are examples of major social institutions."

The etymological usage of the terms like social cooperation versus legal protection of competition is not a matter of passing unimportance. The difference between the two concepts in theory and practice, one reinforcing the other, is a significant social issue. Let us examine this issue.

Conceptually first: Rawls treats the correction to wellbeing of the underprivileged by configuring a point of resource allocation near or on the 45-degrees line from the origin to the production possibility surface (say in quantities of two goods as substitutes). This marks the desired socially distributive point to establish equality, but at the sacrifice of efficiency, according to his Difference Principle. If efficiency is reduced by such a reallocation of resources, the question then is what output does society optimally produce to realize the goal of distributive equity? The issue is that unless society is able to produce the feasible quantity of goods, distributive equity remains at a lower level. Increasing returns to scale of production and economies of scope in accordance with the values of society remains reduced. On the other hand, in the kind of methodical economic depiction used by Rawls to explain the efficiency and distributive equity relationship, no second-best conditions of welfare economics can be used to restore the allocative optimality of production *on* the production possibility surface (Henderson & Quandt, 1963). Therefore, in the presence of social policies and second-best corrections of distributive equity there will always be price-distortions. This will cause some sort of social wellbeing in favor of the underprivileged. But the production of the social product to enable the desired distributive equity to attain will be difficult.

This leads to the conclusion that a society ought to produce as much as is possible to gain on both the efficiency and the equality sides simultaneously. This is a matter of social discourse in which the episteme of unity of knowledge signified by systemic participation and complementarities remains supreme for the socially simulated optimal combination of efficiency and distribution.

This point brings us to the next Rawlsian goal within the principal conditions of the Original Position and the Difference Principle. The result is social cooperation. But the idea contradicts the meaning of competition as an absolute social right in Rawls' conception of social justice. Social cooperation implies sustainability of a discursive society. A discursive society exercises consciousness and rules for the attainment of the episteme of unity of knowledge by participation and complementarities between mind-matter artifacts. In the socio-scientific sense, such attributes are extended to organic unity of being and becoming. While the concept of competition contradicts that of social cooperation as substantive concepts, so also rule enforcement like taxation to generate distributive correction causes price distortion. Consequently, the potential output (hence revenue and profits) is reduced permanently by the levying of tax to the extent that a tax on revenue can reduce the long-run profits of a competitive firm, small in size as it is in economic theory. The reduction is to the level of the minimum of the average cost curve of production, which marks the optimal-efficient point of competitive production.

Along such lines of argument, Nozick (1974) argued against the morally abhorring practice of levying taxes by legal tenets for redistribution of wealth. But Nozick's arguments bring the entire production system to the neoclassical extreme, which remains mute on the issue of social justice (Phelps, 1989). Economic neoclassicism does not and epistemologically cannot, have a methodology and a method other than that based on the postulates of competition, scarcity of resources, steady-state equilibrium, and optimality of objective function. These states altogether are consequences of the postulate of economic rationality.

Rationality has its roots in rationalism as the basic philosophy of a differentiated way of viewing the relationship between competing self and other. It is depicted by the prevalent principle of methodological individualism (Buchanan, 1999; Holton, 1992). Thus, while Nozick addresses the first-best solution of an optimal and equilibrium world of economic neoclassicism, Rawls addresses the second-best productive and resource allocation situation. Neither of these methods gets off the usual way of treating efficiency and equality as gross substitutes with displacements in market equilibrium caused by price and allocative distortion.

Rawls' (op cit, p. 14) claim of his non-utilitarian approach is therefore questionable: "In the absence of strong and lasting benevolent impulses, a rational man would not accept a basic structure merely because it maximized the algebraic sum of advantages irrespective of its permanent effects on his own basic rights and interests. Thus it seems that the principle of utility is incompatible with the conception of social cooperation among equals for mutual advantage. It appears to be inconsistent with the idea of reciprocity implicit in the notion of a well-ordered society." While

Rawls' observations on the theory of utilitarianism and the immanent utility theory of ethics are correct, yet his treatment for a correction in the second-best situation does not suffice to displace the utilitarian methodology.

Rawls remains a thoroughbred rationalist. Rationalism yields the differentiated worldview of self-interest that establishes the postulate of economic rationality. The resolution of the efficiency versus equality is still carried out within the neoclassical context of the second best. Hence, Rawls cannot be a non-utilitarian. His theory of justice is a deeply neoclassical theory of the second best, and a utilitarian view of economy and society. In the socio-scientific venue, the theory loses its consistency on the issue of social cooperation and competition behavior, and all that these entail.

An Analytical Criticism of Rawls' Second-Best Resource Allocation and Utilitarianism

Consider the following problem of Rawls' theory of justice as fairness that is enforced within social relations: In Figure 1, $W(x_1,x_2) = W_1(x_1) + W_2(x_2)$ is the utilitarian welfare surface expressed as the sum total of the utilities of two individuals 1 (poor), 2 (rich) who enjoy the choices of quantities x_1 (needs) and x_2 (wants), respectively. The dented area is due to the social opportunity cost between distributive equity and economic efficiency. According to Rawls, the area A is the social premium to be paid to repair the shortfall in distributive equity. Consequently, the delivery of the two goods in favor of the underprivileged is shown in the (x_1, x_2)-diagram. The region B shows the greater distribution in favor of the underprivileged.

The conclusion is that, in a discursive society the points 'a' and 'a' ' are unstable of optimality and equilibrium on the welfare surface and the production possibility surface, respectively. Now a continuous supply of resources is required to enhance Rawls' social optimality and 'reflective equilibrium'. The resulting subsequent regions A and B never disappear. Such a dynamic depicts Rawls' evolutionary Difference Principle after temporary attainment of Original Positions and evolution there from. The second-best conditions prevail continuously, carrying along with

Figure 1. Rawls' allocations between efficiency and distributive equity

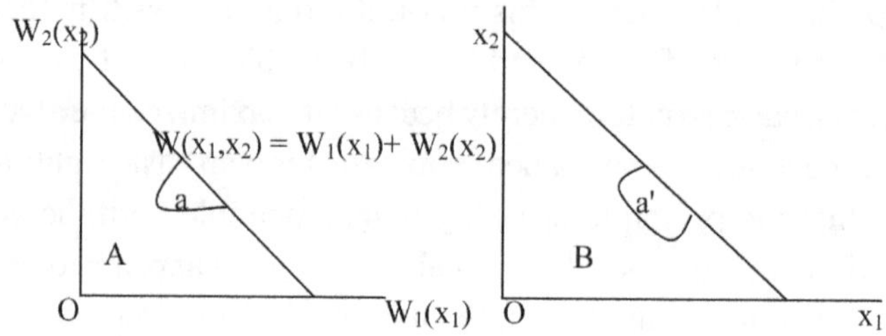

them the permanent semblance of resource distortion and increasing opportunity cost of gaining distributive equity by sacrificing efficiency. The social product in every juncture is sub-optimal and resources remain unemployed.

On the other hand, in a utilitarian society, points 'a' and 'a' ' are attained by social policy correction. The dented surfaces now blow outwards, and if they can, as by the utilitarian argument, then $W_1(x_1)$ increases, whereas $W_2(x_2)$ decreases. The intersection of these curves shows the social contract between the underprivileged and the rich. Likewise, the surface of the goods (x_1, x_2) attains its own optimal and equilibrium point, as shown.

Between the above two cases the former is more plausible in Rawls' arguments, though this analysis is carried out within the second-best neoclassical economic fold. Yet the second case is the one that results in Rawls' case of the Original Position, because the socially unequal situation must be corrected by the Difference Principle to converge into an Original Position to attain equality. Society then starts all over again *ad infinitum*.

In the end, Rawls' theory of justice is tossed between the pure utilitarian case and the second-best utilitarian case of neoclassical welfare economics. In both cases, exogenous inputs of learning in reformed Original Positions continue on the social contracts between the underprivileged and the rest. Because of the infinitely repetitive social game thus played out, morality and ethics in Rawls' social order are permanently of the exogenous type. Learning as *process* fails to exist.

A simple formalism will prove the above points. According to the utilitarian welfare and neoclassical utility function the following maximizing problem exists:

$$\text{Max. } W(x_1,x_2) = W_1(x_1) + W_2(x_2) + \varepsilon'(x_1,x_2) \tag{1}$$

subject to $Y = a_1.x_1 + a_2.x_2 + \varepsilon''(x_1,x_2)$,

Here Y denotes income (budget), a_1 and a_2 are constants (unit costs) for attaining W_1 and W_2, respectively. Let λ denote the Lagrangian coefficient, the Lagrangian 'L' being,

$$\text{Max } L = \text{Max } \{[W_1(x_1) + W_2(x_2) + \varepsilon(x_1,x_2)] + \lambda[Y - a_1.x_1 - a_2.x_2]\}; \tag{2}$$

$\varepsilon(x_1,x_2)$ is a linear function of $\varepsilon_1(x_1,x_2)$, $\varepsilon_2(x_1,x_2)$. These margins denote the social premiums taken from the rich for the improvement of wellbeing of the underprivileged.

For the two cases discussed above, the Lagrangian optimization gives the results: $dW/dx_1 > 0$ because of the Difference Principle. This implies,

$$\partial W_1/\partial x_1 + (\partial W_2/\partial x_2)*(dx_2/dx_1) - \lambda.a_1 - \lambda.a_2*(dx_2/dx_1) + \partial\varepsilon/\partial x_1 \geq 0 \tag{3}$$

The above expression is written as,

$$\partial W_1/\partial x_1 + [(\partial W_2/\partial x_2) - \lambda.a_2)*(dx_2/dx_1)] + \partial\varepsilon/\partial x_1 \geq 0. \quad (4)$$

But since, $\partial W_1/\partial x_1 > 0$; $\partial\varepsilon/\partial x_1 > 0$; $(dx_2/dx_1) < 0$; and $(\partial W_2/\partial x_2) \rightarrow \lambda.a_2$, because of $(\partial W_2/\partial x_2) \rightarrow \lambda.a_2$ = unit cost of attaining W_2 divided by marginal cost = price level, therefore $\lambda.a_2$ denotes real unit cost of attaining W_2.It can likewise be shown that, $(\partial W_1/\partial x_1) \rightarrow \lambda.a_1$ = real unit cost of attaining W_1.

Figure 2 shows how such a mutual social contract is attained by interaction between W_1 and W_2. The result is the second-best approximation to 'a', and thereby, 'a'', by applying the two versions of utilitarian theory as explained above.

There is a final important result here. The utilitarian convergence of Rawlsian social contract characterizes the 'reflective equilibrium' 'b' as a stable point. This implies that, Rawlsian social contract is in fact utilitarian at every point of the Original Position vis-à-vis the Difference Principle.

Peter J. Hammond's Ethical Preceptor in Utilitarian Social Contract

Peter J. Hammond (1987) has interlaced the transformation between extended ethical liberalism and economic consequences. Here is how these concepts are defined.

Ethical liberalism denotes rationality based values of individualism as the sign of human freedom. From ethical liberalism arises the aggregation of such individual ethical preferences in rational choices and decision-making to bring about their social representation. In this way, individual utility indexes are induced by values of liberalism. Such values reflect methodological individualism, independence of decision-making, rational behavior at the core of preferences, and a well-ordered

Figure 2. The social contract in a utilitarian Rawlsian plane

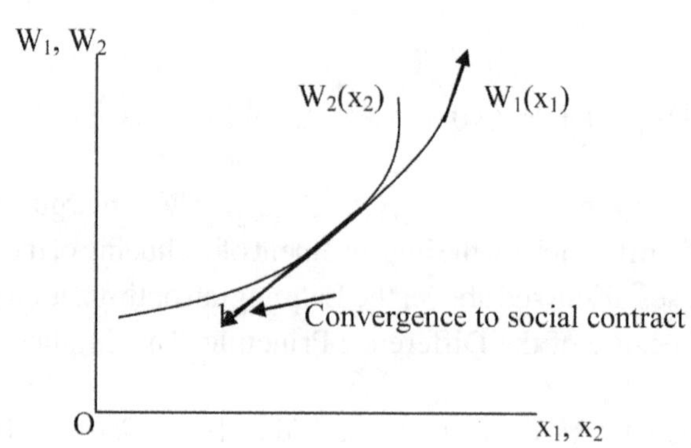

(transitive) social ordering wherein all individuals respond to ideal ethical liberalism. Aggregation of such independent and optimally framed utility functions and preferences map the results in the formation of the well-ordered liberal social welfare function, social preferences, and thereby social choice.

Thereby, a utilitarian welfare function is established as the aggregation of independently distributed individual utility functions. Such a representation of the aggregate social welfare function represents the explanatory core of Hammond's fundamental utilitarianism, an idea that Hammond shares with Harsanyi (1955) and Vickery (1960) social aggregate forms.

Here is how the preference and welfare-utility relations are mapped in Hammond's fundamental utilitarianism: Let $x = (x_1, x_2, \ldots, x_n)$ be socioeconomic variables that are associated with given contingencies of individual attributes denoted by $\eta = (\eta_1, \eta_2, \ldots, \eta_n)$, respectively. For instance, honesty as moral attribute brings about a certain level of fair earnings. Thereby, income is linked with honesty.

A 'consequence' in the individual case is denoted by (x_i, η_i), where $i \in M_i$, the set of all liberal motivated individuals. Such a number of individuals can expand along with the strengthening of the liberal nodes of the social order, like a tree branches out in foliage. Furthermore, every consequence is induced by liberal ethical values, say ν_i, $i \in M_i$. Thereby, the idea of honesty combined by its link with earnings is governed by the meaning of honesty and the resulting consequences (x_i, η_i), where $i \in M_i$. We can then say that the liberal value governing consequence being individualism and enlightened self-interest, there need not be a special conscience in the individual to give charity. Charity remains a voluntary attribute in anyone. Consequently, an individual's income remains independent of the attribute of charity. Therefore, the extended liberal ethical bundle (x_i, η_i, ν_i), $i \in M_i$ comprises independent variables.

The inference then is socially non-integrative: $\{\nu_i\}, i \in M_i$ is an exogenous bundle of values, whereby the utilitarian transmission of such individual values can be transmitted into society at large by enforcement. This is the axiom of dictatorship (enforcement) in Arrow's (1964) Possibility Theorem on Social Choice. Furthermore, the exogenous nature of $\{\nu_i\}$, $i \in M_i$ in the triplet causes its independence between both (x_i, η_i), by its primary independence of relationship with $\{\eta_i\}$. Therefore, there must logically exist independence of relationship between each of the following: $\{x_i\}$, $\{\eta_i\}$ and $\{\nu_i\}$, $i \in M_i$. Thus follows the exogenous nature and methodical independence of the individual extended ethical liberal vector (x_i, η_i, ν_i), $i \in M_i$. Ethical exogeneity is caused primarily by the axiom of methodological individualism that remains entrenched in liberal economic worldview (Taylor, 1967).

Such a perspective of extended liberal ethics can be generalized: God, society, and self are independent matters; competition and cooperation are independent actions. Trade and financial interest are opposed financial instruments. Resource mobilization and bank-savings are contrary household decisions in which banks act as competing institutions between finance and the real economy, etc.

Furthermore, in the words of Buchanan (1999, p. 391) on the axiom of methodological individualism as the core of liberal economics: "Concomitant with methodological individualism as a component of the hard core is the postulate of rational choice, a postulate that is shared over all research programs in economics.". Along the same lines write Buchanan & Tullock, 1990, p. 34): "... all collective action may be converted to an economic dimension for the purposes of our model. Once this step is taken, we may extend the underlying economic conception of individual rationality to collective as well as to market choices."

The above generalization can be proved formally. Let the extended liberal ethical bundle denoted by extended ethical liberal vector (x_i,η_i,ν_i), $i \in M_i$, be set up in subsets A_j corresponding to j-number of dominant values of the type mentioned above (e.g. competition, self-interest, etc.). $A_{ij} = (x_i,\eta_i,\nu_i)_j$, $i \in M_i$, $j \in M_j$ as the number of value-related issues addressed. If possible, let A_{i1} be a bundle of independent elements corresponding to the induction effect of value 1. Let A_{i1} be a bundle of independent elements corresponding to the induction effect of value 1. A_{i2} is then a set of interdependent elements, unlike A_{i1}.

Now, is it possible that, $A_{i1} \cap A_{i2} \neq \phi$, $i \in M_i$? In answer to this impossibility we note that if there is non-nullity of the intersecting sets, the elements of A_{i1} will establish non-null relationship with the elements of A_{i2}. But the relational mapping between the two sets will yield the elements of A_{i1} to be relational. The only feasible way for this to happen is for all the sets to be inter-element-specific relational. Then $A_{i1} \cap A_{i2} \neq \phi$, $i \in M_i$. This is a contradiction to the liberal worldview. Hence, the only other possibility is for,

$$A_{i1} \cap A_{i2} = \phi,\ i \in M_i.\ \text{Likewise, } A_{ij} \cap A_{ij'} = \phi,\ i \in M_i,\ j \in M_j,\ j' \in M_{j'} \tag{5}$$

as many values of the extended liberal ethical genre.

Using the result given by $A_{ij} \cap A_{ij'} = \phi$, $i \in M_i$, $j \in M_j$, $j' \in M_{j'}$ we obtain the following result: $\cup_i(A_{ij}) = \Sigma_i F(A_{ij})$, for given value parameter denoted by $j \in M_j$. F(.) is an order-preserving set. It is of the kind assumed by Hammond, as each of the individuals is assumed to uphold the liberal ethical value in a well-ordered social order. A similar assumption is upheld by Rawls and Arrow to solve their Impossibility Theorems and the nature of justice as fairness in rationalist thought.

Likewise, $\cup_i(A_{ij'}) = \Sigma_i F'(A_{ij'})$, for given valued parameter denoted by $j' \in M_{j'}$. F' is similar to F. Now by adding up the two equations for generalized liberal ethical value we then obtain,

$$\cup_i \cup_j(A_{ij}) = \Sigma_i \Sigma_j F(A_{ij}),\ \text{with } \cap_i \cap_j(A_{ij}) = \phi;\ i \in M_i,\ j \in M_j. \tag{6}$$

Hammond identifies F(.) as the utility evaluation of consequences denoted by (A_{ij}). In the additive form shown above over individual-specific consequences and liberal ethical values the resulting aggregate form is the social welfare function. The additive forms stand for the fundamental utilitarianism as formulated by Hammond along lines of Harsanyi, Vickrey, and Arrow. I have argued earlier that Rawls as a prime liberal rationalist emulating Immanuel Kant, although rejecting utilitarianism, became victim to the utilitarian additive methodology of justice as fairness.

We now carry the explanation of methodological independence caused by the primal value of methodological individualism a step further. The differentiating relations and functions according to additive aggregation methodology as linear representation, with and without weighting, mark circular rounds of cause and effect of exogenous relations between the consequences. If weights are assigned to the linear aggregation of utilities to form social welfare, such weights are assigned by liberal institutions. Weights are thereby carriers of liberal-value emphasis. For instance, a conventional bank's spending in poverty alleviation and microenterprise is non-existent, and there is no such value to make such charity a part and parcel of the financial world. Thus in the allocation of resources by the conventional bank's weighting, the charitable allocation holds the lowest priority. There is also the well-known fact that for the poor there is no bank loans without heavy collateral. Hence, the weighting of charity here too holds a low measure.

A mono-causal relation from the side of liberal ethical value to the formation of individual aggregating to social consequences cannot result in a learning process. Hammond's, and thereby, utilitarian social welfare system and its genre in all of liberal and rationalist vintage, cannot answer the following question in their mono-causal relationships: If conventional banking system is not obliged to ameliorate the poor and the small, this would implicate robust economic growth but no redistribution – a consequence. Yet such an optimal resource allocation result will not generate moral-social reformation of the liberal ethical value; although it will continue on to reinforce the liberal ethical value-commerce-growth-income paradigm in its welfare outlook.

Here then is the difference between Hammond's neo-liberal rationalist welfare system entrenched in utilitarianism and the concept of wellbeing in a learning system with epistemic unity of knowledge:

Hammond, Harsanyi, Arrow, and Rawls' well-ordered social order having utilitarian characteristics can now be summarized in the following generalized form:

$$\{\nu_i\}_j \rightarrow [A_{ij} = (x_i,\eta_i,\nu_i)_j,\ i \in M_i,\ j \in M_j] \rightarrow \cup_i\cup_j(A_{ij}) = \Sigma_i\Sigma_j F(A_{ij}),\text{ with } \cap_i\cap_j(A_{ij}) = \phi;\ i \in M_i,\ j \in M_j \rightarrow \{\nu_i'\}_j \rightarrow [A_{ij} = (x_i,\eta_i,\nu_i)_j,\ i \in M_i,\ j \in M_j] \rightarrow \text{continue repetitively} \quad (7)$$

Learning-type social order in epistemic unity of knowledge, rejecting utilitarianism by complex aggregation, is formalized by (Choudhury, 2000):

$\{\nu\}_j \rightarrow [A_j = (x,\eta,\nu)_j, j \in M_j] \rightarrow$ Simulate $W(A_j)$, subject to circular causation between $(x,\eta,\nu)_j$, (8)

Great Transformation by epistemic unity of knowledge and the world-system relations in unity of knowledge:

$$\Omega, S) \rightarrow \{\theta\}_j \rightarrow [A_j = (x(\theta),\eta(\theta),\theta)_j, j \in M_j] \rightarrow Simulate W(A_j(\theta)),$$

subject to circular causation between $(x(\theta),\eta(\theta),\theta)_j, j \in M_j$ (9)

continue on repetitively towards higher levels of consciousness in unity of knowledge through simulacra of evaluations along the interactive, interactive, and evolutionary (IIE) learning processes in knowledge-time-space dimension.

It is very important to note the distinct ways of formalizing the objective criterion by way of aggregation of preferences, utilities, and the resulting expression of social choice. In the utilitarian expression, the linear additive expression of utilities and underlying preferences for forming social welfare, gives a worldview of differentiated consequences, variables and agents in the social choices. Contrarily, in the wellbeing concept of the epistemic unity of knowledge and unification of the consequences, there are only non-linear relations, by means of which, the wellbeing function is simulated in respect of the learning variable. Such a knowledge-flow variable in respect of its primal epistemic reference of oneness generates simulacra of possibilities to generate unity of knowledge and the consequential unity of world-system. We have pointed out earlier that, even when the expression *appears* to be linear, yet the knowledge-induced variability of the coefficients cause foliation in the solution space of the relations that simulate the variables and the wellbeing index in the light of epistemic unity of knowledge.[2]

INTERGENERATIONAL DISTRIBUTION OF MORALITY AND ETHICS (GAUTHIER, 1986; TEMKIN, 1995)

In line with our examination and criticism of the foundation of rationalism and rationality, and as these are portrayed by the ethics of utilitarianism in most contemporary occidental thinkers, we now move on to the intertemporal distributional question. We have pointed out earlier that 'time' by itself is benign of cause and effect. 'Time' only records the event of cause and effect on corporeal and cognitive matters. We have also argued that the singular epistemological premise of occidental thought in all of socio-scientific domain in 'everything' is the space-time dimensional thought. Such a limited corporeal view of reality does not extend beyond the field of physics devoid of matter, referred to as 'empty space' by Einstein (trans. Commins & Linscott, 1954). This limited understanding of reality remains ontologically dysfunctional on matters of interlinking the epistemic foundations of morality and ethics. Thus, instead of this constricted space-time basis of understanding and measuring reality we invoke the dimensions of knowledge, time, and space of holistic reality. In this context, reality comprises events that are determined primarily by knowledge-flows emanating from foundational episteme of unity of knowledge, as in the monotheistic law. Knowledge-flows and their induced socio-scientific variables are then observed, explained, and measured simultaneously with knowledge of the time-space events.

Upon such a concept of the two opposite categories of dimensional analysis of events there stands the problem of distributing morality and ethics intertemporally. We will begin with some examples to firstly, explain the standpoint of occidental thinking on such issues. Thereafter, we will examine the same concepts critically in the context of their logical problem and critical evaluation by the alternative precept of evaluating intertemporal allocation of resources by cause and effect in connection with the emergent precept of morality and ethics.

In the investigative area, the concept of sustainability plays a significant role. Sustainability is a concept and value for morality and justice, life-fulfillment and the production, ownership and continuity of resources that relate with events happening in space-time domain (Coombs, 1990). But despite this noble understanding of the concept, the questions remains: Why does a relational idea of sustainability always run into problems in occidental intertemporal view? Important references here are of Gauthier (1986) and Inglott (1990).

Gauthier's idea of morality by agreement is a strictly relational one. According to him the present generation should be concerned with the wellbeing of its most contiguous future generations, that is the asset valuation associated with redistribution and equality is spread over contiguous overlapping generations. Only across such generations the individuals can interact to establish preferences, utilities, and wellbeing as social contracts; and thereby address the conformable conscionable allocation of resources. The next generations of surviving individuals will look after the wellbeing of the following generation, and in this way, all the way along intertemporal conscious actions and responses between contiguous generations.

Why should there be an invisible social contract in and by which the intertemporal savings problem remains unresolved? What then would be the meaning of morals and sustainability if there is no relational order between surviving intertemporal partners? Besides, if the moral and ethical attitude in terms of overlapping generations is not re-generated and repeated intertemporally, can the attribute of sustainability be upheld across generations?

Gauthier is correct in my view, to examine the intertemporal resource redistributive case of overlapping generations in the sense of relational order. In this regard, Gauthier writes (op cit, p. 299): “Each person interacts with others both older and younger than himself, and enters thereby into a continuous thread of interaction extending from the most remote human past to the farthest future of our kind … creat[ing] indirect co-operative links extending throughout history.”

Yet Gauthier’s viewpoint has been questioned by Temkin (1995) in the light of equality of resource distribution and holding it across generations. The controversial issues pointed out are as follows: The present generation will be overly consumptive of current resources, the consequence of which will be to leave less for the future generation despite the social contract formed between them to allocate resources for the future. Intra-generational equity may mean a greater present consumption and the higher intra-generational utility. By neoclassical economic theory, there will be higher preferences for present consumption with higher consumer utility and social welfare index. Besides, there will be political actions and institutions subservient to this attitude in order to carry on and implement the individual preferences. A utilitarian climate of intra-generational distribution for present welfare is generated. The result of higher present-generation taxes to attain intra-generational equity would reduce the intra-generation national wealth. Consequently, a decreased level of wealth would be transferred into the next generation, and thereby to overlapping generations ever after.

But this argument can be taken on the reverse as well. A higher tax on wealth of the present generation to look after the welfare of the overlapping generations may increase the welfare of the overlapping generations at the expense of the present one. In either of the two cases mentioned here, taxes and likewise, other acts of egalitarianism lead into inequality despite the objective of attaining equity in resource distribution, production, and ownership intertemporally.

There is also the questionable method of resource evaluation intertemporally. Neoclassical economics offers the present-value and cost-benefit methods of evaluation. Yet in such measures the discount rate must be known, one that will assign present-value of cash flows higher than the future expected cash flows. But there is no way of exactly knowing such futuristic discount rates, even in the best of foresight. The state of best foresight is tantamount to there being no risk. A deterministic intertemporal cash-flow regime is a figment of thought that cannot be realized. The problem is not solved by taking expected values of probabilistic cash-flows. Thereby expected discount rates for such probability distributions are unknown over time. Besides, the risk premiums that present generations pay for future probabilistic cash-flows are like taxes on present goods for securing future ones. The resulting inequity caused by such intertemporal income, savings, and consumption problem was pointed out above.

In the end, none of the existing methods of intertemporal resource valuation is acceptable in the resolution of the equality issue intertemporally. Temkin refers to this as the irresolvable problem of inter-generational equity. The method underlying such conflicts is the perennial issue of resource scarcity between competing and conflicting agents in any given stage of development. This kind of competition and conflict is true always and everywhere in neoclassical economics and the related socio-scientific theory immersed in social and biological Darwinism. The postulate remains unchanged despite increases of resources and technology, for intra-generationally the pressure of competition and claims over expending resources over time remains intact.

The intertemporal resource distribution, allocation, ownership and equity problem is cast in the neoclassical framework of competition between the present and future generations. These may be overlapping generations and otherwise. The goods and services they so allocate are competed for intertemporally. The relational issue between overlapping generations remains unresolved in the inter-generational allocation problem due to the indeterminacy of the discount rate and the nature of probability distributions of consequences in the uncertain future.

This kind of perennial result of the space-time structure applied to inter-generational resource allocation problem is a neoclassical trade-off on sustainability, for which, sustainability as valued partnership and complementarities between agents and variables cannot be attained. Temkin quoting Epstein (1992, p. 91) writes: "[W]here the freedom of the present generation to make unfettered dispositions is crimped, the alterations in its consumption patterns will reduce the total stock of wealth available in the future .... The effort to redistribute wealth within the second generation reduces the amount of wealth passed on to that generation. We cannot have it both ways."

The above-mentioned problems of intra-generational and inter-generational relational concepts of allocation of resources can be resolved in the framework of epistemic unity of knowledge. That is, the extension of the field of social action and response is to the knowledge, time, and space dimensions, with knowledge as the primal determining factor of all. The objective of every node of the overlapping generation string from the present to the future is a decision-making point centered on the simulation of wellbeing function subject to existing and corrective interrelationships between the interacting variables. Such variables describe both – the existing state of affairs and the objectively aspired for moral and ethical transformation. The resulting conception of social participation in such simulated wellbeing functions along the path of learning possibilities is the objective of the intra-generational and inter-generational transfers for the objective of attaining degrees of participatory unity of being and becoming between the overlapping generations. Likewise, there is the consequential unity of knowledge simulated between the variables that realize the epistemic oneness of being and becoming.

Equity and equality that obsess both the utilitarian and the egalitarian utility and welfare indexes of overlapping generations are not the objective for moral-social reconstruction. The perspective thereby, is to attain participatory social contracts between overlapping generations out of simulated knowledge-flows that generate and continue in the light of epistemic unity of knowledge. Equity and equality, redistribution, ownership, and sustainability are all the attributes derived from the social contract of a unified society by participative wellbeing as so formed and simulated. The attainment of such participative nature of wellbeing out of a continuous reproduction of knowledge-flows arising from discourse in the light of epistemic unity of knowledge conveys the principle of sustainability. At the foundation of such epistemic unity of knowledge and the sustained world-system of its kind is the unique law overarching across 'everything'. This is where God enters and abides in the realm of soul and mind and matter interconnected reality.

So by way of an example, we inquire on the role of God in the financial and social system. The role of God is conveyed by the sustainability of the discursive society in the midst of its objective criterion of wellbeing function. This is induced pervasively by the divine law of oneness and its induction on unity of being and becoming of things in the world-system.

The bank is the institution for mobilizing resources into the gainful ends in this substantive direction of being and becoming out of organic oneness. Money, finance, and the economy now become various institutions that along with their diverse instruments of the appropriate kinds, realize the resource mobilization into the good things of life. In the context of intertemporal allocation, production, ownership and sustainability of resources, the bank as an institution plays the role of moment-to-moment simulation of the social objective of wellbeing as we have defined it, subject to continuous Interaction, Integration, and Evolution (IIE) of the interrelated variables and their artifacts over the dimensions of knowledge, time, and space.

Unlike the relational models presented by Gauthier and others in evaluating intertemporal equity and equality question backwards in time to correct for historical mistakes, the way of understanding overlapping generation in the sense of epistemic unity of knowledge is forwards. The principle in this is that mankind as social ensemble corrects for its past mistakes by moral and ethical reconstruction of itself and its progeny, in which the past gets forgotten by the birth and continuity of the new moral worldview. To look back and demand compensation by survivors for the past or their progeny in a social ensemble is to extort an undetermined resource off the morally reformed present and future generation. This is sheer anger and avenge for which there is no appropriate compensation except repentance and moral reformation of the present and the future social ensembles. Indeed, all faithful and good societies acclaim the motto: "Forgive and forget". This is the ultimate sign of moral and ethical sustainability of a good and discursive society.[3]

Now for the sake of arguments here let us say that rationality invokes in individuals and their construction of social preferences by utilitarian type aggregation the transitivity rule in the following cases:

Past generation (A) prevails Present generation Future generationon its preferences (demand) for asks for forgiveness has its preferences compensation for the wrongs and moral reconstruction for moral that were perpetrated to the (B) re-generation (C) dead in the past. Consider the following preference possibilities (denoted by >) and their utility ($U_i(.)$) implications; i = A, B, C:

1. **A > B > C:** This is a contradiction. For if true then, $U_A > U_B > U_C$. The society has not gained on learning over the past to the present and does not expect to learn in the future including its relationship with the overlapping generation.
2. **A > B; C > B:** This leads to a contradiction. For since B is the 'past' of C, therefore, if A > B, then at the same time it is not possible for C > B. But if B > C by this contradiction then the further contradiction of (1) will hold.
3. **B > A; C > B; then C > B > A:** By the transitivity axiom. Then $U_C > U_B > U_A$. But such a higher learning in the future cannot be guaranteed. It may be an exception.
4. **B > A; B > C; implying, $U_B > U_A$; $U_B > U_C$:** This preference ordering does not withstand a guarantee that the present learning is necessarily better than the past. This may be an exception.

Thus in the intertemporal framework, the transitivity axiom of rational choice cannot abide (Condorcet, 1785). Therefore, there is no sound reason to argue along lines of a rationalist or rationality axiom of the utilitarian making. The annulment of the transitivity axiom also applies to the egalitarian case, if such a case is embedded in rationalism and economic rationality. Yet it is along such transitive lines that the rationalist philosophers have explained their models of intertemporal resource distribution for equality and equity. Political standpoint, institutional policies, and social beliefs have been established as taboos upon the misguided epistemological premise.

AMARTYA SEN ON ETHICS AND ECONOMICS

The important first issue to study regarding Sen's (1990) profound treatment of ethics and economics is the method of ethical aggregation of preferences. While we have covered this topic earlier, the new ground now is to inquire on the micro-ethical foundation of economic and social aggregation to their macroeconomic level. In this context it would then be possible to treat the ethical function that banks ought to perform within the development complex. The latter traditionally has been a macroeconomic study. But in the micro-ethical foundation of macroeconomics, ethics becomes an endogenously active factor. The macroeconomic policy-making, particularly those that involve the social embedding of monetary policy, fiscal policy and human resource development policy, now reflect the micro-foundational nature of preference formation in the ensemble of the banking system. Thus through this foundation at the microeconomic level arises the macroeconomic design of policy-making with its endogenous ethical embedding.

In light of the above-mentioned kind of observation made by Sen (op cit, p. 7) who writes: "I would argue that the nature of modern economics has been substantially impoverished by the distance that has grown between economics and ethics". This points out to the relevance of a solid place for immersion of the engineering approach in the treatment of ethics and economics. Such a complemented approach takes the form of a general-system modeling combining normative and positivistic studies of economic reasoning in one integrated methodology.

Sen (1990) carries further his critique of economic theory in the light of its assumptions, but not in reference to the alternative vast possibilities for reformation that economics holds out for society and science in socio-scientific analysis. The important criticism at the fundamental levels of axioms is against the postulate of economic rationality. Abandon this axiom and the whole self-acclaimed edifice of economic reasoning crumbles. Thereby, the subsequent assumptions wither away. These are the postulates of scarcity of resources, self-interest, and marginal rates of substitutions between goods, services and productive factors, even at the household level of production, and between the socially privileged and underprivileged. The latter is the case of household decision-making respecting marriage, divorce and other forms of cohabitation, conflict and conflict-resolution between the preferences of members of the household, the present, the future and the past generations (Becker, 1989).

Sen does not bring forth the debilitating consequences of lateral addition of linear preference mappings in social welfare formulation. But we have identified earlier the social implication of such linear preference aggregation. We have denied social preferences and individual rationality on the basis of the impossibility of full-information in a learning plane. Learning constitutes our entire life experience. Learning experiences complex aggregation, which even in the apparent linear form, was really foliation of geodesics of learning paths (Kupka & Peixoto, 1993).[4] Thus we introduced for the first time in economic reasoning the pertinence of mathematical complexity, though this may be explained in terms of verbal lucidity, in which Sen has a profound place.

Linear social preference is the result of disjoint linear individual preferences. They make up the utilitarian ethical world-system. Consequently, no complexity generated by crossing meandering paths along learning geodesics of human and scientific experience can be logically possible. Economic theory erected upon its postulate of economic rationality does not have the methodology for studying complexity. Likewise, the same kinds of linear, independent, and methodologically individuated preferences cannot offer the endogenous theory of ethics and economics.

Sen points out the dysfunctional role of rational choice and the postulate of economic rationality in social welfare function as not being a truly ethical valuation approach to the broader context of social relations. Social aggregation in such a case simply adds up individual preferences premised on self-interest and expressed by the individual and household utility functions. When self-interest assumption is relinquished, along with it the ethical context of social preferences in social choice also gives way. The utility function and the utilitarian contexts of social ethics fall apart. Along with this demise of traditional notions of methodological individualism many of the axioms and assumptions of economic behavior, prediction and sheer analytical nicety disappear. The conclusion then is that in the truly ethical treatment, economic theory remains unready to address the broader context of morality and ethics that dismisses the postulate of self-interest, and thereby all the postulates of methodological individualism.

Sen (1990, p. 55) writes regarding such a contrasting picture of social ethics versus methodological individualism: “This is most obviously so when importance is attached to the ‘agency aspect’ of a person. Indeed, the person himself or herself may have reasons for pursuing goals other than personal well-being or individual self-interest. Respect for the agency aspect of others can also lead to similar departures. Self-interested behavior can scarcely suffice when agency is important on its own (and is not simply reducible to the pursuit of self-interest).”

The end result of such arguments as critique of economic theory and welfare economics based on the utility and utilitarian background suggests that, the specific contexts of morality and ethics must be the basis of consequential evaluation and the social agency. Whenever any shade of rationalism is invoked, then along with it in direct or indirect derivation enters the postulate of rational choice from the side of the political philosophy of utilitarianism and self-interest. Ethics can be seen as individualistic altruism when the rational derivation of individual preferences on morality and ethics remain the definitional groundwork. But when the theme of morality and ethics are invoked by the epistemic origin of unity of knowledge then learning and organic relationships as ‘agency’ become intrinsic values. Such values to abide strictly by unity of knowledge must have a unique and universal epistemological basis. We have argued in this book (see Preface) that the uniqueness and universality are found in strict abidance with the monotheistic law and as it establishes the grand design of human reality.

Along with the demise of the neoclassical and traditional postulates of economic theory, the understanding and applications of standard economic indicators and their extensions in various fields of economics must be replaced. Among such economic indicators is the concept of efficiency produced by the concept of Pareto optimality in welfare economics, and minimum average cost of production in the theory of the firm. Sen points out this important fact. It heralds the emergence of new economic postulation.

Welfare economics exemplified by Pareto optimality, and prevailing in utilitarianism (consumer theory based), and the Walrasian general equilibrium system in multi-market analysis (consumer-production-factor based), become distorted in explaining agency social behavior. Now behavior is always a social consequence of valuation and conformable choices in the framework of such social consequences. Man is not an island. He belongs to, is developed in, and is enriched or decays along with the nature of the social whole. Consider the family for instance, as the greatest institution of man that represents the fullness of a social miniscule. The family then must be treated as a conglomerate of cooperating individuals (Choudhury, 1996).

Visualize the following kind of Walrasian general equilibrium system that is figuratively shown as the tangential meeting sets of optimal-equilibrium points of production possibility and commodity indifference curves. Can such a unique point exist in the midst of continuous learning that embeds in social agency and inter-variable (commodities and prices) interaction? No. In the learning case of interrelations there are only fuzzy points of complexly distributed variables for which relative prices cannot exist. Hence, relative prices and commodity bundles cannot exist either in the deterministic sense or in the straightforward probabilistic sense. We have explained earlier that in learning fields, in place of straightforward probabilistic distribution of variables, what we have are repetitive probabilistic distributions (Choudhury, 2011c). Indeed, such compounded probabilistic distributions are explained as frontiers of new thinking in quantum physics (Hawking & Mlodinow, 2010)[5]. In the embedded world-system of morality, ethics, science, and society (hence economics), there are interrelated systems and cybernetics with circular causality between them and their variables.

On the role of deontological ethics (duty bound), welfare choice, and consequences, Sen's criticism of Nozick's theory of justice is noteworthy. But in the knowledge-centered social choice problem with consequential evaluation of the wellbeing function having no trace of utilitarian or welfarism with the self-interest postulate, our deontological explanation of ethics and economics is quite different. We summarize this wellbeing formulation of deontological-based social choice here.

KENNETH J. ARROW AND SOCIAL CHOICE WITH IRRELEVANT PREFERENCES FOR SOLVING THE IMPOSSIBILITY PROBLEM

The utilitarian approach to preference aggregation and maximization of the summation of individual utility functions to comprise the social welfare function does not contribute to the field of ethical dynamics in our learning model of unity of knowledge. In the financial world, the banking system forms a social miniscule, like that of the family, which overarches individuals, values, communities and the social whole. Consequently, the utilitarian methodology cannot be applied with its aggregate preferences, utilities and interpersonal comparisons of utilities to explain the endogenous role of ethics and morality formed by the complex medium of discourse and learning.

What is the social worldview with ethics and morality as the manifestation of the divine law that the financial system ought to stand for? Does Arrow's theory of social choice and individual values (Arrow, 1964) contribute to such an area of social formalism? In other words, is the technical meaning of welfare function as presented by Arrow, valid in our case of endogenous learning model driven by the episteme of the monotheistic law as the manifestation of God in 'everything', and thereby in the financial system? The answer is in the negative.

The majority rule of Arrow's social choice under democracy allows for the ultimate division of the space of rational choices into two disjoint categories. Let these be represented by the vectors $\{X_1\}$, $\{X_2\}$ of n_1 and n_2 members, respectively, $n_1 > n_2$, with the strict preference relation P, such that the relation, X_1PX_2, as long as $n_1 > n_2$. However, in case of $n_1 > n_2$, say due to death, retirement, migration, and hegemony of members, the independence of irrelevant preferences says that, X_2PX_1, as long as $n_2 > n_1$. The preferences P_1, P_2 thus remain independent. Arrow considers the majority rule in terms of numbers, not in terms of the strength of values that a diminishing community can bequeath to others. Arrow writes in regard to the social consequences of such a perspective of his postulate on the independence of irrelevant preferences as follows (op cit, p. 26): "... the choice to be made among the set S of surviving candidates should be independent of the preferences of individuals for candidates not in S."

When applied to the study of financial practices, the stakeholders and shareholders asset evaluation modeling is at point. According to Arrow's postulate of majority rule in social decision making, a shareholder model need not address the stakeholders' interests out of value premises. That is because of the disjoint nature of the preferences of $\{X_1\text{=shareholders}\}$ and $\{X_2\text{=stakeholders}\}$, as explained above.

In the end thereby, the meaning of welfare function of mainstream economics *a la* Arrow, becomes untenable in our case of social wellbeing. This rejection is due to both of the following attributes: Firstly, the utilitarian nature of aggregation of individual preferences and utilities to the social level does not function in the moral-social plane. Secondly, the incompleteness concept of Arrow's welfare function disables its extension to the realm of universal values. On the other hand, the universality of the monotheistic law configures the generalized-system and cybernetic fields of knowledge-induced socio-scientific variables. Among these are the backward and forward continuums of circular causality encompassing intertemporal sociality of all. Nothing is left out, whereas 'everything' is corrected to their moral-social reconstruction by the universal value premise of unity of knowledge and details of the world-system.

An example pertaining to the banking system in this regard is the continuum of intertemporal unity of relations between money and real economy with the gold standard. We will study this theme as the money-real economy unified arrangement determining value in terms of price stability, socioeconomic development, and the human resource factor. Arrow's postulate of majority rule and independence of irrelevant preferences fall apart in such extension of the meaning of value. So also does Arrow's meaning of aggregation in the welfare function.

The present book argues within its moral-social perspective of unity of knowledge that, the monetary, financial, and real economy sectors are not independent of each other. These sectors do not predominate over one another, so that otherwise the preferences of savers remain inclined towards the financial sector. The result then would otherwise be the predominance of the rate of interest as the rate of return in the financial sector. The real economy would then remains marginalized by the rate of interest as the principal financial instrument.

The utilitarian dysfunction of separable aggregation rule and the analytical semblance of independence between individuals in social entities is inherent in Arrow's definition of the welfare function (p. 23): "By a social welfare function will be meant a process or rule which, for each set of individual orderings $R_1, \ldots, R_n$ for alternative social states (one ordering for each individual), states a corresponding social ordering of alternative social states, R." The implications of relational epistemology of unity of knowledge caused by circular causation and wellbeing concepts are contrary to Arrow's conception. In the wellbeing function and the circular causation relations explaining the degree of existing or socially transformable complementarities between variables, there is no substantive meaning of priorities. Inter-causal variables are all circularly interrelated in the sense of their systemic and cybernetic unity of knowledge and organic relations.[6]

On the topic of ethics and morality in the banking system, the welfare function assumes the role of principal-agent relationship. Such a welfare function is maximized according to Arrow's dictatorship criterion by the dominance of the agent's decisions over the principal's preferences. On the other hand, in the wellbeing function there cannot be any less than three alternatives to be chosen by the principal and agents. One of these three choices is the endogenous ethics and morality variable, which is induced by the knowledge-flow variable. It is derived from the epistemic foundation of the monotheistic law of unity of knowledge. Following the determination of knowledge-flows there is extensive discourse on determining laws, rules in reference to issues at hand. Thus, consensus follows. Such interactively generated integration leads into creative evolution. The learning processes arise and span across continuums of systems. The underlying IIE-learning model universalizes the methodology of unity of knowledge for every socio-scientific issue. Independence between endogenous ethical values, preferences, social actions and responses and the social choices are thus co-evolutionary.

The implication then is an alarming one on moral-social construction. The IIE-learning worldview implies that, other than the monotheistic epistemological origin of the socio-scientific law, endogenous ethics arising from the moral law cannot be induced into the financial order in any other way. It is equally true of the ethics-benign socio-scientific order. Consequently, in the absence of the monotheistic epistemological consciousness institutional preferences cannot be changed in the direction of moral-social reconstruction. IIE-learning process worldview of epistemic oneness gives the other, new foundation of economic, financial, social, and scientific architecture.

CONCLUSION

Our review of the contemporary literature on the possibility of ethics and morality in the framework of an organically symbiotic world-system, within which is embedded the domains of economics, finance and society, shows that a cogent theoretical and practical framework is lacking in the entire of mainstream methodology. Bridging the missing gap of endogenous integration of morality and ethics with the economic, financial, and social systems is a deeply epistemological theme of study. This chapter has continued on to show the dividing line between the epistemology of unity of knowledge and the rationalistic approach on this theme. The result is the consequential moral and ethical void in narrowed rationalist reasoning. Its analytics, empirics and application, and the resulting moral-social reconstruction, do not and cannot extend beyond the limited vision of the material domain. God, the monotheistic law, and the ethical and moral dynamics all remain incapable by their dissociative treatment of explaining the otherwise essentially holistic study of te endogenous relations between God, man, society, and science. Such a socio-cybernetic treatment comprises the methodology, consciousness, explanation, and application of God to the world-system.

Now to bring God into the socio-scientific and cybernetic world-system system, the methodology, moral-social consequences and analytical implications, intellection and application, must all lie in the framework of the comprehensive worldview of systemic unity of knowledge and the world-system. Such a worldview arises in logical and analytical ways from the monotheistic law and its substantive explanations of and application in human experience.

A comparative review of the literature in contrast to the monotheistic worldview regarding most mundane matters points out the following facts:

1. Mainstream socio-scientific thought is uniformly premised in rationalism, despite some moral and ethical background of these studies. When it so happens the reliance is once again on the rationalistic way of understanding morality and ethics. Barriers to the res extensa domain of morality and ethics as consciousness of unity of knowledge in socio-scientific thought prevail (Uittenbogaard, online).
2. In Islamic socio-scientific thought there are two contesting schools. Those that rely on the exogenous treatment of monotheistic oneness expressed through the divine law belong to the school of rationalism. The difference merely is that tis school invokes the monotheistic origin of Islamic episteme but do not know how to make this structural and functional in a methodology emanating from the law of monotheism and its application in constructing a unified world-system in its generality and particulars.

The second category of Islamic thinkers belongs to the primordial episteme of the Qur'an and the Sunnah, and derived the episteme of unity of knowledge from this ontological primal foundation. Such Islamic thinkers have developed a methodology of the structural and functional use of the monotheistic law in real life. The development is in progress.

The example of such different approaches to worldly issues is found in the treatment of money, finance, and real economy. But the depth of the difference is methodologically substantive and res extensa over the knowledge, time, and space dimensions.

REFERENCES

Allen, C., Smit, I., & Wallach, W. (2005). Artificial morality: Top-down, bottom-up, and hybrid approaches. *Journal of Ethics and Information Technology*, *7*(3), 149–155. doi:10.1007/s10676-006-0004-4.

Arrow, K. J. (1964). *Social choice and individual values*. New York: Wiley.

Becker, G. S. (1989). Family. In Eatwell, J., Milgate, M., & Newman, P. (Eds.), *The New Palgrave: Social Economics* (pp. 64–76). New York, NY: W.W. Norton.

Breuer, R. (1991). *The anthropic principle, man as the focal point of the universe.* Boston, MA: Birkhauser.

Bruteau, B. (1997). *God's ecstasy.* New York, NY: The Crossroad Publishing Co..

Buchanan, J. M. (1999). The domain of constitutional economics. In *The Logical Foundations of Constitutional Liberty.* Indianapolis, IN: Liberty Fund.

Buchanan, J. M., & Tullock, G. (1990). Individual rationality in social choice. In *The Calculus of Consent, Logical Foundations of Constitutional Democracy.* Indianapolis, IN: Liberty Fund.

Choudhury, M. A. (1996). A theory of social systems: Family and ecology as examples. *Kybernetes. The International Journal of Systems and Cybernetics, 25*(3).

Choudhury, M. A. (2000a). *The Islamic worldview: Socio-scientific perspectives.* London, UK: Kegan Paul International.

Choudhury, M. A. (2000b). A social contractarian theory of markets: Rawls, Gauthier, neoclassicism and the alternative. *International Journal of Social Economics, 27*(3). doi:10.1108/03068290010384268.

Choudhury, M. A. (2011a). The future models of Arab political economy. *World Futures: The Journal of General Evolution, 67*(6), 437–448.

Choudhury, M. A. (2011b). Family as socioeconomic management system. *International Journal of Management Systems, 18*(1).

Choudhury, M. A. (2011c). A probabilistic model of learning fields. *The Journal of Muamalat and Islamic Finance Research, 7*(1).

Condorcet, M. J. A. N. (1785). *Essai sur l'application de l'analyse a la probabilite des decisions rendues a la pluralite des voix.* Paris, France: Imprimerie Royale.

Coombs, H. C. (1990). *The return of scarcity: Strategies for an economic future.* Cambridge, UK: Cambridge University Press. doi:10.1017/CBO9780511552281.

Dawkins, R. (2006). *The god delusion.* London, UK: Transworld Publishers.

Einstein, A. (1954). The problem of space, ether, and the field in physics. In Commins, C., & Linscott, R. N. (Eds.), *Man and the Universe: The Philosophers of Science.* New York: The Pocket Books, Inc..

Epstein, R. (1992). Justice across the generations. In Laslett, P., & Fishkin, J. (Eds.), *Justice between Age Groups and Generations, Philosophy, Politics, and Society*. New Haven, CT: Yale University Press.

Etzioni, A. (1988). What is rational? In *The Moral Dimension: Towards a New Economics*. New York, NY: The Free Press.

Gauthier, D. (1986). *Morals by agreement*. Oxford, UK: Oxford University Press.

Gel'fand, I. M., & Shenitzer, A. (1961). Introduction to tensors. In *Lectures on Linear Algebra* (pp. 164–185). New York, NY: Interscience Publishers, Inc..

Gleick, J. (1987). *Chaos, making a new science*. New York, NY: Viking Penguin.

Hammond, P. J. (1987). On reconciling Arrow's theory of social choice with Harsanyi's fundamental utilitarianism. In Feiwel, G. R. (Ed.), *Arrow and the Foundations of the Theory of Economic Policy* (pp. 179–221). London, UK: Macmillan.

Harsanyi, J. C. (1955). Cardinal welfare, individualistic ethics, and interpersonal comparisons of utility. *The Journal of Political Economy*, 63.

Hawking, S. W., & Mlodinow, L. (2010). *The grand design*. London, UK: Transworld Publishers.

Henderson, J. M., & Quandt, R. E. (1971). *Microeconomic theory*. New York: McGraw-Hill.

Holton, R. L. (1992). *Economy and society*. London: Routledge.

Inglott, P. S. (1990). The rights of future generations: Some socio-philosophical considerations. In Busuttil, S., Agius, E., Inglott, P. S., & Macelli, T. (Eds.), *Our Responsibilities Towards Future Generations* (pp. 17–27). Malta: Foundation for International Studies & UNESCO.

Kant, I. (1949). *The philosophy of Kant* (Friedrich, C. J., Trans.). New York, NY: Modern Library.

Korten, D. C. (1995). *When corporations rule the world*. London, UK: Earthscan.

Kupka, I. A. K., & Peixoto, M. M. (1993). On the enumerative geometry of geodesics. In M.W. Hirsch, J.E. Marsden, & M. Shub (Eds.), *From Topology to Computation: Proceedings of the Smalefest*, (pp. 243-253). New York, NY: Springer-Verlag.

Kuran, T. (2004). *Islam and mammon: The economic predicaments of Islamism*. Princeton, NJ: Princeton University Press.

Moore, G. E. (1962). *Principia ethica*. Cambridge, UK: Cambridge University Press.

Myrdal, G. (1957). An unexplained general traits of social reality. In *Rich Lands and Poor, the Road to World Prosperity*. New York, NY: Harper & Row.

Nozick, R. (1974). Distributive justice. *Philosophy & Public Affairs*, 3.

O'Donnell, R. M. (1989). Types of probabilities and their measurement. In *Keynes: Philosophy, Economics & Politics* (pp. 81–105). London, UK: Macmillan Press Ltd..

Phelps, E. S. (1989). Distributive justice. In Eatwell, J., Milgate, M., & Newman, P. (Eds.), *The New Palgrave: Social Economics*. New York, NY: W.W. Norton.

Pindyck, R. S., & Rubinfeld, D. L. (2001). *Microeconomics*. Upper Saddle River, NJ: Prentice-Hall, Inc..

Rawls, J. (1971). *A theory of justice*. Cambridge, MA: Harvard University Press.

Sen, A. (1977). Rational fools: A critique of the behavioural foundations of economic theory. *Philosophy & Public Affairs*, 6.

Sen, A. (1990). Freedom and consequences. In *On Ethics and Economics* (pp. 58–89). London, UK: Basil Blackwell.

Shipler, D. (1986). *Arabs and Jews*. New York, NY: Times Books.

Sztompka, P. (1991). *Society in action, the theory of social becoming*. Chicago, IL: The University of Chicago Press.

Taleb, N. N. (2007). *The black swan: The impact of the highly improbable*. New York: Random House.

Taylor, O. H. (1967). *Economics and liberalism*. Cambridge, MA: Harvard University Press.

Temkin, L. S. (1995). Justice and equality: some questions about scope. In Paul, E. F., Miller, F. D. Jr, & Paul, J. (Eds.), *The Just Society* (pp. 72–104). Cambridge, UK: Cambridge University Press. doi:10.1017/S0265052500004684.

Uittenbogaard, A. (n.d.). *A brief history of monotheism, from the desert to the grand unification*. Retrieved from http://www.abarim publications.com/Book_Review/index.html#.UWpA1rWmh30

Vickery, W. S. (1960). Utility, strategy, and social decision rules. *The Quarterly Journal of Economics*, *74*, 507–535. doi:10.2307/1884349.

Witham, L. (2010). *Marketplace of the gods: How economics explains religion*. Oxford, UK: Oxford University Press. doi:10.1093/acprof:oso/9780195394757.001.0001.

Zohar, D., & Marshall, I. (2004). *Spiritual capital*. San Francisco, CA: Berrett-Koehler Publishers, Inc..

ENDNOTES

1 The Prophet Muhammad said so about the mother: Who has the highest rights on you? The prophet said, the mother. Who has the next highest rights on you? The prophet said, the mother. Who has the next highest rights on you? The prophet said, the mother. Who has the next highest rights on you, the prophet said, the father.

2 This can be proved as follows: Let the equation in which variables (x,y,z) and coefficients (a,b) are all knowledge-induced by θ-values (not explicitly shown) be written as, x = ay + bz. Since on the IIE-learning process model any function is continuously differentiable and hence analytical, therefore Taylor's expansion of analytical functions around a point of learning (simulated equilibrium) will exist. We then write such Taylor expansions for the functions of θ-induced variables,

$$x(\theta) = x(\theta_0) + (\theta - \theta_0).(dx(\theta)/d\theta)_{\theta 0} + \text{higher terms;}$$
$$(ay)[\theta] = (ay)[\theta_0] + (\theta - \theta_0).(d(ay)[\theta]/d\theta)_{\theta 0} + \text{higher terms;}$$
$$(bz)[\theta] = (bz)[\theta_0] + (\theta - \theta_0).(d(bz)[\theta]/d\theta)_{\theta 0} + \text{higher terms.}$$

Each of these expansions is foliated by parametric variations of the learning values θ_0 on the **IIE**-learning process string. Hence the functionals (x,y,z)[θ] are non-linear in the coefficient values. Thereby, the entire simulation system comprising the wellbeing function and the equation constraints is a non-linear one. Such simulation equation constraints with parametric variation of θ-values along various expansion paths of the series will cause nexus of intersections of the generated equations. In the non-linear space such spans of intersections become manifolds of nexus. Formalism concerning such spans can be found in the manifold foliation theorem given by Kupka and Peixoto (1993). I adapt their theorem to the following enunciation here:

Given the analytical properties of functionals in nonlinear spans that can be Taylor-expanded in a manifold M of m-dimension with (n/2)-codimensions, n/2 being number of paired foldings in the space of (**R**xM), **R** is real space. Hence, all lines that belong to **R** become manifold spans in **R**xM.

3 These points can be examined formally as follows: Let the present value of discounted aggregate stream of future utility ($U_f(x,t)$) functions of present, including the overlapping generation of living persons in social ensemble, discounted by δ_f, be denoted by $\int_0^T U_f(x,t).e^{-\delta f.t}dt$.
Likewise, let the present terminal value of aggregate utilities of past deceased generation of persons, ($U_p(x,t)$), considered in the social ensemble at the zero-time at a rate of growth of δ_p be denoted by,

$\int_{-t}^0 U_p(x,t).e^{\delta p.t}dt$. For equality as argued by Gauthier, the welfare of the two sectional generations must be equal at zero-time (the present). Thereby, by $\int_0^T U_f(x,t).e^{-\delta f.t}dt = \int_{-t}^0 U_p(x,t).e^{\delta p.t}dt$.
The social welfare function at zero-time is denoted by,
$W(U_p,U_f,\delta_p,\delta_f) = \int_{-t}^0 U_p(x,t).e^{\delta p.t}dt + \int_0^T U_f(x,t).e^{-\delta f.t}dt$
$=$ either $1.\int_{-t}^0 U_p(x,t).e^{\delta p.t}dt$
or $2.\int_0^T U_f(x,t).e^{-\delta f.t}dt$

That is, intra- and inter- generational social policies on resource claims and distribution will be determined by resorting to either the preferences and weights (δ_p) of past generations in social ensemble today; or by resorting to the same (U_f,δ_f) for present and overlapping and future generations in social ensemble considered today.There is no way of equating the discounted and aggregated utilities in social welfare as stated above, since 'dead men tell no tales'. The demand of survivors forms merely subjective claims.

4 Such a general system of multilinear relationship of evolutionary nonlinear functionals can be represented as a tensor functional (Gel'fand&Shenitzer, 1961). The following is the way to write tensor functionals: $(\mathbf{x}(\theta),\mathbf{f}(\mathbf{x}(\theta));(\mathbf{Fof})(\mathbf{x}(\theta))) = a_{ij}^{\ k}.\xi^i\eta^j\zeta_k$, where, $\mathbf{x}(\theta) = \xi^i.e_i$; $\mathbf{f}(\mathbf{x}(\theta)) = \eta^j.e_j$; $(\mathbf{Fof})(\mathbf{x}(\theta)) = \zeta_k.e^k$. ($e_i$; e_j) are the contravariant basis vectors of region R. e^k are the covariant basis vectors of $(\mathbf{Fof})(\mathbf{x}(\theta))$ in region R^, which is the dual of covariant vector space of region R, meaning the functionals that are linearly additive of nonlinear functionals in R.

5 Hawking and Mlodinow (2010, p. 72) explain such compound (extensive) probability distributions in quantum physics: "According to quantum physics, no matter how much information we obtain or how powerful our computing abilities, the outcomes of physical processes cannot be predicted with certainty because they are not *determined* with certainty…" We have extended this principle of uncertainty to the knowledge-induced multiverse that forever learns from the beginning to the end.

6 Let $W(\mathbf{x}(\theta))$ denote the wellbeing function that is simulated subject to circular causation relations between the vector of knowledge (θ)-induced variables $\mathbf{x}(\theta)$.

In the circular causation system, simulation can commence from any of the equations involving particular candidate of the vector$\mathbf{x}(\theta)$. Hence, no priority of social ordering is pre-assigned. Even if an Islamic bank as an institution, say was addressing the goal of poverty alleviation, it can go ahead in such a project not by spending charity funds (zakat). Rather, it can make productive projects to introduce the poor into the market venue to become able. There are other examples.

We note the following consequences:

Let $\mathbf{x}(\theta) = \{x_1(\theta),x_2(\theta)\}\{dW/d\theta > 0;$

with $dW/d\theta = [(\partial W/\partial x_1(\theta)).(dx_1(\theta)/d\theta) + (\partial W/\partial x_2(\theta)).(dx_2(\theta)/d\theta)] > 0$, identically under the force of learning by complementarities (or diminished by complementary de-learning).

In the **IIE**-learnig process model, as $\theta \rightarrow \theta^*$, so do W(.) and its variables reach temporary equilibriums. But evolutionary learning dynamics preserving or improving the degrees of unity of knowledge cause evolutionary effects on the temporary equilibriums. The result is evolutionary learning equilibriums. These span continuums of intertemporal socio-scientific domains. Hence,

$$(d/\theta)(dW/d\theta) = d^2W(.)/d\theta^2 > 0,$$

is preserved identically with respect to all the knowledge-flows and knowledge-induced variables.

The result here proves that there are no irrelevant preferences, thereby independent relations, and hence the properties of a technical definition of welfare function do not abide, when knowledge induction of the participatory and complementary type is used in social evaluation and reconstruction.

Chapter 5
The Moral Possibility of Islamic Banking System as Institution:
Contrasting Cases

ABSTRACT

This is an applied chapter on the application of the phenomenological model of unity of knowledge to a critical understanding of the Islamic law, economics, finance, and banking philosophy of the Islamic banks in Indonesia. The chapter explains how the Indonesian Islamic banks are trying to introduce the moral and ethical factors in the mundane business of finance and banking as a sign of integrating God (i.e. the monotheistic law) with this world-system. The chapter goes on with its critical examination of the Indonesian case in the light of its theorem of universality and uniqueness of the monotheistic law as functional ontology. An extensive review of the literature is undertaken to establish its critical worldview of the predicament prevailing in the moral premise with Islamic economics, finance, and banking. The alternative prescription is provided in light of the phenomenological model of epistemic unity.

INTRODUCTION

Much of this chapter is a rigorous depiction of the principles of Bank Muamalat as an example of an Islamic bank operating successfully in Indonesia. These principles were explained in their moral context by Riawan Amin (2004). The summary of his work is as follows:

DOI: 10.4018/978-1-4666-4643-8.ch005

Copyright ©2014, IGI Global. Copying or distributing in print or electronic forms without written permission of IGI Global is prohibited.

The Islamic bank Muamalat is charged by three principal motivations. These are firstly, power, information, knowledge and rewards. These attributes make up the Arabic (Indonesian-ised) meaning of *PIKR*. Secondly, a Zero-base (humility) combines with *Iman* meaning faith, to yield *Konsistency* (Indonesian-ised consistency) and Result. Thus these principles together comprise Amin's key principle of *ZIKR*, meaning devotional worship. Thirdly, the attribute of *Militancy* (meaning competitive aggressiveness) combines with *Intellect*, *Kompetitif* (competition) and Regeneration to yield together *MIKR*. Amin's conception of the Islamic bank in the final instance is the organization of interaction between *ZIKR, PIKR,* and *MIKR* in seamless continuity of interrelations. It does not matter at which of these initiating points the organization launches its vision and mission. The end result is the same – the attainment of common wellbeing for all, both within and outside the organization. Between all of them, the moral-social organization as of the institution of Islamic bank interacts to attain the common goal of wellbeing.

Amin's schema of interaction between the value attributes in Islamic Bank Muamalat is improvised by us in Figure 1. In our improvising of Figure 1 the re-statement of *ZIKR* points to the central role of knowledge formed by faith and belief in the

Figure 1. Interaction between ZIKR, PIKR, MIKR, and FIKR in continuity across knowledge, time, and space continuums

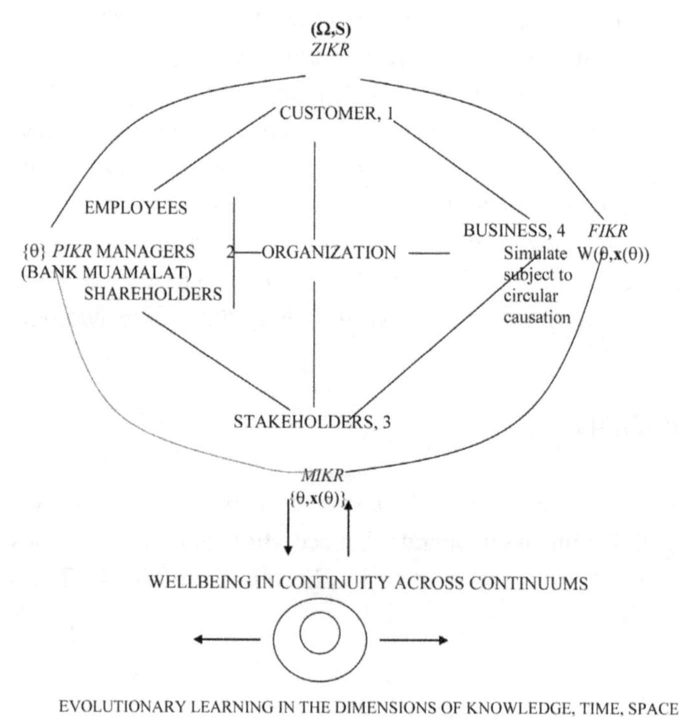

dynamic system of interaction of faith (*ZIKR*) with the world-system, with which the Islamic bank ought to interact. The result then is not a meager solitude of worship. Rather, the rewards in continuity and continuums are made of profitability for the Islamic bank and benefits for the great commons as a whole. The continuity of such benefits to self and other manifests the Islamic bank's intertemporal showering of spiritual and material rewards to all in the midst of knowledge, belief, and action. Note that we have also included *FIKR* as yet another element that carries *PIKR* and *MIKR* into *ZIKR* again in a seamless continuity. This perspective though is not in Amin's characterization.

Inglott (1990) points to such felicitous continuity in his dynamic intergenerational model of environment and ecological sustainability. Several of the themes that we have dwelled upon feature prominent in Agius' effective paper: He mentions the Rawlsian dictum that the present generation can establish its self-interest with the most contiguous progeny in preference to the distant ones. Hence moral behavior to conserve, contribute, and preserve the intertemporal resources is limited to the present most contiguous generation. This is also our meaning of the 'nearest' point of valuation of assets taken over the extended domain of knowledge, time, and space that together define justice and fairness both to the present and future generations.

Furthermore, like in our explanation, there is a substantive gap in the moral thought of Kant, which also appears in Agius' arguments concerning a relational paradigm of intergenerational ethics. That is alerting on the permanent character of dualism between 'the phenomenal aspects of an action' in the space-time domain and the timelessness of the noumenal i.e. moral character. Instead of this meaning of value, in our case there is no relational separation between the variables, their relations, and entities. There are simply explained circular causality between the events of space-time and the episteme affecting the occurrence or non-occurrence of such events. Noumena or the moral law is of the metaphysical ontological nature in all of occidental belief and functions. Thus, space-time and timelessness of knowledge remain independently dualistic domains. Contrarily, the moral law is the worldly mapping of the monotheistic law of epistemic oneness into the events occurring in the dimensions of knowledge, time, and space. This is our stand on the theory of epistemic oneness influencing behavior, applications, and inferences in the world-system. Within that world-system is the defining place of institution-market relational idea.

In the dimensions of knowledge, time, and space there exist the relational cybernetic universes of the present and future. Within these are the microcosms and the cosmic entirety, whose study is a matter of great importance in understanding intra-systemic dynamics. This kind of pervasive intra-systemic dynamics for the social order is explained in the context of markets and institutions (Islamic bank).

The relational order is examined as interactive wholes for the bestowing of wellbeing to all – humans and other.[1] Figure 1 implies that the meaning of sustainability is based on the perpetuation of truth in continuity across continuums of knowledge, time, and space dimensions. We explain this phenomenon as follows.

SUSTAINABILITY IN TERMS OF THE BELIEF SYSTEM CARRIED THROUGH INSTITUTION-MARKET RELATIONSHIP

Sustainable development is a study in social choices that sustain both society and economy intertemporally (South Commission, 1990). The domain of society embraces ethical values that are derived from the moral epistemological roots. Economy embraces material values that support the moral-social contract. Thus society and economy are embedded in each other as being interconnected and inter-causal subsystems within the total world-system. This is the meaning of cybernetic as the study of the extensively inter-relational universe.

Markets and their exchangeables are thus induced by the moral values of moral-social sustainability. Institutions guide the formation of ethical preferences and choices of the morally induced exchangeables. The preference menus of both individuals and institutions interrelate to establish the ethical social contract out of interactive, integrative, and creatively evolving discourse.

The participatory dynamics formed in this way by the intersection of institutions and markets preferences and ethical values arising out of expanding the applications of the epistemic premise of knowledge underlying the moral social contract, forms the key meaning of sustainability. Thereby, the intertemporal path of resource evolution becomes a learning path. Along this path, the participatory complementarities between variables, their relations, and institutions and markets carry forward the moral-social contract.

Figure 1 by its widening domains of interaction established by the continuing effect of belief followed by the positivistic interrelations between institution and agency as shown in the figure, explains our meaning of sustainability along the path of intertemporal moral-social contract. One of the primal areas of such sustainability is empowerment established by the perpetual participation at and by the grassroots in the institution-market learning process. This kind of realization remains the responsibility of Islamic banks as ethical institutions in promoting morally induced exchangeables. Figure 1 explains such realizations.

Integrating the grassroots with the mainstream of development involves choice of appropriate technology, linkage between sectors, and human-resource development at the grassroots, communitarian decision-making, and other ones. Above all, focusing on the primary interrelationships among these activities in the light of attaining social justice, involves issues of intertemporal distribution and protection of the environment and ecology and fair intergenerational ownership and distribution. These issues are examined in the light of the focus on moral-social justice (Ansari & Choudhury, 1991). Questions relating to poverty, entitlement, employment, basic needs, and the choice of appropriate technology are all taken up in the light of the evolutionary integrative and interactive milieu of politico-economic arrangement and social justice as implied by Figure 1.

Truth and Social Justice as Properties of Sustainability

The concept of sustainable development is inextricably linked with the moral-social contract as explained above. Without the moral principle of truth and social justice there cannot be sustainability, despite what we offer to this concept in terms of the measurement of material development. Besides this understanding of the sustainability concept, it is also indispensable in this case to understand the epistemic roots of sustainability as defined by its moral basis. In respect of the epistemic foundations of knowledge and sustainability, ethics is endogenously induced by the force of participation and complementarities—unity of relations—between variables, their relations, and entities.

Participation, likewise complementarities intra-system and inter-systems, form the properties of sustainability along learning processes. In the emergent participatory consequence of a discursive society (Dreyfus and Rabinow, 1983), the idea of institution-market linkages assumes key importance. The resulting holistic system becomes a learning system by virtue of the endogenous nature of ethics in it. Thereby, the ethics of epistemic unity of knowledge induce the Interacting, Integrating, and Evolutionary variables (IIE) and its systemic and cybernetic congeries. Moral-social transformation takes birth, and sustains itself intertemporally by the methodological dynamics of the learning process in IIE.

With the endogenous ethical induction of the variables of the learning curve for the Islamic bank according to Figure 1, the learning function shows up to be quite different from the one in mainstream literature. The difference is borne out by the central impact that changes in learning imparts to the complementary relations between productive and learning factors and the knowledge-induced outputs.

Contrary to the mainstream explanation of learning-type production functions, there is no inverse relationship between *labour input per unit of output* and the *accumulated quantity of output* (Pindyck & Rubinfeld, 2001). An inverse relationship between labour per unit of output and cumulative output, and also between any levels of output in the process of production, means that the production menu is permanently replacing factor inputs for the sake of maximizing output and profits by reducing unit cost of labour. The implication of institutional changes, appropriate technology, participation between factor inputs for codetermining the production menu and the sustainable structure of development are not considered in such a learning experience of the mainstream firm.

On the other hand, endogenous learning experience in production includes these mentioned strategies and structures. Since factor inputs are now participatory and complementary in the codetermined production menu, therefore, they do not experience marginal rates of technical substitution. Resources continuously generated by knowledge-induction are not scarce. The perpetual effect of knowledge regeneration along the IIE-learning processes impacts upon enterprise, innovation, and institutional codetermination of productive choices. Unit cost for factor inputs decline because of 'economies of scope', which cumulative output at any level experiences. Besides, such cumulative output increases by a joint production function with complementary factor inputs. Consequently, there is no need now to reduce inputs of production. Expanding cumulative output and its factor inputs increase in complementary fashion in the presence of endogenous knowledge-induced joint production functions and declining average cost indefinitely.[2]

The fact that the moral foundation of ethical endogeneity arises exclusively from the law of epistemic unity, can be seen by the denial of such intrinsic unity of being in any other epistemological source. Humanism too is a rationalistic behaviour as also is altruism and ethics that arise from rationalistic premises. Buchanan (1999) explains this hedonic idea of the whole of economic reasoning despite any ethical sensitivity, in the following words: "For constitutional economics, the foundational position is summarized in methodological individualism.... Concomitant with methodological individualism as a component of the hard core is the postulate of rational choice, a postulate that is shared over all research programs in economics.... The domain, as such, cannot be extended to include inquiry by those who choose to perceive social interaction differently."

In the endogenously learning organizational system the conscious comprehension and application of human relations in the midst of a primordially determined epistemic unity regenerates and continuously sustains knowledge. The knowledge-flow simultaneously determines and sustains interconnections with the matter-mind comprehension of reality. The event of such systemic interconnection is of an evanescent and efflorescent nature.

The *a priori* and *a posterior* reasoning in the domain of epistemic unity of knowledge are interconnected. Such unified interrelationships are formalized by the emergent circular causation process of unified reality in learning processes by complementarities. Thus the solution domains of circular causation in the phase of moral-social transformation using epistemic unity of knowledge reject the problem of heteronomy otherwise central to Kantian theory of knowledge (Carnap, 1966). The dualistic problem of heteronomy is emphasized by Hegel: "No transition is possible to the specification of particular duties" in Kant's ethical theory. The reason for this dichotomy is the severance of the *a priori* from the *a posteriori* domains of reasoning. The gap between these stand out as heteronomy, being the problem of lack of synthesis in forming a universalized (generalized) theory of knowledge by organic unity of being and becoming.

According to Figure 1, the central repetitive emergence of relations between institutions and the world-system occurs through fresh actualization of *ZIKR*. The subsequent and simulated results from such circularity establish the continuity of the institution-market interrelationship in the light of epistemic unity of knowledge.

EXPLAINING THE ZIKR (Z), PIKR (P), MIKR (M) RELATIONAL DYNAMICS IN THE INTERACTIVE, INTEGRATIVE, AND EVOLUTIONARY (IIE) LEARNING WORLDVIEW OF EPISTEMIC UNITY

We define the following inner variables (denoted by the vectors θ_1, θ_2, θ_3) or attributes of each of the components mentioned here. Thus, $Z = \{\theta_1\}$; $P = \{\theta_2\}$; $M = \{\theta_3\}$. Furthermore, the institutional (Islamic bank) variables, such as the riba-free and trade-related financial instruments are mudarabah or profit-sharing, mushar*akah* or equity participation, *murabaha* or mark-up cost-plus pricing, *ijara* or rental, *bay' muajjal* or deferred payments, *qard e-hasana* or interest-free charitable loans or gifts and grants (Annual Report of Bank Muamalat, 2009). Let this trade vector be denoted by $\{\mathbf{x}\}$. The agent-specific connections shown in Figure 1 are denoted by relations $\{R_i\}$, i = 1,2,3,4, between the institution (Islamic bank) and the wellbeing indexes of each of these agents via (Z,P,M) in terms of their respective sub-vectors.

$\{R_i\}$-relations form circular causation relations between the vectors as stated in respect of the principal value-premise feeding into a set of agent-specific wellbeing indexes, W_j, j = 1,2,3,4 in Figure 1. These indices finally compound into the objective criterion of total wellbeing, W, formed as a compound index of W_j's. One can note the extensively wide and complex number of interactions that can form between the variables, moral values across their attributes, and the agents represented by their respective wellbeing indices. Thus a system and cybernetic approach to such complexity, particularly as the number of interrelations in the complementary mode expands, becomes unwieldy and untenable (Chiang, 1992, pp. 3-12). Now the circular causation system of interrelated functions realizes the system and cybernetic approach in an amenable manner.

$\{R_i\}$-relations in (Z,P,M)-model with the episteme of unity of knowledge

Amin points out various human resource mechanisms that exist and can have the potential in Bank Muamalat towards instilling the (Z,P,M)-attribute values. An examination of interrelations between the attributes points out firstly, the first level of the R_i-relations.

Thus, R_i^1's are schematized as shown in Figure 2.

As it stands, the (Z,P,M)-attributes interact within them by circular causality. This is implied by double arrow heads, except for (Humility, Faith)-attributes that exogenously determine the P-attributes and M-attributes, as shown by arrow-heads. The regenerative cycle is completed by the feedback shown by the return arrows to the $\{R_k^1\}$-system of R_i^1-interelations between the {Z,P,M}-domains. The exogeneity of the (Humility, Faith)-box conveys the meaning that, in any given process of learning by the interactions between the attributes, the moral value plays the initiating function. Upon this effect, the entire system of interrelations is activated. However, the second continuation of the learning process recalls the achievements of the inter-attribute relations caused by an earlier scale of consciousness (simulated θ-values) in the (Z,P,M) attributes-specific interrelations. The learning feedback is thus established in the (Z,P,M)-domain by the 'regenerative' attribute of the learning process. Within the boxes as well, the same kind of interrelations are maintained, with the exogeneity of the (Humility, Faith)-box, though 'recalled' by discursive feedback.

The R_i^1-relations so generated can next be extended by introducing socioeconomic variables that are induced by (Humility, Faith)-attributes box in the (Z,P,M)-circular causation relations. This system of relations is referred to here by R_i^2, which is schematised in the following form:

Let the average θ-value be calculated by ordinal assignment of values (for instance by questionnaire survey responses on value responses). Let, $\theta = \text{Average}\ \{\theta_1, \theta_2, \theta_3\}$, which is now applied for weighting by ranks the value premises of R_i^1. We write,

$$R_s^2(\mathbf{x}) \leftrightarrow R_i^1(\theta); \qquad (1)$$

Figure 2. Characterizing the (Z,P,M)-model

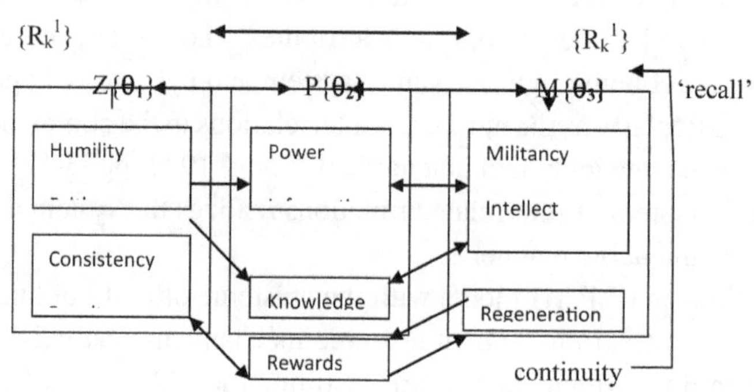

$i = 1,2,3,4$; $s = 1,2,..,n$ as many elements as there are in the vector x.

This system of recursive relations is equivalent to the entire system of relations comprehended between the value base and the induced socioeconomic set of variables, 'n' in number.

We re-write as follows: $R_s^2(x)$ forms the system of relations,

$$x_1 = f_1(x_2,x_3,\ldots,x_n,\theta\in(Z,P,M)) \tag{2}$$

$$x_2 = f_2(x_1,x_3,\ldots,x_n,\theta\in(Z,P,M)) \tag{3}$$

$$x_n = f_n(x_1,x_2,x_3,\ldots,x_{n-1},\theta\in(Z,P,M)) \tag{4}$$

$$\theta = G(x_1,x_2,x_3,\ldots,x_n) \tag{5}$$

The result of simulation of the system of $R_s^2(\mathbf{x})$ feeds into the simulation equation of θ-value to yield the wellbeing index. Theoretically, θ is the functional image of $W(x_1,x_2,x_3,\ldots,x_n)$, the compounded wellbeing index of the agency-specific wellbeing indexes, $W_i(x_1,x_2,x_3,\ldots,x_n)$, $i = 1,2,3,4$. By a suitable choice we can write, $W = \Pi_i W_i^{\alpha I}$; α_i are exponent-coefficients. Yet for simulative empirical purposes only the equivalence of the θ-equation to compounded wellbeing is adequate. But W(.) is conceptually rich and abiding in the entire theoretical model of IIE-learning.

Amin enumerates a number of factors that influence the entire system of simulation relationship comprising (R_i^1,R_s^2). Rational faculties such as reasoning, knowledge, and intellect, empower the mind out of (Humility, Faith)-attributes. Now Z and P interact by way of a rational person self-actualizing in his community while upholding the praises of God. In this way, equilibrium is established between man's self-image and the external environment that he comes to study and utilize. For P to give its worth, the institution (Islamic bank) needs to share its power, knowledge, and information with stakeholders, which truly in the extended meaning, is the society at large.

On the side of M, P interacts through Z to create two interacting and evolutionary dynamics. These are man's duty to the moral cause (referred to as *hablum-min-Allah*). Simultaneously, such moral consciousness is integrated with man's responsibility to others (referred to as *hablum-min-annas*). These two precepts of human development are not independent of each other. They interact, integrate, and evolve across the socioeconomic system of the **x**-vector with the primacy of {θ}-values arising from the epistemic origin of (Ω,S). In regards to the total interactive picture leading to creative evolution, Amin writes (p. 185): "Communications, once again, take place in a two-way fashion. So, the communications model is not only top-down, but also bottom-up. The crew members in a division will communicate ideas to their superiors. They can exchange views with the personnel of other divisions or even with executive directors as part of the search for second opinion."

It needs to be noted where from the exogenous (Humility, Faith)-box is derived that in turn affects all other attributes and is circularly recalled in the Z-box. The emergence of the (Humility, Faith)-box is from our previously explained and formalized epistemic unity denoted by (Ω,S). But as schematized by Amin, it is of the nature of θ-value, which is derived by the moral law and discourse in concert with the socio-scientific world-system, as in the relation with the P and M – boxes. Consequently, the primal premise in our epistemic formalism of unity of being and becoming, and which is recalled across continuums of learning processes forming simulacra of possibilities in $\{\theta,\mathbf{x}(\theta)\}$, is (Ω,S). On the other hand, $\{\theta\}$-values existing in continuity across continuums of socioeconomic systems form regenerative factors of transformation.

A CRITIQUE OF THE (Z,P,M)-RELATIONS BY THE INTERACTIVE, INTEGRATIVE, AND EVOLUTIONARY (IIE) LEARNING METHODOLOGY OF EPISTEMIC ONENESS IN THE WORLD-SYSTEM

There is difference of a substantive epistemic nature between the above two ways of interpreting the primal as against the created forms. The primal (Ω,S) cannot be recreated, as it is meta-ontological in nature. It remains exogenous in the whole system governed on epistemic unity of knowledge. (Ω,S) as the epistemic law of monotheistic oneness is simply recalled for the commencement and continuity of new learning processes; thereby expanding the knowledge-induced socio-scientific vectors, which are regenerative. θ-values are inductive in nature being derived from the *a priori* deductive premise of (Ω,S). As inductive values in the epistemic situation, $\{\theta\}$-values can arise from an interpretive legalistic scholasticism, called in Islamic terminology as *fiqh*. This is the kind of interpretive epistemology that has marked much of the nature of development of the *shari'ah*. The result has been a distancing of Islamic bank financing instruments in the direction of the so-called Islamic financial product development. Yet the essential *objective and purpose* of the *shari'ah* known as the *maqasid as-shari'ah*, have been missed out by the inductive nature of legal scholasticism (Choudhury, 2011).

On the other hand, the primal place of (Ω,S) as the deductive foundation of knowledge in epistemic oneness makes the *Qur'an* and the *Sunnah* as the immutable epistemic origin. *Fiqh* and *shari'ah* remain subject to re-investigation, change and revision by learned discourse followed by consensus in reference to the *Qur'an* and the *Sunnah*, i.e. (Ω,S).

In such a case, the recalling of (Humility, Faith)-box is subject to change and revisions, and even overhaul of certain doctrines when referred to the more primal episteme of (Ω,S). In this sense therefore, (Ω,S) remains permanent and continuous across participatory and complementary systems signifying unity by learning linkages. On the other hand, inductive *a priori* reference to $\{\theta\}$-values can become discontinuous by replacement and change. If and when this situation occurs the regenerative process of continuous learning across continuums of systems and socio-scientific variables break down. Every semblance of the episteme of unity of knowledge ceases to exist.

There are many disruptive examples and consequences that have arisen in the Islamic choice of laws, financial instruments, and legal rulings (*fatawa*). The four schools of Islamic jurisprudence differ in the application of the financial instruments of *mudarabah, musharakah, murabaha* (Usmani, 2004). The plethora of secondary financing instruments that has arisen in Islamic banks, such as *tawarruq* (financial murabaha, see below), *sukuk* (participatory bond), *bay' salam* (deferred payment), *murabaha* (cost-plus mark-up on hire-purchase of equipments), are legitimated in Malaysia by the Islamic Shafei school of thought. Yet these are questioned by the Islamic learned in the *Wahabi* orthodoxy. It has thus become impossible to unify the learned legal experts (*shara'ee*) by a universally agreed upon code of the *shari'ah* on financial matters. At the end of all these cantankerous differences between the differing Islamic schools of thought the (Humility, Faith)-box governed by $\{\theta\}$-values leaves the cycles of its regenerative capacity and falls into rationalist thinking on financial choices.

In the case of epistemic unity of knowledge premised strictly in (Ω,S) the continuation of learning processes is not of the rationalistic kind. Indeed, religious discourse now loses its metaphysical value and is replaced by the functional ontological mapping of the moral law into the world-system in details. In this kind of learning processes, discourse and rediscovery of subtle and higher levels of knowledge premised in epistemic unity are interactively made to lead into consensus (integration) by the recall of (Ω,S) in every new discourse relating to the evaluation of wellbeing criterion. Interaction and integration thus lead into evolutionary learning processes through heightened re-commencements following discourse.

The precept of universality of (Ω,S) in the IIE-learning methodology now replaces the narrow meaning of rationalistic or religious beliefs that can be different not only within religious sects, but also between different peoples. Only participation, complementarities in the good things of life made to relate in ways to increase wellbeing through the act of unity of being and becoming, are empowering common tenets of all events. In the *Qur'an*, such a medium of knowledge formation is established in concert with the issues and problems of the world-system. It is called the institution of the *shura* (consultation). The *shura* as learning process is both institutional and consciousness (*tasbih*). We refer to this integrated evolutionary learning experience as *tasbih-shura* (conscious discourse).

Interpreting Figure 1 in Terms of Unity of Knowledge

The concept of *tasbih-shura* is premised on a rectangle of circular relations that can be further disaggregated into subtleties. In Figure 1, according to the *tasbih-shura* evolutionary learning experience, the starting vertex is of Ω (*Qur'an*). Ω is explicated by the ontological mapping of S (*sunnah*), thus forming the epistemic origin of the moral law. The moral law as an explanatory origin of worldly forms is liberated from the metaphysical ontology of oneness.

The second vertex now forms (Ω,S) in this sense of functional ontological mapping. (Ω,S) now maps onto the domain of primal functional knowledge of edicts of the moral law. Its understanding by learned discourse is denoted by the derivation of primal textual knowledge from (Ω,S), and can be denoted θ^*. The source of such understanding is the moral text (*Qur'an* and *sunnah*). It thereby signifies the derivation of rules from discourse on the comprehension of the monotheistic law of epistemic oneness, called *ijtihad*, derived out of *tasbih-shura* experience in discourse.

The third vertex in the tuple of knowledge formation at this vertex is the worldly knowledge of epistemic unity. This stage signifies the understanding of organic oneness by *tasbih-shura* discourse in respect of specific issues and problems under investigation. The knowledge-flow in this stage is denoted by θ. Thus this vertex of knowledge tuple is made up of (θ^*,θ). (θ^*,θ). Next, 'θ' leads to its material induction of the socioeconomic variables. The knowledge-induced socioeconomic vector is denoted by $\{\mathbf{x}(\theta)\}$, with $\{\theta\}$ being derived from θ^*, which in the first instance is derived from (Ω,S). The tuple (θ^*,θ) is derived discursively and by devotional attributes, as in the case of the (Humility, Faith)-box.

The fourth vertex shows the recalling of the epistemic origin (Ω,S) in terms of the relational evaluation of the system of organically unified circular causation relations in terms of $\{\theta,x(\theta)\}$ arising from the simulation of the wellbeing function. Knowledge formation of both the moral law and the knowledge of specific problems under the universal criterion of acceptability are discoursed in the light of the unified nature of inductive reasoning and deductive reasoning integrated together through rounds of recalling (Ω,S) for regeneration of new learning processes. The three parts of the methodological worldview namely, interaction (discourse), integration (epistemic unity attained by discursive consensus), and evolution (IIE) caused by post-evaluation of wellbeing by deductive-induction functioning of epistemic unity in all issues and problems, are established by the rectangular depiction. It can be disaggregated into its subtleties in reference to the stakeholders and shareholders model of asset-valuation. We take this up in the next section.

A CRITIQUE OF SHAREHOLDER MODEL OF ASSET-VALUATION BY THE EPISTEME OF UNITY OF KNOWLEDGE IN FIGURE 1

The (Z,P,M)-model of Islamic Bank Muamalat is a distinctively shareholder model, not even a stakeholder model that could call in community representation in decision- making, and which could then relate the bank with the community by an extension of the participatory dynamics. (Z,P,M)-model is thereby a way of making unilateral decisions that regulate the whole banking institution in the light of shareholders' interest. The shareholder model is thus upheld as the sole legitimate financial arrangement under the *shari'ah* postulate of safeguarding property rights.

The adoption of the shareholders model as opposed to a community-wide participatory stakeholder model causes a breakdown in the circulation of $\{\theta\}$ across continuums of the (Z,P,M)-systems. Also the continuity property of the knowledge-domain is abandoned. Here a substantive difference arises between the (Z,P,M)-system and the (Ω,S)-learning system. (Z,P,M)-model, exemplified here by the shareholders model emulating only the property-rights feature of the *shari'ah*, relents to rationalistic origin of *fiqh* (interpretation).

The (Ω,S)-model instead, calls for continuous revisiting the *Qur'an* and the *Sunnah* in the framework of ever-new discourse, as in the case of *ijtihad*, *tasbih* and *shura*. The central function of *shura* is to inductively evaluate and deductively (normatively) reconstruct the simulacra of possibilities according to the episteme of unity of knowledge and the knowledge-induced unified world-system. This is accomplished by the learning processes in the socio-scientific order. A particular example of the learning process of epistemic unity of knowledge is the phenomenon of institution-market interrelations. The extension of such learning processes in the embedded totality is the study of events in the dimensions of knowledge, time, and space.

RETURNING TO THE UNIVERSALITY OF THE MONOTHEISTIC LAW AS FUNCTIONAL ONTOLOGY

The strictly epistemic origin of (Ω,S)-worldview in unity of knowledge makes this moral law and its derived ethical worldview universally acceptable. The principle of universality that was established earlier is proved analytically by conceptualization of the self-referencing theorem relating to this topic in regards to uniqueness and its mathematical explanatory power. But universality here also means the principle of institutional practice that can be commonly accepted by most people under the guiding principle of unity of knowledge that instils them. At the conceptual level, the primal epistemic premise is oneness of being and becoming in the light of the moral law of oneness. The search for such a law is done by intellection and discourse, and search and discovery.

The self-referencing result of (Ω,S)-epistemological model leads to the conclusion that no purer truth of oneness of the moral law and its symbiotic relationship with the world-system can be found except in the *Qur'an*. The *Qur'an* accepts no place for rationalist divide, as in Kantian heteronomy. The latter makes the separation between the *a priori* (moral) and the *a posteriori* (world-system) reasoning; between deductive and inductive reasoning; and between *noumenon* and *phenomenon*. Consequently, there is extension of scope of the moral law of epistemic oneness to interconnect events occurring in the dimensions of knowledge, time, and space, such as the *functional* ontological relationship between God and the World-System, between the Hereafter and the World-System, in every detail and subtlety including institutional and market behaviour..

The same is true of the domain of practical application of the moral law, which remains universal. An example is the argument against interest as impediment to wellbeing and resource mobilization. This universal precept has been in the writings of all great economic and social thinkers.[3] For example, the quantity of money exchanged for goods in a free market exchange or induced to attain such a state of exchange by monetary policy, is the function of prices and quantities of goods (transactions) in exchange. Money is thereby a convenience to value prices, but it does not exist in the absence of goods in exchange in the first place. The subtleties of the money-market relations in the good things of life are left out of the (Z,P,M)-model, as they are otherwise addressed in revolutionary freshness in the (Ω,S)-model.

Due to the questionable epistemic origin of (Z,P,M)-model many of the most revolutionary ideas emanating from (Ω,S)-epistemic premise and its socio-scientific implications remain absent in intellectual comprehension and practice. There are several instances of this significant remiss: The extension of the theory of epistemic unity to the revolutionary idea of pervasive complementarities, and thereby to intra-system and inter-systemic participation between entities and agents, are unknown in the other intellection sources of Islamic economics, finance, and social embedding. Consequently, many of the mainstream economic principles have remained unchallenged. They are copied in straightforward way to analyse any and every problem of Islamic economics, finance, and society.

Among these are models of marginal rates of substitution, non-learning behaviour, absence of a theory of endogenous ethics, and thereby of endogenous learning in consumption and production, and of the new knowledge-induced endogenous growth models and cost functions etc. The implications of the terms 'competition', 'scarcity of resources', 'optimization', a constriction to 'time-dynamics' in the absence of the substantive way of endogenous learning fail to be known. Thereby, failure to bring such ideas into practice in the light of organic symbiosis that is otherwise generated by epistemic unity in the world-system, is equally absent. Islamic scholarship has thus failed to set up a challenge and search and discovery of alternatives in both intellection and practice.

Islamic economics and finance have run into errors by using incorrect terminologies by importing them from the mainstream field. Language deficiency and incorrect comprehension have impeded the rise of a revolutionary worldview as in (Ω,S)-model. Thus we find in the (Z,P,M)-model the persistence of terms such as 'militancy (aggressiveness)', 'competition', and 'power'. While the use of such terms may be excused, while the exogenous ethical connotation is retained, the problem remains at the conceptual level.

Networking according to the principle of pervasive complementarities and participation encourages excellence in participation and productivity, efficiency, and rewards so earned, rather than individualism to earn the optimum for self-interest. The latter is a concept of competition and self-interest. New dimensions of understanding such alternative analytical terms are as follows: 'simulation' replaces 'optimization'. Cooperative networking replaces 'competition'. Abundance by way of resource reproduction replaces 'scarcity of resources'. The individual within society replaces 'individualism'. Wherewithal, the idea of participatory discourse replacing institutionalized 'methodological individualism'. The ethical nature of goods, exchange, preferences, and menus in institution-market learning interrelations, replace a differentiated model of the economy (Holton, 1992).

The entire epistemological substance of unity of knowledge and the world-system is not known in the whole of Islamic economics, finance, and society. The problem is emulated by the (Z,P,M)-model. Consequently, the epistemic place of the moral law in universal socio-scientific explanations remains simply a rationalistic pursuit in this model – the sheer shareholding model.

No analytical understanding of the power and application of themes of symbiotic organic unity of systems have entered in a theory of being and becoming of the Islamic genre. The entire philosophy of science and its induction in the paired universe of organic unity by the moral law is not known, except in the framework of (Ω,S). The Hereafter is studied as the *Great Event* in the process-model of evolutionary learning of the symbiotic world-system driven continuously and across continuums by the episteme of $\{\theta\} \in (\Omega,S)$. Much is thus lost in the absence of the (Ω,S)-worldview as the monotheistic meta-epistemology of total reality.

THE EMERGENCE OF THE IIE-LEARNING WORLDVIEW FROM THE QUR'AN AND THE SUNNAH

Some of the verses of the *Qur'an* can be noted here in respect of the fundamental *Qur'anic* combined with the *sunnah* origin of the IIE-learning process methodology of epistemic unity:

Behold! In the creation of the heavens and the earth, and the alternation of Night and Day—there are indeed Signs for men of understanding. (Qur'an 3:190)

These verses establish the fundamental place of reason induced by the episteme of conscious oneness to recognize truth and the moral entirety along with the experienced domain. *Qur'anic* consciousness of the universe, is at the centre of experience and history.

O you who believe! Obey God, and obey the Apostle, and those charged with authority among you. If you differ in anything among yourselves, refer it to God and His Apostle, if you believe in God and the Last Day: That is best for you, and most suitable for final determination. (Qur'an 4: 59)

These verses point out the way to certainty in knowledge and its acquisition in relation to the socio-scientific world-system. The discursive function of agency in such derivation of knowledge is grounded in (Ω,S)-model.

And thus have We, by our command, sent inspiration to you: you knew not (before) what was Revelation, and what was Faith; but we have made the (Qur'an) a Light, wherewith we guide suchof our servants as we will; and verily you do guide (men) to the Straight Way (Qur'an 42:52)

The Way of God to Whom belongs whatever is in the heavens and whatever is on earth, behold (how) all affairs tend towards Allah! (Qur'an 42:53)

These verses bring together the immutable premises of universality of knowledge and truth: The moral foundation of oneness (Ω) is mapped onto the world-system to form knowledge via the functional ontology of S. The extension of the moral law over knowledge, time, and space and its unified relational mappings are established by the process rising from the epistemic conscious premise of oneness of the moral law, followed by its impact on the learning world system, and moving in continuity and continuums of systems towards the Hereafter, the Final Event of 'everything'.

Glory be to God, Who created in pairs all things that the earth produces, as well as their own (human) kind and (other) things of which they have no knowledge. (Qur'an, 36:36)

These verses point out the very nature of symbiosis on which the learning universe is premised as ensemble of pairs that exist in the dimensions of knowledge, time, and space.

Oh you people! Eat of what is on earth, lawful and good; and do not follow the footsteps of the Evil One, for he is to you and avowed enemy. (Qur'an 2:168)

Consumption and the concomitant production of the good things of life are put down as principles for individuals and societies to discourse upon for a beneficial determination.

God commands justice, the doing of good, and liberality to kith and kin, and He forbids all shameful deeds, and injustice and rebellion. He instructs you, that you may receive admonition. (Qur'an, 16:90)

The universal principle of respect and decent personal and social behaviour are laid down for the guidance of all of humanity. Such guidance is based on the time-immemorial values that span every society always. Only those who revolt against them are the social recalcitrant, who needs to be guided with admonition.

See they not how God originates creation, then repeats it: truly that is easy for God. (Qur'an 29:19)

The evolutionary essence of learning, observation, and assertion, as in the ensemble of histories of everything is laid down for the socio-scientific understanding of processes of change and transformation. This essence is centred in the moral law.

Such is God, your real Cherisher and Sustainer: Apart from Truth, what (remains) but error? How then are you turned away? (Qur'an 10: 32)

The return to God through the inculcation of the divine law in human historical experience in every respect, is the ineluctable proof of the supreme truth. This marks universality and uniqueness of the moral law of epistemic oneness in 'everything'.

In such ways, the *Qur'an* unravels the truth that is easy and universal to comprehend by all. The philosopher-poet Goethe once remarked, "If this is Islam, are we not all in it?" Truth appears clearly to everyone, although it is comprehended differently according to beliefs and texts. Truth par excellence is thus universal. Truth is clear and disclosed. It denies all that is cluttered in shadowy arguments, unreasonable and dark elements of rationalism.

Such is the nature of *Qur'anic* truth that flies against the meaning given to relative truth as by Nozick (2001, p. 43) in the occidental light, asserting that, "Our theory places truth *within* space-time." Thus truth becomes a relative concept, in which, to be ethical can morally abhor according to Nozick. This problem of relativism of truth occurs in all of occidental reasoning because it is not taken as an integrated connection between *noumena* and *phenomena* in the knowledge, time, and space dimensions. If it is so, as in the *Qur'anic* philosophy of epistemic unity, the moral law (monotheism), then the knowledge tuple (θ^*,θ) as derived from (Ω,S) is primordially determined by the organic complementarities between *a priori* and *a posteriori* reasoning, likewise between deductive and inductive reasoning, and normative and positivistic reasoning. Consequently, relativism is annulled by the pervasively unitary (complementarities) axiom. The relativism exists because of the partitioning of dualistic reasoning upon which Occidentalism rests its fundamental epistemology.

THE OCCIDENTAL INTELLECTUAL PREDICAMENT

Qur'anic intellection marks the extension of worldly relations to the entirety of the knowledge, time, and space dimensions of reality – not merely limited to the space-time structure of physical reality, and to the Darwinian dualism that is imparted into all of occidental socio-scientific reasoning. Such is the pervasiveness of occidental epistemology of the socio-scientific 'everything'.

In the study of money, finance, and real economy, such a dualistic rupture is shown by the separation between these domains due to the existence of interest rates that automatically create a cleavage of competition and diversion of funds from the real sector into the financial sector. The reverse can happen. But not all forms of interest rates are annulled. Speculation and bank-savings in delayed investments abound. A conventional bank cannot be an interest-free bank, and thereby, not an agent of wellbeing in society, as long as its portfolio is dichotomized between the two ends – the financial sector (liquid bank-savings) and the productive sector (real economy). Such a state of banking severes any hope of complementing money and real economy via the route of interest-free, hence trade-oriented mobilization of resources.

The socio-scientific dualism found in money-finance-real economy relationship is equally found to exist in the physical sciences. This would prove the pervasiveness of the principle of dualism and differentiation in all of occidental epistemology.

Examples are of the postulate of Darwinism pervading all the academic disciplines, as recognized by Popper (1978) in his theory of emergence of mind. Other examples are dualism between deductive and inductive reasoning; micro and macro worlds in space-time that are framed in contesting theories, and consciousness that is based on materiality by negating immateriality i.e. essence. This is particularly the case, on the one hand, with the Newtonian worldview that relies on the optimal universe and its physical events; and Relativity physics that too holds up an optimal World Line of space-time curvature. On the other hand, Quantum physics is non-optimal science. Hawking & Mlodonow (2010, p. 82) writes in this regard: "Quantum physics tells us that no matter how thorough our observation of the present, the (unobserved) past, like the future, is indefinite and exists only as a spectrum of possibilities. The universe, according to quantum physics, has no single past, or history."

THE ISLAMIC INTELLECTUAL PREDICAMENT

While such dichotomous developments are deeply rooted in the emergence and continuity of western mind, the same kind of intellectual leanings are to be found in the study of Islamic economics, finance, and society today. That is because the advent of the field of Islamic economics and finance has been intellectualized and practiced upon mainstream thoughts carried through by no fresh demand on the epistemological foundations of truly Islamic origin. The starting point of concept and practice has been traditional *fiqh* (clergy interpretation), and thereby rationalized *shari'ah* in the clergy for which the investigative doors never opened beyond certain traditional thought. New ideas were never visited by the great institution of consultation and discourse that the *Qur'an* offers to humanity. This is the exercise of the *shura* with conscious reflection on reality (*tasbih*). Within this a search for an ever-fresh labyrinth of thought, research and discovery called *ijtihad* is launched.

Nowhere among the Islamic social scientists there has been an analytical theory of epistemic oneness that functionally shapes the world-system and its details in the framework of *Qur'anic* symbiosis (pairing), the organically learned universe of unity signified by complementary and participatory entities representing the good things of life for all. The borrowed tradition of Islamic economics, finance, society and science could not shed light on the emergence of the *functional* ontology of epistemic unity of knowledge. Yet the epistemic worldview of unity of knowledge is able to explain the differentiated world of competition and de-learning caused by methodological individualism.

The debility arising from the absence of proper epistemology has continued on in the Muslim fold for a long time now, because the role of the clergy subdued novelty in legitimate discourse (*ijtihad*) by their traditional and sometime defunct ways. It was mentioned earlier in this book about the failure in the field of Islamic economics and finance to evolve standardized *shari'ah* rules of financing, and identifying the permissible from the forbidden or the non-recommendable. A singular work of Yusuf Qaradawi (1999) is a far cry from intellectual substance. The variant Islamic schools of *fiqh* (legal interpretation) have contributed to this intellectual dismay.

On the other side, the modernists have lost the forest for the trees of true *Qur'anic* essence of socio-scientific thought. This fact is glaringly projected in Islamic economics and finance, with its sorry effect upon Islamic banks. See Choudhury (2006) for a critique of developments in Islamic social sciences.

Likewise, there has gone by futile research, cantankerous debates and opposition and intolerant schools of scholars, *sufis* (*tariqas*), and dynasties that indulged in the question of the nature and theology of God. Such wasted time went against the entire spirit of the *Qur'an* that exhorts the believers to study the creation of God, not his essence, nature, and theology (*dhat*) of God.

A good coverage of such a cantankerous plateau of wasted scholarship is given by Guessoum (2009). Yet Guessoum's scholarship descends into a substantive *problematique*. He misses completely on the central role of epistemic oneness in *Qur'anic* science. Thereby, despite being professor of physics and astronomy, he fails to understand and expound the analytical façade of epistemic oneness in the building of a worldview and methodology in science -- in all sciences, not parochially limited to the caption Islamic science, which is a misnomer.

In the same way, Nasr's Gnosticism (1992) finding its place in a depiction of Islamic science has resulted in mere speculation and *sufi* philosophy. It bears no scope of application and sound future in intellection and its application in the world of science and society, the socio-scientific order.

In the end, it becomes suspect whether Islamic history and science are the same as the *Qur'anic* concept of historicism and scientific paradigm. The inferential standpoint of our present work is an example of the widest socio-scientific generality in *Qur'anic* intellection as being different from Islamic intellection by the lineage of scholars, jurisprudential schools, political oppressors, and divisive communities. This difference is important to note in its generality so as to assess the role that Islamic scholarship plays within the intellection and application of Islamic economics, finance, and society.

The *Qur'anic* philosophy of history is yet another example to contend with. We identify this discipline as the field of historicism or historiography as epistemologically premised in unity of knowledge and its ontological formalism in explanatory and applied models of emergent complex symbiotic nature. Thereby, the evidential proof of epistemic unity of being and the unifying interrelation of all things, re-establishes the same truth of epistemic unity arising from the evidential premises.

This is the idea of consciously understanding the Signs of God in the order and scheme of things.

In various ways the circularity between cause and effect, between action and response among entities, interrelate in reproducing the continuing evidences of epistemic unity in everything. From the passage of such knowledge-centred discourses and evidences, simulations and inferences, arise the analytical meaning of participation and complementarities as the inexorable affirmation of epistemic unity. This kind of dynamics of knowledge and the world-system is in the heart of reality. Thus *Qur'anic* methodology is a further projection into the field of philosophy of history. It awaits explanation in terms of epistemic unity in the field of historical principle of transformation and narration.[4]

Islamic Historicism as Another Case for Critical Study

The *Qur'an* presents history as a body of events that always unravels conflict between truth and falsehood in the process of generating the knowledge and inferences on how to conduct life in its ever-changing perspectives, while keeping it steered to the learning path of epistemic unity as the permanent fact. This is the meaning of *Qur'anic* historicism as its philosophy of history. It is divided into a part that explains the cause of change in everything on the basis of the incessant production of knowledge-flows emerging from the epistemic core. This is the (Ω,S)-worldview. Historicism marks the re-originating conscious process emulating the explanation of the (Ω,S)-worldview.

Also according to the same *Qur'anic* praxis, the system based on falsehood can also be studied. Falsehood forms the opposite category to truth within the completeness of reality. The formalism of the IIE-process methodology in the extended framework of *Qur'anic* historicism provides the structure of processual interrelationships explained by the circular causation and continuity model of unified reality.

Confirmation of unity through the complex system of relations among knowledge-induced entities re-affirms the worldview of epistemic unity in the order of things. A simulation methodology emerges. This methodology carries the process of systemic interrelationships to their higher levels of conscious comprehension. Re-originated learning and inferential processes emanating from one level to circularly recursive higher levels of knowledge form the incessantly creative dynamics of the *Qur'anic* historical process. It also denotes the knowledge-centred praxis of *Qur'anic* world-systems.

Islamic depiction of scholarship is a positivistic enumeration as narrative of the facts of history among Muslims. Much of this span of Islamic history, except for the contributions of the great *mujtahids* (the learned exponents of the age of Islamic scholasticism), has been a narrative one. Thereby, no fresh normative and deductive worldview emerged in the light of the *Qur'anic* core of epistemic oneness to explain the order and scheme of things.

WHAT IS THE PLACE OF GOD IN THE GENERALIZED MODEL OF THE WORLD-SYSTEM?

The Resource Allocation Predicament

The history of Islamic economics and finance, the only one in this discipline that is capable of bringing God into the banking system, has been a dismal confusion. For example, there is no intellectual theory that would fire the field of a truly Islamic idea of money and its productive relationship in respect of the good things of life. It was mentioned that Islamic economics and finance have nothing challenging to contribute in the light of the truly *Qur'anic* worldview, except to offer product development claimed to be *shari'ah*-compliant. Yet this may not be serving the greater goals and objective of wellbeing (*maslaha*) as enunciated by *maqasid as-shari'ah*. As a result, an overly shareholders model is pursued instead of stakeholders model that would otherwise aim at the wellbeing of the conscious world nation of Islam, the *ummah*, wherein development, money, monetary system and policy, and institutional objectives and public policies will assume their distinctive endogenous interrelationship.

Examples here would be the emergence of Islamic common market, monetary union, monetary policy and regulations with gold standards. Some efforts in the direction of monetary transformation with the gold standard are presently being promoted via the medium of the gold *dinar*. The emergence of Islamic capital markets with the monetary multipliers has proved to be a venture in global capitalism. None of these goals are in the mind and matter of Islamic banking and its underlying intellection in Islamic economics and finance or in the drawing boards of Muslim nations.

As it stands today, no Islamic bank is found to statistically declare through databanks its charitable spending by way of mandatory Islamic wealth tax payment called *zakat* and other forms of spending for poverty alleviation. Yet all Islamic banks declare high returns on equity and financial efficiency ratios (Choudhury, 2011b). This state of calculative culture among scholars presents a contrasting view of efficiency on the one hand. On the other hand, the impact of Islamic finance on poverty alleviation remains authentically undeclared, and is unknown.

The neoclassical postulate of marginal rate of substitution in its welfare function comprising competing sides of economic efficiency and distributive equity is reflected in the calculative culture of crass empiricism. In other words, Islamic banks by being so undisclosed in their charitable spending, remain neoclassical institutions. They promote maximization of shareholders' wealth, and exclude stakeholding via a greater scope of social participation. Some central banks of Muslim countries have departments of the *shari'ah* to guide and regulate Islamic bank performance (Bank Indonesia, 2002). Yet the absence of a clear direction of ethical funds in poverty alleviation shows that central bank policies pursue no such active poverty alleviation policy.

Monetary policy is adhered to as macroeconomic pursuit. Yet what otherwise ought to be the case, is the development of micro-level monetary policies of Islamic banks for poverty alleviation. Islamic banks are disabled to contribute in this direction in the absence of any proactive government, public and social policy framework for investigating the micro-foundation of complementary macroeconomic monetary and fiscal policies in Islamic perspectives.

In the end, it matters little how much profits and funds the Islamic banks in total mobilize and earn for shareholders' benefits in capital markets. For example a cursory examination of the Zakat Fund of the Organization of Islamic Conferences brings out the following picture: Recently, the Organization of Islamic Conferences (OIC) handed over its *Zakat* Fund of $3billion to be managed by BMB Fund under the aegis of the Rayo Withanage asset-management theory and approach based on an express efficiency criterion of business and management. Yet if we compare this *Zakat* Fund to the total Islamic fund of $700 billion that circulates in the capital market today, the *zakat* percentage is a mere 0.04 percent, much below the 2.5 percentage required for *zakat* disbursement to the poor and needy by enterprises and otherwise. This ratio if not substantially improved will dip to zero percentage with the expected growth of Islamic capital market funds to reach $4trillion in the next five years.

UNDERSTANDING ISLAMIC BANKING IN THE GENERALIZED THEORY OF EPISTEMIC UNITY

The generalized theory of epistemic unity is a systemic and cybernetic participatory and complementary model. In it Islamic banking ought to share with what goes on in the socio-scientific world of intellection. The question to investigate in this light is the delineation of interrelationships – say for one, between Islamic banking functions and the scientific function of the learning dynamics in the midst of epistemic unity of knowledge. Such an example can be the model of epistemic unity formalizing the money-finance-real economy interrelationship. But since we have already mentioned this case earlier and will return to it later, we turn to another example that for once will be construed as distantly related, but that is not so.

We consider a bifurcation model of social being and becoming expounded by Sztompka (1991) and Prigogine (1980). This is a dynamic causality model of evolutionary learning in which every node of change is a simulated point attained by circular causation relations. These drive the system of variables across simulacra of possibilities.[5] Every node is generated by circular causation relations between critical variables, whose interrelations need to be known by a mix of policy-theoretic quantitative and analytical means to develop the simulation possibilities out of the prevailing imperfect situation of complementarities between the good things of life.

Now invoking the circular causation system given earlier in terms of its various selected variables, Islamic banks or a conglomeration of them, such as the Association of Islamic banks ought to be equipped by human resources, database and analytical system comprising such circular causation relations that can be empirically simulated, and inferences obtained. From the results, simulation possibilities can be engineered by institutional and policy alternatives. None such institutional capabilities exist today despite that it has been over seventy-five years now for Islamic economics in the literature and over thirty years for Islamic banks.

Establishing such a shared arrangement requires institutional development, as with the Association of Islamic Banks or the Islamic Development Bank (IDB). The services can be used by the network of Islamic banks internationally and by the Islamic Research and Training Institute (IRTI) in concert with the Statistical, Economic and Social Research and Training Center (SESRTCIC). Yet while the wish to be more proactive in the area of Islamization of the national economies of members countries remains, IDB has not moved in this direction in organic participatory cooperation with her sister organizations and the commercial Islamic banks. The need remains in the light of the comprehensive objectives of *maqasid as-shari'ah* that integrates God with the mundane and analytical vision as the worldly mission of epistemic unity of knowledge.

Networking among Islamic banks remains weak, whereas this ought to be a key attribute of participatory development and wellbeing in a self-actualizing social system. Networking is an attribute of participation not only between Islamic banks, but also between Islamic and conventional banks. This can proceed in areas where they can objectively cooperate for the overall mission of socioeconomic development with moral values and ethically embedded efficiency parameters. Among the central ones of such values are poverty alleviation and human resource development. These are addressed in complementary ways side by side with efficiency, profitability and growth as goals. Inter-bank networking also increases the capital base, which then can be used to finance small and large projects and enterprises. Without networking there cannot be effective risk and production diversification. These results otherwise are central for the sustainability and growth of Islamic banks in the comprehensive socioeconomic directions interrelating money, finance, and the real economy.

Annual Reports of Islamic banks and the IDB do not publish inter-bank networking project and financing data as part of the equity-participation and co-financing information, important as such information are for evaluation and enhancing development of Islamic banks in the social economy. The principle of participatory cooperation has not dawned on Islamic banks even as the scientific analytics, promotion and dissemination of ideas towards networking, remain subdued.

In the end, it is difficult to understand how Islamic banking can attain its moral responsibility—the corporate social consciousness and responsibility (CSCR)—by addressing in organically unified ways the multitude problems of socioeconomic development. The weakness arises due to the absence of epistemic oneness of the moral law premised on (Ω,S,θ^*) mentioned earlier as the primal intellectual worldview. Instead, the intermediate positioning of the *shari'ah*, as issues regarding shareholders' interest on wealth maximization and the *fiqi* implications have together characterized the pursuit of Islamic banking, economic, finance, and social issues.

In the bifurcation model of evolutionary learning dynamics, it is quite possible for learning nodes to be differentiating between each other. When this happens, the nodes of the learning tree break down. The property of continuity, and thus sustainability of the interactive systems weakens. At the end, a wishful Islamic bank model degenerates into a conventional model with the traditional beliefs on the postulates of profit-maximization, resource scarcity, competition and self-interest economic, financial and social goals. Such is the impression one gets from the assessment of Islamic banks to date. They are found to fast join the capitalist globalization race (*Business Islamica*, March 2008, "Gulf mega-sukuk issues a rich man's club", *Islamic Finance Forum* 13-17 April 2008, pp. 18-19).

CONCLUSION

A great gap between theory and practice, ideals and reality of Islamic economics, finance, and banking remain at large. These problems leave the Islamic banking only marginally different in their ideals from the conventional finance and banking system. Profit-making; the shareholding model of valuation of investments and assets; and competing optimization behaviour; a shallow detached understanding of the goals of the monotheistic law at work through the economic, financial, and social world-system in the light of the episteme of unity of knowledge, remain empty of notice. Instead, globalization, survival, and profit-maximization objectives hold their sway. The result is oblivion of the moral-social objective of wellbeing through Islamic banking system. Islamic banking is therefore for the rich and wealthy shareholders and scantily for the spillover benefits for the poor who form the stakeholders groups in the Muslim world.

A close example of practical orientation of the monotheistic law nonetheless exists in the case Bank Muamalat of Indonesia. But other major Islamic banks have their slacks in development. A major drawback that denies the episteme of unity of knowledge to play its role in the construction of the unified world-system is that of failure of institutional networking.

Yet this relationship between God, money, and society is a permanent topic of belief and quest in the Judea-Christian tradition as well (Kirkpatrick). For example, on the trusteeship of the earth and wealth in it by man the Psalm 24:1 declares: "The earth is the LORD's, and all its fullness . . ." God is the creator and owner of everything. All our wealth ultimately comes from the ground (the earth), and the earth belongs to God. This is a universal and unique message of monotheism with its distinct methodological way of explaining reality.

REFERENCES

Al-Qaradawi, Y. (1999). *The lawful and prohibited in Islam*. Indianapolis, IN: American Trust Publications.

Amin, R. (2004). *The celestial management*. Jakarta, Indonesia: Bening Publishing.

Ansari, M., & Choudhury, M. A. (1991). The idea of sustainable development in Islam. *The Journal of Development Studies*, *9*, 1–21.

Bank Indonesia. (2002). *The blueprint of Islamic banking development in Indonesia*. Jakarta, Indonesia: Bank Indonesia.

Bank Muamalat. (2009). *Reinforcing our business foundation*. Jakarta, Indonesia: Bank Muamalat.

Buchanan, J. M. (1999). The domain of constitutional economics. In *The Logical Foundations of Constitutional Liberty*. Indianapolis, IN: Liberty Fund.

Business Islamica. (2008,). Gulf mega-sukuk issues a rich man's club. *Islamic Finance Forum.*

Carnap, R. (1966). Kant's synthetic a priori. In Gardner, M. (Ed.), *Philosophical Foundations of Physics*. New York: Basic Books, Inc..

Choudhury, M. A. (2006). Development of Islamic economic and social thought. In Kabir Hassan, M., & Lewis, M. (Eds.), *Handbook of Islamic Banking*. London, UK: Edward Elgar Publishing Company.

Choudhury, M.A. (2011a). The dynamics of the Shari'ah and the world-system. *King Abdulaziz University Journal: Islamic Economics, 23*(2).

Choudhury, M. A. (2011b). *Islamic economics and finance: An epistemological inquiry*. Bingley, UK: Emerald.

Fisher, I. (1911). *The purchasing power of money*. New York: Macmillan.

Fitzpatrick, T. (2003). Postmodernism and new directions. In Alcock, P., Erskine, A., & May, M. (Eds.), *Social Policy* (pp. 125–133). Oxford, UK: Blackwell.

Foucault, M. (1983). *Beyond structuralism and hermeneutics, the archeology of the human sciences* (Dreyfus, H. L., & Rabinow, P., Trans.). Chicago, IL: University of Chicago Press.

Guessoum, N. (2011). *Islam's quantum question*. London, UK: I.B. Tauris.

Hawking, S. W., & Mlodinow, L. (2010). *The grand design*. London, UK: Transworld Publishers.

Hayek, F., & Kresge, S. (1999). Intertemporal price equilibrium and movements in the value of money. In *Good Money Part I, the New World*. Chicago, IL: The University of Chicago Press.

Henderson, J. M., & Quandt, R. E. (1971). *Microeconomic theory*. New York: McGraw-Hill.

Holton, R. L. (1992). *Economy and society*. London, UK: Routledge.

Inglott, P. S. (1990). The rights of future generations: some socio-philosophical considerations. In Busuttil, S., Agius, E., Inglott, P. S., & Macelli, T. (Eds.), *Our Responsibilities Towards Future Generations* (pp. 17–27). Malta: Foundation for International Studies & UNESCO.

Keynes, J. M. (1963). Economic possibilities for our grandchildren. In *John Maynard Keynes Essays in Persuasion* (pp. 358–373). New York: W.W. Norton.

Kirkpayrick, T. (2012, September 23). God, money, and you. *Good News: A Magazine of Understanding*. Retrieved from http://www.ucg.org/marriage-and-family/god-money-and-you/

Ledger, C., & Pickard, S. (Eds.). (2004). *Creation and complexity: Interdisciplinary issues in science and religion*. Adelaide, Australia: ATF Press.

Nasr, S. H. (1992). The Gnostic tradition. In *Science and Civilization in Islam*. New York, NY: Barnes & Noble.

Nozick, R. (2001). *Invariances: The structure of the objective world.* Cambridge, MA: The Belknap Press of the Harvard University Press.

Popper, K. (1978). Natural selection and the emergence of mind. *Dialectica, 22*(3), 339–355. doi:10.1111/j.1746-8361.1978.tb01321.x.

Prigogine, I. (1980). *From being to becoming*. San Francisco, CA: W.H. Freeman.

South Commission. (1990). *The challenge to the south.* Oxford, UK: Oxford University Press.

Sztompka, P. (1991). *Society in action: The theory of social becoming*. Chicago, IL: The University of Chicago Press.

Usmani, M. T. (2004). *An introduction to Islamic finance*. Karachi, Pakistan: Maktaba Ma'Ariful Qur'an.

ENDNOTES

1 The *Qur'an* refers to community of other like the human communities, thus being bestowed by the ends of wellbeing between humankind and all others in a seamless interaction across knowledge, time, and space dimensions.

2 The learning curve with endogenous knowledge (θ) induced in it is written as, $L(\theta) = A + B.N(\theta)^{-\gamma} + f(\theta)$; where L denotes labour input in production; N denotes cumulative output; A, B, γ are coefficients with γ denoting the speed of learning, these coefficients being non-negative. $f(\theta)$ is the learning function of knowledge input θ in the whole learning curve.
Firstly, by assuming that the coefficients are independent of θ we obtain, $dL/d\theta = f'(\theta) - B.\gamma.N^{-(1+\gamma)}.(dN/d\theta) > 0$, because of learning induction in the complementary factor input with its other inputs (such as capital).
We further write the above expression as, $f'(\theta) = dL/d\theta + B.\gamma.N^{-(1+\gamma)}.(dN/d\theta) > 0$ identically. Hence, $L(\theta)$, and likewise $K(\theta)$ (capital input), as complementary inputs under θ-induction, both increase along with N increasing. This result is contrary to that of the learning curve in which L and K remain substitutes. L per unit of output decreases (likewise K per unit of output decreases) because there is a continuous burst in productivity. But since θ-induction is continuously in operation; therefore, the average productivity curve perpetually shifts upwards. Along with such a shift the total productivity curve shifts upwards,

but not in an optimal fashion, rather by way of simulation caused by θ-induction of the variables. The marginal productivity curve remains undefined. The total productivity and average productivity curves are the results of simulation in θ-induction of variables. Consequently, these form perturbation paths in (L,K,N)[θ] along with their relations, such as production menu and wellbeing functions.

The role of θ in generating such changes is due to institutional changes in conjunction with markets and technology, all being influenced by endogenous preferences carrying the force of learning.

3 Keynes wrote (1963, p. 369):

"The love of money as a possession—as distinguished from the love of money as a means to the enjoyments and realities of life—will be recognized for what it is, a somewhat disgusting morbidity, one of those semi-criminal, semi-pathological propensities which one hands over with a shudder to the specialists in mental disease."

Hayek (1999) argued in favor of private market for money in his idea on the future value of money, just like the free exchange markets of goods. In the Islamic case of money-real economy linkage by virtue of the principle of epistemic unity, free market of money will set its value in terms of the prices of goods in exchange. Thus money will have no intrinsic value of its own. The true money value will be reflected in the relative prices of exchangeables.

In Walrasian general equilibrium system (Henderson and Quandt, 1971) with money (m) treated as commodity, money and goods in exchange as having constant marginal substitution rate denoted by λ_x for good x, will yield, $p_{m,x} = \lambda_x . p_x$, where p_x denotes price of a good x. The total price of money would then equal $P_{m,x} = (\Sigma_x \lambda_x . p_x)/\Sigma_x \lambda_x$. Once again value of money denotes the prices of exchangeables. Such prices are primal. Upon them money seeks its true value. The quantity theory of money in its form of the classical equation of exchange (Fisher, 1911) is a clear manifestation of the same argument: Money has no intrinsic value of its own. Its value is determined by the prices of exchangeables in the first place.

4 *Qur'an* (29:20): "Say: 'Travel through the earth and see how God did originate creation; so will God produce a later creation: For God has power over all things.' "

5 Fitzpatrick (2003, p. 128) writes: "Ours, then, is an age of simulations that endlessly refer only to other simulations. The infinite circularity of these self-references is what Braudrillard calls the *simulacra*: everything is a reproduction of other reproductions. Society explodes in on itself and we cannot liberate ourselves from the *simulacra*...."

Likewise Immanuel Kant wrote I. Kant (*Critique of Judgment* quoted in Ledger & Pickard op cit, p. 8): "Parts bind themselves mutually into the unity of a whole in such a way that they are mutually cause and effect of one another."

Chapter 6
Corporate Social Consciousness and Responsibility with an Ethico-Economic Idea of Productivity and Efficiency

ABSTRACT

The concept of Corporate Social Consciousness and Responsibility (CSCR) is introduced in the model of measurement of its effect as moral and ethical value on production. Thus, a financial production function as well as a real-value production function is endogenously induced by the learning parameters of the phenomenology of unity of knowledge. This is shown to yield a new concept of complementarities between ethically induced economic efficiency. Empirical directions are prescribed.

BACKGROUND

Corporate Social Consciousness and Responsibility (CSCR) is about ethical behavior in the governance and decision-making of a firm. The firm's principal decision-making items in its choice of technology and factor inputs to produce goods and services are based on physical units of such factors. But beyond this limited view of production menu the modern firm is concerned with ethical issues that enhance the learning prospects of the firm as an organization, and also brings about economies

DOI: 10.4018/978-1-4666-4643-8.ch006

Copyright ©2014, IGI Global. Copying or distributing in print or electronic forms without written permission of IGI Global is prohibited.

of scale and economies of scope in the production of goods and services. Thus the modern firm is not a competitor; rather it is a cooperator with other firms, locked in a network of interactive and integrative choices in an evolutionary learning environment of production, productivity, and efficiency. Such attributes of the modern firm comprise not an exogenous enforcement of social responsibility. The enforcement comes about by endogenous actions and response, whose roots are in ethical consciousness. Thus we use the term Corporate Social Consciousness and Responsibility (CSCR) in the study of a firm's production function ad its financing.

OBJECTIVE

The objective of this chapter is to examine the ethical roots of firm's behavior and its measurement in respect of CSCR with ethical induction of critical variables. A quantitative model of circular causation between the variables is established to explain pervasive inter-variable complementarities. The principle of pervasive complementarities presents the sure sign of unity of knowledge between the good things of life in an organic learning system. Thereby, socioeconomic sustainability is established through such a learning system. A firm's ethically induced indicators of productivity and efficiency are therefore unreadable in a theory of economics and finance that fails to endogenize ethics in the production menu.

This chapter will develop an ethically induced perspective of production function. Such a production function is then used to develop and quantify the ethically induced productivity and efficiency measures. A quantitative model of unity of knowledge signified by the circular causation between participatory variables, as in the case of a socioeconomic organic learning system, is established and empirically evaluated with analytical conclusion.

REVIEW OF THE LITERATURE

The above-mentioned points have been well exhibited by the Japanese firms (Kobayashi, 1988), which emphasize the team-work and coordination in Japanese business and corporation. Kim and Mauborgne (2005) wrote their prolific best-seller in this area of cooperative management of production for firms and strategic businesses. Indeed, within the system and cybernetic idea of decision-making in management and organization (see various issues of *Kybernetes, International Journal of Cybernetics, Systems and Management Studies*), with the firm being an example of the idea of interactive and integrative decision-making in a learning environment, ethical issues of business and production management have taken center-stage for some time now (Simon, 1957, 1960; Johannessen, 2006; Xuemou & Dinge, 1999).

The methodology of productivity and efficiency analysis introduced below is different from the ones done for Data Enveloping Analysis (DEA) and Stochastic Frontier Analysis (SFA) (Majid, Saal, Battisti, et al., 2009). These other methods do not question the neoclassical paradigm and methodology in measuring production, productivity, and efficiency. Hence, the production function and production possibility surface characterized by marginal rate of substitution and smooth non-learning frontiers, despite the probabilistic methods of SFA, abounds. A gamut of complementary effects and participation generated by continuous endogenous learning is not addressed. The existence of these latter phenomena causes perturbations and non-probabilistic convergences referred to as being fuzzy consequences (Kellert, 1993). They defy sound predictive measurements.

Endogenous learning models of the type introduced here by continuous perturbations and extensive complementarities, form a new genre. However, in the estimation and simulation methods underlying the formulation of the learning models of production, productivity and efficiency presented here, a sophisticated class of probabilistic methods can be tried out as tools of refined analysis (Choudhury, 2011).

MODEL

Production Menus with Corporate Social Responsibility

Corporate Social Consciousness and Responsibility (CSCR) assumes a picture of interactive, integrative, and learnt decision-making by firms through the process of understanding common technological futures. In the gambit of issues that now comprise the soft-technology basket there are the physical environmental issues, social contracts that are mutually suitable to factors of production, and sustainable future of firms that are friendly to physical and human ecology (Hawley, 1986; Goodland, Daly, and El-Serafy, 1992; Martinez-Alier, 1987; Coombs, 1990). CSCR takes up a further deepening meaning when it is extracted out of the ethical decision-making of corporations and is made to link up with the common interests of ecology and the grassroots for poverty alleviation and gaining human capabilities (Walker and Unterhalter, 2010; Ekins, 1992; Daly, 1992). Korten (1995) refers to such an emergent age of business decision-making as 'ecological revolution'.

The business world we have inherited calls for different kinds of strategies in production, organizational decision-making, and delivery of its social image to the consumer, society and development scenario. These dimensions are quite different from those we have learnt and practiced in a bookish way in view of the neoclassical world. Myrdal (1987) calls upon this kind of challenge to neoclassicism in his words (slightly edited): "I have always wondered why the psychologists and philosophers have left the economists alone and undisturbed in their futile exercise (neoclassicism)."

THE NATURE OF SOCIO-SCIENTIFIC ARGUMENTATION

This chapter formalizes the ethically induced concepts of organic learning in production function and measurements of total productivity and efficiency under the impact of CSCR. The meaning and scope of CSCR is substantively premised on organic learning of an extensively and widening participatory form of interrelations. Total productivity and efficiency measures are used here as concepts linked with the aggregate ethical index comprising a gambit of production related variables. The study is a microeconomic one, and it shares views on the themes of economies of scale and economies of scope (Pindyck and Rubinfeld, 2001) by virtue of the attributes of interactive and integrative learning between firms, as is found in endogenous growth theory (Romer, 1986).

We formalize one such model below. From the formulation and measurement of the strategic ethical indexes of productivity and efficiency that emanate from the model a due set of corporate and developmental implications for guidance of national policies can be derived. This is the case of injecting national development plans and corporate responsibility with the environmental ethical futures.

Methodology

The following symbols are defined:

Q: $\{Q_i\}$ denotes the vector of m-number (i = 1,2,..,m) of 'joint production' outputs in a joint production function.

M: $\{M_j\}$ denotes the vector of n-number (j = 1,2,..,n) of participatory development-financing instruments that generate resource interdependence and inter-firm output and resource (cost) flows in response to the cooperative production and technological organization of the 'joint-production' system.

N: $\{N_k\}$ denotes the vector of s-number (k = 1,2,..,s) of factors of production that together form social contracts on sharing resources in new forms of technological choices in cooperative production menus that are for the common good of productive factors and business and society at large.

θ: $\cup_r \cap_l \{\theta_{rl}\}$, denotes a consensual (interactive) knowledge-variable formed by averaging out a sequence of knowledge-flows corresponding to a system of *integrative* decision-making ($\cap_l$; integrations, l = 1,2,,..L) that are generated by corresponding systems of interactive ($\cup_r$; interactions, r = 1,2,.., R) decision-making premised on partnership and participation. In the ethico-economic learning model of production defined by the gambit of variables, the emergent θ-value governs *all* the variables. Hence, as in the concept of *Gaia* (Primavesi, 2000; Maturana & Varela, 1980) the interactive and integrative learning variables of participatoriness denoted by θ-induction applies to both human and non-human (socioeconomic) domains.

Hence θ generates an extensively endogenous system of causal relations between all the variables. The result is a general-system model of interactive, integrative, and organic learning in the business world of production and organization. Productivity and efficiency are defined according to this kind of a scenario of CSCR in production and business organization.

Further details on the above-mentioned variables are now noted. The variable Q forms a 'joint production' function (Henderson & Quandt, 1971), in which every output is related to the rest of the other outputs. This involves inter-production causality and expected values of prospective productions. The idea of production interrelations here is of the input-output type.

M is characterized by a pool of interest-free variables of project financing (Choudhury, Mufeedhul, 2009), such as profit sharing, equity-participation, shareholding, trade-financing, co-financing, all of which mobilize resources into productive spending. By virtue of their participatoriness to generate capital in real projects, and thereby establish cooperative networking and choices in the production and technological environment, M is treated as a vector of development financing instruments.

N promotes trade in a productive environment. Hence its elements are of interest-free categories. They together form an organically relational cooperative vector as opposed to a competition vector in social contracts between productive factors and diverse projects. For instance, the Blue Ocean (Kim and Mauborgne, 2005) type of cooperative business strategy is argued to lead into co-determination of factor services as opposed to marginal substitution (competition) between them found in Red Ocean strategy.

The continuous burst of learning in the production and business environment ensemble within the greater ecology causes complementary possibilities between N, M, and Q. The role of θ is fundamental in these kinds of endogenous knowledge-induced participatory (complementary) *inter*-relations. They imply organic unity between the interacting variables in view of the circular causation between the variables signifying unity by participative complementarities that are governed by epistemic oneness.

θ-variable thereby induces all the variables. Consequently, we have the set of variables to form the index of productivity, and efficiency measure comprising the CSCR as the ethical bond of learning in the system of endogenous causal interrelations. This vector is denoted by $\{Q(\theta), M(\theta), N(\theta)\}$, written down as $\{Q, M, N\}[\theta]$, or implied so by suppressing θ. The same symbolization holds for the component variables of the respective vectors. Because of the extensively complementary relations between the learning variables, there exist circular causation (circular interrelations) between them.

The end result of the estimation and simulation of the resulting circular causation relations is the ethical index. It is represented by the θ-function in terms of the expected complementary relations between the variables. In the contrary actual case of absence of complementarities, simulation is carried out to turn the non-complementary relations into complementary or progressively complementary ones. This kind of transformation involves policy-making and learned changes in social preferences by a discursive process. Non-complementary relations are shown by the negative coefficient values in terms of marginal rate of substitution between the variables *ceteris paribus*.[1] Thereby, CSCR implications are derived specific to the financial firms and projects that are studied empirically.

Estimation

We suppress the common induction of the variables by θ and write by implication a specific form of the 'joint production function' for the financial sector as:

'Joint financial production function' (not a vector notation):

$$Q = \prod_{i=1}^{m} Q_i^{\alpha i} \tag{1}$$

The empirical version of expression (1) is generated firstly out of the estimated equations and the predictor values of the circular causation variables. The circular causation estimations by Equations 2-4 below signify the *prevalent* state of complementarities or absence of complementarities between the variables in the learning ethical sense of CSCR in business and financial joint production menus.

$$Q_i = Q_i(Q_1, Q_2, .., Q_{i-1}, Q_{i+1}, \ldots, Q_m, M_1, M_2, .., M_n, N_1, N_2, \ldots, N_s) \tag{2}$$

$$M_u = M_u(Q_1, Q_2, .., Q_m, M_1, M_2, .., M_{i-1}, M_{i+1}, \ldots, M_n, N_1, N_2, \ldots, N_s) \tag{3}$$

$$N_v = N_v(Q_1, Q_2, .., Q_m, M_1, M_2, \ldots, M_n, N_1, N_2, \ldots, N_{j-1}, N_{j+1}, \ldots, N_s) \tag{4}$$

$i = 1,2,.., m;\ u = 1,2,..,n;\ v = 1,2,.., r.$

The ethical index $\theta = E(.)$ invokes the intra-firm CSCR issues. The estimated results here are amenable to examination, analysis and interpretation in the estimated form of E(.).

$$\theta = E(Q, M, N) \tag{5}$$

$\{\theta\}$-values are institutionally set by discussion among members of research groups, and are thus assigned ranks given to the column-wise socioeconomic variables in respect of their levels of complementarities. These are then averaged across inter-column $\{\theta\}$-variables so calculated as ranks compared to the columns of socioeconomic variables (Choudhury & Hossain, 2009). A very interesting way of assigning similar-to θ-ranks is done by Anwar et al, (2011) by way of neural systems.

The estimated form of the financial production function is thus obtained by expression (1). From this estimated form, interpretations of the results on joint production function, productive factor use, effectiveness of participatory financing variables are empirically determined. Thereby, the effect of learning (θ-flows) in CSCR, and finally, the productivity and efficiency measures are computed and studied.

Productivity of Financing: Q/M_j; $j = 1,2,..,n$ (6)
Productivity of Factors: Q/N_k; $k = 1,2,..,r$ (7)
Inter-Joint Production Mix: Q_i/Q; $i = 1,2,..,m$ (8)
Production Efficiency: Elasticity $\in_{\theta,\mathbf{x}} = \partial \log\theta/\partial \log\mathbf{x}$, (9)

where, **x** denotes all the variables in expression (5) taken one at a time via circular causation. Induction by ranked $\{\theta\}$-values is implied in the variables.

One notes how the ethical impact by θ-variable has endogenized the various variables. In expressions (6)-(9) for instance, $Q = Q(\theta)$ is the result of incorporating the multivariate results of complementarities generated by the circular causation relations (2)-(4), as shown by the direction of the arrows between these equations. Likewise, the $(\mathbf{Q}_i, \mathbf{M}_j, \mathbf{N}_k)[\theta]$ vector-values are the results of predictors generated from the estimated regression equations.

Simulation

The estimated Equations 1-5 are next simulated (meaning ethically reconstructed) by improving the estimated coefficients by discursive choices in view of establishing better degrees of complementarities between the variables. This is a normative ethical issue and depends upon the degree of feasibility of the complementarities that can possibly be gained, given various short-term constraints in resources and possibilities. The simulated predictor values are thereby generated from the new versions of (1)-(5) in respect of such simulated changes. Expressions (6)-(8) are re-evaluated as simulated productivity and efficiency values.

The arrows as shown between the Equations 1-5 give the direction of the steps of the empirical processes to be taken between these equations. The same relations are repeated for the simulative case. Further statistical and empirical analyses are followed up.

Results

Only the estimated phase of the model empirics is done in this chapter. The estimated result (A5) given in the appendix shows that the specified financial production function suffers from decreasing returns to scale, as $\in_{Q,F} + \in_{Q,D} < 1$.

The productivity indexes for F and D are estimated by Equations (A7) and (A8), respectively. Although F and D are complementary in their movements as signified by the Equations (A9) and (A10), yet their contributions to economies of scale are declining. Along the average cost curves of administering F and D towards the output Q, the implication is that increasing quantities of F and D do not contribute to economies of scale. These are signs of weak financial and ethico-economic performance of the recorded Islamic banks in Indonesia in respect of economies of scale related to D. The ethico-economic implication is shown by way of low complementarities between M and D variables.

The empirically based inference is that Islamic banks in Indonesia remain well advised to initiate structural changes and better portfolio management to become contributors to the productive climate of the economy at large. This calls for simulation of the estimated equations in substantive ways by intra- and inter- institutional discourse and networking between Islamic banks in Indonesia along lines of desired technological change, portfolio selection, and joint ventures vis-à-vis CSCR (i.e. complementary relations). The simulation part of this chapter remains a pending undertaking because of its extensive empirical work.

Figure 1 shows how endogenous changes by participatory learning between financial instruments (F), depositor instrument (D), and by intra-firm discourse signified by $\{\theta\}$-values take place in respect of their contributions to the economic output Q.

In Figure 1 the widening iso-cost surfaces exhibit decreasing returns to scale as indicated by the decreasing productivity and efficiency measures with the growth of output in the estimated Equations (A7) and (A8). The surface of $\{Q,F,D,\theta\}$ made up of OQ-paths is the production surface induced endogenously by θ-values. This surface is a gamut of interconnecting paths (not shown) that jut out of specific paths and interconnect with the other ones. This kind of nexus of organic inter-relationships conveys the system-meaning of circular causation relations between the variables.

CONCLUSION

The above kind of knowledge-induced business strategy and production functions of firms leads to a substantive way of understanding CSCR as complementary learning relations, signifying sustainability in business strategy and production function. A range of pertinent implications can be read off the estimated and simulated forms of the production function, the circular causation relations, and the productivity and efficiency measures. Such results can convey a substantively new picture on developing new CSCR outlooks on business strategy and productivity and efficiency alternatives comprising the CSCR issues of endogenous learning.

A further direction of research in the area of measuring endogenously learning types of production models and their genre of productivity and efficiency measures is by using the stochastic optimal control theory (Kumbhakar & Lovell, 2000). However, the emergent consequences are too elaborate to be reproduced in this chapter. See Choudhury and Korvin (2002) as an example on estimating learning models of firm behavior by optimal control theory. This direction of further research on the theme as of this chapter, using stochastic control theory in non-neoclassical financing and production environment, remains a potential area of research (Choudhury & Korvin, 2002).

Main Points

The concepts of Corporate Social Conscious Responsibility and Corporate Social Responsibility are distinct from each other.

Figure 1. The nature of evolutionary production surfaces induce by θ-learning

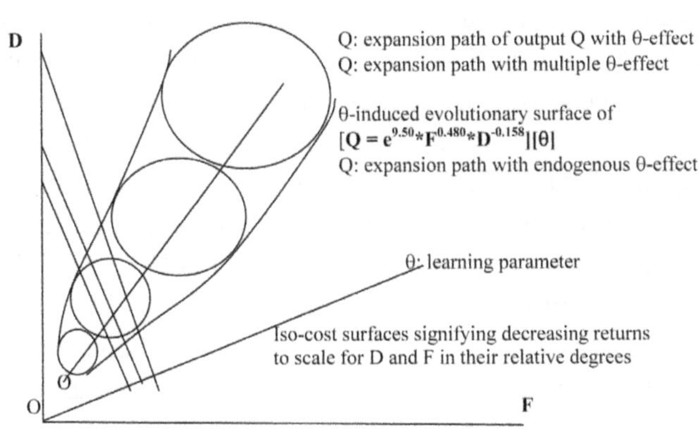

1. **Corporate Social Responsibility:** An institutional arrangement targeted by exogenous policy enforcement to attain certain social goals. Such targets and policies are set at the governmental level under the supervision of international bodies.
2. **Corporate Social Conscious Responsibility:** An endogenous outcome of interactive learning to set targets ans and goals of social corporate behavior. The participants in the derivation of policies, programs, and guidance in CSCR collectively determine these directions out of consciousness, which is formed by knowledge. In this chapter the foundation of such knowledge-induced social conscious realization was premised on the episteme of unity of knowledge.

The theme of corporate social responsibility from the viewpoint of consciousness, as in businessmen who instill such socil consciousness into the realm of business is a theme that found deep roots in Protestant ethics. The works of Howard R. Bowen are lansmarks of such contributions in the area of Corporate Social Consciousness Responsibility. Acquier, Gond and Pasquero (2011, p. 615) write on the contributions of Bowen to the consciousness theory of social corporate responsibility of businessmen: Bowen considered the ideal social in " 'individual self-determination tempered by consideration for social welfare' (Bowen, 1953, p. 27), within a mixed-economy framework. The businessman was thus called on to "recognize the social implications of his decisions and to consider the social interest—so far as is possible and reasonable" (Bowen, 1953, p. 30). Pragmatic considerations, however, were only part of the argument. Bowen also introduced a deontological side to his rationale: Power involves responsibility. "It is becoming increasingly obvious that a freedom of choice and delegation of power such as businessmen exercise would hardly be permitted to continue without assumption of social responsibility" (Bowen, 1953, p. 6). This argument, later theorized as the "iron law of social responsibility" (Davis, 1960), was hereafter to become a key tenet of business ethical thinking."

In the light of his protestant religious background Bowen also talkd of this religious way of understanding social corporate responsibility with human consciousness in it. On the matter Acquier et al (2011, p. 617) further write: "Protestant thinkers, he found, do not unconditionally support capitalism. For example, they explicitly dispute the assumption that quasinatural market laws can regulate human choice; to them, what explains behavior best is the force of *human character*. Their views are also critical of the classical dogma of private property, a central tenet of capitalism, and in response to which they present (two) countervailing principles."

All these points establish the fact that, Social Corporate Consciousness Responsibility is a theme embedded in a universal way among deontological thinkers of the social order and human future by business. A generalized knowledge-inducing model of the type we have discussed in this work applies.

REFERENCES

Acquier, A., Gond, J.-P., & Pasquero, J. (2011). Rediscovering Howard R. Bowen's legacy: The unachieved agenda and continuing relevance of social responsibilities of the businessmen. *Business & Society*, *50*(4), 607–646. doi:10.1177/0007650311419251.

Anwar, S., Romansyah, D., Sigit, P., & Watanabe, K. (2011). Treating return of mudharabah time deposit as investment instrument: a utilization of artificial neural networks (ANNS). *Humanomics: International Journal of Systems and Ethics, 27*(2).

Blaug, M. (1970). *An introduction to the economics of education*. London, UK: Penguin Press.

Bowen, H. R. (1953). *Social responsibilities of the businessman*. New York, NY: Harper.

Choudhury, M. A. (2009). *Money, finance, and the real economy in Islamic banking and finance: perspectives from the maqasid as-shari'ah*. (Unpublished Masters Dissertation). Department of Economics, University of Stirling, Stirling, UK.

Choudhury, M. A. (2011). A probabilistic model of learning fields. *The Journal of Muamalat and Islamic Finance Research*, *7*(1).

Choudhury, M. A., & Hossain, M. Z. (2010). A socio-statistical study of a composite index of human wellbeing. In Priya, A. (Ed.), *Handbook of Human Development and Management*. Serials Publication.

Choudhury, M. A., & Korvin, G. (2002). Simulation versus optimization. *Kybernetes: International Journal of Cybernetics. Systems and Management Studies*, *31*(1), 44–60.

Coombs, H. C. (1990). *The return of scarcity, strategies for an economic future*. Cambridge, UK: Cambridge University Press. doi:10.1017/CBO9780511552281.

Daly, H. (1992). From empty-world to full-world economics: Recognizing an historical turning point in economic development. In Goodland, R., Daly, H., El-Serafy, S., & von Drost, B. (Eds.), *Environmentally Sustainable Economic Development: Building on Brundtland* (pp. 29–41). Malta: Center for Development Studies.

Davis, K. (1960). Can business afford to ignore social responsibilities? *California Management Review*, *2*(3), 70–77. doi:10.2307/41166246.

Ekins, P. (1992). *A new world order, grassroots movements for global change*. London, UK: Routledge.

Goodland, R., Daly, H., El-Serafy, S., & von Drost, B. (Eds.). (1992). *Environmentally sustainable economic development: Building on brundtland*. Malta: Center for Development Studies.

Hawley, A. H. (1986). *Human ecology*. Chicago, IL: The University of Chicago Press.

Henderson, J. M., & Quandt, R. E. (1971). *Microeconomic theory: A mathematical approach*. New York, NY: McGraw-Hill.

Johannessen, J.-A. (2006). Organizations as social systems: The search for a systemic theory of organizational innovation processes. *Kybernetes: International Journal of Systems and Cybernetics*, *27*(4), 359–387. doi:10.1108/03684929810219404.

Kellert, S. H. (1993). *The wake of chaos, unpredictable order in dynamical systems*. Chicago, IL: The University of Chicago Press. doi:10.7208/chicago/9780226429823.001.0001.

Kobayashi, Y. (1988). An economic analysis of Japanese beauracracy. In Choudhury, M. A. (Ed.), *Political Economy of Development in Atlantic Canada* (pp. 25–47). Sydney, Canada: University College of Cape Breton.

Korten, D. C. (1995). The ecological revolution. In *When Corporations Rule the World* (pp. 261–276). London, UK: Earthscan.

Korten, D. C. (1995). Restore money's role as a medium of exchange. In *The Post-Corporate World* (pp. 195–197). San Francisco, CA: Berrett-Koehler Publishers, Inc..

Kumbhakar, S. C., & Lovell, C. A. K. (2000). *Stochastic frontier analysis*. Cambridge, UK: Cambridge University Press. doi:10.1017/CBO9781139174411.

Mariani, A.-M., Saal, D. S., & Battisti, G. (2009). The impact of Islamic banking on the cost efficiency and productivity change of Malaysian commercial banks. *Applied Economics*.

Martinez-Alier, J. (1987). Methodological individualism and inter-generational allocation. In *Ecological Economics, Energy, Environment and Society*. Oxford, UK: Basil Blackwell.

Maturana, H. R., & Varela, F. J. (1980). *Autopoiesis and cognition: The realization of the living*. Dordrecht, The Netherlands: Reider. doi:10.1007/978-94-009-8947-4.

Myrdal, G. (1987). Utilitarianism and modern economics. In Feiwel, G. (Ed.), *Arrow and the Foundations of the Theory of Economic Policy*. London, UK: Macmillan.

Pindyck, R. S., & Rubinfeld, D. L. (2001). *Microeconomics* (5th ed.). Upper Saddle River, NJ: Prentice-Hall.

Primavesi, A. (2000). *Sacred gaia*. London, UK: Routledge. doi:10.4324/9780203451786.

Romer, P. M. (1986). Increasing returns and long-run growth. *The Journal of Political Economy, 94*, 1002–1037. doi:10.1086/261420.

Saif & Dadang. (2011). Treating return of mudharabah time deposit as investment instrument: A utilization of artificial neural networks (ANNS). *Humanomics: International Journal of Systems and Ethics, 27*(2).

Simon, H. (1957). *Models of man*. New York, NY: John Wiley & Sons.

Simon, H. A. (1960). Decision making and organizational design. In Pugh, D. S. (Ed.), *Organization Theory* (pp. 202–223). Hammondsworth, UK: Penguin Books.

Walker, M., & Unterhalter, E. (2010). The capability approach: Its potential for work in education. In Walker, M., & Unterhalter, E. (Eds.), *Amartya Sen's Capability Approach and Social Justice in Education*. London, UK: Palgrave Macmillan.

Xuemoue, W., & Dinghe, G. (1999). Pansystemic cybernetics: Framework, methodology and development. *Kybernetes: International Journal of Cybernetics. Systems and Management Studies, 28*(6/7), 679–694.

ENDNOTES

1 $\partial \ln x_i / \partial \ln x_j = (x_j/x_i)*(\partial x_i/\partial x_j) = -\alpha$, as an estimated coefficients of x_j in a log-linear relationship involving x_i and x_j, with $\alpha > 0$, means that $\partial x_i/\partial x_j < 0$. Hence, x_i and x_j are partial marginal substitutes of each other.

APPENDIX: A SIMPLE CASE OF ESTIMATION AND SIMULATION USING THE FINANCIAL PRODUCTION FUNCTION

Let $Q = f(F,D) = A.F^{a}D^{b}$, (A1)

where Q denotes a concept of output of the financial sector, understanding that the financial sector by virtue of its production of papers and services is not endowed by a well-defined concept of output, that is production function. This is similar to the classical problem of defining a fuzzy educational production function (Blaug, 1970). We will proxy Real Gross Domestic Product (RGDP) by Q.

The coefficients 'a' and 'b' are not constrained by any specific values. But $a + b > 1$ would imply economies of scale in production. $a + b = 1$ will imply constant returns to scale in production. The efficient impact of learning should imply increasing returns to scale. But this is left to the estimation (prevalent state) result to prove. This result can then be improved by simulation (ought-to-be normative state) in the perspective of normative social reconstruction towards gaining complementarities between the variables.

The circular causation relations are,

$$\ln F = \ln a_0 + a_1.\ln Q + a_2.\ln D \quad \text{(A2)}$$

$$\ln D = \ln b_0 + b_1.\ln Q + b_2.\ln F \quad \text{(A3)}$$

$$\ln\theta = \ln c_0 + c_1.\ln Q + c_2.\ln F + c_3.\ln D \quad \text{(A4)}$$

1. Estimation Forms

$$\ln Q = 9.50 + 0.480 \ln F - 0.158 \ln D \quad \text{(A5)}$$

The generic estimated form is,

$$Q = e^{9.50}*F^{0.480}*D^{-0.158} \quad \text{(A6)}$$

The productivity indexes are,

$$(Q/F) = e^{9.50}*F^{-0.52}* D^{-0.158} \quad \text{(A7)}$$

$$(Q/D) = e^{9.50}*F^{0.480}*D^{-1.158} \quad \text{(A8)}$$

$$\ln F = - 12.9 + 1.50 \ln Q + 0.480 \ln D \quad \text{(A9)}$$

$$\ln D = 11.7 - 1.65 \ln Q + 1.60 \ln F \quad (A10)$$

$$\ln\theta = - 5.61 + 0.007 \ln Q + 1.05 \ln F - 0.111 \ln D \quad (A11)$$

The generic estimated form of (6.A11) is,

$$\theta = e^{-5.61} * Q^{0.007} * F^{1.05} * D^{-0.111} \quad (A12)$$

This ethical index (A12) ratifies the results mentioned above in respect of productivity and efficiency of Islamic banks. That is, in respect of Q and F, the contributions are as detailed below. The statistical results are given in Tables 1-11.

2. Statistical Results in Detail

The regression equation is: lnQ = 9.50 + 0.480 lnF - 0.158 lnD

Table 1. Regression Analysis: lnQ versus lnF, lnD

Predictor	Coef	SE Coef	T	P
Constant	9.5042	0.8664	10.97	0.002
lnF	0.4802	0.1728	2.78	0.069
lnD	-0.1583	0.1537	-1.03	0.379

S = 0.0758327 R-Sq = 95.8% R-Sq(adj) = 93.0%

Analysis of Variance

Table 2.

Source	DF	SS	MS	F	P
Regression	2	0.39275	0.19638	34.	15 0.009
Residual Error	3	0.01725	0.00575		
Total	5	0.41000			

Durbin-Watson statistic = 1.49575

The regression equation is: lnF = - 12.9 + 1.50 lnQ + 0.480 lnD

Table 3. Regression Analysis: lnF versus lnQ, lnD

Predictor	Coef	SE Coef	T	P
Constant	-12.856	6.426	-2.00	0.139
lnQ	1.4998	0.5397	2.78	0.069
lnD	0.4804	0.1514	3.17	0.050

S = 0.134015 R-Sq = 98.7% R-Sq(adj) = 97.8% R-Sq(pred) = 91.23%

Analysis of Variance

Table 4.

Source	DF	SS	MS	F	P
Regression	2	4.0659	2.0329	113.19	0.001
Residual Error	3	0.0539	0.0180		
Total	5	4.1198			

Durbin-Watson statistic = 1.53311

The regression equation is: lnD = 11.7 - 1.65 lnQ + 1.60 lnF

Table 5. Regression Analysis: lnD versus lnQ, lnF

Predictor	Coef	SE Coef	T	P
Constant	11.70	16.62	0.70	0.532
lnQ	-1.651	1.602	-1.03	0.379
lnF	1.6037	0.5054	3.17	0.050

S = 0.244852 R-Sq = 96.5% R-Sq(adj) = 94.2% R-Sq(pred) = 79.97%

Analysis of Variance

Table 6.

Source	DF	SS	MS	F	P
Regression	2	5.0299	2.5150	41.95	0.006
Residual Error	3	0.1799	0.0600		
Total	5	5.2098			

Durbin-Watson statistic = 2.04321

The regression equation is: $\ln\theta = - 5.61 + 0.007 \ln Q + 1.05 \ln F - 0.111 \ln D$

Table 7. Regression Analysis: lnθ versus lnQ, lnF, lnD

Predictor	Coef	SE Coef	T	P
Constant	-5.607	8.901	-0.63	0.593
lnQ	0.0067	0.9251	0.01	0.995
lnF	1.0518	0.5235	2.01	0.182
lnD	-0.1105	0.2865	-0.39	0.737

S = 0.121510 R-Sq = 99.2% R-Sq(adj) = 98.0%

Analysis of Variance

Table 8.

Source	DF	SS	MS	F	P
Regression	3	3.5850	1.1950	80.	94 0.012
Residual Error	2	0.0295	0.0148		
Total	5	3.6145			

Durbin-Watson statistic = 2.54637

The regression equation is: $\theta = - 107 + 10.1 \ln Q - 2.94 \ln F + 3.02 \ln D$

Table 9. Regression Analysis: θ versus lnQ, lnF, lnD

Predictor	Coef	SE Coef	T	P
Constant	-107.37	35.15	-3.06	0.093
lnQ	10.143	3.653	2.78	0.109
lnF	-2.936	2.067	-1.42	0.291
lnD	3.015	1.131	2.67	0.117

S = 0.479763 R-Sq = 99.1% R-Sq(adj) = 97.8% R-Sq(pred) = 70.33%

Analysis of Variance

Table 10.

Source	DF	SS	MS	F	P
Regression	3	52.214	17.405	75.62	0.013
Residual Error	2	0.460	0.230		
Total	5		52.675		

Durbin-Watson statistic = 2.60569

Table 11. Equations (A1)-(A4) were estimated using the following data

Years	Q	F	D	θ
	(Millns.USD)	(Millns. USD)	(Millns USD)	
2001	164,520	228	2.007	1.00
2002	194,930	364	3.242	1.97
2003	237,330	614	3.361	2.98
2004	256,680	1,258	12.988	5.51
2005	289,480	1,692	17.309	7.21
2006	369,280	2,271	22.062	9.35
		Generating θ-Values		
Year	**θ1**	**θ2**	**θ3**	**θ=(θ1+θ2+θ3)/3**
2001	1.00	1.00	1.00	1.00
2002	1.30	2.36	2.24	1.97
2003	1.73	4.86	2.36	2.98
2004	1.92	11.30	3.32	5.51
2005	2.25	15.64	3.75	7.21
2006	3.04	20.79	4.23	9.35

The θ-ranks have been computed by distributing the differences between the values given by columns and dividing them each by 100, but this scale of division does not matter. Source: Bank Indonesia, Islamic Banking Directorate

Chapter 7
Productivity Analysis in Ethically Induced Financing Environment:
A Case Study of Indonesian Islamic Banks

ABSTRACT

This chapter carries further the content of Chapter 6 to the measurement of an ethically value-induced index of productivity. A learning-form of the endogenously ethics-induced production function is formulated. This is empirically simulated for the case of Islamic banks in Indonesia that claim to introduce the moral and ethical elements of the Islamic Law in the affairs of finance and banking. Inferences are drawn for instructive purposes in the area of introducing the moral and ethical law in the study of business affairs, which is a significant subsystem of the grand world-system.

BACKGROUND: THE NEOCLASSICAL IMPOSSIBILITY IN MEASURING PRODUCTIVITY AND EFFICIENCY IN SOCIAL FINANCIAL ENVIRONMENT

In common parlance, the term, 'factor productivity' means the ratio of output to specific factor inputs. In the input-output sense, productivity can also be measured by the input-output technical coefficients of production. The technical input-output coefficient a_{ij} is defined by the ratio (technical coefficient) $a_{ij} = x_{ij}/x_j$, meaning the

DOI: 10.4018/978-1-4666-4643-8.ch007

Copyright ©2014, IGI Global. Copying or distributing in print or electronic forms without written permission of IGI Global is prohibited.

intensity with which the output of ith sector (or project, source) is used as input to produce a unit of total output in the jth sector (project, source), i,j = 1,2,..,n.

In the case of an endogenous technologically induced factor input over time, $x_1(t)$ [hence $x_2(t)$], such a time-dynamic factor-productivity is explained by the expression (Solow, 1980, pp. 33-38),

$$Q(t)/x_1(t) = x_1(t)^{\alpha}f(k(t))/x_1(t) = f(k(t)).x_1^{(\alpha-1)},\ k = x_2(t)/x_1(t).$$

$\alpha > 1$ denotes the degree of the homogenous production function, $Q(t) = f(x_1(t),x_2(t))$, which stands for the production function in the factor inputs $x_1(t)$ and $x_2(t)$. $\alpha > 1$ equivalently also denotes the degree of economy of scale of production in the formal production function.

The above form of the neoclassical production function and the underlying input production isoquants necessitate existence of well-defined formal expressions for these cases. Accordingly, the neoclassical economic theory implication is that, there will abide marginal rate of substitution between the production outputs, as between different competing sectors and projects. There will likewise be opportunity costs of substitution between the factor inputs along their production isoquants. The same implication is borne out by the assumption of smoothly defined production possibility curves and isoquants.

Scarcity of productive resources, competition between opposites in outputs and inputs, and the concurrent need for smooth production possibility surfaces define the opportunity costs of substitution between outputs and inputs. The resulting definition of the production function in terms of outputs and inputs are permanently premised on the above axiomatic premises of neoclassical theory of production and cost. The resulting productivity and efficiency analyses are then carried out.

Yet the same axiomatic premises are untenable when participatory financing is studied by its relevant different models of fuzzy joint production functions and social contracts based on complementary relations between the factor inputs and output distribution by productive linkages across sectors, regions, and other socioeconomic environments. The idea underlying complex forms of production relations is that there exist extensive linkages between the production menus, their inputs, other outputs, technology, and sustainable development of the firm's structure and organizational behavior. Such organic interrelations result in extensive fields of circular causation relations, backward and forward. A joint production function and a dynamic form of input-output system of learning relations between complementary interactive possibilities establish a financial-productive social nexus (Choudhury, 2010).

In the neoclassical case, the outputs such as all of the paired types of variables $\{y_i(t)\ y_j(t)\}$, and thereby all of $y_{ij}(t)$'s, i,j = 1,2,..n; likewise all of $\{x_1(t),x_2(t)\}$, exist as marginal substitutes of each other. Hence the production possibility surfaces and the production isoquants so formed remain smoothly convex and concave to the origin, respectively. Such a result is premised on the assumptions of marginal substitution and smooth production surfaces and isoquants mentioned above. They then lead to a production cost line and price relatives that are deterministic or are valued probabilistically to obtain expected values for the production indicators. It is therefore, logical that the relations between outputs and inputs in various sectors and kinds, must remain observable as datum. Consequently, productivity as a computed measure related to such assumedly well-determined production menus and isoquants related to minimum average cost is a deterministic or probabilistically quantifiable economic indicator.

The problem of lack of well-definition of the production functions due to ethical and organizational learning and decision-making factors in the financial firm also means that the underlying institutional relations must be incorporated in the firm's production menu. An example here is the case of Islamic banks. These financial institutions must undertake deliberations over issues of compliance of their financial products with the Islamic Law. Their organizational behavior invokes institutional discourse over legal tenets of the Islamic Law relating to economic, financial, social, and ethical issues.

The result is the emergence of financial matters in Islamic banks that are different from those examined in the neoclassical firm. In the neoclassical case there is no endogenous presence of innovation and ethics to be embedded in the production relations. Ethics, technology, and learning in evolutionary processes, remain exogenous to neoclassical production relations. On the other hand, the presence of ethical factors in new forms of financial production menus that influence organizational behavior of Islamic banks, leads into simulation of the production models beyond just their empirically estimated results. The estimated results reflect just the sheer positivistic observations concerning the use of financial data for Islamic banks. The simulated results yield the normative future, structural change, and social transformation of financial rules of Islamic banks that must comply with the Islamic Law.

REVIEW OF THE LITERATURE

New Outlooks and Strategies on Production in Global Financial Firms

Indeed, many global firms are changing their strategies and production processes on the aftermath of global financial crisis. See for example Kim and Maubourgne's (2005) most popular best-seller entitled *Blue Ocean Strategy*. It argues in favor of the change of strategy away from competition to cooperation, and financial strategic alliances through networking and sustainability concepts in the present-days' world of participatory business environment. The expectation is that such a strategy would reduce costs by providing access to sharing -- in technologies, inputs, markets, and information. Such an approach is particularly helpful to Microenterprises and Small and Medium size Enterprises (MSMEs). MSMEs cannot survive on hard-pressed competition for gaining market shares. They need more caring incubators to protect, nurture, and sustain them in an environment of complementary development and strategic innovation (World Bank, 2000; United Nations Development Program, 1998; Batbeck & Blackburn, 2008).

Herbert Simon and Bounded Rationality in Financial Decision-Making and Choices

Herbert Simon's (1960) and his classical works (1952-53) were early harbinger of the arguments in support of satisfycing behavior of bounded rational choices as opposed to optimal utility and profit-maximizing behavior of neoclassical thought. Bounded rationality is different from rational choices of perfectly competitive markets. Instead of full-information in the case of perfectly competitive rational choice behavior of firms, the prevailing environment of asymmetric information has caused failed choices. To safeguard firms from such failures protection is deemed necessary. Financial protection can be gained by networking and strategic alliances in business, intra-firm and inter-firm discourse, transparency and disclosure with good corporate governance and corporate social responsibility. Thereby, the study of organic causality as opposed to full-information based optimal market choices has entered business planning deeply. Such is the message from Herbert Simon.

Simon's bounded rationality explains the emergence of perturbations in organization behavior. The assumptions and consequences in bounded rationality defy the traditional models of resource allocation. The specification of well-defined production functions in the face of institutional complexity becomes moot. Thereby, the measurement of productivity and efficiency in neoclassical framework remain seriously flawed. This is all the more real during these post-financial crisis times that affect the behavior of the financial firm (Farmer, 2010).

Three kinds of interaction apply in Simon's causality approach to business decision-making as organizational behavior:

R1: Intra-firm interaction $\rightarrow$ cohesion (C).
R2: C $\rightarrow$ Diversity of strategies and decision (D).
R3: D $\rightarrow$ C (recursive decision-making).
R4: C $\rightarrow$ I (interactions).

The continuity of causal relations in bounded rational decision-making, namely, [R1→R2→R3→R4] represents an institutional enforcement of the process internal to the firm, as information evolves within a bounded rationality set of financial alternatives. However, there is a problem of incompleteness of the relationship here. That is, a *recursive* satisfycing process in the above-mentioned bounded causal relationship does not exist. Contrarily, an extension of causality frontward and backwards would explain also the reversal of the relations. Furthermore, such relations can be of very complex types between {R1, R2, R3, R4}. Such is the nature of circular causality in organic interrelations.

Perturbations of Welfare Function and Social Choices Contra Neoclassical Theory

Similar kinds of inconsistency in social decision-making that results in proving the non-existence of smooth type production possibility surfaces can be found in social welfare theory (Arrow, 1951; Henderson and Quandt, 1971). By a cursory examination of the non-smooth surfaces of social choices it can be deduced that multiple irregularities of convex welfare surfaces implicate complexity in social choice theory. This situation causes mismatching of social choices with optimal choices on smooth social welfare surfaces, and likewise, on smooth production possibilities surfaces. The consequence of non-smooth surfaces in such cases defies measurements of productivity and efficiency indicators of the neoclassical genre of optimal welfare, production, profits, costs, and utilities (Nikaido, 1968; Bator, 1957; Henderson & Quandt, 1971).

In order to get over this anomaly of social choice, Arrow (1951) prescribed his theorem on the existence of a dictator to announce an end to the discursive game of democratic openness. Arrowian institutions (1974) are empowered to enact such a game-theoretic closure. This kind of institutional ruling takes the form of an announced end to the discursive game by means of the postulate of 'irrelevant preferences'. Because of the inexactness of indeterminate social choices in Arrowian social choice theory *qua* institutional democracy, Whittaker points out that Arrow's social choice theory remains devoid of prescriptions for policy. Whittaker (1987, p. 574) writes: "The most obvious point to make about Arrow's discussion of organizations … is that it conveys merely a broad vision rather that a specific theory. The speculation is on the grand scale, with few clues as to how the general perspectives can be applied to concrete cases and issues, let alone the formulation of precise refutable hypothesis."

The Impossibility of Neoclassical Production Possibility Surface to Resolve the Social Issue of Entitlement Failure

Amartya Sen's (1986) formalism concerning an optimal correction to restore a 'starvation' point in entitlement failure on to a neoclassical production possibility surface is another example that leaves to question the received analysis of economic theory of second-best resource allocation with ethics and government presence. The basis of this argument against the socioeconomic reality by way of neoclassical ideas of production function and concepts of productivity and efficiency measures is that public intervention always disturbs market efficiency. The resulting state of resource allocation displaces the points of optimality and equilibrium on the production possibility surface. Sen recognizes this fact, but continues on to explain his theory of entitlement failure by means of a neoclassical method of optimal allocation of resources.

Such a problem of social choice due to the non-existence of identifiable optimal points on the social welfare surface is recognized in the case of policy-induced transmission of an interior 'starvation' point of Sen (1986) on to the optimal surface. Policy distortions of market equilibriums cause such social aberrations to occur. The consequence is failure of market equilibrium and optimality to be attained. All these consequences relate to a failure in measuring productivity and efficiency in the second-best sense of competition and resource allocation in production milieu as described by the opportunity cost and optimal production frontier, be these deterministic or expected value reduction of stochastic frontiers.

Such aberrations in resource allocation methods, production and productivity and second-best efficiency questions are also the consequences of Rawls' (1971) social choice theory involving his Difference Principle and Original Position along shifting neoclassical welfare surfaces in respect of the distribution of social welfare to the most underprivileged segment in society.

The Greater Domain of Financial Decision-Making Qua Social Domain

Myrdal (1987) took exception to the simplistic approach of utilitarian and welfare analysis by its use of models of optimality, equilibrium, and stable forms that do not represent the actual perturbed complex reality of social choice. Myrdal (1987, slightly edited) wrote: "I have always wondered why the psychologists and philosophers have left the economists alone and undisturbed in their futile exercise (neoclassicism)."

Complexity is most thoroughly embedded in financial issues that interface with social choices. Examples of such social perturbations within economics and finance are found in the complex nature of the product that these disciplines service. The financial products defy their commoditization because of the ethical, and thereby, the public and social issues that underlie the production and cost-sharing decisions. In Islamic banks and their clientele the consumers, firms and shareholders, the production mix is determined by extensive discourse along lines of the ethical appropriateness and practices of Islamic banks and their financial products and project outlets on grounds of compliance with the Islamic Law (Haniffa & Hudaib, 2007).

Stochastic Frontier Analysis and Neoclassical Production Possibility Surface

To overcome the neoclassical problems of production specification and quantification of the productivity and efficiency measures of performance of Islamic banks, Abdul-Majid, Saal, and Battisti (2009) have shown that efficiency of Islamic banking performance is more appropriately studied by Stochastic Frontier Analysis (SFA). The authors use the idea of efficiency of bank performance measurement equivalently with that of bank productivity. However, this theoretical notion of equivalence between productivity and efficiency is true only in the case of perfect competition (Debreu, 1959). The same is not true of resource allocation by imperfectly competitive firms.

Besides, when firms do not produce tangible outputs as if they were quantities of goods as fungible, their production functions remain not merely stochastic in nature, but also, such functions defy well-definition of substance. Production functions in such complex cases fail to comply with the smoothly behaved states of increasing returns to scale. Contrarily, increasing returns to scale induce the Islamic bank's production function by induction of ethical factors, organizational discourse leading to decision-making and legal compliances with the Islamic Law for Islamic banks. The decision and strategy centering on cooperation and networking are expected to affect the production and cost-sharing environment. Consequently, the absence of well-definition of output and inputs, and thereby, the fuzziness in the formal nature of neoclassical production function and price relatives cause the productivity and efficiency measures to defy both deterministic and stochastic measurement when ethical factors are induced in them.

Consequently, in the case of ethically induced issues of production, the SFA becomes problematic in ethically induced productivity measurement. SFA continues on to rely on the convex-to-origin production possibility frontiers of the neoclassical genre albeit randomness of such a surface. On the other hand, under institutional complexity generated by ethical induction in discourse, legal matters and decision-making, the observed price relatives either between substitute outputs or inputs, cannot truly be read off the resultant ethically induced complex production relations. Stochastic Frontier (SF) continues on simply as a probabilistic method rather than as means towards explaining structural change in financial firms. The probabilistic optimal and equilibrium locus of production and input point(s) continue on to be governed by neoclassical production possibility surfaces that become independent of ethical nuances.

Kumbhakar and Lovell (2000) have explained the use of SFA to smoothen market failures and instability of output, profit, and revenue frontiers that lead to random production inefficiency. The dual problem of productivity and efficiency failures along the SF is similar to the dual problem of neoclassical production possibility curves subject to bounded rationality and inefficient information flow. To smooth the probabilistic production related surfaces is equivalent to searching for the availability of conditions that would be otherwise available for 'fully' optimized profits, revenue and output, and minimum cost.

In reality, the financial production menu is bedeviled by market failures as is amply proven by global financial volatility and the inability to bring down such volatility to market correction (Greenspan, 2010). But the most pertinent inadequacy of SFA in defining the functioning of financial production function arises from the side of its inability to reflect upon the pervasive institutional learning and participatory behavior, and co-determination of social contracts by inputs of a financial production menu. These attributes are the abiding signs of endogenous ethical learning in a participatory venue of the financial firm. An example of such a case is an Islamic bank. Islamic banks are faced with the legal and ethical requirements of the Islamic Law governing products and their delivery to the public domain.

Multiple points on the social welfare surface taken as an SF do not help. That is because multiple points of inflexion on the social welfare surface cause problem of identifying the optimal points of social choice. This situation results in the well-known theorem of existence of a dictator in the social welfare function to call an end to the otherwise continuous simulative game (Arrow, 1951; Hammond, 1987).

Fuzziness of Educational Production Function as Another Example of Neoclassical Problem

Yet another area of study of such productivity measures and their problems of estimation is found in the area of human capital theory and economics of education. The classical contributions in this area of educational production functions, their specification and estimation, are those of Blaug (1970), Griclichez (1970), Denison (1962). The same methodological approach as the SFA is used to smooth out a probabilistic ill-defined production possibility curve of educational output. The analytical problems apply, related with the definition of the production function, the production possibility frontier, and production isoquants. The problem of estimating the cost and price relations and the measurements of productivity and efficiency prevail in the case of educational production function as in the case of SFA.

PRODUCTION MENUS IN ETHICALLY INDUCED INSTITUTIONAL DECISION-MAKING AND SOCIAL CHOICES

The nature of production function in the presence of ethical questions combined with fuzzy production outputs and inputs, such as ethics, technological choices, and public policy issues, becomes blurred in the neoclassical economic analysis of production related questions. Probabilistic correction and exogenous intervention by means of ethical rules do not help in generating self-governed artifacts of structural change (Krugman, 1996), behavior and ethical consequences in the productive venue.

So the problem of production measurement is one of reading the effects borne out by the presence of institutional structures, policies, and ethical effects that underlie participatory choices and decision-making. The result is that all such frontiers related with production, social welfare and utilities, together define the greater venue of production and social linkages as ought to be done by financial firms. Thereby, the meaning and measurement of productivity and efficiency with ethical and sustainability meanings in them is denied by the neoclassical production function and its prototypes. Production menus and measures of fuzzy goods and services in today's global contagion remain differently valued than in the neoclassical case.

In recent times, the fuzzy nature of the financial outputs and the absence of well-specified inputs to define a financial production function, plus the often disequilibrium trends in price-*tatonement* process in globally volatile and non-corrected capital markets have raised serious questions of optimization and efficiency (Schiller, 2000). Inefficient capital market performance has become the norm rather than the exception during these days of global financial volatility and economic stability. A good paper establishing this aspect of uncertainty and suggesting alternative measurement approach is by Saif and Dadang (2011). These authors use neural non-linear model for testing the performance of Islamic banks in Indonesia.

Yet in the end, no serious attempt has been launched toward initiating a methodological approach in constructing the *financial* production function with the endogenous ethical effects involving institutional structures, decision-making, and learning behavior. These interventions together in their complex but explainable relations convey the meaning of ethical induction. A revision in this direction within the prevalent neoclassical theory of production and cost is not methodologically possible.

OBJECTIVE AND APPROACH

The foregoing review of the literature and the background of the problem of measurement in production relations establish firstly, that a new methodology ought to be adopted for the study, estimation and measurement of productivity and efficiency analysis connected with production functions that are endogenously embedded in fuzzy elements of complexity. Examples of such fuzzy elements in productivity and efficiency analysis are ethics and sustainability that invoke participative dynamics with public and social choices. Economics, finance, and accounting professions serve these important issues by way of being a system *ensemble*. Secondly, the study of such endogenous institutional elements embedded in the measurement of hybrid concepts of productivity and efficiency cannot be limited to sophistication of analytical methods alone. Rather, the relevant method for studying such embedded system-ensemble of complex elements emerges from the recognition of the institutional decision-making structure.

EXPLICATION OF THE OBJECTIVE

In the above-mentioned two-pronged areas impinging upon production issues, due recognition ought to be given to the epistemic basis of the institutional structure and decision-making. The resulting approach is most appropriate for Islamic banks and financial and accounting entities. On ethical grounds such institutions must discourse within their decision-making structure in accordance with the Islamic Law on product development. The ethical element here is explained by the extensively participative decision-making, learning and social, economic and financial linkages that the Islamic firms establish. Hence the productivity and efficiency concepts in such a case are deeply influenced by the participative nature of the financial instruments and the choices of goods and services that Islamic banks must deliver for the greater social good. Included in the ethical purview of outputs are alleviation of social malaise, such as poverty, inequity and justice, and fairness within an environment of development sustainability (Choudhury, 1993).

The third characteristic of Islamic production milieu is continuity of the structure and formalism of the interactive and participative nature of production and its related productivity and efficiency measures. With ethical endogeneity, defined by the extensively participatory and discursive form of decision-making centering on the selection of goods and services in the light of the Islamic Law, makes the production relations of Islamic banks to be of a non-neoclassical type (Holton, 1992).

The emphasis in this chapter is on Islamic banks by virtue of their characteristics that match the descriptive properties of the learning institutions. In such business institutions, complexity of decision-making and its ethically embedded episteme challenges with new insight in the measurement of productivity and efficiency indicators.

The above-mentioned three goals comprise the objective of this chapter. Quantitative modeling further opens the way to conceptualization of the ethically induced elements that are endogenized into production relations. The empirical part simplifies to a specific application of the theory to the formulation of a simple form of the production function, and productivity and efficiency measures for Islamic banks in Indonesia.

METHODOLOGY

The joint production function underlying the financial and ethical participative nature of the Islamic banking idea in the light of the Islamic Law can be formalized as follows:

$$F(\theta, x(\theta)) = A(\theta).x(\theta)^{\alpha} \quad (1)$$

Where, F denotes the money value of total financing done by Islamic banks. F is related to the intrinsic variables as a joint production function in relation to its inputs: $x(\theta) = \{m_1, m_2, m_3, m_4, D_d, D_s)[\theta]$. m_1 denotes money value of *mudarabah* (profit-sharing), m_2 denotes money value of *musharakah* (equity financing); m_3 denotes money value of *murabaha* (mark-up pricing); m_4 denotes money value of *istisna* (financing of prospective manufactures). D_d denotes money value of deposits by common depositors; D_s denotes money value of deposits by principal shareholders. θ denotes a parameter representing values derived from the Islamic Law. These derivations of values are embedded in institutional decision-making (*shura*). In the form of expression (1), an organic relationship between the variables, as inputs is defined. The resulting output is denoted by F. Klein (1946) has used such a kind of relational orientation in his economic aggregation concept of econometric modeling.

$\{\theta\}$-values are assigned ordinally by discursive selection within research and development institution by members of research and development group or project group in reference to trends in the financing variables. These variables comprise the $\{m\}$-vector comprising the financing instruments mentioned above. The financing instruments are selected by virtue of their participative and trade-related nature, which are opposed to interest-based financing instruments. It is the complementary participative nature of the $\{F,m,D_d,D_s\}$-variables that represents the true performance of the Islamic participatory perspectives on financing and socioeconomic change. Incidentally, such a perspective is also pronounced in the received theory of a participatory economy (Vanek, 1971).

In this sense of participative relations between the variables as the true reflection of the Islamic nature of a financial and social economy, each of the variables and the coefficients of expression (1) is induced by {θ}-values. θ appears as the principal endogenizing variable of Islamic learning institution and decision-making in the light of the Islamic Law. This common embedding of θ-value in all the variables is shown by the appearance of [θ] outside the sequence of the x(θ)-vector. θ-value also induces the parametric learning coefficient A(θ), thus causing endogenous shifts in the total financing variable F due to learning within institution (Islamic bank). The vector of power-coefficients $\alpha(\theta) = \{\alpha_1, \alpha_2, \alpha_3, \alpha_4, \alpha_5, \alpha_6\}[\theta]$ is assigned to each of the variables in x(θ)-vector, respectively. By virtue of simulation based on ethically-induced issues affecting changes in these coefficients, they experience pollination by θ-value, as is shown.

The multiplicative (variable elasticity coefficients α in Cobb-Douglas form) form of expression (7.1) as a production function is chosen by virtue of the following properties of Islamic financing in an institutional epistemic structure: Firstly, the participative nature of financing requires complementarities and balanced elasticity values of each of the financing variables in the vector x(θ) to the total financing variable F. Secondly, while such participatory dynamics continue on in the system *ensemble* and cybernetic of interrelations between the variables by virtue of circular causality, so also learning intensifies monotonically within institutions on the epistemic grounds of participation (organic unity) between the Islamic institutions (Islamic banks) by virtue of their compliance with the Islamic Law. Thirdly, the conceptual form of the production function under the postulate of participative performance of Islamic banks, is a normative statement as opposed to the positivistic state of the Islamic banks as they are. The prevalent case is to be estimated. Estimation would then be followed by normative simulation. See below.

The participatory nature of Islamic bank-financing as output in the production relation given by expression (7.1) presents the scope of studying the following measures in our objective: Firstly, the embedded participatory nature of ethics in Islamic financing and social choices of goods and services by the firm and clientele are inherent through the primal effect of θ-variable. Secondly, this form of characterization of the production function gives it the complex essence that makes it non-neoclassical in nature.

PRODUCTIVITY ANALYSIS

The productivity analysis is done by using the transformation of expression (1) in the following form:

$$f_d = (F/D_d) \qquad (2)$$

ratio provides the total financing-to-common depositor financing ratio.

$$f_s = (F/D_s) \tag{3}$$

ratio provides the total financing-to-shareholder financing ratio.

$$f_m = (F/m) \tag{4}$$

ratios ratio provides the total financing-to-specific 'm' financing ratio.

The differentiation between D_d and D_s is made in order to bring out the desired degree of complementarities that ought to exist between common depositors and shareholders as privileged depositors in Islamic bank financing.

From expression (1) we obtain the following circular causation regression equations that will be estimated. They are followed by simulation of the coefficients on the normative ground of social reconstruction of the structure and choices of Islamic banks. Circular causation method is invoked because of the inherent complementary relationships between the variables in the light of organic unity as the episteme of oneness of the Islamic Law.

$$\ln F = \ln A(\theta) + \Sigma_{i=1}^{4} \alpha_i.\ln m_i(\theta) + \alpha_5.\ln D_d(\theta) + \alpha_6 \ln D_s(\theta); \tag{5}$$

$$\ln m_i(\theta) = \ln A(\theta) + \Sigma_{j=1}^{4} \alpha_j.\ln m_j(\theta) + \alpha_5.\ln D_s(\theta) + \alpha_6.\ln D_s(\theta) \tag{6}$$

$i \neq j$

$$\ln D_d = \ln A(\theta) + + \Sigma_{i=1}^{4} \alpha_i.\ln m_i(\theta) + + \alpha_6 \ln D_s(\theta) \tag{7}$$

$$\ln D_s = \ln A(\theta) + \Sigma_{i=1}^{4} \alpha_i.\ln m_i(\theta) + \alpha_5.\ln D_s(\theta) \tag{8}$$

$$\theta = \ln A(\theta) + \Sigma_{i=1}^{4} \alpha_i.\ln m_i(\theta) + \alpha_5.\ln D_d(\theta) + \alpha_6.\ln D_s(\theta) + \alpha_7.\ln F(\theta) \tag{9}$$

PRODUCTIVITY MEASURE

Estimation followed by simulation of expression (5) provides the complete outlook on the financial production function. From the estimation (followed by simulation of the coefficients) of the Equations 5-9 the productivity measures given by expressions (2)-(4) can be computed for various financing variables. Expression (9) gives the estimate of the embedded ethical parameter or learning parameter that drives the whole system of participative interrelationships between the variables of the production function (1). Measures of financial productivity are computed below.

It is noted that in the log-linear form of the equations, the α-coefficients represent the partial elasticity coefficients of each of the independent variables to the dependent ones in the respective equations: Thus for instance in Equation 5,

α_i = (percentage change in f_s)/(percentage change in m_i) (10)

i = 1,2,3,4

α_5= (percentage change in f_s)/(percentage change in D_d) (11)

$\alpha_{6=}$(percentage change in f_s)/(percentage change in D_s) (12)

α_7 = change in θ per unit of a change in lnF (13)

Other elasticity coefficients can be similarly defined.

These elasticity coefficients are similar to the input-output coefficients we pointed out at the beginning of this chapter. However, due to their induction by θ-values through the simulated (normative) version of the estimated Equations 5-9, the semblance of these input-output coefficients is of the dynamic learning kind.[1] The elasticity-coefficients (10)-(12) measure the production efficiencies related to the corresponding variables.

PRODUCTION EFFICIENCY MEASURE

The idea of production efficiency is invoked with the elasticity-coefficients by virtue of the following kind of relationship: As the elasticity coefficients increase in their values toward and across positivistic estimated and normative simulated values, the usage of the participatory finances instruments increases. Consequently, the total financing increases through this kind of systemic participation (complementarities) between the inputs and outputs. With the increase in such financing inputs resulting in the increase in production of total financing caused by increased participatory learning in the financial system, the average cost of production, i.e. the average financing cost decreases. Thus financial production efficiency caused by participation (complementarities) vis-à-vis endogenous learning in the financial system conveying the meaning of endogenous ethics in the financial production and cost-sharing milieu is increased.

Summary of Conceptual Formalism

We have now conceptually completed the analytical groundwork that addresses the objectives of this chapter. These are firstly, a non-neoclassical analytical definition of the financial production function. Upon this non-neoclassical form of financial production function, measures of financial productivity, and efficiency measures are formalized with dynamic embedded endogenous effects of learning-by-doing. This conveys the ethical meaning of sustainability of the financing system in the Islamic banking case. Secondly, the resulting formal system has been theoretically explained using the principle of pervasive complementarities as the sure sign of participation in the case of Islamic financing contra interest-based financing. Such complementarities between the circularly causation interrelations between the ethically induced financing variables represent the participative nature of the emergent system *ensemble* of financing variables that are all induced by the embedded ethical context of the Islamic Law. Thirdly, we now move into the empirical work involving the relations (1) and (5)-(11) to examine firstly the positivistic estimation case of financing by Islamic banks, and then to simulate a normative picture of the same under a better exercise of the Islamic Law.

EMPIRICAL WORK, A SIMPLIFIED CASE STUDY

Positivistic Results for Islamic Banks in Indonesia

The statistical tables are given in the appendix. The following statistical results and observations are obtained:

Note in Table 1 that, due to missing data on D_d and D_s, we could use only the total deposit values denoted by D. But from the empirical results we deduce inferences on productivity measures linked with D_d and D_s. It is also noted that due to a limited time-series data available on the variables to fit the regression results it was necessary to aggregate the m_i-variables (i = 1,2,3,4) into the aggregate financing variable 'm' as shown.

In this way, the equations corresponding to the following ones are estimated:

$$\ln F(\theta) = \ln A(\theta) + \alpha_1 . \ln M(\theta) + \alpha_2 . \ln D(\theta) \tag{14}$$

$$\ln M(\theta) = \ln A(\theta) + \beta_1 . \ln F(\theta) + \beta_2 . \ln D(\theta) \tag{15}$$

$$\ln D = \ln A(\theta) + \gamma_1 . \ln F(\theta) + \gamma_2 . \ln M(\theta) \tag{16}$$

$$\theta = \ln A(\theta) + \delta_1 . \ln F(\theta) + \delta_2 . \ln M(\theta) + \delta_3 . \ln D(\theta) \qquad (17)$$

ESTIMATION RESULTS

Production Function

$$\ln F = 1.11 + 0.777 \ln M + 0.223 \ln D \qquad (14')$$

(4.06) (1.35)(1.16)

$R^2 = 99.3$; DW = 1.65898

The generic equation of the financial production function is,

$$F = e^{1.11} * M^{0.777} * D^{0.223} \qquad (14'')$$

The signs are found to be as expected in the production function of an Islamic bank. The financial production function is of constant returns to scale type; rather than of the increasing returns to scale type that should be appropriate to instill ethical values and learning between variables in a climate of sustainability of the Islamic bank financial process.

In the estimated case,

$$\in_{F,M} + \in_{F,D} = 0.777 + 0.223 = 1.$$

Circular Causation of M with F and D

$$\ln M = -0.44 + 1.09 \ln F - 0.115 \ln D \qquad (15')$$

(-0.33) (4.06) (-0.48)

$R^2 = 98.9$; DW = 2.16663

The generic equation, the financial production function is,

$$M = e^{-0.44} * F^{1.09} * D^{-0.115} \qquad (15'')$$

The meaning in equation (15') is that the proportion of major shareholders' funds M in projects ought to be related in participatory way with the common shareholders' funds D. In such a relationship between M and D, D influences M by virtue of enhancing M by the introduction of common shareholders funds D into M. Likewise, the existing size of total financing F will influence the size of M.

Circular Causation of D with F and M

$$\ln D = -5.28 + 1.70 \ln F - 0.62 \ln M \quad (16')$$

(-5.63) (1.35) (-0.48)

R2 = 95.6; DW = 2.08814

The generic equation is,

$$D = e^{-5.28} * F^{1.70} * M^{-0.62} \quad (16'')$$

The meaning of equation (16') is similar to that of equation (15') but in the reverse causality. The size of M ought to be related in a participatory way to D by showing its presence in the depositors fund mix. F would clearly influence the size of D by way of diversification of the total Islamic bank assets.

The Ethical Indicator Index

$$\mathrm{Ln}\theta = -0.27 + 0.35 \ln F + 0.57 \ln M + 0.123 \ln D \quad (17')$$

(-0.09) (0.22) (0.43) (0.22)

R2 = 96.8; DW = 2.63771

The generic equation is,

$$\theta = e^{-0.27} * F^{0.35} * M^{0.57} * D^{0.123} \quad (17'')$$

Here the signs of the coefficients are as they ought to be for Islamic bank financing. {F,M,D} contribute positively to the ethical decision-making and participatory nature of Islamic banks' financing operations.

SIMULATION RESULT

The estimated equations (14') and thus (14") show no particular weakness in the coefficients in explaining underlying complementarities between the variables. This fact establishes the existence of a participatory nature of the financial sector in respect of total investment related to Islamic bank financial instruments and depositors' contribution. Likewise, the same confirmation on the participatory nature of Islamic bank financing in respect of the ethical basis of Islamic bank financial sustainability is exhibited by equation (16') and thereby equation (17").

However, equations (15') hence (15") and equations (16') hence (16") have opposite signs between M and D recursively. For complementary financing by means of a balanced use of all the source of financing investments, Islamic banks ought to establish complementarities between these diverse instruments. In the absence of such complementarities (participatory nature) between the diverse financing instruments, the signs reflected are of a weakly diversified portfolio of instruments. This case would result in a weak risk and production diversification out of a learning institutional structure and its epistemic decision-making premised on the Islamic Law that fundamentally invokes a participatory economic, financial, and development system. The result of marginal substitution between M and D in the actual observed case suggests that sustainability of the participatory nature of Islamic bank financing is questionable. The negative coefficients in equations (15'), hence (15"), and equations (16') and (16") need to be simulated into positive or less negative values. Such a process would indicate a phased out adaptation into complementarities between M and D over processes of learning between these variables. The learning process here reflects the institutional structural and decision-making changes.

The simulation part of the revision in the complementary relations between M and D has not been done here. But to point out here only, such a revision can be effectively done by the use of Spatial Domain Analysis (SDA) of Geographical Information System (Norhea, Ahmed, & Choudhury, 2011). The method would invoke selection of appropriate elasticity coefficients out of a field of such SDA-generated coefficients. This requires structural changes in Islamic bank financing following institutional discourse in and across these financial institutions. As mentioned above, such a structural change in Islamic bank financing would result in a greater degree of diversification of the financing portfolio towards risk diversification and production diversification.

COMPUTATION OF PRODUCTIVITY MEASURES

By our definition of productivity in the case of the value-embedded concept of a certain concept of output per unit of financial input, the productivity measure is generated by the estimated production function (14").

Computed values of Productivity of M and D, respectively, are generated by,

$$\text{Prod (M)} = F/M = e^{1.11} * (D/M)^{0.223} \quad (18)$$

$$\text{Prod (D)} = F/D = e^{1.11} * (M/D)^{0.777} \quad (19)$$

Actual and estimated trends in the productivity measures of M and D in the financial production function are computed in Table 1.

CONCLUSION

This chapter presents a combination of a critical review of the literature on financial productivity and efficiency measurements in reference to the background of financial production function that is always of a fuzzy type caused by the complexities of ethics, sustainability of decision-making and choices surrounding it. In Islamic banks whose products must comply with the Islamic Law, ethics and discursive decision-making play very critical role. Thereby, institutional interface with market forces intertwine to cause perturbations in the financial production milieu. Such a case is also displayed by institutional and social contractarian interrelations and networking as ways of strategic alliance following the financial crisis.

The conceptual and empirical aspects of the chapter establish the various ramifications of this chapter. A statistical analysis is performed on the essential points of this chapter. The chapter contributes to a new dimension of understanding and measuring production function, and productivity and efficiency indicators in the presence of ethical and discursive institutional phenomenon.

REFERENCES

Abdul-Majid, M., Saal, D. S., & Battisti, G. (2010). Efficiency in Islamic and conventional banking: An international comparison. *Journal of Productivity Analysis*, *34*, 25–43. doi:10.1007/s11123-009-0165-3.

Arrow, K. J. (1951). *Social choice and individual values.* New York, NY: John Wiley & Sons.

Arrow, K. J. (1974). *The limits of organization.* New York, NY: W.W. Norton.

Batbeck, S., & Blackburn, K. (2008). *On the macroeconomics of microfinance* (Discussion Paper No. 106). Manchester, UK: Centre for Growth and Business Cycle Research, University of Manchester.

Bator, F. M. (1957). The simple analytics of welfare maximization. *The American Economic Review*, 47.

Blaug, M. (1970). *An introduction to the economics of education.* London, UK: Penguin Press.

Choudhury, M. A. (1993). *Comparative development study: In search of the world view.* New York: Macmillan Press Ltd., & St. Martin's Press.

Choudhury, M. A. (2010). A neurocybernetic theory of management system. In Gunasekaran, A., & Sandhu, M. (Eds.), *Handbook on Business Information Systems.* Singapore: World Scientific Publications. doi:10.1142/9789812836069_0010.

Colander, D. (2003). Integrating ethics and altruism with economics, or altruism, economics, and Hume's dictum – A response to Morris Altman. *Journal of Economic Psychology*, *26*, 758–761. doi:10.1016/j.joep.2005.06.003.

Debreu, G. (1959). *A theory of value.* New York: John Wiley & Sons.

Denison, E. F. (1962). *The sources of economic growth in the U.S., & the alternatives before us.* Washington, DC: Committee for Economic Development.

Farmer, R. E. A. (2010). *How the economy works.* Oxford, UK: Oxford University Press.

Greenspan, A. (2010, August 2). *Alan Greenspan: US 'risks double-dip recession'.* Retrieved from http://www.bbc.co.uk/news/business-10835176

Grilichez, J. (1970). Notes on the role of education in production function and growth accounting. In Hansen, L. W. (Ed.), *Education, Income and Human Capital.* Washington, DC: National Bureau of Economic Research.

Hammond, P. J. (1987). On reconciling Arrow's theory of social choice with Harsanyi's fundamental utilitarianism. In Feiwel, G. R. (Ed.), *Arrow and the Foundations of the Theory of Economic Policy.* London, UK: Macmillan Press.

Haniffa, R., & Hudaib, M. (2007). Exploring the ethical identity of Islamic financial institutions via communications in the annual reports. *Journal of Business Ethics, 76*(1), 103–122. doi:10.1007/s10551-006-9272-5.

Henderson, J. M., & Quandt, R. E. (1971). *Microeconomic theory: A mathematical approach*. New York, NY: McGraw-Hill.

Holton, R. J. (1992). *Economy and society*. London, UK: Routledge.

Kim, W. C., & Mauborgne, R. (2005). *Blue ocean strategy*. Boston, MA: Harvard University Press.

Klein, L. R. (1946). Remarks on the theory of aggregation. *Econometrica*, 14.

Krugman, P. (1996). *The self-organizing economy*. Cambridge, MA: Blackwell Publishers.

Kumbhakar, S. C., & Lovell, C. A. K. (2000). *Stochastic frontier analysis*. Cambridge, UK: Cambridge University Press. doi:10.1017/CBO9781139174411.

Myrdal, G. (1987). Utilitarianism and modern economics. In Feiwel, G. (Ed.), *Arrow and the Foundations of the Theory of Economic Policy*. London, UK: Macmillan.

Nikaido, H. (1968). *Convex structure and economic theory*. New York: Academic Press, Inc..

Noreha, H., Ahmed, M. S., & Choudhury, M. A. (2011). Circular causation relations using Malaysian data on money and real GDP. In Choudhury, M. A. (Ed.), *Islamic Economics and Finance, an Epistemological Inquiry*. London: Emerald Publishing.

Pham, H. (2009). *Continuous-time stochastic control and optimization with financial applications*. Berlin, Germany: Springer. doi:10.1007/978-3-540-89500-8.

Rawls, J. (1971). *A theory of justice*. Cambridge, MA: Harvard University Press.

Schiller, R. J. (2000). *Irrational exuberance*. New York, NY: Broadway Books.

Sen, A. (1986). Exchange entitlement. In *Poverty and Famines, an Essay on Entitlement and Deprivation* (pp. 167–173). Oxford, UK: Clarendon Press.

Simon, H. A. (1960). Decision making and organizational design. In Pugh, D. S. (Ed.), *Organization Theory* (pp. 202–223). Hammondsworth, UK: Penguin Books.

Simon, H. A. (1952-53). A behavioural model of rational choice. In *Models of Man*. New York, NY: John Wiley & Sons, Inc..

Solow, R. (1980). *Growth theory, an exposition*. Oxford, UK: Oxford University Press.

United Nations Development Program (UNDP). (1998). *Human development report*. New York, NY: Oxford University Press.

Vanek, J. (1971). The participatory economy in a theory of social evolution. In *The Participatory Economy: an Evolutionary and a Strategy for Development* (pp. 51–89). Ithaca, NY: Cornell University Press.

Whittaker, J. K. (1987). The limits of organization revisited. In Feiwel, G. R. (Ed.), *Arrow and the Foundations of the Theory of Economic Policy*. London, UK: Macmillan.

World Bank. (2000). *World development report 2000-2001*. New York, NY: Oxford University Press.

ENDNOTES

1 Elasticity coefficient, say, $\in_{i,j}$ = (xj/xi).(dxi/dxj) of xi to xj, should be positive in sign in the perspective of the participatory nature of the relationship between these variables in the epistemic meaning of organic unity under the perspective of the Islamic Law (Choudhury, 2009). But such a case may not be actually reflected by the estimation results. If so, then the estimated (positivistic) values of the elasticity coefficients need to be improved to positive or less negative signs as per the available resource possibilities in making such changes. Note that no negative sign is affixed to the above elasticity coefficient. This is because the postulate of negatively sloped production possibility curve and the observable existence of price relative of the neoclassical type are not assumed postulates. Rather in the normative sense these assumptions are denied by virtue of the θ-induced learning experience in the participative case of Islamic bank financing according to the Islamic Law.
The θ-induced learning experience reflected in the participative case of Islamic bank financing in the circular causation interrelations (5)-(9) explains the dynamic nature of the institutional learning experience in the normative (simulated) case of Islamic bank financing and the complementarities between the variables of these equations. The financial production function expression (1) as the objective criterion now summarizes the inter-variable complementary relations with the embedded ethical meaning of learning in it.

APPENDIX: STATISTICAL RESULTS

Table 1. Comparative productivity measures, actual and estimated by the production function

Time	Prom (M)		Prod (D)	
	Actual (Eqn 17)	Estimated	Actual (Eqn 18)	Estimated
2001	1.002	1.0560	113.48	120.0075
2002	1.056	1.0718	112.30	114.0115
2003	1.033	0.9658	96.600	168.1740
2004	1.037	1.1637	96.860	85.5680
2005	1.030	1.0985	97.750	104.6185
2006	1.052	1.0936	98.900	106.1934

Table 2. Data generated from secondary data source

	F	M	D			
Time	Million USD	Million USD	Million USD	F/M	F/D	θ
2001	227,77	227.14	2.007	1.002	113.48	100
2002	364,11	344.82	3.242	1.056	112.30	268
2003	614,44	594.57	3.361	1.033	96.600	319
2004	1,258	953.76	12.988	1.037	96.860	611
2005	1,692	1643.29	17.309	1.030	97.750	987
2006	2,271	2150.16	22.062	1.052	98.900	1359

Source: Bank Indonesia report on Islamic banks in Indonesia The assignment of the θ-values by columns and average over column values is done in the following way: Intra-column θ-values = [(Difference between subsequent values)] + previous θ-value so generated starting from a rank of 100; Inter-column average θ-values = $\theta = (\theta_1 + \theta_2 + \theta_3)/3$

A brief review of the statistical analysis in this appendix shows that the log-linear specification in circular causation between the selected variables does not yield 95% levels of significance for the variables and their coefficients in every case. The lower levels of significance in such relations only testify to the need for better (possibly non-linear) regression specifications that can be formulated to replace the log-linear ones.

But despite the statistical estimation problem noted above, the similar consistent results in several other linear relations tried out but not reproduced here, suggest that, complexity is indeed inherent in the estimation and simulation of the learning kinds

Table 3. Rank assignment of θ-parameter on the basis of observed degree of participatoriness intra- and inter- columns

Time	F θ_1	M θ_2	D θ_3	Avg $\theta = \theta = (\theta_1 + \theta_2 + \theta_3)/3$
2001	100	100	100	1.00
2002	236	218	101	268
2003	386	469	101	319
2004	894	828	110	611
2005	1328	1518	114	987
2006	1907	2024	118	1359

of inter-variable relations on the basis of their complementarities, i.e. participation, as reflected in the circular causation approach. Consequently, as pointed out in the text of the chapter, the usual kinds of neoclassical economic specification of the production function, and of the productivity and efficiency measures derived there from, cannot answer the issues of inherent complexities in such relations. Learning kinds of non-linear models of production function but of the non-neoclassical types should be tried for reasons of more reliable statistical estimation results.

It is interesting to note in the comparative literature review that the endogenous treatment of ethics in production function has been invoked. A work in this direction is by Collard (2003). In his paper Collard points out the need for inductive and experimental value of ethical conduct of producers. This kind of a deontological value finds its place as consciousness, and is therefore, of an endogenous nature. But the fact that ethics despite being endogemous is required to be revealed in content to make an ethical production function and utility function amenable to empirical facts converges with the treatment of ethics and consciousness in the production function as an empirically revealed consciousness. Thus a practical confirmation of such ethical facts is sought and this is possible.

Yet in the way we have defined ethics as learning in unity of knowledge, so the episteme of such a formal expression of the production function must be premised on the *functional* ontology of unity of knowledge. This is the rare thesis of this book as also particularized in the case of the endogenous production function in unity of knowledge as the episteme and the foundation of ethics.

THE REGRESSION EQUATIONS

Table 4.

lnF = 1.11 + 0.777 lnM + 0.223 lnD				
Predictor	**Coef**	**SE Coef**	**T**	**P**
Constant	1.1147	0.9608	1.16	0.330
lnM	0.7772	0.1915	4.06	0.027
lnD	0.2228	0.1649	1.35	0.269

S = 0.0996405 R-Sq = 99.3% R-Sq(adj) = 98.8% R-Sq(pred) = 94.06%

Analysis of Variance

Table 5.

Source	DF	SS	MS	F	P
Regression	2	4.0917	2.0458	206.06	0.001
Residual Error	3	0.0298	0.0099		
Total	5	4.1214			

Durbin-Watson Statistic = 1.65898

Table 6.

lnM = - 0.44 + 1.09 lnF - 0.115 lnD				
Predictor	**Coef**	**SE Coef**	**T**	**P**
Constant	-0.444	1.344	-0.33	0.763
lnF	1.0885	0.2682	4.06	0.027
lnD	-0.1146	0.2385	-0.48	0.664

S = 0.117917 R-Sq = 98.9% R-Sq(adj) = 98.2% R-Sq(pred) = 74.77%

Analysis of Variance

Table 7.

Source	DF	SS	MS	F	P
Regression	2	3.8225	1.9113	137.46	0.001
Residual Error	3	0.0417	0.0139		
Total	5	3.8642			

Durbin-Watson Statistic = 2.16663

Table 8.

lnD = - 5.28 + 1.70 lnF - 0.62 lnM				
Predictor	**Coef**	**SE Coef**	**T**	**P**
Constant	-5.2848	0.9388	-5.63	0.011
lnF	1.698	1.257	1.35	0.269
lnD	-0.624	1.298	-0.48	0.664

S = 0.275051 R-Sq = 95.6% R-Sq(adj) = 92.7% R-Sq(pred) = 88.61%

Analysis of Variance

Table 9.

Source	DF	SS	MS	F	P
Regression	2	4.9828	2.4914	32.93	0.009
Residual Error	3	0.2270	0.0757		
Total	5	5.2098			

Durbin-Watson Statistic = 2.08814

Table 10.

Lnθ = - 0.27 + 0.35 lnF + 0.57 lnM + 0.123 lnD				
Predictor	**Coef**	**SE Coef**	**T**	**P**
Constant	-0.266	3.129	-0.09	0.940
lnF	0.351	1.562	0.22	0.843
lnM	0.571	1.320	0.43	0.708
lnD	0.1226	0.5660	0.22	0.849

S = 0.269638 R-Sq = 96.8% R-Sq(adj) = 92.1% R-Sq(pred) = 0.00%

Analysis of Variance

Table 11.

Source	DF	SS	MS	F	P
Regression	2	4.4310	1.4770	20.32	0.047
Residual Error	3	0.1454	0.0727		
Total	5	4.5764			

Durbin-Watson Statistic = 2.63771

Chapter 8
Financial Interest and Human Depravity:
Emergence of the Theory of Interest from the Philosophical Roots of Occidental Epistemological Thought

ABSTRACT

The analytical study of theory, the contributions in the literature, and the study of wellbeing as the primal objective pursued in this whole work are shown to face the permanent predicament of interest rates prevailing in these concepts and systems in its various forms and values. Interest rate is singled out to be the central factor of human predicament in terms of wellbeing and progress. Thus, a new monetary theory arising out of the morally induced concept of quantity theory of money is developed. An extensive review of the literature is carried out in light of the phenomenological model of unity of knowledge. The measured configuration of unity of knowledge in such world-system issues is shown by means of the principle of pervasive complementarities, equivalently participation between the good things of life. The good things of life are equated with those found in the value-laden basic-needs, life-fulfillment regimes of human development, thus moral sustainability.

DOI: 10.4018/978-1-4666-4643-8.ch008

Copyright ©2014, IGI Global. Copying or distributing in print or electronic forms without written permission of IGI Global is prohibited.

INTRODUCTION

The theory of interest is a complex theme. It though rests on a key point that distinguishes it from the moral and ethical potentialities. This forms the contrast that interest rate erects, in degrees of its impact, between trade in the good things of life and the hoarding and *bank-saving* behaviour, on the ruse of creating income out of capital accumulation and spreading this out over consumption and investment futures. Contrarily though, Keynes throughout his life pondered on the nature of savings in relation to the financial and social impediment that interest rate creates in resource mobilization for sustaining the common good.

Such was an ethical reflection of Keynes' impress of Moore's *Principia Ethica* (1962). Yet it is noted that to the question raised by Moore—What is good and thus goodness?—Keynes in his attempt to make Economics as the handmaiden of ethics as the answer could not acquiesce to Moore's explanation of metaphysical ethics. Rather, he constrained himself to naturalistic ethics. Moore's treatment of naturalistic ethics was different from metaphysical ethics.

On this issue Moore wrote (op cit. p. 38-39): "The theories I propose to discuss may be conveniently divided into two groups. The naturalistic fallacy always implies that when we think 'This is good,' what we are thinking is that the thing in question bears a definite relation to some one other thing. But this one thing, by reference to which good is defined, may be either what I may call a natural object—something of which the existence is admittedly an object of experience—or else it may be an object which is only inferred to exist in a supersensible real world. These two types of ethical theory I propose to treat separately. Theories of the second type may conveniently be called 'metaphysical'...." Obviously, Keynes was moved much by Moore's theory of naturalistic ethics, which he used for his own advantage for the economic construction of rationalism.

Thereby came about Keynes' ethical concept of full-employment and a low-level liquidity trap at which money could be expanded to meet with the expansionary needs of the income multiplier in sustainable economic growth. To reach this goal of full-employment in a regime of low rates of interest, high monetary expansion, price stability, expansion in employment with sustainable real economic growth, all together constituted Moore's naturalistic ethics. Rationalism in this notion of naturalistic ethics coloured Keynes' liberal philosophical design of man, society, and the world as the ultimate discursive determiner of truth, Moore's 'good thing – goodness.'

Yet Moore's theory of metaphysical ethics was also a constrained notion that renders dysfunctional the social and economic thinking along such epistemological lines. Metaphysics to Moore meant the worldview arising from Kant and Hegel and then carried over in some form by Marx and the classicists (Marx. edited. Engels,

1892). But Hegel emulating Kant, both run into the problem of heteronomy – Kant in his unbridgeable separation of *a priori* reason from *a posteriori* reason. This caused the problem of lack of synthesis between mind and matter; between perception, consciousness and reality; between deductive and inductive reasoning. Thus dualism entered the philosophy of science in its fullest way. It caused similar semblances in social and economic ordering. Yet in all of such speculative philosophy, God remained a divided other who has no functional relationship and role in the experiential world governed by laws, enlightened human consciousness, and their consequences. Such was the legacy of metaphysical ethics, which continues on to abide without further investigation on the basis of its speculative moorings.

Keynes' convenience to relent on naturalistic ethics wrapped up in the garb of rationalism along the line of the philosophers was a permanent debility of occidental mind. Thus the material world and its consequences under the law of mind-matter dualism ever after remained a partial view of reality. The question as to 'what is the good – goodness' remained a partial explanation.

The economic and social world as a great expanse of mankind's quest for morality, ethics, and goodness, came to be coloured by a desire for goodness, but was unable to give the answer to Moore's relenting question, 'what is the good – goodness?' Such a pent up search would be acceptable if it framed the dialectics of a non-ending search for knowledge, rising from lesser to higher levels of correctness. Yet the muddle of indefiniteness remained entrenched in all of occidental socio-scientific thought due to the separation between naturalistic and metaphysical ethics. Thereby, the place of the Pure and Ideal Law was absent in these philosophical moorings.

THE REASONING DEPARTING FROM THE NATURE OF DICHOTOMY BETWEEN METAPHYSICAL AND NATURALISTIC TYPES OF ETHICAL CATEGORIES

Therefore in this book, our search for the ultimate order of reasoning continues. The end of our search is to reach for unison between the naturalistic and metaphysical conception of morality and ethics ensuing from the conception of what is good – goodness. The end is to arrive at that principal Law, which in one *functional* ontological sense, bridges up the gap caused by the heteronomy of thought in Kant. Hegel's conception of the World Spirit in dialectical historical evolution, as the design of occidental thought, also identified with the end of rationalism (Hegel trans. Sibree, 1956); Hume's inductive reasoning causing the divide between deductive and inductive reasoning (Popkin & Stroll, 2003), are other examples suffering from the problem of heteronomy. This is the separation between pure and practical reason; between *a priori* and *a posteriori* truths; between noumenon and phenomenon.

The monotheistic law declares its challenge to human consciousness on this matter of searching and discovering the ultimate truth: If you have that rational capability to reason out the true reality by the episteme then bring it forth in the world-system. This exists as the challenge of the monotheistic law to all generations, civilizations, and to all shades of thought over all time. The issue is a deeply epistemological one. The challenge occupies the *raison d'etre* of the monotheistic law in connection with the world-system in every detail. This marks emanation of moral and ethical reasoning arising from the episteme of oneness. Such epistemic foundation establishes the *functional* ontological formalism in living experience. The immanent learning process, which is driven by the episteme, marches into an evolutionary construction of the world of unity of knowledge, being, and becoming. The evolutionary learning process ends the learning gap of the dynamics of search for goodness at the point of the Great Event. The Great Event is as certain as is the primordial ontology of the oneness of God as represented in the monotheistic law.

THE LAW OF FINANCIAL INTEREST IN ECONOMIC AND SOCIAL PERSPECTIVES

We will argue that, if there is one root cause of human depravity causing instability, deprivation and inequity in participation, ownership and resource distribution in the whole history of mankind until the present day, this is the rate of interest in resource allocation, production, ownership, and distribution of wealth. In other words, the entire economic and social injustice to mankind has been due to the continuation of the rate of financial interest and its concomitant disorders in everything. Furthermore, we will argue that the interest-centered predicament cannot be changed unless there are conceptual, structural, and instrumental changes in social, financial and economic relations. At the end we are searching for what is the 'good – goodness'. The answer is offered by the ends of a new financial architecture that can be erected in the light of the monotheistic law relating to the replacement of the rate of interest by a productive real economy in trade in the good things of life.[1]

THE QUESTION OF BANK-SAVINGS, CAPITAL ACCUMULATION AND EQUITY

We define national savings 'S' as the sum-total of household savings defined by the holding of assets in the form of (1) bonds (B), (2) shares (Sh), (3) a mix of bonds and shares (B+Sh). We define savings by financial firms using equivalent financial instruments; and Government savings defined as the surplus of tax-revenue (T) over government expenditure (G) plus surplus in the total balance of payments accounts. We define the total balance of payments as the sum of trade surplus (X-M) and surplus in capital accounts (KAB).

We write S in the given symbols as,

$$S = B(i,Y_d) + Sh(r,Y_d) + (T\text{-}G)(i,r,Y) + [(X\text{-}M) + KAB](i,r,e,Y), \quad (1)$$

Here 'i' denotes nominal rate of interest;

- r denotes nominal rate of return on assets;
- Y_d denotes disposable income;
- Y denotes nominal GDP;
- e denotes effective exchange rate.

Bank-saving is defined here as the savings motivated by financial instruments offered by banks to hold savings in cash-balance. Banks though also finance real investments out of savings at home and abroad. But in this component of savings there exist a mix of portfolios between interest-bearing ones and trade related ones. Interest-bearing portfolios represent the holding of bank-savings in financial instruments as cash-balance. The rest of the bank-savings may be mobilized as financial resource in productive real assets.

Conventional saving theory stands on the postulate of opportunity cost between such savings and spending. Besides, if we further invoke the Keynesian income multiplier model then movements in interest rates and productive rates of return form inverse relationships. Since investments (spending) and savings are intertemporal in nature, therefore, by using the time-dependent discount rates of cash-flows in terms of rates of interest, we obtain the result on the inverse relationship between rate of return and interest rate.[2] Because of the intertemporal implication here, this inverse relationship prevails everywhere in both the static and the intertemporal cases.

Now by using this result on the inverse relationship between rates of return belonging to the real economy and the rates of interest belonging to the financial economy, bank-savings drawing funds into the financial economy always stands as marginal substitute for spending in the real economy. A given amount of savings as resource is thus driven by the substitution of resource allocation between the real and financial sectors as opportunity cost. This opportunity cost is denoted by the (interest-rate/yield) relative denoted by i/r.

In expression (1) we obtain the signed results for:

$$S = B(i,Y_d) + Sh(r,Y_d) + (T\text{-}G)(i,r,Y) + [(X\text{-}M) + KAB](i,r,e,Y) \quad (2)$$

By total differentiation in respect of 'i' we obtain,

$$dS/di = \overset{-}{(\partial B/\partial i)} + \overset{+}{(\partial B/\partial Y_d)}.\overset{-}{(dY_d/di)} + \overset{+}{(\partial Sh/\partial r)}.\overset{-}{(dr/di)} + \overset{+}{(\partial Sh/\partial Y_d)}.\overset{-}{(dY_d/di)}$$

$$+ \text{[BANK-SAVINGS EFFECT]} \qquad (3)$$

$$\overset{-}{(\partial(T\text{-}G)/\partial i)} + \overset{+}{(\partial(T\text{-}G)/\partial r)}.\overset{-}{(dr/di)} + \overset{+}{(\partial(T\text{-}G)/\partial Y)}.\overset{-}{(dY/di)}$$

$$\text{[MACROECONOMIC POLICY EFFECTS]} \qquad (4)$$

$$+ \overset{-}{\partial[(X\text{-}M) + KAB]/\partial i} + \overset{+}{\{\partial[(X\text{-}M) + KAB]/\partial r\}}.\overset{-}{(dr/di)} \left\{ \text{EXTERNAL} \right.$$

$$+ \overset{\pm}{\{\partial[(X\text{-}M) + KAB]/\partial e\}}.\overset{-}{(de/di)} + \overset{+}{\{\partial[(X\text{-}M) + KAB]/\partial Y\}}.(dY/di) \left\{ \text{SECTOR} \right. \qquad (5)$$

REPERCUSSION BY EXPRESSION (2) EFFECTS

The net value of expression (2) in terms of the signs as shown is controlled by the negativity of total bank-saving effects on potential resource mobilization. It shows that interest rates cause negative impact on real-economy variables in terms of endogenous relations in the economy. When endogenous forces deepen in the economy, the policy effects diminish. The external sector repercussion effects heighten; but the negative relation between r and i is preserved. In the end we note that savings converted to resource mobilization by means of real-sector development financing instruments in favor of the real economy is reduced by the growth of bank-savings following increasing interest-rate trends.

In Keynesian economic arrangement the role of exogenous macroeconomic policy effects increases. Consequently, interest rate plays an important role in governing policy. For that reason, unless such interest rates are maintained at a low level of prime rates, the real economy cannot be stimulated by means of the income multiplier by expansionary aggregate expenditure policies. The effect then is continuing underemployment and unstable conditions between price, resource mobilization, employment, real economy variables, and interest rates. The end result is that, social policies such as poverty alleviation, non-inflationary economic growth and socioeconomic development sustainability remain difficult to attain. Consequently, the subdued or publically expensive macroeconomic policy regimes cannot effectively establish the naturalistic ethics of full-employment that Keynes wished to attain by the economic dynamics as a rationalist philosopher emulating G.E. Moore. The full-employment level remains unattainable. The economic relations between interest rates, price level, income and aggregate spending in the real economy remain volatile and uncertain even as the income multiplier heightens spending effect of income by the presence of exogenous forces enacted by government and the monetary authority.

INTEREST RATE EFFECTS ON THE RICH AND THE POOR

Conventional economics holds that capital accumulation is necessary for economic growth. Capital accumulation is caused by bank-savings that cause liquid capital to be turned into interest income over time. Bank-savings thereby always cause a substitution of liquid capital for real capital investments. The financial economy is substituted for the real economy as two competing and dichotomous activities in the eyes of mainstream economic reasoning. Those who own initial stocks of money capital can accumulate quick wealth out of capitalized interest income ensuing from liquid bank-savings. Higher capital accumulation enables deepening ownership and power in the acquisition of wealth. Competition and market sharing of opportunities, wealth, power and profits heighten in favor of the rich owners. Extensive command over resource in the competitive and technological ownership and accumulative wealth game of the rich deepens. Along with this, the expansion of the capital base and the challenges to compete also heightens. Consequently, the scope for redistribution of resources in the social order diminishes. The endogenous effects of morality, ethics and values diminish, and give way to the exogenous presence of public policies to correct market failures with compensations.

The social ills that engender fall on the poor and the small enterprises. Unequal redistribution as opposed to self-reliant participatory entitlement and empowerment generated by engaging the poor and the small in the market economy takes over. Economic productivity and sustainability of the productive power, and creativity of the real economy, where the poor and the small enterprises toil, remain subdued by the expanding financial economy marginalizing the real economy.

The problem of equitable resource redistribution, ownership, and the rise of morality and ethics through the learning dynamics of consciousness in market exchange mechanism is never resolved. Over and above this social predicament the non-sustainability of stable price, employment, monetary, financial, and marginalized employment relations in the real economy compound with the widening poverty gap in the presence of the interest-bearing regime.

INTEREST RATE REGIME VS. THE PARTICIPATORY WORLDVIEW CONCEPTION OF ETHICO-ECONOMIC VALUE

Gauthier (1986, p. 337, slightly edited) writes on a perspective of participatory social contract between entrepreneurs: “Morality takes on different colouration when viewed in relation to participation. For asocial seekers and strivers morality could be no more than a needed but unwelcome constraint. But for those who value participation, a morality by agreement, although still a source of social constraint, it makes their shared activity mutually welcome and so stable, ensuring the absence of coercion or deception. As our analysis of co-operation has shown, agreed constraint is a condition of the rational acceptability to the actors of the division of benefits realized by their shared activity. And so it is a condition of their finding participation in such activity intrinsically valuable.”

We can adapt the participatory and cooperative perspectives in their epistemological meaning to the relationship between money, finance, real economy, and the banking system as an institution that can carry the essence of wellbeing, justice and fairness to the extensive domain of ‘everything’ that justice affects. In such a context, Gauthier’s and for that, the whole of the rationalistic philosophy of law and justice for the understanding of general and particular issues of society, economics, and finance, must be critically reviewed. This is because rationalism is incapable of attaching epistemological credence to the substantive reality of God and the monotheistic unitary law of ‘everything’. Within this situation the general and the particular issues are enmeshed for a unique and universal explanation. The issues are thus so resolved under the *functional* ontological phenomena interconnecting God, the world-system, and the learning process embedded in the episteme of unity of knowledge. The rationalists, and for that Gauthier, do not attach value to such a holistic perspective of ‘everything’.

Gauthier’s entire work is on the philosophical translation of the idea of economic rationality, in which the conception of justice, morality and value is based on the individual preference summation to the social level. As a result, the participatory nature of society is erected on the foothold of such a rationally motivated individual preference and utility aggregation to form social utility. These were also the ways of Rawls, Arrow, Harsanyi, Hammond and Benthamite utilitarian philosophers. We have discussed them at length before.

The rationalists are completely mute on the nature and effects of interest rates as impediments to value socioeconomic reality as being premised on relational unity that otherwise exists between value, price, money and financial and real sectors. To the rationalists in general, and thereby to Keynes, the monetarists, and to Gauthier, interest rate remains a measure of value. The argument made is that interest rate is a measure that is human derived out of agreement by discourse. Gauthier thereby claims the relevance of moral agreement between lenders and borrowers as the legitimacy for the presence of interest rates. The argument intensifies in macroeconomic policy formulation as it is induced exogenously by the rate of interest and its concomitant financial environment.

On the meaning of value, which Stigler (1970) remarks, is the most complex issue of economic theory, Gauthier remains ambivalent. There is no ontological argument given to the meaning of value that arises from the embedded social structure. Gauthier simply attaches a meaning of morality that is gained by social agreement between rationally discoursing agents. Value becomes the result of such a social discourse. On this point, Gauthier (op cit p. 47) championing the cause of the rationalists, and thereby their sanctified liberal methodological individualism, writes: "Value is then not an inherent characteristic of things or states, not something existing as part of the ontological furniture of the universe in a manner quite independent of persons and their activities. Rather, value is created or determined through preference. Values are products of our affections."

Such a notion of value is contradicted by its detachment from the ontological roots. Our premise of reasoning is the episteme of the monotheistic unitary law and its impact on the knowledge-induced unified world-system. A few examples are given here.

Consider a farmer who in his roaming through the forest discovers an exotic fruit. He has never seen it before. He takes it home and finds out that the fruit has inherent medicinal value. He could sell the fruit for a high price as measure of value. This would result in a monopolistic market exchange generating price as value out of bargaining between the buyer and seller (farmer). Furthermore, if a utility function for the fruit exists for the buyer and seller then the price would be equal to the marginal utility of that joint social utility.

Contrarily, the farmer can decide to open up a farming enterprise of the fruit so as to grow more of it and sell it in the midst of market exchange. The farmer's and buyers' monopolistic and monopsonistic powers respectively, are broken up by such an expanded market exchange. The endogenous process of market transformation bestows moral and ethical values of medicinal good to many buyers.

The question in either of the above two case is this: What level of price can be considered as economic value for the farmer? In the rationalistic sense, mutual bargaining for a monopolistic value would be considered as morally acceptable. Yet on moral basis, the farmer is not the owner of the intrinsic substance of medicinal value of the fruit. The medicinal value is ontologically inherent in the fruit. The farmer can at best claim the cost of his effort to bring the fruit down from the tree, preserve and export it to the market, and the like. Consequently, only these components of the delivery of the fruit into market exchange can qualify as value.

The ontologically inherent medicinal value of the fruit remains as the exogenously endowed value in the market valuation of the fruit.

The fruit thereby fetches its true value in price in the second case of market exchange, which is an endogenous activity. The true value of the medicinal fruit is now determined by the ethical transmission of the ontologically inherent medicinal value into an ethicized (farmer conscience) market exchange. The market exchange mechanism is thus the true medium to determine total value. In this case of a rare good in exchange, the moral law determines the just pricing as value in the midst of the socially transformed market exchange by farmer's consciousness. Robust interaction is engendered between market and polity (institutionalized and affective moral law) to generate the medium of ethical market exchange. The ontological category of original medicinal substance of the fruit forms the ethical parameter of just pricing. The ethical market transformation realizes the morally and ethically induced value by market exchange. Such a determination of value renders ineffective the rationalistic idea of value as being independent of the ontological initial state of the fruit. For further details on the theme of value see Choudhury (2011, pp. 50-61).

Next, consider the following example, which proves that there remains inconsistency in determining the object of value in the rationalist approach to resource *allocation*. The rationalist approach to value does not make any difference in the choice between interest rate and the rate of return. Consequently, much of the moral depravity by the rate of interest in terms of the financial and real sector dichotomy of resource allocation remains ignored. Ethical determinism is now set by a rationalist idea of the liberal discursive society.

To formalize further, let the rationalist social welfare function be denoted by W = W(i,r). 'i' represents the interest-rate as return caused by the disjoint and competing financial sector with the real economy. 'r' represents the rate-of-return caused by the disjoint and competing real economy with the financial sector. Gauthier's championing of the rationalist liberal doctrinaire accepts the postulates of utility maximization subject to the budgetary constraint. That is, the following is accepted as an acceptable criterion of morality under rational choice:

$$\text{Max } W(S(i),I(r)), \tag{6}$$

subject to the budget, $B = i.S + r.I$, where S denotes bank-saving; I denotes spending.

By Lagrangian classical constrained optimization of W(.) we obtain:

$$(\partial W/\partial S)/i = (\partial W/\partial I)/r = 1/P; \tag{7}$$

P being an index compounding i and r.

Thereby, $dS/dI = -(r/i)$ (8)

Now if 'i' is the object of value then it is solely chosen exogenously. Let the optimal point on the welfare surface be say, the northern (S,0), with S denoting bank-saving. Conversely, if 'r' is the object of value in moral agreement by discourse between the financial sector and the real sector, with I denoting investment, then the optimal point on the welfare surface is say, at the southern corner (0,I). These are mutually exclusive choices of value. Hence, there is a contradiction in terms of the nature of 'r' and 'i' in social choice.

Finally, any other point on the welfare surface is an unstable point. It therefore results in social depravity by inefficient allocation of resources between the financial sector and the real sector, as we have discussed this point earlier.

Conclusively therefore, by various examples it can be proved that the idea of value as rationally assigned to market and by humanly discoursed rationalists, is at best a notion not a precept. This fact is established both conceptually and analytically. We now go on to investigate this theme regarding the impossibility of the interest-ridden financing, economic, and social arrangement on the wellbeing of the poor. We will continue on to invoke the principle of social contract in the mold of the world-system with participatory empowering involving a rationalistic discursive society and its ontological moral impossibilities in this issue (Sztompka, 1974). The topic is poverty alleviation in the midst of the rationalist design of the financial and real sectors and the emergent social order out of this.

CONTRASTING MODELS OF SOCIAL JUSTICE

In the models of social justice championed by Rawls, Nozick, Gauthier, and Keynes in terms of his ethical persuasion of G.E. Moore, and many other rationalists, the inherent axiom of the model construct and the social contract that ensues are neoclassical in nature. The authors are unable to liberate their arguments from the axiom of scarcity. This darkens the human side of the social contract. There have been social thinkers on the other side who have written and produced evidences to negate the axiom of scarcity in many human societies (Polanyi, 1957).

Contrarily, the rationalists' understanding of scarcity as the necessary evil against the social desire and necessity for cooperation and participation is contrary to the axiomatic meaning of scarcity that is attached to the axiom of economic rationality. So strong and irrevocable is the core axiom of scarcity in economic theory that without it, the entire economic reasoning and social philosophy collapses. On this point Gauthier states (op cit p.335): "scarcity is the humanly necessary evil. Faced with scarcity, choice as a device that, in selecting some activities, rejects others is necessary, and the rule of rational choice is maximally to fulfill one's preferences."

Scarcity as a postulate of economic rationality is a necessary and sufficient condition for the existence of optimal allocation of resources. Thereby, the postulate links up with rational choice, and all the optimization criteria, individual and aggregate social preference pre-ordering, and competition and contest of market exchange. An example is at point here. The state is adequately well off by its tax revenues. But she still encounters the scarcity problem of allocating a given budget for development of villages and the urban sector; for poverty alleviation and industrialization. The resource allocations, in all such cases, result in marginal rates of substitution between alternatives. This is equivalent to the existence of opportunity cost of resource allocation between competing ends.

Now, how does the banking system react to such an order of optimal allocation of budget as scarce resource? The socioeconomic development and growth patterns feed into the banking system via the investment, savings, and industrialization programs. Such a climate of development and growth planning, productivity and profitability means the inevitable rise of the market and private economy by endogenous forces. The Government addresses the underlying issues exogenously. In this, a government action is linked with the residual wellbeing of the social sector. The private sector and the social sector remain permanently opposed as marginal substitutes under the axiom of resource scarcity.

Thus, no matter what, even as the Western society advances to its highest abundance, the core axiom of resource scarcity in economics, finance, and socio-scientific thought by social Darwinism that affects both society and science as competing processes in the western mold, will prevail always. Along with this permanent characteristic of Western socio-scientific order embedded in a rationalist worldview of liberalism, participatory social contract will be colored by the axiom of resource scarcity and all the social impediments of competition and conflict this axiom and behavior bears.

Now bring in the optimal resource allocation problem for poverty alleviation in the rationalist worldview. We cannot envision now that the axiom of resource scarcity can be supplanted by something better; as long as the endogenously functioning moral-social consciousness does not prevail in the first place. Moral-social consciousness can arise only by the necessary and sufficient prevalence of the good things of life. Such a state of moral-social attainment requires endogenous reflection on and acceptance of human goodwill for the good – goodness. Goodness and wellbeing would then be instilled by the morality, ethics, knowledge, and moral-social consciousness emanating from the law of symbiotic oneness (organic relational epistemology of the monotheistic law). Now together with the new vision of social reality and human participation in it to derive and advance the just social contract, the much needed design of the moral socioeconomic order can be realized.

Stability of the emergent moral-social economic, financial, and social order, replacement of interest rate in bank-saving by tradable instruments, empowerment in a truly participatory (complementary) form of social reformation can be actualized by the interactive, integrative, and evolutionary learning world-system model (IIE-model). The human society along with the domain of resources, and markets and institutions that bring these together in symbiosis by discourse in the light of the epistemic law of unity of knowledge and the world-system, form the paired universe of epistemic unity for the moral-social purpose.

REPRESENTING THE ASOCIAL NATURE OF RELATIONSHIP BETWEEN SOCIAL PARTICIPATION AND THE ECONOMIC POSTULATE OF SCARCITY: THE RATIONALISTIC QUAGMIRE

Figure 1 shows how uncertainty, instability, loss of wellbeing by exclusiveness of the poor cause fuzzy allocations, unstable pricing of returns, and volatile equilibriums everywhere in the presence of unpredictable relations between interest rates and real yields. The endogenous nature of social change is lost to the power of markets and methodological individualism, as the expansion of the resource trajectory OU moves in the direction of urban welfare. Consequently, the trajectory on the goods-plane moves in the direction of capital goods away from the basic needs of life.

Figure 1. Wellbeing and resource depravity caused by interest rates

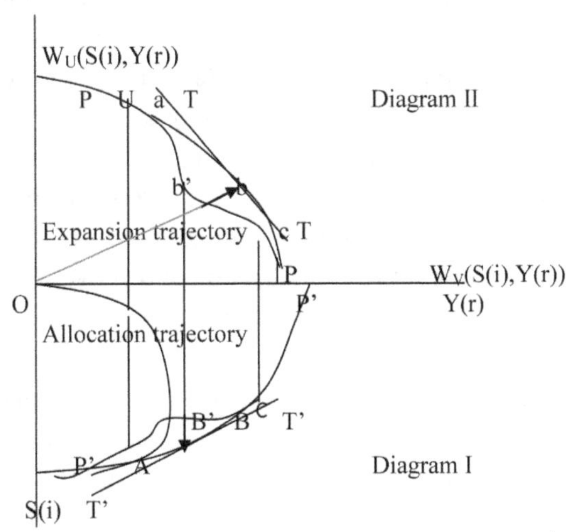

In such a scenario of contest for scarce resources between the rich and the poor; between the village and the urban sector; between the financial sector and the real sector; and between self and other, any social intervention to correct such a demeaning situation is by the exogenous policies of institutions, state, government and powerful external governance. Every such action distorts the smooth functioning of the economic, financial, and social order by the burden of taxes, declining real output, and deficits that the human generations pay for without let up. In the end, the market process fails because resource scarcity makes self-centered individualism as the driving force of the social contract. The state fails because of its heavy-handed exogenous governance. This distorts the efficiency of markets to function well. Neither the market process nor the government intervention taken exogenously or solely is appropriate for moral-social reconstruction of the fallen pathos of resource scarcity coloring the human outlook.

As Figure 1 shows, the rate of interest returns full circle to haunt the entire set of moral-social relations. Participation is just a wishful name invoked. It is not a reality in such a contested view of mind-matter dichotomy. Participation is a social arrangement for sharing resources by discourse. Yet participatory arrangement upholds the commercial, political, and social power, and the exogenous nature of institutions to enforce policies and will. The human nature and human will remain unchanged. The consequences thereafter take different sets of stratagem and interests. In the end therefore, once again the absolutely unfailing need for moral and ethical endogeneity of values, consciousness and learning derived from the epistemic origins of unity of knowledge remains the invincible answer to the brotherhood of humankind.

Certain questions arise. They were raised earlier in the history of political economy, but never adequately answered by Marx due to his belief on the one-dimensional man who does not submit to morality and ethics. Marx saw in individuals and society simply the reign of politico-economic power, conflict, and self-interests. Marx failed to understand the rich dimensions of the moral worth in the making of human psyche and the human future (Berman, 1989). Marx painted the bloody picture of capitalism in terms of what he claimed as its success in overcoming scarcity by economic abundance. Yet the question of scarcity in the framework of economic rationality, and the limits of social contract resting on power and competition, remain permanent in rationalism and neo-liberalism. True that abundance has increased by the growth of technology, the acquisition of resources, and control over them across the globe (Wallerstein, 1974). But methodological individualism in the socio-scientific sphere involving mind and matter and the neo-mercantilist and neo-colonial governance and control over global resources has deepened. Power, want, and opportunities aggrandize the self-interested agent to seek the ever more. Competition and contest in the postulate of scarcity of resources deepen to configure the adverse mind-matter relationship, even at the heights of abundance. The consequential nature of demand,

and the alteration of social power, the meaning of self and other, and ownership and acquisition of wealth, remain predominant (Palan, 2000).

Diagram I of Figure 1 explains the well-known way of allocation of the budget line denoted by T'T' between the two goods, namely, bank-savings (interest (i)-bearing) S(i), and the real output in terms of real yield 'r', thus Y(r). The slope of the budget line is (r/i). But as shown, anywhere randomly along the production possibility surface P'P' the region B'B is policy-corrected exogenously to establish optimal point on P'P'. There is a random premium (insurance) on this exogenous policy correction, such as payments of taxes and levies connected with the transaction costs on policy development and implementation. Consequently, the occurrence anywhere randomly along the surface P'P' causes the price relative (r/i) to become random. This is a result that would otherwise hold as well due to the uncertainty caused in the financial and real sectors, which is caused by the presence of interest rates, as explained earlier.

Every point in Diagram II is connected with a point in Diagram I. Diagram II explains the equivalent kind of resource allocation between the welfare distribution of the village sector (rural poverty) and the urban sector (industrialization). These are denoted by W(..) for the two sectors, respectively. The same consequences of randomness, volatility, instability and indeterminateness of relative prices hold true along the welfare distribution surfaces. These are caused by similar exogenous correction of market failures when neither market system nor institutions can respond to the much-desired endogenous social behavior of conscious agents instilled by learning in the epistemic domain of unity of knowledge arising from the moral law. This is contrary to the episteme of rationalism. Now both the regions denoted by (B,B') and (b,b') cause distortions of the surfaces where interest-rate depravity of sustainable development prevails all over.

We can now write,

$$-dY(r)/dS(i) = (i/r) \text{ is random and fuzzy in the (B,B') region} \tag{9}$$

$$\Leftrightarrow dW_v(S(i),Y(r))/dW_u((S(i),Y(r)) \tag{10}$$

is undefined in the fuzzy region (b,b'),[3] according to the first order conditions of welfare-maximization (Henderson & Quandt, 1971).

It is no doubt then that Phelps (1989) points out that, economic theory is not methodologically poised to answer the predominant social question, namely of wellbeing, social justice and poverty alleviation. We have now proved that the rate of interest is the central cause of the social predicament.

INTEREST RATE AND THE INCIDENCE OF POVERTY

Table 1 gives the relationship between the incidence of poverty and the rate of change of real GDP in the global scene. The data shows that for all cases shown, the slim percentage annual increases in HDI are not significantly affected by percent increases in growth rates of per capita GDP, despite the high rates shown. The implication then is that the other factors of HDI, such as longevity rates, enrolment ratios, adult education levels, and nutrition levels have not contributed significantly towards changes in HDI as related to annual rates of growth of GDP per capita.

OTHER THEORIES AND MODELS OF POVERTY ALLEVIATION AND SOCIAL JUSTICE IN RELATION TO THE RATE OF INTEREST

Is there a way out of poverty, conceptually and practically in received social and economic theory, and the organization of social contract thereby? To investigate this question critically, it is necessary to understand the causes and nature of poverty as the most debilitating condition of humankind, worse than the human health issue and global resource allocation problem. We emphasize this point, because the condition of human health may be based on personal familial adaptations to consumption and environment. Such conditions have been with human beings for a long time by cultural, social, economic and civilizational causes. Beyond such accrued experiences on health, the process of public health delivery will always cater

Table 1. Distortion relations between annual rates of change of HDI, poverty line, and GDP per capita, selected regions

Regions (%) (1990-2010)	HDI (%) (1990-2004)	GDP Per Capita HDI to GDP Per Capita[4]	ε Elasticity of
Developing Countries	1.15	3.00	0.38
Arab States	1.00	1.30	0.77
East Asia & Pacific	1.75	5.80	0.30
Latin America & Caribbean	0.80	1.10	0.73
South Asia	1.55	3.39	0.46
OECD	0.35	1.80	0.19
World	0.90	1.40	0.64

Sources: UNDP (2010). *Human Development Report 2010: The real wealth of nations, pathways to human development.*UNDP (2006). *Human Development Report 2006, Beyond scarcity: power, poverty, and the global water crisis*

to the needs of the seriously afflicted. Likewise, basic education has always been mankind's necessity. To build upon this and thereafter to deliver additional levels of tertiary education is always practiced by public authority. Consequently, as long as health and human resource development of the basic-needs kind are accessible by all, there is no particular cause of poverty due to these acquired conditions. It then remains for the public and social authority to engineer and enforce the social contract of a just and inclusive society of opportunities for all. Indeed, such basic-need guarantees of education and health are the very conditions promoted by the Millennium Development Goals (http://www.undp.org/mdg/basics.shtml).

Beyond acquiring the life-sustaining conditions of basic needs the rest of the needs become wants, except when residual caring is needed for the weak and distressed. Yet a whole population cannot be distressed; otherwise social collapse will follow. The poverty conditions on a balance between headcount, family income and entitlement, nutrition, human resource, health, participation and empowerment, public policy of a caring society, and above all, contentment and the balance of wellbeing of familial and community life, are sufficient for a good life according to the *dynamic* basic-needs regime of development in a learning and conscious social order. To avoid and alleviate abject and hard-core poverty is the goal of moral-social transformation into a learning society. Its principal objective criterion then is to attain simulated (learnt) levels of wellbeing in the good things of life. These comprise the essence of the *dynamic* basic-needs regime of development.

To demand more, over and above the *dynamic* basic needs of life-fulfillment along the learning trajectory of a participatory moral-social order, is to enter the gates of economic and social competition. Upon this condition, the depriving states of scarcity and methodological individualism, the conflict between self and other, and similar depravity, enter society lock, stock and barrels. Welfare is acquired at the expense of wellbeing by self-interested and competing social groups. Individuals and society inculcate social preferences that are based on self-interest, governing the welfare concept in economic theory. The institutions of banking, economics, finance, and society at large follow suit. Technology deepens the depriving consequences on the basis of power and ownership. Markets fail in their endogenous function of mobilizing resource by conscious preferences of individuals, institutions and the state. The exogenous power of governments takes over. Thereby, distortion effects on market exchange in basic-needs appear. Social wellbeing is diminished. Wellbeing and welfare are contrasting concepts in socio-scientific and cybernetic theory of an evolutionary learning worldview driven by epistemic oneness. In the real world, such oneness is manifest by pervasive complementarities and participation enabled by the monotheistic law and its worldly instruments.

In the end, we note that abject and hard-core poverty is not the cause, and its nature is not defined in the presence of a dynamic basic-needs regime of development with participation and discursive learning. Contrarily, poverty is the result of a demand for *wants* over *needs* (Levine, 1988). The impoverishing human state then follows in scarcity, competition, and individualism. The state of abundance reflected in the basic-needs regime of development by its intrinsic learning worldview under epistemic unity of knowledge is lost.

To cure this most heinous human state of abject poverty in any society, the moral and ethical premise of unity of knowledge and life (Choudhury, 2011) must be endogenously engineered into the model and implement of poverty alleviation within the entire socioeconomic development framework. Social wellbeing becomes the objective social criterion for simulating levels of poverty alleviation. The wellbeing function represents simulated balance between the good things of life as expressed through participatory social choices of the good things of life. Can such an epistemic worldview be found in the prevailing literature? That is, has mainstream scholarship engaged a worldview of unity of knowledge to develop an organically unified world-system?

An argument is made in favor of expanding the capital base for low-interest access to capital by labor to increase ownership. Following are examples: Consider banks that network to share expertise, equities, and costs to increase shareholding in the interest of profitability and sustainability of the networked business entity.

What would be the nature of capital formation in this case? The larger the business expansion, the more the capital need, and the cost and risk. Consequently, the premium for investment coming in the form of yields must be maintained high to meet the operational capital and long-term prospects. The short and medium term yields are a mix of interest rates and rates of returns on investments. According to the explanations provided earlier the resource allocation between the liquid and real assets, between short and medium term, and long-term assets, the field of (i/r) remains volatile. Consequently, capital accumulation takes the interest-rate bias. The real sector is ignored. From our arguments given earlier, poverty-alleviation is defeated.

Consider next government bonds and joint ventures that can be used to network investments between the private and public sectors. In this case too, long-term interest rates and rates of return combine together to de-stabilize the process of capital formation. The end result then is to move into interest-based bond financing or the like of it by shadow interest rates, such as coupon rates and discount rates used for capitalizing long-term cash-flows as yields from bond-financed assets. Thereby, the volatility, instability, riskiness and indeterminateness of the financial and real asset portfolio continue. Interest rates must thereby, re-enter as premium for capitalizing such uncertain conditions of capital expansion. The predicaments of poverty in the face of such adverse conditions of interest rate and socioeconomic instability are never reduced, even in the well-intended models of Binary Economics (Ashford, 1994).

An argument is made that the long-run rate of return from productive investments will outgrow the interest rates to create a capital base that can then be accessed by labor. This kind of financial argument is a mistaken article of faith. For consider the long-run capitalization series given below and apply the discounting by interest rate (i) with the Cash Flows (CF) being affected by rates of return (r).

$$PV(i,r) = \Sigma_{t=1}^{\infty} CF(1+r)^t/(1+i)^t = \Sigma_{t=1}^{\infty} CF.(1+r-i)^t \sim CF\int_0^{\infty} e^{-(i-r)t}dt \qquad (11)$$

The infinite cash-flow series (11) will be convergent if and only if, r < i. This is a mathematical condition that must hold always over time. Hence capital accumulation and the expansion of the capital base must always be in the direction of interest-based financing. Now if easy access to the capital base is allowed at a cost of capital say i', such that i > i'; then there would be r' < r. A series of i's and r's can thus be generated for which there are increasing sequences of PV(i,r) for such decreasing sequences of i's and corresponding r's. The implication then is that the financial firm would make increasing intertemporal profits by such a capitalization method. Hence, the capital base will forever be tied to the sequences of interest-based financing above the rates of return. The predicaments of ownership, equitable distribution, and poverty alleviation, are thereby never diminished in reference to our concept of wellbeing.

What is the answer to the various approaches to poverty alleviation under the offers of interest-based financing of soft-loans, financial accessibility, ownership by deferment, and charitable assistance by the state? Upon this we will also discuss the structure of small to medium size asset accessibility and development as microenterprises and SMEs within the same interest-rate regime of financial and real sector relationship of wellbeing and sustainability.

A low-interest loanable capital base and asset ownership requires a long-term payment schedule to capitalize the total value of the held assets along with the progressively increasing rate schedule on property taxes. Consequently, the debt capital held is not amortized over long time periods. This causes the net value of property to remain lower than the purchase price. The experience has been in the case of subprime mortgage rates in South USA during the Great Recession in the U.S.A. While mortgage rates remained low, the expected future price of real estates could not be amortized by the net lower prevailing value, thus leading into property foreclosures. Such public calamity was a mighty lever to hit all stakeholders alike during the Great Recession in present times as during the Great Depression of the thirties.[5]

Other forms of ills also darkened the subprime-rate financial crisis. There was the ethical failure on the part of buyers. They were led astray by the lower mortgage rates and market-led liberal lending by mortgage companies. Consequently, such buyers indulged in excessive acquisition of un-capitalized wealth. When the financial bubble burst, the ethical failing led into market devaluation of wealth, status and buyers' satisfaction. The owner became a debtor and an insolvent dreamer of failed wealth.

On the aftermath of such financial cataclysm there came about exogenously applied disciplining of the buying spree. This happened by financial regulations. Yet the government expanded debt capital on public funds through government bonds. There never was any conscience to control the debt problem *per se*. The net capitalized value of financial assets mortgaged, leased, and bonded by credit expansion, did not effectively recover from the financial crisis of subprime mortgage rates. Not to speak of the very poor, who might be seen as the happy noncompeting groups in the American poverty slumps, but even the small and medium size entrepreneurs and prospective owners were worse off in recent years (Stiglitz, 2003). Non-sustainability and acquisitive wants in the market venue as built-in endogenous American reign of capitalism on the one hand, and the heavy and failed exogenous governance by the state and monetary authority on the other hand, have together failed in their task to attain stability.

KELSONIAN AND ALTERNATIVE ECONOMICS FOR AMERICAN SOCIAL EQUALITY

Kelso (Ashford, 1994) gave the idea of 'productiveness' as an enlarged capital ownership by free access to a supply-side economy. The idea of productiveness in Kelsonian economics is different from factor productivity (Kelso & Patricia, 1965). Productiveness measures the ratio of the sum of value of factor input services to the value of total output generated by the inputs. Yet neither the notion of productivity of capital and labor (total productivity) nor productiveness can explain the social, economic and financial causes of poverty, and then explain how poverty can be addressed as social evil to contend with.

Along the same lines of arguments of received economic and financial reasoning embedded in capitalization theory other forms of innovative ideas fall into the same impossibility to alleviate poverty. An example is the Employee Stock Ownership Plan (ESOP). On the financial aspect, an ESOP comprises a tripartite financial contract involving the company that sells stocks to the employee trust fund. The trust fund then borrows the sale value of loan from a bank and pays the company this amount. The company guarantees this loan to the bank. The company then pays annual amount to the trust along with interest. This amount is then returned to the bank. Out of these periodic payments of loans, a formula-determined amount is saved in the employee savings fund (Nightingale, 1982).

The capitalist problem of ESOP as with similar financing methods is with the capitalization formula, which is based on the interest incentive on the part of the bank as a partner in the deferred debt-financing method. The effect of such a financing method is to extend the interest-financing culture intertemporally in and across the continuums of social systems.

The total amount of interest so earned by the trust fund and returned to the bank is the principal incentive to uphold the company's altruism to fund the employees' retiring fund by the shares bought by the company. The alternative to this kind of financing on the basis of ownership in the company assets by means of employees' shareholding would be to convert the funds of the trust company into investment shares, with the bank being a participant in this along with the company, the trustees, and the employees.

THE MARXIAN IMPOSSIBILITY IN POVERTY ALLEVIATION

The methodological impossibility to alleviate poverty exists also in Marxian ideas. The development of Marxian economic and social theory has taken place within the paradigm of scarcity and conflict. The difference from the capitalist economic treatment of resource allocation is in the unit of analysis and its impact on preference formation and preference aggregation to comprise social preferences. The Marxian unit of analysis is the aggregation of individual preferences to the state level, and to explain how preference aggregation is realized in Marxian social transformation (Heilbroner & Milberg, 1995).

In every case nonetheless, be it political economy, world-system theory or social theory, the continuance of the core postulate of scarcity and competition and methodological individualism have marked every shade of politico-economic and social thought. Buchanan (1999, p. 391) has emphasized this viewpoint in his words: "Concomitant with methodological individualism as a component of the hard core is the postulate of rational choice, a postulate that is shared over all research programs in economics."

Marx's theory of socialism was a prognosis of the theory of capitalism based on the labor theory of value emulating Ricardo. Marx tried to explain the inherent theory of value in terms of the circulation of capital by his M-C-M model, with the intervening production part in C representing the division of money-capital into payment for labor value and other means of production, like capital and land. But we can make the third most important element of payment in the M-C process. This is the conversion of M into pseudo-money, such as bonds sold and bought in the capital market in the generalized form of C. Otherwise too, in the complete and complex cycle of money capital across the economy, many other pseudo-monies can enter in the production of C. C thus becomes embodied interest-accrued in money form arising from pseudo-money. The path M-C-M is then wholly embodied interest. The capital structure is caused by debt capital, which is interest bearing. The productive part of this capital structure enters a similar process of formation.

Only labor remains a different category of productive factor in such an interest-washed circulation of capital in the M-C-M model. According to Marx, in the capitalist economic system labor is deprived by surplus value taken by the capitalist. This surplus value arises by the force of interest rates. Consequently, we have noted that in the usual economic model the price relative of intertemporal allocation of resources is denoted by (i/r), where 'i' is the rate of interest (of any kind) in total capital formation in terms of its plethora of term-structure of interest rates crossing across the economy-wide capital circulation process. 'r' is the return on assets in the real economy, real or nominal in value.

According to Marx's theory, such real asset must be solely a positive function of *living* labor. Consequently, 'r' is a direct function of wages 'w'. By missing out the debilitating role of interest rate in capital formation in the generalized economy-wide perspective of M-C-M model, Marx and Ricardo overlooked the interest-rate impediment in human possibility. Thereby, none of these theories could effectively incorporate the role of morality and ethics in economic science. Consequently, as in the case of the non-ethical behavior characterizing irrational exuberance, the buying spree of property in the subprime rate regime could not be molded by reversal of conscience. Likewise, no financial phenomenon could be explained by any alternative analytical approach that would be different from the method of endogenous ethics integrated with economic and social preferences.

Economics and social theory thus remained entrenched in their assumed exogenous ethical intentions. This is the case with Binary Economics, Marxism, and social choice theory. Exogenous treatment of ethics reflected logical positivism. The normative possibilities are sidelined (Friedman, 1953). Consequently, a robust theory of ethics and economics never emerged. Public and social policies reflect the exogeneity of ethics. This perspective prevails in economic and financial theory and practice.

THE NATURE OF POVERTY AND POVERTY ALLEVIATION IN REFERENCE TO INTEREST-BASED FINANCING REGIME

Our review of the literature and critical examination of prevalent ideas show conceptually and empirically that in spite of the tremendous technological advancement that the world experienced in its state of modernity, there remains the serious post-modern question of social justice and poverty alleviation. Among the many deconstructive features of post-modernity we have studied here, the debilitating impact of any and every interest-based theory and regime on the critical issue of poverty alleviation, that otherwise comprise a core theme of morality and ethics, prevails. The core moral issues are social justice, fairness, sustainability, and within them the trend towards equality, distribution, participatory empowerment, and poverty alleviation.

In spite of the exuberance over technological power and affluence of the modern age, the poor and deprived are no better off. In fact, they are worse off today than ever before. This fact points to a permanent ethical debility of the continued conceptualization, as by the core axiom of scarcity in the *allocation* of resources, and its application through economic, finance, and social theory into institutional and policy effects. Likewise, we have noted that any exogenously induced program to establish moral and ethical sustainability for long-lasting impact on social justice, empowerment and poverty alleviation cannot realize human consciousness in its flight towards morality and ethics.

This otherwise is accomplished by an endogenous trait of the true moral worth. Likewise, markets that do not learn on moral and ethical consciousness by the dynamic transformation of individual preferences forming social preferences, and thereby social wellbeing, are not the answer of endogenous realization of human consciousness.

In the end, we infer from our various arguments that, poverty is caused by the desire to acquire possessions beyond means. This is true of both the rich and the poor. The rich by not meeting their responsibility to share with the poor in a participatory social contract acquire what they are not entitled to. The rich then take for themselves that which he ought to give away as sharing in life-sustaining means. The poor on the other hand, by *desiring* to acquire more than what his means allow, including what he is entitled to duly have in a participatory society, enters a contested social framework. From such conflict-ridden social situations the rich and the poor do not establish a complementary sharing social arrangement. That is, the core axiom of resource scarcity found in the rational economic sense, distorts the moral-social contract.

Along with the visage of contest in society between the rich and the poor, the dynamic intertemporal basic-needs regime of development disappears and is replaced by the wants economy. Wellbeing and the capacity for happiness and sustainability of life-sustaining goods and services are reduced, as prices increase. Among these, the rate of interest remains the financial collateral on real assets. Ownership and equitable distribution are thwarted in the short run and long run.

Poverty alleviation can therefore be the result not of plenty but of lack of moderation, with the just and balanced entitlement and empowerment capability for the poor and the rich. Only in a participatory society both the rich and poor can self-actualize on *needs*, not on *wants*. It is said that a rich man who has no craving for acquisition and hoarding is a citizen of the spiritual world. A poor man who has all the craving for material wealth and acquisition is a man of the acquisitive world.

The intertemporal dynamic basic-needs social order embedded in the exchange of the good things of life forms the good and just society (Paul, Miller, Jr., & Paul, 1995). The connection between law and a just society via the process of the moral order is the essence of the good society. Its goal is not to attain a rich and acquisitive society, where the teeming many live in poverty and deprivation. Hart (1997, p. 156) quotes regarding such an acquisitive society: "What are states without justice but robber-bands enlarged".

Poverty alleviation is thereby a grand circular causation field of interactions leading to social consensus by participation in a discursive society. This issue was earlier penned by Myrdal (edited by Streeten, 1958). Such a society invokes learning dynamics of an intertemporal basic-needs regime of development and wellbeing. Such is the sustainable development characteristic of our interactive, integrative, and evolutionary model (IIE) of learning dynamics in knowledge, time and space dimensions that we have presented in this book. More on such a design of development by the moral and ethical consciousness will be studied in the next chapters using the IIE-learning process model.

The participatory nature of social contract between the rich and poor is a circularly causal functional interrelationship between these two groups; and of the two together with the participatory nature of the social, economic, and financial system. Within the complex of interrelationships are the lubricating functions of economy, finance, banks, institutions, the public authority and community. Figure 2 explains such a participatory circular causation dynamics (Wunsch, 1988).

CONCLUSION

The rule of justice and equality in a participatory model of the social, economic and financial order is enabled in a dynamic basic-needs regime of development. Such a regime is established and sustained as life-fulfilling one in a system that complements every part of it by automatically releasing resources for social wellbeing. Resource scarcity thus becomes untenable in such an order both by generating abundance and by rejecting the postulate of rationalism that breeds on scarcity, competition, and methodological individualism. A rationalist society reflects its utilitarian transformation in its welfare criterion, far removed from the wellbeing concept of epistemic unity of knowledge in the learning world-system.

The central theme that the participatory social, economic, and financial order replaces is the debilitating function of the rate of interest. Interest rate is a surplus over and above the productive returns of an economy. It thereby segments the social

Figure 2. Participatory interrelations in a unified social, economic, and financial system

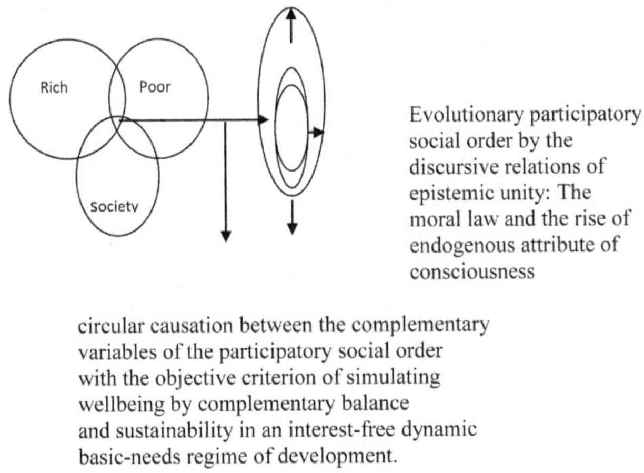

order between the real economy and the disjoint financial economy causing competition as opposed to complementarities between the financial sector and the real economy. The participatory social contract is systemically denied in the interest-bearing regime of development, resource allocation, and change. The existence of interest rate in every model of the capitalist genre, despite the good intention that rationalist thinkers may have, becomes debility everywhere across society today, and in the intertemporal sense of resource allocation, productive participation, and distribution.

Poverty alleviation along the lines of a concerted and participatory approach involving the poor and the government, the urban sector, and the rural sector, is being sought as panacea by the world development organizations. On this issue the World Bank (2000, p.12) writes:

The strategy in this report recognizes that poverty is more than inadequate income or human development—it is also vulnerability and a lack of voice, power, and representation. With this multidimensional view of poverty comes greater complexity in poverty reduction strategies, because more factors—such as social and cultural forces—need to be taken into account.

The way to deal with this complexity is through empowerment and participation—local, national, and international....

On the same topic UNDP (1999, p. 75) remarks:

Participation in the process must be widened. Knowledge is needed not only of the latest technologies but also of local ecosystems and food chains, local culture and systems of exchange, socio-economic conditions and political and market stability. This calls for broad collaboration.

In all such studies and pioneered by this book, the context of system and cybernetic methodology in participatory development remains predominant. The systemic worldview of addressing the sustainable development problem and issues in it, such as social justice, poverty alleviation, money and real economy and many attenuating instruments for attaining the evolutionary learning kind of systemic and cybernetic model has not been developed otherwise. This missing theme is the originality of our work.

REFERENCES

Ashford, R. (1994). The binary economics of Louis Kelso: A democratic private property system for growth and justice. In Miller, J. H. (Ed.), *Curing World Poverty, the New Role of Property* (pp. 99–132). New Hope, KY: Saint Martin de Porres Press.

Berman, H. J. (1989). Beyond Marx, beyond Weber. In McCullough, H. B. (Ed.), *Political Ideologies and Political Philosophies*. Toronto, Canada: Wall & Thompson.

Buchanan, J. M. (1999). The domain of constitutional economics. In *The Collected Works of James M. Buchanan: The Logical Foundations of Constitutional Liberty* (pp. 377–395). Indianapolis, IN: Liberty Press.

Choudhury, M. A. (2011). *Islamic economics and finance: An epistemological inquiry*. Bingley, UK: Emerald Publications.

Friedman, M. (1953). The methodology of positive economics. In *Essays in Positive Economics*. Chicago: University of Chicago Press.

Friedman, M. (1956). The quantity theory of money – A restatement. In Friedman, M. (Ed.), *Studies in the Quantity Theory of Money* (pp. 3–24). Chicago, IL: The University of Chicago Press.

Friedman, M. (1962). *Capitalism and freedom*. Chicago, IL: The University of Chicago Press.

Hart, H. L. A. (1997). Justice and morality. In *The Concept of Law*. Oxford, UK: Oxford University Press.

Hegel, G. W. F. (1956). *The philosophy of history* (Sibree, J., Trans.). New York, NY: Dover Publications.

Heilbroner, R., & Milberg, W. (1995). The crisis of vision. In *The Crisis of Vision in Modern Economic Thought*. Cambridge, UK: Cambridge University Press.

Henderson, J. M., & Quandt, R. E. (1971). *Microeconomic theory*. New York: McGraw Hill.

Kelso, L., & Patricia, H. (1965). *Two-factor theory: The economics of reality*. New York: Random House.

Levine, D. (1988). *Needs, rights, and the market*. Boulder, CO: Lynne Reinner.

Marx, K. (1892). Capital, a critique of political economy vol. II: The process of circulation of capital. (F. Engels, Ed.). Moscow, Russia: Progress Publishers.

Millennium Development Goals. (n.d.). Retrieved from http://www.undp.org/mdg/basics.shtml

Moore, G. E. (1962). *Principia ethica*. Cambridge, UK: Cambridge University Press.

Myrdal, G. (1958a). Ends and means in political economy. In Streeten, P. (Ed.), *Value in Social Theory, a Selection of Essays on Methodology by Gunnar Myrdal* (pp. 206–230). New York, NY: Harper & Brothers Publishers.

Myrdal, G. (1958b). The logical crux of all science. In Streeten, P. (Ed.), *Value in Social Theory, a Selection of Essays on Methodology by Gunnar Myrdal* (pp. 231–236). New York, NY: Harper & Brothers Publishers.

Myrdal, G. (1958c). The principle of cumulation. In Streeten, P. (Ed.), *Value in Social Theory, a Selection of Essays on Methodology by Gunnar Myrdal* (pp. 198–205). New York, NY: Harper & Brothers Publishers.

Myrdal, G. (1958d). *Value in social theory: A selection of essays on methodology by Gunnar Myrdal* (Streeten, P., Ed.). New York, NY: Harper & Brothers Publishers.

Nightingale, D. V. (1982). *Workplace democracy: An inquiry into employee participation in Canadian work organizations* (pp. 165–169). Toronto, Canada: University of Toronto Press.

Palan, R. (2000). New trends in global political economy. In Palan, R. (Ed.), *Global Political Economy, Contemporary Theories* (pp. 1–18). London, UK: Routledge.

Paul, E. F., Miller, F. D. Jr, & Paul, J. (Eds.). (1995). *The just society*. Cambridge, UK: Cambridge University Press.

Phelps, E. S. (1989). Distributive justice. In Eatwell, J., Milgate, M., & Newman, P. (Eds.), *The New Palgrave: Social Economics*. New York, NY: WW. Norton.

Polanyi, K. (1957). *The great transformation*. Boston, MA: Beacon Press.

Popkin, R. H., & Stroll, A. (2003). Hume's analysis of causation. In *Philosophy* (pp. 265–275). Oxford, UK: Made Simple Books.

Stigler, G. J. (1970). The influence of events and policies on economic theory. In Rima, I. H. (Ed.), *Readings in the History of Economic Theory*. New York: Holt, Rinehart & Winston, Inc..

Stiglitz, J. E. (2003). *Globalization and its discontents*. New York, NY: W.W. Norton.

Sztompka, P. (1974). *System and function, towards a theory of society*. New York, NY: Academic Press.

United Nations Development Program (UNDP). (1999). *Human development report*. New York, NY: Oxford University Press.

Wallerstein, I. (1974). *The modern world systems theory: Capitalist agriculture and the origins of the European world-economy in the sixteenth century*. New York, NY: Academic Press.

World Bank. (2000). *World development report 2000-2001*. New York, NY: Oxford University Press.

Wunsch, G. (1988a). Theories of causation. In *Causal Theory and Causal Modeling, Beyond Description in the Social Sciences* (pp. 21–66). Leuven, Belgium: Leuven University Press.

Wunsch, G. (1988b). Causal modeling in the social sciences. In *Causal Theory and Causal Modeling, Beyond Description in the Social Sciences* (pp. 169–196). Leuven, Belgium: Leuven University Press.

ENDNOTES

1. *Qur'an* (2:175) on interest (*riba*) and trade.
2. $U_0 = -I + U_1(1+r)/(1+i)$ as discounted utility (U_1) in a two-period case (0,1). I denotes investment. By maximization of the present-value (U_0) we get, $dU_0/dU_1 = (1+r)/(1+i)$. Consequently, the intertemporal discounted utilities form inverse relationships between as opportunity cost denoted by r/i.

3 $dW_v(S(i),Y(r))/dW_u((S(i),Y(r)) = [(\partial W_v/\partial S).(dS/di) + (\partial W_v/\partial Y).(dY/di)]/[(\partial W_u/\partial S).(dS/di) + (\partial W_u/\partial Y).(dY/di)] = (dS/di)[(\partial W_v/\partial S) - (\partial W_v/\partial Y).(i/r)]/(dS/di)[(\partial W_u/\partial S) - (\partial W_u/\partial Y).(i/r)] = [(\partial W_v/\partial S)/i - (\partial W_v/\partial Y)/r]/[(\partial W_u/\partial S)/i - (\partial W_u/\partial Y)/r] = 0/0$, undefined in the case of *welfare(W(.))*-maximization for $W_v(..)$ and $W_u(..)$, the (weighted) sum total of which is the social welfare function.

4 Elasticity $\varepsilon = (GDP)/(HDI).(dHDI/dGDP) = (dGDI\%)/(dGDP \text{ per capita}\%)$, meaning for every 1 percentage increase in GDP, HDI increases by ε factor of 1 percent, as shown in Table 1.

5 Let cash flow CF be netted by mortgage payment on the property purchase price p, say p.i. Then there is the property tax T_t deduction on p, say $p.T_t$ over time t. Net cash-value now at time 't' is $NCF_t = CF_t(1 - p.i - p.T_t)^t$. The capitalized value during the subprime financial regime is $PV = \Sigma_t NCF_t/(1+s)^t$, with 's' as discount rate. Let the expected capitalized value on property buyers be E(PV) with expectations that p will increase over the short-run; 'i' will remain low; and in a property-friendly market for marginal owners, $(i-T_t)$ would remain low. It can then be shown, that in the end the E(PV) could be realized if the following condition held: $(1/p).(dp/dt) > (ds/dt).(1/(i-T_t).p)$. Intertemporal increase in the rate of growth of property value (p) would be determined by changes in the discount rate 's' over time. Since p declined during the subprime financial crisis, it shows then that 's' declined as well. Future risk could not be adequately capitalized by such decreasing discount rates, even though the sanguine expectation of property futures remained high on irrational exuberant buyers.

Chapter 9
Social Reconstruction by Replacing Interest Rates with Trade Instruments

ABSTRACT

The way to replace interest rates in economic, financial, and social issues by using trade-related instruments is formally developed in great detail. The world-system meaning of unity of knowledge derived from the episteme and applied to the complementarities of the Mind-Matter universe of three dimensions, namely knowledge-time-space, is formalized. Methods of the measurements underlying such conceptual ideas are introduced. This takes us to the field of circular causation and its implications around statistical "estimation" and "simulation." The simulation results are followed by ethical, policy, and institutional implications. Many equilibrium results, devised now in the evolutionary world-system of process learning, are formalized and presented.

INTRODUCTION

This chapter is in continuation to Chapter 8. We pursue the theme of moral-social development by replacing the financial instruments related to the rate of interest with trade-related ones while dealing with the good things of life. We continue to define the 'good things of life' as those arising in the dynamic basic-needs regime of economic arrangement induced by the epistemic unity of knowledge.

The objective of this chapter is thus to establish the nature of circular causation interrelationships between the following three sets of variables: the trade-related participatory development financing instruments phasing out the interest-based fi-

DOI: 10.4018/978-1-4666-4643-8.ch009

Copyright ©2014, IGI Global. Copying or distributing in print or electronic forms without written permission of IGI Global is prohibited.

nancing instruments; the consequential moral-social simulation towards wellbeing, and thereby attaining poverty alleviation. Towards making a comprehensive study in this direction this chapter will invoke original ideas in monetarism in the areas of micro- and macro- foundations of Quantity Theory of money, output and prices, and the Keynesian fiscal policy bias. The post-monetarist and post-Keynesian fiscally integrated theory of money and the real economy is developed to study the tripartite and related integrated problem of development financing, wellbeing, and poverty alleviation in a regime of phased out interest rates.

EXPLANATIONS OF TERMS

A few terms need to be explained at the outset.

1. Trade-Related Financial Instruments Contrary to the Rate of Interest

Firstly, we recapitulate why trade-related financing instruments are contrary to interest-based instruments in attaining sustainable development. In this regard we identify the objective criterion of social development to be the wellbeing function. The wellbeing function was defined earlier as the measure of organic unity and balance in the complementary *inter*relationships between the variables representing the good things of life. Simulation of the wellbeing criterion is thereby the primary objective. Within this objective criterion are embedded several other ones as they are studied and remain within the domain of investigation, conceptualization, and empirical and applied possibility. We have shown earlier in the chapters that simulation of the wellbeing objective criterion is carried out subject to circular causation relations between the selected variables.

Circular causation method establishes a comprehensive exercise in 'estimating' followed by simulating the social reconstruction to higher and more explainable levels of unity of relations between the good things of life. While simulating the relations, the emergent empirical configuration of the circular causation model leads into policy and institutional changes based on the moral and ethical perspectives of social reconstruction. Circular causation also has an analogy with organic interrelations in natural sciences. However, when discussing social organism, strict equivalence with natural sciences organism cannot be maintained. Only by tying down the organic behavior of social phenomenon to the uniqueness of the evolutionary learning worldview and formalized by the IIE-model, the organic structure of the learning system in epistemic unity of knowledge can be preserved.

In describing social order as organism of collectivity in the light of the organic and structure preserving nature of epistemic unity of knowledge and the unified world-system, we can resort to Sztompka (1974, p. 49) words: ".... First, human beings, the basic elements of society, are linked by a definite network of social relations. Thus there exists a certain social structure which makes a society something more than a simple aggregate of people; namely, it is specific integrated whole. Second, continuity of the whole is preserved, despite the constant changes and transformations at the level of the individual and, specifically, despite the continual replacement of persons making up a given society. And third, this continuity of structure is preserved by virtue of the specific functions performed by the elements of social structure."

The theme of poverty alleviation that we studied in Chapter 8 in relation to the debilitating effect of interest-rate regime in this moral-social reconstruction is an embedded goal in the wellbeing objective criterion. That is because poverty alleviation appears in the circular causation relations of the wellbeing criterion as one of the interactive, integrative, and evolutionary relations that sustains the dynamic basic-needs regime of development.

To summarize, our earlier explanation of interest-bearing, impeding and sector dichotomizing effect of resource mobilization by way of scarcity of resources, the presence of interest divides inter-sectoral relations barring unification between them. This causes a sure breach of unity of knowledge by organic moral-social relations between life-sustaining possibilities. On the other hand, trade marks the exchange of goods and services between participating agents. Here resource mobilization is essential. While interest rate impedes resource mobilization, trade lubricates it. The good things of life emanating from the emergent trade-related resource mobilizing development regime are dynamic basic needs as opposed to the wants of life. Dynamic basic needs comprise necessaries, comforts, and refinements taken at these levels as the dynamic diversification of basic needs across diversity but yet not denoting wants.

Cumulative causation (Myrdal, edited by Streeten, 1958) in the development process with interest is marked by accumulation of capital driven by interest rate. Thereby, interest rate prevailing throughout such social order restricts trade always. The neoclassical consequence of the resulting relationship between interest rate, resource scarcity, and capital accumulation, is denoted by a permanent move of the economic expansion path towards bank-savings. This is seen as a substitute for trade in the real sector. In the Keynesian case, the same effect of resource scarcity by interest rate, barring resource mobilization by trade into the real economy, shows up in the permanent postponement and the high instability of the point of full-employment output.

Monetarist version of the quantity theory of money is deeply entrenched in the term-structure of interest rates that are used for various types of asset valuation. Consequently, resources are permanently driven away from unification between productive factors and real goods and services. Scarcity of resources in the meaning of competition and tradeoff between opposing forms of asset ownership deepens. The result is concentration of social groupings according to their self-interests. In all therefore, widening access to resources by trade; and access to the good things of life by exercising participation and pervasive complementarities between the good things of life, is forever denied.

2. The Term: Good Things of Life

Next to explain is the term, "the good things of life". The good things of life are those that establish sustainability along the evolutionary epistemology of learning in unity of knowledge and the moral-social regeneration of the consequential unified world-system. Sztompka (1974, pp. 124-132) writes in regards to the unitary perspective of systemic relations as the unique symbol of a meaningful society: "The assumption of boundary interchange, states that there are definite relationships binding all the systems together. In an operational sense this means that any changes in elementary, partial, or global states of one of the systems have definite consequences with respect to the elementary, partial, or global states of the other systems. In some cases, there is also a sort of mutual interpenetration of the systems; the elements of one being simultaneously the elements of the other."

Yet reflecting on the meaning of the good things of life in the framework of socio-scientific unity, the moral and ethical implications are inherent in the meaning of goodness. Consequently, a conception such as that of statistical correlation, marginal rate of substitution in resource allocation between competing goods or between multiple 'bads', and prioritizing the use of one good over another, or accepting the better of the 'bads', do not convey the substantive meaning of organic unity in the moral and ethical sense. These ways of interrelating alternatives do not represent the unity between the good things of life.

Contrarily, good things are characterized by their property of derivation by rules of the epistemic origin of the moral text. This forms the axiomatic core. It defies rationalism and all that rationalism entails in economics, finance, society and the socio-scientific disciplines. The essence of unity in the morality axiomatic reference is not one of biological organism. Rather, it is formed by the knowledge-induced regenerating of possibilities that carry on heightened learning by resource mobilization. The result is the enabling of capability and functioning in development (Sen, 1999).

3. Schematic Explanation of the Determinants of Good Things of Life

The following selection criteria determine the choices of the good things of life: (1) The moral axiomatic text is premised on the epistemic unity of knowledge. We have argued that such a primordial moral characterization necessary arises from the monotheistic law in its purest form.[1] (2) The laws emanating from this axiomatic text in respect of particular and generalized themes are discoursed to yield interpretative rules of action in real world issues. Such rules comprise classification of their understanding, of the emanating ethical goods, and the nature of instruments that can help attain the essence of the epistemic laws now derived as rules of life pertaining to general and particular concepts. The totality of (1) and (2) and its continuation across systemic and cybernetic processes of learning over continuums of domains forms the purpose and objective of the Islamic Law.

In the Islamic case of the the pure monotheistic law, the above principles are found to be ingrained in the Islamic Law. The underlying objective and purpose of the Islamic Law is known as the *maqasid as-shari'ah.*

We also note: (3) The worldly acceptance and further adaptation of such epistemic rules enter the determination of things as the good things. They comply with the process from (1) onto (2). This phase represents the formation of the worldly tenets of the Islamic Law. At this stage, the empirical testing followed by social simulation causing moral-social reconstruction, proceeds on continuously. One thereby notes that, neither in meaning nor in practice the idea of Islamic Law (*shari'ah*) or of *shari'ah*-compliance is identical with the meaning of *maqasid as-shari'ah* (Crane, 2011). Yet well-determination of rules, operational instruments, and the substantive meaning of wellbeing criterion in respect of specific and general problems under investigation establish comprehension, application, and thereby, continuity of the moral and ethical learning processes in moral-social reconstruction.

The fourth (4) phase of moral functionalism denotes recalling the axiomatic epistemic unity of knowledge to continue the learning process established in phases (1)-(3). Phases (1)-(3) are thus continued on intra-system and inter-systems as cybernetic learning processes across the dimensions of knowledge, time, and space. The learning processes over evolutionary epistemology thus sustain the determination of the good things of life as life-sustaining artifacts.

Moral-social inter-causality for determining the good things of life is established in the learning process from (1) – (4):

3.1. Moral-Social Causality for Determining the Good Things of Life

1. **Moral Law (in Islam the Law of Monotheism) (Invariance and Exogeneity):** *Maqasid as-shari'ah* (objective and purpose of Islamic Law originally derived from the monotheistic law). Leading to:
2. **Inter-Causality:** *Shari'ah/shari'ah*-compliance. Leading to:
3. **Inter-Causality:** [Wellbeing with circular causation premised on epistemic unity → (1) testing the positive nature of social reality ('estimation') → (2) 'simulating' by circular causation to attain moral-social reconstruction into better levels of unity of knowledge and unifying relations between the representative variables as complements and participative].Leading to:
4. **Inter-Causality:** Determination of good things of life arising from the simulation. Note that all good things are knowledge-induced in the epistemology of unity of knowledge. Thus, because of the functional interdependence between embedded artifacts by the core of knowledge-flows, knowledge breeds knowledge. Materiality is a diversified and flippant construction of knowledge. Materiality is thus a temporary state of 'being' responding to the continuous 'becoming' of evolutionary knowledge-flows The example here is the medicinal fruit of the farmer mentioned earlier. A fruit is a fruit is a fruit by materiality (being). But they are differentiated by quality, essence, and the ethical purpose. Thus the learning property of 'becoming' remains indelible in knowledge formation.[2] Leading to:
5. **Inter-Causality:** Evolutionary epistemology into emergent learning phases of unity of knowledge and the unified (participatory, complementary) world-system by continuously recalling the Moral Law.

The important point to note in level (5) is how the continuity of the learning process is established, and how the deductive reasoning continues into inductive consequences, and how the inductive reasoning reverts thereby into deductive reasoning, and so on in continuity across systemic continuums. Such an endogenous property of the learning process is a high-water mark of unity of knowledge and of its epistemic effect on the moral-social construction of the unified world-system. This dynamics of the learning process is now explained.

The evolutionary epistemology between processes is characterized by two phases of learning. Firstly, new knowledge-flows evolve from the moral-social reconstruction based on the circular causation simulation of wellbeing in a given process. This knowledge-flow as measured configuration of wellbeing is represented by the ethical index. It is the last equation of the estimated/simulation system in the circular causation model. The evolutionary knowledge-flow denotes consciousness moving towards the epistemic core of level (1). The moral-ethical correctness of the estimated/simulated wellbeing index thus enters further simulation as benchmark of social change in reference to level (1) in the second learning process, and so on.

In this way, the deductive reasoning based on level (1) goes into the inductive stage (4) through the empirical and applied reconstructive stage. Thereafter, the inductive consequence of level (4) further evolves into level (5) by referring to level (1). The sequences of deductive to inductive to deductive cycles continue on. In such cycles of reasoning, interconnecting along the continuous learning processes, only level (1) remains the axiomatic point of reference. It initiates new phases of evolutionary learning. All other parts of the learning system in the details of deconstructions are endogenously linked by knowledge-flows. Upon this, time and space become datum of information flow in different evolutionary processes. But these are all axiomatically guided by the only exogenous phenomenon in the learning system. This marks the recurrence of level (1) 'everywhere' and in 'everything'.

Here is the schematic explanation of the recursive learning processes unifying the deductive and inductive reasoning in continuous rounds. The same model also establishes the continuity between positive and normative states of the world-system in 'everything'.

LEARNING RELATIONS BETWEEN THE HUMAN AND NON-HUMAN WORLDS

Both the human and non-human worlds learn in continuity across continuums. But it is the human world that unravels the mysteries of the non-human world. Interaction leading to integration, followed by creative evolution in learning processes, characterizes the interrelated domains of the human and non-human worlds. While the non-human world unravels its mysteries by the intrinsic nature of its essence endowed in balance and unity of being and becoming, the human world taps the intrinsic knowledge and converts it into artifacts of socio-scientific information and utilization for the non-human and human worlds.

The balance of interrelations in such interdependent processes of learning between the two worlds establishes the life-sustaining regime of wellbeing for all. Indeed, it is only in the human world that there is classification, interpretation and processes of cognitive learning. Stepping over such balance results in the breakup of unity and learning between the two worlds. Sustainability, balance and perpetuity as elements of the epistemic unity of knowledge in the shared knowledge domain between the human and non-human worlds (mind-matter inter-causal universe), thus mark the learning process premised on the monotheistic law as the moral law.

The non-human world is endowed by embodied knowledge of balance, homogeneity, and organic unity. The human world is not so optimally endowed. Yet the interactive, integrative, and evolutionary (IIE) learning processes ensue from the human world and interrelate with the observed phenomena and abstraction. Social order is thereby not simply made up of human groupings. Rather it is formed by the organic and wellbeing unity in and between the human and non-human worlds. This conveys the widest meaning of social relations and sustainability, and hence the learning process intra-system and inter-systems.

Human knowledge suffers from the limits of perception. Bergson remarked that perception is the lowest state of mind; it is like mind without memory. Therefore, in the IIE-learning process the complete mystery of creation is never unraveled. Knowledge of the non-human world is thereby constrained by the limits of human capability to know it. In the human world, the dynamics of knowing and the perpetual flow of knowledge, as were shown in Table 1, take up incessantly many paths of possibilities. About such evolutionary epistemological paths of learning of the natural world-system wrote Hawking and Mlodinow (2010, p.80): "…for a general system, the probability of any observation is constructed from all the possible histories that could have led to that observation. Because of that this method is called the 'sum over histories' or alternative histories' formulation of quantum physics." Variations in probabilities determined by the knowledge, time, and space dimensions of occurrence of information along such diverse paths of histories imply the random, temporary, and evolutionary properties of human learning about creation.

Human learning, being so constrained in the IIE-learning processes, cause evolutionary equilibriums to occur along the variant paths of socio-scientific histories.

Table 1. Deductive/inductive, normative/positive recursive relations in unity of being and becoming

	Process 1	**(Deductive∩Inductive) (Normative∩Positivism)**	**Continuity Process 2**
	------------------	↓	--------------
Monotheistic Law (Moral Law)	World-System (specific/ general):	Checking for convergence of Simulated Knowledge Estimation Simulation of Wellbeing by Circular Causation	Commencement and repetition
(Exogenous)	Discourse		Law: Episteme (Wellbeing) to the Moral Law
			(Recalling the Monotheistic Law)
	(Endogenous Relations)		(Exogenous Epistemic Reference)
Deductive/ Normative	Inductive/ Positivism	Deductive/ Normative	Inductive/ Positivism

But no optimum exists anywhere except in the infinitesimal and instantaneous point. Such an event is uninteresting in the learning and cybernetic world-system. Hence with temporary and evolutionary equilibriums, but with absence of optimality in the dimensions of knowledge, time, and space, there cannot be absolutely undisturbed, reductive observation and understanding of the non-human world by the human mind. Thus in the IIE-learning processes between the two worlds, both of them yield to the same conditions of temporary and evolutionary equilibriums by the absence of optimality and incompleteness of knowledge everywhere and in 'everything'.

All of socio-scientific analysis, despite the continuously intrinsic nature of learning in the non-human world, makes up the human and non-human IIE-learning system as shown in Figure 1. In this figure, consider the knowledge (θ)-induced relationship in terms of the vector, $(x_1(\theta),x_2(\theta),\theta)$. The surface S is spanned by many trajectories denoted by T-space. This describes evolutionary paths of the vector $(x_1(\theta),x_2(\theta),\theta)$. The surface S' is the coplanar projection of S. S is non-optimal in evolutionary θ-values inducing $(x_1(\theta),x_2(\theta),\theta)$-vector. Likewise, the corresponding projection space S' spanned by θ-induced trajectories T' is non-optimal in $(x_1(\theta),x_2(\theta))$. Yet each of the evolutionary sub-spaces of S being temporarily closed within evolutionary open sets has a temporary and evolutionary equilibrium point. There are many such points, emerging as the sub-spaces expand horizontally due to inner learning dynamics, and expand upwards due to evolutionary learning dynamics.

BRINGING BACK THE TRADE, POVERTY ALLEVIATION, AND WELLBEING INTERRELATIONS

We extract from Figure 1 the knowledge-induced variables that define the wellbeing function in terms of its property of pervasive complementarities (participation). Let the vector $x_1(\theta)$ denote trade related variables and instruments relative to interest rate. Let $x_2(\theta)$ denote poverty alleviation as a complex vector of variables as determinants of poverty alleviation (World Bank, 2000). θ is a monotonic positive representation of wellbeing function (W(.)) in the circular causation system of equations interrelating $(x_1(\theta),x_2(\theta),\theta)$. We write the circular causation simulation system as follows:

Simulate $W(x_1(\theta),x_2(\theta))$, (1)

say that $x_1(\theta) = \{(z = Y_N/Y_W), P\}[\theta]$, $x_2(\theta)$ = index of poverty

Y_N denotes GDP in basic-needs sector;
Y_W denotes GDP in the wants sector (non-basic needs);

Figure 1. Interrelationship between human and non-human worlds in knowledge-induced evolutionary equilibrium without optimality

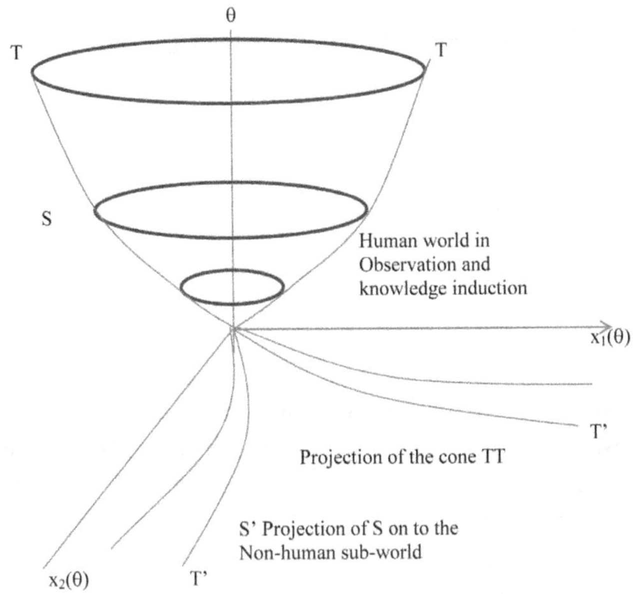

P denotes financing by the aggregate of participatory instruments relative to interest rate.

The normative properties of epistemic unity of knowledge in expression (1) subject to the following circular causation Equations 2-5 are as follows:

$$dW/d\theta = \underset{>0}{(\partial W/\partial z(\theta))}.\underset{>0}{(dz(\theta)/d\theta)} + \underset{>0}{(\partial W/\partial P(\theta))}.\underset{>0}{(dP(\theta)/d\theta)} + \underset{<0}{(\partial W/\partial x_2(\theta))}.\underset{<0}{(dx_2(\theta)/d\theta)} > 0$$

The induction by θ means firstly 'estimation' of the prevalent state of the circular causation relations (inductive/positivistic), which may not be in conformity with epistemic unity (deductive/normative). 'Estimation' is followed by simulation in reference to the goal of attaining levels of moral-social transformation by epistemic unity of knowledge and complementarities between the good things of life. These are denoted by increasing (z,P)[θ] and decreasing $\mathbf{x}_2(\theta)$ after 'simulation' of the first-round 'estimation' results.

The circular causation relations thus exist at two stages. First there is the 'estimation' stage (inductive/positivistic as in Table 1). The second stage is the 'simulation' of the estimated results by changing the coefficients to establish better semblance of the epistemic unity of knowledge, and thereby, wellbeing. This is the deductive/normative derivation out of the 'estimated' (inductive/positivistic) stage.

1. Estimation Stage (Inductive/Positivistic)

$$z(\theta) = f_1(P(\theta), x_2(\theta), \theta) \tag{2}$$

$$P(\theta) = f_2(z(\theta), x_2(\theta), \theta) \tag{3}$$

$$x_2(\theta) = f_3(z(\theta), P(\theta), \theta) \tag{4}$$

$$\theta = F(z(\theta), x_2(\theta)) \tag{5}$$

The functional similarity of expressions (1) and (5) means each of these expressions is a scalar representation of the other expression. Hence, while expression (1) defines the conceptual version of the wellbeing function, expression (5) gives the empirical version of the ethical index that ensues from the state of the circular causation relations. The first step, namely that of estimation of the circular causation system with existing data is now complete.

2. Simulation Stage (Deductive/Normative)

The estimated equations are simulated by changing the coefficients in the light of desired transformation to attain better semblance of unity of knowledge in the system by way of improved complementarities between the good things of life; or negative signs in the opposite case. These coefficients in the log-linear form of the (f,F)-functions in the circular causation system (1)-(5) stand for inter-variable elasticity coefficients. With the simulated values of the variables by coefficient-changes in the structural Equations 2-5 as normatively/deductively desired out of social discourse, the final version of the ethical index in Expression 5 follows.

The simulated value of the ethical index (wellbeing measure) is the normative result in reference to the epistemic unity of knowledge to be attained, and is set discursively. The result is reflected in coefficient changes. Once the estimated and simulated variables and the ethical indexes are set, the comparisons between the actual (statistical), estimated and predictor (simulated) values can be studied. This stage results from expert discourse on the goals of desired moral-social transformation. The policies and institutional structural changes that need to be reconstructed to attain moral-social transformation become the inferential basis of decision making. The epistemic unity of knowledge and its unification by complementarities and participation are established in the broadest context of the social order formed by organic learning between the human world and the non-human world (Figure 1). All the elements of the deductive/normative and inductive/positivistic stages of reasoning have now been unified by organic synergies emanating from the circular causation system of wellbeing simulation.

By this way of integration and continuity between the normative and positivistic aspects of economics and socio-scientific models we have agreed with, but not fully succumbed to the methodology of economic reasoning raised by Friedman (1953, pp. 42-43)[3], and his subsequent followers. The fact is that no science can be built upon either too much of given set of hypotheses or rationalized hypotheses. There are premises of intellection that remain universal to the social order and to the terrain of history that may not be observed, but they form abiding social lessons. Such epistemological beliefs can become premises for conjectures and refutation out of falsification, verifiability, and affirmation (Boland, 1989).

In this book, we have premised all reasoning on the unassailable episteme that no one denies. This is the episteme of unity of knowledge and its induction of unification in the generality and particularity of diverse issues, problems, and the world-systems. Its possibility to study the positivistic nature of reality (estimation) followed by moral-social reconstruction (simulation) of such positivistic realities bring together the positivistic and normative together in unison with the design of society of the future. It renders the accepted hypothesis to critical investigation to discover fresh and newer ways of explaining social reality that the simplified linear vision and maximization calculus of existing economics and socio-scientific system cannot explain.

Even in the most ordinary economic case for instance, the axiom of scarcity of resources cannot explain the learning worldview. But the reverse is true – from the learning worldview to specificity of resource scarcity problem by assigning $\theta = 0$, and then studying the concomitant process of this ethically fallen world-system characterized by exogeneity of ethical behavior, assumption of competition, and inter-variable and inter-entity conflict shown by marginal rates of substitution caused by competition.

INFERENCES DERIVED FROM 'ESTIMATION' AND 'SIMULATION' ASPECTS OF CIRCULAR CAUSATION

Nature of Learning Equilibriums in the IIE Processes

An interesting result is derivable from the estimation and simulation stages of the circular causation equations of the wellbeing simulation problem. We note here that the equations of the circular causation are structural in type. Thereby, every variable is endogenously related to other ones, and thereby, such variables are estimated and simulated thereafter. Such regenerated variables stand for functional transformations of the observed statistical variables. Therefore, a set of compact solution in any specific learning process (Table 1) maps it onto itself, but evolves there from.

The enunciation of the Fixed Point Theorem can now be extended to state that, a temporary compact set of solutions of the circular causation system maps itself onto itself with the property of evolution from such a temporary state of topological compactness. Such a topology generates temporary but evolutionary equilibriums across learning processes. In this statement of the problem, the Fixed Point Theorem (Nikaido, 1989) has been extended to include evolutionary equilibriums that temporarily map themselves into themselves by continuously differentiable functions (Choudhury, 2011a).

The moral-social implications of this Fixed Point Theorem result are several. The epistemology of unity of knowledge and the actionable domains exist in 'everything' with diversity in unity of being and becoming. This conceptual result is true of specific and generalized problems of world-systems. Thus the infallible property of universality and uniqueness of the monotheistic law as the epistemology of unity of knowledge and its knowledge-induced world-systems is established (Choudhury & Zaman, 2009). This inference yields the fundamental premise of establishing the moral-social reconstruction possibility. That is realized by the sole function of the monotheistic law in terms of its strict unitary principle of the law and induction of the world-systems in every detail.

We also deduce from the evolutionary version of the Fixed Point Theorem that, because evolutionary equilibriums exist across continuums of the knowledge, time, and space dimensions, therefore, predictability is possible but 'near' to the points of occurrence of probabilistic events. This result yields the overlapping generation model of asset-valuation that addresses true valuation 'near' to the points of occurrence of probabilistic events, rather than using present-value and its generic models of asset-valuation with intertemporal cash-flows of the uncertain future (Choudhury, 2011b).

This result on asset-valuation is a revolutionary alternative to the usual kinds of mainstream models that are presently used by Islamic banks and financial institutions everywhere. The moral and ethical implications of the overlapping generation model are to introduce the discursive dynamics. This is simultaneously combined with analytical ramifications at the 'near' nodes of decision-making along the evolutionary process-driven path of intertemporal evaluations. Contrarily, the mainstream asset-valuation models, presently being used by Islamic banks and financial institutions, are thoroughly benign of moral and ethical sensitivity.

Inferences for Islamic Economics and Finance

In Islamic economics and finance the moral and ethical implications of the *maqasid as-shari'ah* are altogether forgotten as an endogenous force of preference conduct. Today's clamor of '*shari'ah*-compliance' in Islamic banking products remain substantively devoid of consciousness in the epistemic law of unity of knowledge and its functional relations with the specifics of systemic unification.

Contrarily, the preference behavior of Islamic bank shareholders and managers remain of the utilitarian type. These agents state that, if they are pious groups making good financial decisions according to the *shari'ah*, then the consequences of their actions will be good. The moral and social effects of their decisions will be transmitted to society at large. Such a transmission of institutional decision-making and preferences would then be equivalent to moral and ethical social choices.

Such an attitude is a thoroughly utilitarian viewpoint. In it the socially discursive dynamics and the emergent consequences are subdued. Morality and ethics do not arise from the socially participatory spectrum as an endogenous force. Thereby, in the present milieu of Islamic banking, we do not find sound funding programs and database to back up Islamic banks' functions in poverty alleviation. Yet paradoxically the financial efficiency ratios are calculated to be high (e.g. Islamic Bank Bangladesh). Consequently, both the meaning of morality and ethics in Islamic banking and the relevance of statistical calculations to prove financial efficiency remain null and void in the eyes of the *maqasid as-shari'ah*. Contrary to these prevailing implications of Islamic economics, finance and banking in their intellection and practitioner milieu, the substantiation of the concept and application of ethical endogeneity, as we have presented, negate and alter the situation into a *maqasid*-friendly worldview.

Micro-Foundation of Macroeconomics

Other inferences can be drawn from the evolutionary version of Fixed Point Theorem. One of these is to reflect upon and formalize on the micro-foundations of economic and social theories. An example of this is poverty alleviation by means of microeconomic and community and village based policies. The end result is a complex system of impact on the economy-wide aggregate level. In fact, for bringing back God into the financial world through the paths of morality and ethics, economic theory must be solely microeconomic and epistemologically grounded.

Macroeconomics, and thereby the morally and ethically benign empiricism and models of finance and society, do not reveal the preferences of actors on the scene. This is equally true even in the case of the study of microeconomic foundations of macroeconomics. For instance in rational expectations theory (Minford, 1983) the problem of utility maximization in price level and unemployment rate results in a tradeoff between these variables. This is an untenable choice according to the moral and ethical precept of pervasive complementarities between the good things of life in the knowledge-induced economic system. Knowledge-induction takes place in 'everything', as we have explained (Figure 1). Yet its dynamics is possible only by human agency, which is micro in nature. The micro responses can be aggregated by complex learning dynamics to the social level.

It is therefore a misnomer to theorize upon Islamic macroeconomics as a bearer of the divine law at the economy-wide system by way of moral and ethical endogeneity (Choudhury, 2006). Such a project is impossible. All of Islamic economics, finance, banking, and society, are truly an intellection at the microeconomic level with complex, not utilitarian, aggregation of micro-preferences, choices and functions to the economy-wide level prevailing in the dimensions of knowledge, time, and space.

The result on the evolutionary, ethically endogenized preferences and choices studied by the Fixed Point implications of learning systems is absent in all of Islamic economics, finance, and banking theory. Consequently, no fresh challenge either in academia or modeled practice has been introduced by the mainstream imitation of a fading field of Islamic economics and finance. Islamic economics in its mainstream orientation has disappeared in a distant din of clamor only.

THE MICRO- AND MACRO-IMPLICATIONS OF ECONOMIC AND SOCIAL THEORY

Two specific academic areas that can be revolutionized by the theory of ethical endogeneity in formalizing the microeconomic foundations of complex macro-aggregation are monetary and fiscal economics. But in revolutionizing change it is necessary to go beyond and to include the embedded nature of economics with moral, ethical and social valuations in models and formalism of complex interface between the human world and the non-human world. This is the mind-matter inter-related dynamics.

Money and fiscalism have traditionally been treated as macroeconomic entities. Yet the study of micro-foundations of monetary and fiscal variables is a sparing exception to be found in the works of the Austrian School (Yaeger, 1997). But here too, the moral and ethical implications of microeconomic theory of money were not expounded. Should we then imply that in the minds, thoughts and writings of the prominent schools of economics the role of morality and ethics remained exogenously linked with microeconomic preference formation as the objective criteria of economic behavior?

In Chapter 8 we have maintained that, any economic and financial thought that does not liberate itself analytically, and by institutional and policy-driven practice, from interest-based financial reasoning, remains incapable of alleviating poverty, rendering equality, and generating access to ownership and empowerment. Summarily, that is because of the epistemological groundings of all such thought in liberalism, which is premised on methodological individualism. This subsequently associates with the axioms of scarcity of resources, and concomitantly with competition, maximization of objective criteria, and methodological self-interest (Quinton, 1989).

Thus, certain fundamental axiomatic corrections premised on human nature and on the intrinsic participatory nature of the world-system are required to establish the endogenous theory of morality and ethics in micro-foundations of complex macro-aggregation. The approach then is to develop thought and application on the micro-foundations of economic and social policies with moral and ethical endogeneity.

Our theme of microeconomic policy-theoretic investigation will thus take us to the study of interface between money, fiscalism, socioeconomic variables, and the endogenous domain of morality and ethics. We will interface them according to our IIE-learning formalism with the objective of simulating wellbeing, as explained by the circular causation method relating to poverty alleviation, distributive equity, empowerment, and ownership of the good things of life.

In the moral and ethical domains of the monotheistic law of epistemic unity of knowledge between the human world and the non-human world, Figure 1 yields the embedded nature of its evolutionary spaces in S(θ) and S'(θ). Thereby, in the IIE-learning space denoted by (S∩S')[θ], Figure 2 explains this case.

In Figure 2, representative subspaces of S and S' when embedded by the organic unification of epistemic unity of knowledge, that is by θ-knowledge-flow, is identical with the sub-space (S∩S')[θ]. This identity between the embedded human and non-human world-systems and their epistemic unification is true of every evolutionary learning space of the same type. A substantive point needs to be noted here in respect of the inner intra-systemic evolutionary dynamics and the outer inter-systemic evolutionary dynamics of the total organic system of evolution intra-cum-inter-systems.

The micro-world of intra-systemic evolutionary dynamics corresponds with internal processes of learning in Table 1. On the other hand, the inter-systemic evolutionary dynamics corresponds with the learning continuity over continuums of subspaces shown by multiple learning processes (Table 1). And then by the dynamics and epistemic formulation of wellbeing simulation objective criterion, subject to the circular causation system, the IIE-methodology is operational in all such intra-inter systemic evolutionary learning dynamics.

Figure 2. Intra-system and inter-system learning with temporary and evolutionary fixed points in learning spaces

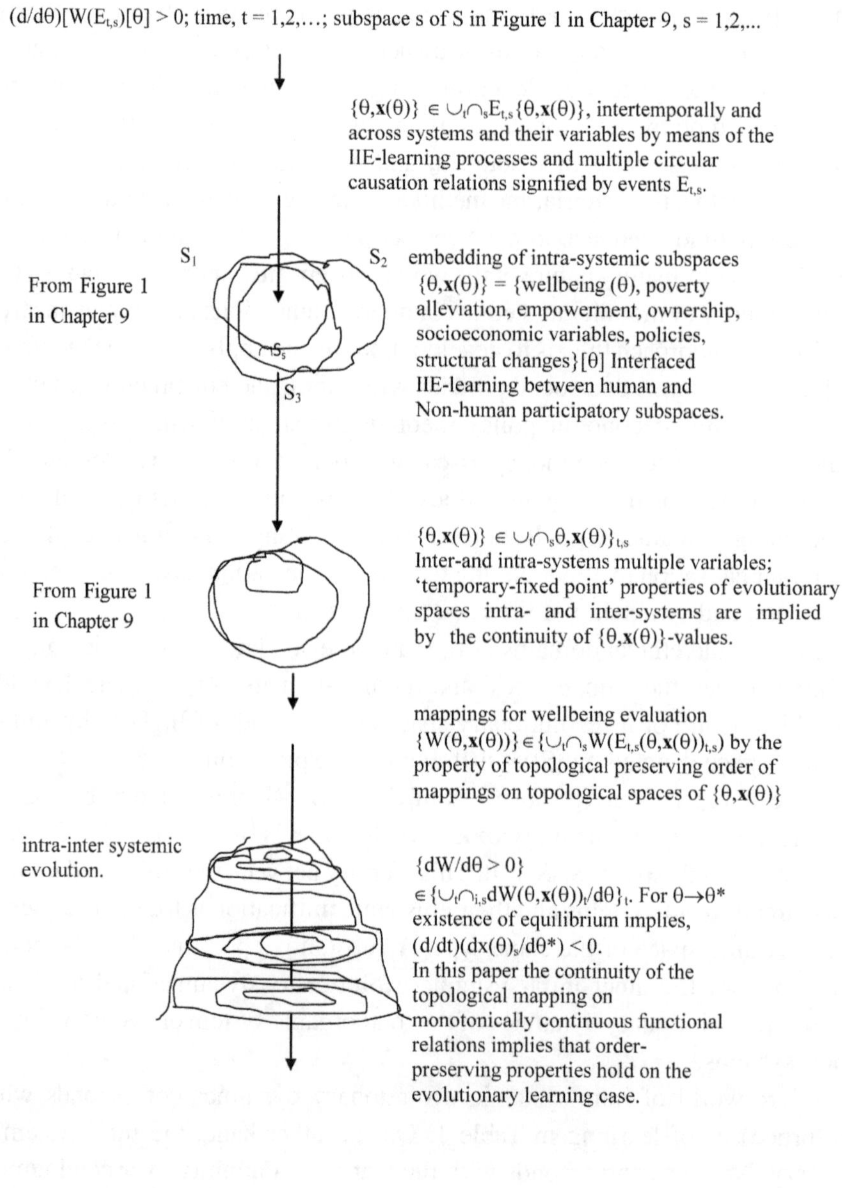

The questions to ask then are these: Does the real world of mind and matter accede naturally to the micro-foundations of agent-specific behavior? Is the macro-perspective a natural state of the mind-matter relationship?

The answers to these questions are akin to the river that throws out its debris and leaves them by the shore as she flows. In the macroeconomic simile, the river once it throws out the debris manifests no relationship between the two except for two different bodies of matter separately performing their functions: the river throws out the debris; the debris floats by the side of the flowing river. On the other hand, in the micro-foundational sense, we would study the hydrodynamics of the river and the response of the debris to this in order to study the causality of the two in the wellbeing of the human and non-human environments. As an example, the buoyancy of boats and the power of Tsunami are studied in this latter purposive way for the wellbeing of all.

Economics likewise is a behavioral science. But its dichotomy between the exogenous nature of policy and extraneous variables in macroeconomics does not accomplish the full interactive nature of the discipline. However, this state of macroeconomics can be changed, but only by transforming its foundation into microeconomic reasoning, formalism, and its application as a fully behavioral science with extensive endogenous causal relationships between all variables. Included in these relationships are the endogenous variables of morality and ethics. In the end, the kind of socio-scientific reasoning that we have explained above by unifying the deductive and inductive, normative and positivistic reasoning opens up new frontiers of policy-theoretic knowledge.

In the field of macroeconomic dynamics, variables are grouped into endogenous and exogenous kinds. For example, while poverty alleviation remains endogenously affected by income level and human resource development; monetary and fiscal policies act as exogenous variables. Thereby, it is untenable in macroeconomics to relate monetary policy, signified say by statutory central bank reserve ratio, to the endogenous variables. Likewise, it is untenable to relate fiscal policy signified by autonomous government expenditure, to the multidimensional nature of poverty alleviation and income generation. Likewise, there is no predictable relationship between economic growth and poverty alleviation. A neoclassical growth model or a Keynesian/monetarist expansion will define economic growth path by the efficiency context of production and cost. They would then use a distributional variable for income compensation effect on poverty alleviation.

The result then will be as follows: The endogenous effects of growth (income generation) and poverty alleviation will continue on in the direction of economic efficiency. Economic efficiency and distributive equity as of poverty alleviation will prevail in their great tradeoff. Phelps (1989) has pointed out that, indeed the economic methodology is not adept to answer the question of social justice.

Our conclusive argument is that, all of economic, and in fact socio-scientific reasoning, is bereft of an *endogenous* treatment of morality and ethics. The implication of this conclusion is that, methodologically socio-scientific reasoning is not built upon moral and ethical foundations. Rationalism, upon which all of socio-scientific reasoning of liberal scholarship is premised, does not help out with an outlook on morality and ethics. We have explained this point abundantly in Chapter 8.

It is now necessary to establish moral and ethical sensitivity in socio-scientific reasoning to incorporate morality and ethics as foundational endogenous elements in the monotheistic epistemological basis of the worldview. Furthermore, without the moral and ethical consciousness of socio-scientific thought, the otherwise *exogenous* treatment of such elements cannot internalize them in our preferences, attributes and practices. Policies and institutional structures that build upon the exogenous treatment of morality and ethics will always sideline them in belief and practice. The immanent instruments of practicing morality and ethics as exogenous factors in human preferences will not lead into the alleviation of social problems. Among these instruments are the interest-rate related ones. We have argued this point in Chapter 8.

Our arguments now lead us into establishing the moral and ethical reconstruction of monetarism and fiscalism in the light of the theory of wellbeing that we have propounded in this work. Some critical definitions and concepts are needed to launch the new monetary-fiscal formalism based on their complementarities. Also we need to examine the complementarities of such policies with the socioeconomic variables, which define the wellbeing objective function. Through the inherent simulation via circular causation between the variables and policies, poverty alleviation, empowerment, real socioeconomic variables, policy changes, and structural institutional changes are attained. All of these relations and more are taken up in the light of their endogenous nature, as formalized by the IIE-evolutionary learning methodology. The implications of Figure 2 are thereby invoked.

EXPLANATION OF SELECTED TERMS

This section reiterates the central focus on human dignity gained by poverty alleviation, empowerment, and socioeconomic security that is everyone's fundamental right. We ask the question: Which one is primordial for raising human functioning in relation to the non-human world, now expanded by the widening vision of complementarities and participation? Is it poverty alleviation and all of the other goals that go along with poverty alleviation, or is it the goal of wellbeing being primal?

As we have noted in the wellbeing simulation problem, subject to circular causation relations between the variables, poverty alleviation is a *derived* target variable of circular causation equations of wellbeing simulation. Indeed, poverty alleviation is a multidimensional task. On this issue the World Bank (2000, p. 6) writes: "The choice and implementation of public actions that are responsive to the needs of poor people depend on the interaction of political, social, and other institutional processes. Access to market opportunities and to public sector services is often strongly influenced by state and social institutions, which must be responsive and accountable to poor people. Achieving access, responsibility, and accountability is intrinsically political and requires active collaboration among poor people, the middle class, and other groups in society. Active collaboration can be greatly facilitated by changes in governance that make public administration, legal institutions, and public service delivery more efficient and accountable to all citizens—and by strengthening the participation of poor people in political processes and local decision making. Also important is removing the social and institutional barriers that result from distinctions of gender, ethnicity, and social status. Sound and responsive institutions are not only important to benefit the poor but also fundamental to the overall growth."

The state of poverty and poverty alleviation are not pre-assigned states of human life. These human conditions are social states. Being so, the affliction of poverty is caused by the inter-causal effects of many social problems and issues. These have to be changed and corrected. Including in this vector of variables and their causal effects is the will and effort of the afflicted ones to wrestle out of the demeaning states of poverty in concert with the social order of participation. Being a social issue for the existence and alleviation of poverty in relation to the overarching objective of wellbeing, an individual, group, community, region, and country, measures its own depth of poverty by interrelating across the extant of social relations.

The problematic depth of poverty is based on the inadequacy of basic needs. Poverty is not caused by a lack of wants. When disparate entities are made to compare by way of emulating their standards, individuals then enter the domain of relative-poverty alleviation. Relative poverty is governed by the aspiration for wants. This kind of poverty alleviation should not be a goal of alleviation by specific policies and structural changes, for which otherwise, much public expenditure and unnecessary social cost can arise. The perception on the incidence of poverty ought therefore to be determined by the target group or individuals within the scope of their adequacy in meeting provision of basic needs. This kind of attitude towards poverty on the basis of adequacy of needs reflects an attitude of contentment in the specific needs basket. Such an attribute belongs to the needs basket that is induced by epistemic knowledge determining wellbeing via contentment and social balance. When viewed in this comprehensive way of epistemic knowledge and its induction of the adequacy level of the needs basket, much of the cost of alleviating poverty can be reduced, and poverty alleviation made possible.

Systemic complementarities and participation are fundamental for understanding wellbeing, and thereby empowerment and its causal relationship with the incidence of poverty and poverty alleviation. Participation is a concept that cannot be restricted to human domain alone. Participation extends over the use and management of resources, goods and services, all types of socioeconomic and experiential artifacts. The IIE-learning model defines participation as the overarching creative interaction and integration between the human world and the non-human world. We have explained this point earlier.

Variables, relations, and events are the results of causality in the circular causation system of interrelations. Variables are received information in the IIE-learning processes. Yet such variables may be initially crude in ethics, but subsequently transformed into learning variables that enable extensively endogenous causality with all other variables. This kind of social participation takes place by the induction of knowledge-flows relating to the unity of knowledge and the world-system. The eventuality of the simulated variables by knowledge-induction is the station to be reached for developing moral-social relations signified by their circular causation interrelations. Such a knowledge-induced moral-social state of the ethically reconstructed variables is the idea of event that becomes functional by the complementary characteristics of knowledge-flow and the knowledge-induced variables.

Socioeconomic variables (including policy, instrumental, and institutional variables) are the ethically reconstructed variables by the induction of knowledge-flows as in the IIE-process model of simulation of wellbeing, subject to the circular causation relations between the wellbeing functional variables in the good things of life. The straightforward socioeconomic data are not the end-point of socioeconomic information for moral-social transformation with which wellbeing simulation is involved. Incidence of poverty and poverty alleviation as stand-alone variables are therefore not acceptable data in the learning model for wellbeing simulation. No model is acceptable, and therefore variables useful, that do not enter circular causation for moral-social reconstruction and analysis. Critical indicators are calculated in the comparative scale of estimated values and simulated ones, as we have pointed out earlier.

Bertrand Russell (1903) defines scientific model as abstraction of reality. He also goes on to define our state of the conscious world, remarking: It is strange that we know so little and yet we know so much; and so little a knowledge we have can give us so immense a power. We combine such immanent attributes of modeling to describe our reality by the use of specific variables and their states: Modeling is thereby abstraction of the moral-social reconstruction of interrelations between the defining variables. In the end thereby we find, that socioeconomic variables used in modeling ought to explain the specific and the generalized model of moral-social reconstructed reality.

Policy and instrumental variables and those of institutional structural change fall in the same purview of endogenously related variables resulting from circular causation. Consequently, macroeconomic variables of these types lose their morally and ethically benign character. The wellbeing model of simulation by circular causation subsumes these kinds of variables within the endogenous group calling forth micro-foundational choices in them. Institutions are treated as discursive organizational entities (Arrow, 1974). In the moral-social context, institutions are non-utilitarian and non-rationalistic. Instead, they are endogenously defined by the wellbeing objective criterion that the members discourse upon in light of the epistemic unity of knowledge.

Money and fiscal variables and polices are the two subsets of socioeconomic variables that become ethically knowledge-induced when entered in the wellbeing model that is simulated subject to circular causation relations. These variables, and the policies premised on them are then transformed into knowledge-induced variables with their important synergistic role in the circular causation system. Being so, money and fiscal variables and policies must be aggregate concepts of primitive microeconomic concepts with behavioral properties in the specific and generalized model interrelating money and fiscal variables with the rest of the socioeconomic variables.

Generalization of the model of wellbeing simulation subject to circular causation relations applies to 'everything', thus forming the model of socio-scientific phenomenology. Only the problems of different disciplines and categories remain distinct, not the model of unity of knowledge and its induction of the learning world-system. The latter category remains universal and unique. Generalization also means that it encompasses every specific application and conceptualization in the form of the interactive, integrative, and evolutionary phenomenon along the path of learning processes. This nature of specificity within the generalized worldview is clearly manifest in the wide and evolutionary form of wellbeing model that is simulated subject to large equation system of circular causation relations. Thereby, the equation of poverty alleviation presents a specific problem within the generalized system of wellbeing simulation, and so on. Dealing with poverty alleviation, money, fiscal variables, real economy variables, prices, employment, and human resource development in a system of interrelated equations, constitutes a larger specific model system within the evolutionary generalized system.

MICRO-PERSPECTIVES OF MONEY, FISCALISM, REAL ECONOMY, PRICES, AND POVERTY ALLEVIATION

Friedman's (1960) formulation of Quantity Theory of money, output, and prices was at the aggregate level using methods that straddled the model with a plethora of interest rates in various assets. The model then took the following form:

$$M = (1/v).Y, \tag{6}$$

Where, M denotes the nominal value of the quantity of money in circulation.

- Y denotes nominal value of GDP. Thus Y = P.y, P as price level, y as real value of GDP.
- v denotes the velocity of money circulation in generating the real output.

In terms of real value of money in demand, the exchange Equation 6 is re-written as,

$$M/P = (1/v).y \tag{7}$$

Equations 6 and 7 convey the following results: When $v < 1$, $M > Y$. The nominal quantity of money exceeds the nominal output value. Likewise, the quantity of real money exceeds the real output value. In these cases, money is withdrawn from the real economy circulation into interest-bearing financial assets. When $v > 1$, $M < Y$. The nominal quantity of money in circulation is less than the nominal output value. It is likewise the case with real money and real output relationship. In these cases, the quantity of money in circulation does not meet the expected demand for producing real output. In both cases, any departure of v from its unitary value causes disequilibrium between the monetary sector (hence financial sector) and the real economy. This kind of substitution between the two sectors is similar to the case of neoclassical model of resource competition and allocation by substitution of the financial sector for the real sector.

The velocity of money circulation is thereby of critical importance in the exchange equations over time. Friedman characterized the velocity of money circulation in terms of interest rates in various kinds of financial assets in the following functional form in real economic variables:

$$v = v(i_b, i_e, p^\wedge, i, w, Y/P; u) \tag{8}$$

where, i_b denotes real interest rate on bonds;

- i_e denotes real interest rate on equity;
- $p^\wedge$ denotes rate of change in price level;
- i denotes the average interest rate on all kinds of financial assets;
- w denotes real value of wealth;
- Y/P denotes real output;
- u denotes random statistical variable incorporating other effects.

For our case of reading the exchange equation, we consider a plethora of financial assets bearing various interest rates. Then 'r' is interpreted as the term structure of these interest rates. We also allow for time variations in all the variables. Consequently, the time-variation of v^ will include the resulting functional variation of all the included variables over time. Now a number of differences arise between Friedman's version of the exchange equation and our proceeding formulation of Quantity Theory of Money in respect of the micro-foundations of preferences, choices, prices, money and output.

Firstly, time-variation of the variables introduce instability in the time-variation of 'v'. Consequently, unless there are endogenous controlling dynamics that gravitate 'v' towards a value of unity, money and output will remain in gap away from the economic expansion path that defines the use of money in spending in the good things of life, and thereby annuls the use of money in bank-savings. Only in the case of v =1 can a full utilization of money in generating real sector output be realized. Banks now work as intermediaries to mobilize savings into the real sector. The financial sector and the real economy sector now establish continuous bridging to mobilize resources of all kinds, and money circulation perfectly through the economy as needed of the monetary function. In all other cases of values of 'v' there is departure from the ideal case. Approximation is accepted by narrowing down the variations of 'v' away from the value of unity.

What does the value of 'v' equal to unity signify? This question was explained earlier in this work by treating aggregate money of Quantity Theory as micro-money. In the latter case, money is parceled fully in quanta into project needs. The level of such micro-money disaggregation depends upon the size and diversification of projects.

What is the idea of an economy in such a case as being distinct from the lateral aggregation of market functions, but yet aggregated in terms of complex micro-functional relations? For example, projects exist in participatory networks. Thereby micro-money divides into plethora of inter-project product diversification and cost-sharing for development. Now the total quantity of money in circulation economy-wide through all projects and their inter-projects networks amounts to the final convoluted aggregation of money across all such diversifications.[4]

In Friedman's equation of exchange, variations in 'v' causing demand gaps between monetary aggregates and real output stand for the positivistic state of monetary circulation as spending in the economy. The adverse positivistic effects are transmitted on price level. This can be shown by Equation 7 along time-variation:

M^ - P^ = y^ - v^ greater or less than 0 (9)

in terms of time rates of change in the variables signified by (^). Thus, for time-variations in v and y the following result is obvious:

M^ greater or less than P^ (10)

However, the important point to note is that when M^ > P^, price-stabilization results in deficiency of demand gap between the prevalent and potential level of output. As a result, underemployment and unemployment persist. When, M^ < P^, then inflationary pressure builds up. Now along the upward rising short-term aggregate supply of output, underemployment and unemployment are not effectively removed. The only way by which such conditions can be removed, but without removing the prevalent states of money, output, price level, and employment relationship, is for governments to enact exogenous policies – the monetary policy targets and fiscal policy targets. There is no endogenous adjustment between these policies and aggregates.

The micro-money case of relationship between money, product diversification, prices, and employment is hinged on the systemic knowledge induction of market variables combined with similarly induced institutional forces. The epistemic consciousness of unity of knowledge appears now as organic complementarities between the mentioned variables. Knowledge induction of the economic system corrects market actions into dynamic basic needs of life. The simulated θ-values in the money aggregation equation affects the entire set of variables by their circular causation relations in simulating the wellbeing function. The resulting θ-ethical index (equivalently the measured level of wellbeing) explains the nature of pervasive complementarities between the variables. Such θ-induced variables stand as examples of the good things of life in the dynamic basic-needs regime of development.[5]

The micro-money version of the exchange equation interrelating money, output, price level, and employment circular causation relationships is now possible:

$$\text{Simulate } W(M_{i...k}, Y_{i...k}, P_{i...k}, r_{i...k}, L_{i...k})[\theta] \tag{11}$$

Subject to the circular causation relations:

$$M_{i...k}(\theta) = f_{i...k}(Y_{i...k}, P_{i...k}, r_{i...k}, L_{i...k})[\theta] \tag{12 – 16}$$

This equation (12) truly marks the micro-money expression of equation of exchange. If we further re-write expression (12) as,

$$M_{i...k}(\theta) = A.Y_{i...k}^{a} P_{i...k}^{b} r_{i...k}^{c} L_{i...k}^{d} \theta^{e} \tag{17}$$

each of the variables is θ-induced. A, a, b, c, d, e are coefficients that are firstly estimated, and subsequently simulated by discursive or statistical methods. Consequently, the coefficients have their own probability distributions that can be mapped by the Spatial Domain Analysis of Geographical Information System (Choudhury & Hossain, 2010). The coefficients a, b, .., e in expression (17) and other similar ones in the system of such multiplicative forms of the circular causation relations denote elasticity coefficients of the dependent variables in respect of the independent variables.

All the equations of the circular causation system taken together explain the complementary interrelationships representing the epistemic unity of systemic knowledge induced in the micro-foundational variables. A *dynamic* basic-needs regime of development must prevail as representation of the good things of life.

At the end, there is the ethical index of unity of knowledge,

$$\theta = g(M_{i...k}, Y_{i...k}, P_{i...k}, r_{i...k}, L_{i...k})[\theta] \tag{18}$$

This expression too can be estimated and simulated in the multiplicative form of expression (18). The sum of the estimated/simulated coefficients can take all three numerical values – equal to unity implying constant returns in the wellbeing function; greater than unity implying increasing returns in the wellbeing function; less than unity implying decreasing returns in the wellbeing function.

i,j…,k denote diversified sub-systems of sectoral network formed by interaction, integration and evolution (IIE-learning processes) (Figures 1, 2) (Choudhury, 2000).

SPECIAL NOTES IN THE MICRO-MONEY SYSTEMS OF EQUATIONS OF EXCHANGE

Operational Venue of the Dynamic Basic-Needs Regime of Development

The operational dynamic basic-needs model of money-real economy exchange comes out of the functional ontological effect of unity of knowledge on issues of sustainability and wellbeing by organic complementarities and extensively discursive participation between variables, their relations and the representative entities of the variables. Such is a logical characteristic of the epistemic system. Given such characterization of the epistemic system in unity of knowledge, the participatory nature of the learning system with $v \to 1$ as $\theta\uparrow$, causes monetary aggregate to be mobilized into the real economy by participatory development financing instruments. Now all forms of interest rates are replaced progressively by asset-backed rates of return (also profit-sharing rates, yields on real assets). In such a case, the relational explanatory monetary equation (9.12 or 9.17) takes the form of accounting identity in the real output form,

The Monetary Accounting Identity

$$M_{i...k} = v\,(r_{i...k}).P_{\,i...k}\,.y_{\,i...k} \qquad (19)$$

Also the aggregate accounting identity form is,

$$M = v(r).P.y \qquad (20)$$

All the variables are θ-induced. $v(r_{i...k})\rightarrow 1$ as $\theta\uparrow$ and $v(r)\rightarrow 1$ as $\theta\uparrow$, meaning the monetary and real sectors are unified by a 100 per cent mobilization of financial savings into the real economy without bank-savings. Interest rates are thus replaced by rates of return in the good things of life.

In the limiting case of fully 100 per cent mobilization of resources, Equations 19 and 20 become spending equations interconnecting the monetary sector and the real economy.

Poverty Alleviation in the Monetary Relationship

The moral and ethical worth of money is realized by its fullest circulation (mobilization) in the good things of life. Among such good things of life to attain is poverty alleviation. Poverty alleviation variable (Pv), like employment variable (L), enters as additional candidate in the Equations 11-18. The rest of the analytics go through, though with the explanation of the money and poverty alleviation relationship taking place through the circulation causation with all the other complementary variables.

Indeed, now we have come full circle on the topic of poverty alleviation in its absolute and hard-core form. That is, any system that harbors interest rate, upholds the notion of economic rationality premised on scarcity of resources, competition, and maximization of self-interest goals by methodological individualism, cannot realize poverty alleviation. Contrarily, poverty alleviation is the possibility of the learning system in unity of knowledge among the good things of life comprising the dynamic basic-needs regime of moral-social development. Only in such a participatory socioeconomic system the use of money is realized as financial resource mobilization into the real economy. Logically thereby, interest is phased out by rates of return by cause and effect between trade and money circulation.

UNIFYING THE MONETARISM-FISCALISM DYNAMICS IN THE SIMULATION MODEL OF WELLBEING

Blaug (1993) has rightly pointed out that monetary policy and fiscal policy are opposite arms of attaining non-inflationary economic growth. Contrarily, in the context of the model of epistemic unity of knowledge in the learning worldview, the two approaches would be unified by their complementarities. Monetary and fiscal policies are endogenously unified by the induction of knowledge-values in the framework of their micro-foundational forms that interrelate between themselves and the vector of socioeconomic variables in an extended form of the circular causation system of equations that simulate the wellbeing function.

Here is how we represent the complementarities between the knowledge-induced variables. In the reduced form of the monetary equation of exchange (Equation 20 derived from Equation 19, which in turn is derived from the explanatory Equations 11-9.18), monetary aggregate is equated to spending in the sense of accounting identity conveyed by the simplified equations. In the relational explanatory system of equations money has been endogenized. Likewise, the spending relations are also endogenized as explained by the Equations 12-18. Therefore, both the monetary and fiscal functions are endogenous relations of the same set of variables. They now appear as functional images of each other in the equations of exchange and their deconstructed micro-foundational forms.

To these initial observations in modeling monetary and fiscal unification we add the domain of moral and ethical actions in the dynamic basic-needs regime of development. The result takes shape in working coherently between the ingredients of this substantive area of post-monetarism and post-Keynesian now formalized in terms of their microeconomic foundations. The premises of action comprise firstly, the axiom of epistemic unity of knowledge. This is followed by its truly possible realization in the domain of dynamic basic-needs regime of development, and the micro-foundation of complex aggregation in to the economy-wide level. Extensive endogeneity of circular relations in wellbeing simulation everywhere forms the applied basis of the comprehensive theory. Thus the entirety of the IIE-learning model is brought forth consistently, as with the earlier diverse model formulations.

The dynamic basic-needs regime of development concurs with the convergence between the demand and supply curves of basic-needs. This is a classical economic fact. But in the θ-induced case of socioeconomic variables of the dynamic basic-needs regime of development, the perfectly elastic supply and demand curves of basic-needs carrying forward the market equilibriums across given prices and quantity, experience perturbations along the locus of market equilibriums. The dynamics of temporary and evolutionary market equilibriums are linked with innovations occurring continuously by knowledge-induction.

When the above classical microeconomic perspective is brought into the complexity of diversified networks, then Equation 19, subject to $v \rightarrow 1$ with $\theta\uparrow$, implies that spending of micro-monetary aggregates in appropriately diversified projects of the good things of life pervade the dynamic basic-needs regime of development. The resulting so-called aggregate demand curve in its microeconomic context, equivalently the microeconomic context of IS-curve now represents accounting identity of the total expenditure in dynamic basic needs. Consequently, such an accounting identity becomes a perfectly horizontal IS-curve in terms of the micro-foundational concept. In the θ-induced regime of temporary equilibriums of the evolutionary type Equation 19 implies that the money-fiscal equilibrium prevails always, subject to $v \rightarrow 1$ with $\theta\uparrow$.

The tripartite equilibrium is now established simultaneously between the monetary sector, the fiscal sector, and the *dynamic* basic-needs pricing and quantity of goods and services in the real economy. In this way, the quantity of micro-money equates with the demand for real good and services. This demand is enabled by spending, which takes the form of micro-foundational perspective of fiscalism – that is spending. A micro-foundational model of general equilibrium is thus established with pervasive monetary-fiscal equilibrium, stable prices, elastic output, increasing employment, and replacement of interest rates by rates of return. The dynamics of such a tripartite system of circular causality are fully controlled by the evolution of $v \rightarrow 1$ with $\theta\uparrow$.[6]

The pervasiveness of demand and supply of money at all price levels of quantities demanded and supplied is claimed by the real bills hypothesis (Green, 1989) and by the *laissez-faire* theory of money, prices and output (Greenfeld & Yaeger, 1963; Black, 1970; Fama, 1980; Hall, 1985, 1997). Friedman's (1967, p. 17) remarks explain the real-bills stand regarding quantity theory of money: "… that changes in the demand for money call forth corresponding changes in supply and that supply cannot change otherwise, or at least cannot do so under specified institutional arrangements…. The same forces affect both the demand for and the supply of money, and in the same way."

The reality of unison between monetarism and fiscalism in the way explained above is particularly true of a regime with balanced budget. In such a situation, budget deficits (surpluses) would conform to an increase (decrease) in the quantity of money (Friedman, 1953). Approximation to the dynamic basic-needs regime, a causation of which is $v \rightarrow 1$ with $\theta\uparrow$, reduces the displacements between money and fiscalism and brings about effective stabilization. As long as such a situation prevails, sustainability is attained.

In our methodological critique of the entire dichotomous development between monetarism and fiscalism in macroeconomics, the underlying effect of knowledge-induction along the learning model negates the meanings of demand and supply of money as invalid concepts. All that prevails in the money-fiscal-prices-goods inter-relational case is the idea of a quantity of money in circulation through the money-finance-real economy linkage. Such a unified linkage by circular causation between the variables of these sectors is the manifest meaning of the epistemic unity of knowledge arising from the monotheistic roots by law, rules, guidance, and instruments across the good things of life. Such is the epistemological feature of Islamic economics, finance, and society in its learning worldview.

CONCLUSION

The convergence of arguments on moral-social reconstruction of thought, intellection, institutions, policies and practices, has appeared on the poverty question. Alleviating absolute poverty rather than eliminating *all* forms of poverty, except the abject, absolute and hard-core kind, is a process involving a spectrum of inter-related activities, ways of thinking, and human attitude in community and society, and the moral behavior, and conduct of such behavior towards the attainment of wellbeing. Within the overarching objective of attaining wellbeing through a moral rather than a rationalistic society, lies the undeniable and pressing derivation of the moral rule to alleviate poverty.

Within the process of the goal of attaining wellbeing, and thereby eradicating poverty of the abject, absolute and hard-core, lies the normative and positivistic social construct, deductive and inductive reasoning, as separately construed opposite polarities. This is the mark of moral debility, even of maturing modernism and post-modernism. The point has been expressed in the erudite writings of Husserl (1965), Dampier (1961), and Dilworth (2008).

The normative and positivistic perspectives of political economy have thus been integrated to present a unified worldview of diversities (Streeten, 1994). All of these together change the vision and mission of moral-social experience. Rationalism and its offshoots based on the axiom of rationality of thought are to be found entrenched in mainstream economics, and social and socio-scientific thinking. Such postulates and practices based on them are inextricably tied to ethically constraining postulates. These comprise the core postulates of resource scarcity, maximization, competition, and self-interest arising from methodological individualism in its varied human and institutional forms. The situation is like what Shackle (1971) characterizes: the end of novelty in learning in the state of maximization and steady-state equilibrium. This equivalently marks the end of the learning, discursive, and innovative process, unless these factors are further induced exogenously by extraneous factors of resources, technology, and policies. That is the way of bringing about change in mainstream socio-scientific thought. It fails to be of the cybernetic and inter-causal essence.

Among many of the kinds of such exogenous factors, and the consequential morally and ethically benign intellection of economic and socio-scientific optimality and steady-state equilibrium, there is the rate of interest and its pervasive presence in financial indicators. We have explained the existence of the rate of interest in all its manifestations as the core problem of moral debility of any society. Poverty alleviation cannot be attained, and the morally meaningful construct of socioeconomic development cannot be realized in the presence of *any* semblance of interest rate and its regime of financial and social relationship. Thus, we have argued that not only is any form of interest-rate regime of development finance untenable for moral-social reconstruction, but contrarily it is possible to replace interest rates for a progressive social economy. Such replacement of interest rate and its related transactions are possible by simulating wellbeing with trade-related instruments of finance in relation to the real economy. The underlying dynamics of such a trade-related regime of development and wellbeing has been explained in the context of a participatory and complementary model of dynamic basic-need development. Macro-wide variables and policies now take the micro-foundational basis of complex aggregation.

Dynamic basic-needs regimes of socioeconomic development then acquires a substantive meaning and intellection on a learning processed based worldview premised on the episteme of unity of knowledge and the knowledge-induced world-system, with its generality and specifics. The characterization of dynamic basic-needs regime of sustainability is a wellbeing objective criterion. From this, the interrelationships between many other variables, their relations and institutional practices, structures and micro-endogenous policies, are derived. Dynamic basic-needs evolving across evolutionary learning processes induced by the epistemic of unity of knowledge and its unified world-system, is not simply a domain of the poor. Quite the contrary, economies and societies at every stage of their development have basic-needs models of wellbeing, balance, and moral-social construction on sustainability enabled by participation in respect of the wellbeing criterion.

Streeten (1981, p. 331) writes his thoughtful words in regards to the substantive meaning of basic-needs for development sustainability: "... basic needs spells out in considerable detail human needs in terms of health, food, education, water, shelter, transport, energy, simple household goods, as well as non-material needs such as participation, cultural identity and a sense of purpose, which interact with the material needs. Basic needs is a more positive concept than the double negatives of eliminating or reducing unemployment or alleviating poverty."

Streeten (1981, p. 331, edited) continues on to emphasize the micro-foundational type of disaggregation of macroeconomic approach for poverty alleviation through basic-needs paradigm: "...Our concepts have become decreasingly abstract and increasingly disaggregated, concrete and specific.... GNP and its growth is a highly abstract and unspecified conglomerate of goods and services, irrespective of what and for whom."

In the context of a similar complementary concept of grassroots development, the ethical values are all intellectualized and practiced by the participation of *all* in a discursive society (Choudhury, 1998). The episteme of unity of knowledge and its unification functions in the generality and specifics of the socio-scientific order forms the circular cause and effect of the intrinsic learning worldview of a discursive society.

The emergent kind of social intellection can be summarized in Foucault's words (Foucault, 1983, p. 191): "By *episteme* we mean … the total set of relations that unite, at a given period, the discursive practices that give rise to epistemological figures, sciences, and possibly formalized systems.… The episteme is not a form of knowledge (*connaissance*) or type of rationality which, crossing the boundaries of the most varied sciences, manifests the sovereign unity of a subject, a spirit, or a period; it is the totality of relations that can be discovered, for a given period, between the sciences when one analyses them at the level of discursive regularities."

Substantive original ideas of the micro-foundation of economy wide and social reasoning in dynamic basic-needs conception of wellbeing have emerged. In the end, our micro-foundational formalism of aggregate economy-wide variables, their relations, and the underlying entities dealing with monetarism, fiscalism, and the real economy in a dynamic basic-needs regime of socioeconomic development led us to propose such a money-finance-real economy circular causation model.

Our study throughout this work and specifically in this chapter in respect of the major ethical issue of social justice, poverty alleviation, and sustainability, point out a common focus on wellbeing in both the Islamic economic, finance, and social view and the many who have thought with the heterodox perspective among the occidental thinkers. We have given the example of Paul Streeten on Gunnar Myrdal's circular causation method.

Such a convergence in ideas and ideals is made possible by the endogenous treatment of consciousness that needs to be induced in preferences and choices at the individual level and its complex aggregation by the IIE-learning process methodology under unity of knowledge as episteme. It is this particular methodological formalism of the wellbeing function with circular causation model that carries the epistemic unity of knowledge into the real world from its ontological origin, as manifested by the monotheistic law. The message of this work and chapter in respect of some key issues of ethical sociality is the building blocks of a monotheistic consciousness of unity of knowledge with its methodological details applied to the issues at hand and studied in the system and cybernetic worldview.

REFERENCES

Arrow, K. J. (1974). *The limits of organization*. New York, NY: W.W. Norton.

Black, F. (1970, Autumn). Banking and interest rates in a world without money. *Journal of Banking Research*, 8-20.

Blaug, M. (1993). *The methodology of economics*. Cambridge, UK: Cambridge University Press.

Boland, L. A. (1989). On the methodology of economic model building. In *The Methodology of Economic Model Building* (pp. 39–63). London, UK: Routledge.

Choudhury, M. A. (1998). *Studies in Islamic science and polity*. London, UK: Macmillan Press Ltd. doi:10.1057/9780230378032.

Choudhury, M. A. (2000). *The Islamic worldview, socio-scientific perspectives*. London, UK: Kegan Paul International.

Choudhury, M. A. (2001). On the existence of evolutionary learning equilibriums. *Journal of Science*, *16*, 1–13.

Choudhury, M. A. (2006). Islamic macroeconomics? *International Journal of Social Economics*, *33*(2). doi:10.1108/03068290610642238.

Choudhury, M. A. (2011). Overlapping generation model for Islamic asset valuation: A phenomenological application. In *Islamic Economics and Finance: an Epistemological Inquiry* (pp. 173–188). Bingley, UK: Emerald Publications.

Choudhury, M.A., & Hossain, M.S. (2010). Neuro-cybernetics of socio-scientific systems. *Mind and Society, 9*.

Choudhury, M.A., & Zaman, S.I. (2009). Self-referencing as socio-scientific methodology in contrasting paradigms. *Kybernetes: International Journal of Cybernetics, Systems and Management Studies, 38*(6).

Crane, R. D. (2011). Foreword. In Choudhury, M. A. (Ed.), *Islamic Economics and Finance: An Epistemological Inquiry*. Bingley, UK: Emerald.

Dampier, W. S. (1961). *A history of science and its relations with philosophy and religion*. Cambridge, UK: Cambridge University Press.

Dilworth, C. (2008). *Scientific progress: A study concerning the nature of the relation between successive scientific theories*. Berlin: Springer Science.

Fama, E. (1980). Banking in the theory of finance. *Journal of Monetary Economics*, *6*, 39–57. doi:10.1016/0304-3932(80)90017-3.

Foucault, M. (1972). *The archeology of knowledge and the discourse on language* (Sheridan, A. M., Trans.). New York: Harper Torchbooks.

Foucault, M. (1983). *Beyond structuralism and hermeneutics: The archeology of the human sciences* (Dreyfus, H. L., & Rabinow, P., Trans.). Chicago, IL: University of Chicago Press.

Friedman, M. (1953). The methodology of positive economics. In *Essays in Positive Economics*. Chicago: University of Chicago Press.

Friedman, M. (1953a). The methodology of positive economics. In *Essays in Positive Economics* (pp. 3–46). Chicago, IL: University of Chicago Press.

Friedman, M. (1953b). Monetary and fiscal framework for economic stability. In *Essays in Positive Economics* (pp. 133–156). Chicago, IL: University of Chicago Press.

Friedman, M. (1960). *A program for monetary stability*. New York, NY: Fordham University Press.

Friedman, M. (1960). *A program for monetary stability*. New York, NY: Fordham University Press.

Green, R. (1989). Real bills doctrine. In Eatwell, M., & Newman, P. (Eds.), *New Palgrave: Money* (pp. 310–313). New York: W.W. Norton.

Greenfeld, R. L., & Yaeger, L. B. (1963). A laissez-fare approach to monetary stability. *Journal of Money, Credit and Banking*, *15*, 302–315. doi:10.2307/1992481.

Hall, R. E. (1997). The government and the monetary unit. In Yaeger, L. B. (Ed.), *The Fluttering Veil, Essays on Monetary Disequilibrium* (pp. 383–391). Indianapolis, IN: Liberty Fund.

Hawking, S. W., & Mlodinow, L. (2010). *The grand design*. London, UK: Transworld Publishers.

Husserl, E. (1965). *Phenomenology and the crisis of philosophy* (Lauer, Q., Trans.). New York: Harper & Row Publishers.

Minford, P., & Peel, D. (1983). Rational expectations models: The basic method. In *Rational Expectations and the New Macroeconomics*. Oxford, UK: Martin Robertson.

Myrdal, G. (1958). The principle of cumulation. In Streeten, P. (Ed.), *Value in Social Theory, a Selection of Essays on Methodology by Gunnar Myrdal* (pp. 198–205). New York, NY: Harper & Brothers Publishers.

Phelps, E. S. (1989). Distributive justice. In Eatwell, J., Milgate, M., & Newman, P. (Eds.), *The New Palgrave: Social Economics*. New York, NY: W.W. Norton.

Quinton, A. (1989). *Utilitarian ethics*. La Salle, IL: Open Court.

Russell, B. (1903). Relations. In *Principles of Mathematics* (pp. 95–100). New York, NY: W.W. Norton.

Sen, A. (1999). Functioning and well-being. In *Commodities and Capabilities* (pp. 17–21). New Delhi, India: Oxford University Press.

Streeten, P. (1994). Positive and normative political economy and normative political economy. In *Strategies for Human Development, Global Poverty and Unemployment*. Copenhagen, Denmark: Handelshojskolens Forlag.

Streeten, P. A. (1981). *Development perspectives*. London, UK: Macmillan.

Sztompka, P. (1974). Systemic models in functional analysis. In *System and Functions, Towards a Theory of Society* (pp. 47–57). New York, NY: Academic Press.

Sztompka, P. (1974). Functional-subsystemic analysis. In *System and Functions, Towards a Theory of Society* (pp. 124–134). New York, NY: Academic Press.

World Bank. (2000). *World development report 2000-2001*. New York: Oxford University Press.

Yaeger, L. B. (1997). *The fluttering veil, essays on monetary disequilibrium*. Indianapolis, IN: The Liberty Press.

ENDNOTES

1 *Qur'an* (112): "In the name of *Allah*, the Beneficent, the Merciful: Say: He is *Allah*, the One! *Allah* the eternally besought of all! He begets not nor was He begotten. And there is none comparable unto Him."
Qur'an (2:255): "God! There is no god – but He – the Living, the Self-subsisting, Eternal. No slumber can seize Him nor sleep. His are all things in the heavens and on earth. Who is there can intercede in His presence except as He permits? He knows what (appears to His creatures as before or After or Behind them. Nor shall they compass aught of His knowledge except as He wills. His Throne does extend over the heavens and the earth, and He feels no fatigues in guarding and preserving them for He is the Most High, and Supreme (in Glory)?

2 *Qur'an* (13:4): "And in the Earth are neighboring tracts, vineyards and ploughed lands, and date-palms, like and unlike, which are watered with one water. And We have made some of them to excel others in fruit. Lo! Herein verily are portents for people who have sense."

3 "Progress in positive economics will require not only the testing and elaboration of existing hypotheses but also the construction of new hypotheses. On this problem there is little to say on a formal level. The construction of hypotheses is a creative act of inspiration, intuition, and invention; its essence is the vision of something new in familiar material. The process must be discussed in psychological, not logical, categories; studied in autobiographies and biographies, not treatises on scientific method; and promoted by maxim and example, no syllogism or theorem."

4 In discreet monetary flows, $M(\theta) = \cup_s \cap_{i...k} M_{i...k}(\theta)$ = convoluted network value = $\int\{\cap_{i...k} M_{i...k}(\theta)\}d\theta$, the continuous case. These terminal values of the quantity of micro-money post-aggregation by complex network relations can be inferred in Figure 2.

5 $M(\theta) = \cup_s \cap_{i...k} M_{i...k}(\theta)$ transforms into $M(Y,P,r,L)[\theta] = \cup_s \cap_{i...k} M_{i...k}(Y,P,r,L)_{i...k}(\theta)$, and likewise in the continuous case of learning.

6 $\{[C(y) + I(r,y) + G(r,y)[\theta]\}_{i..k} = IS_{]i..k} = [v(r).p.y]_{i..k}$ = Spending function $(r,y,p)_{i..k} = M_{i..k}(r,y,p)_{i..k}$. All variables are micro-foundational and θ-induced. C denotes consumption expenditure. I denotes investment expenditure. G denotes government expenditure. 'r' denotes rate of return replacing interest rate in the dynamic basic regime with extensive complementarities and participation prevailing. 'y' denotes real income. 'p' denotes prices of goods and services in the dynamic basic-needs regime of development. Dynamic basic-needs regime of development is characterized by non-inflationary economic growth. The monetary variables and policies complement the fiscal variables and policies through the spending function. Hence money-real economy and financial sectors are complemented in the learning model subject tov→ 1 with θ↑.

Chapter 10
Money, Price, Output, Interest Rate, and Factor Employment:
Comparative Theory

ABSTRACT

This is a chapter in general-equilibrium study of the Walrasian type. It is extended to money, output, and prices along with their other important economic effects (e.g. employment and stability). The Walrasian monetary model and the quantity theory of money model are both compared and contrasted with the endogenous theory of money model in light of the systemic view of unity of knowledge that grounds the phenomenological model in this book.

INTRODUCTION

The objective of the chapter is spelled out in its four parts. These are firstly, to lay out a general perspective of monetary theory in mainstream economics so as to lay down how money and real economy are treated in the way as we understand monetary theory and policy and the evolution of monetary history. Secondly, we lay down a universal theory of interactive, integrative, and evolutionary (IIE) worldview of unity of knowledge, which is understood as organic circular causal unifying inter-relationship between the good things of life. Among these blessed artifacts of life are money and production, price stability and factor utilization, trade and productivity in the phased out regime of interest rates (Choudhury, 2007). The underlying economic perspective follows the IIE-learning methodology that emanates from the

DOI: 10.4018/978-1-4666-4643-8.ch010

Copyright ©2014, IGI Global. Copying or distributing in print or electronic forms without written permission of IGI Global is prohibited.

foundation of the universal theory of unity of knowledge. All the variables appear as complementary possibilities rather than the kinds of mainstream understanding of marginalism and trade-off between them.

The mainstream theory of economics, finance, and 'everything' as in the generalized world-system is thus critiqued and replaced rigorously in this chapter by the worldview conception of organic (learning) unity in the interactive, integrative, and evolutionary methodology of epistemic unity gained by continuous learning. Money in Islam in its contrasting study with mainstream theory overviewed in the first part of this chapter is presented in a substantive way in part three of this chapter. Part four of this chapter presents an empirical exercise in the light of the theory of money in Islam using the estimation/simulation method of circular causation.

The chapter concludes by establishing the Islamic methodological worldview of unity of knowledge as the episteme for explaining the learning dynamics of all issues and problems of the human domain. In a specific case we establish the model and the learning dynamics of complementary relations between money and real economy through the function of the financial instruments/sector in the model of unity of knowledge. Thus a contrasting result emerges between the marginalist axioms of mainstream economics and finance characterizing the nature of goods or 'bads', and the continuously learning dynamics in complementarities between ethical possibilities and their induced variables.

THE MAINSTREAM GENERAL EQUILIBRIUM MODEL OF MONEY, PRICES, GOODS, AND PRODUCTIVE FACTORS

The Pareto optimal general equilibrium model of goods, prices and productive factors has been elegantly established by Henderson and Quandt (1971). We will firstly explain textually and then summarize the mathematical result in this chapter.

The Pareto optimal general equilibrium model comprises the simultaneous solution for goods, prices, and factor utilization between the demand side shown by consumer utility, and the supply side shown by the production function. The utility function $U_i(q_{i1}^*,\ldots,q_{is}^*, x_{i1}^o-x_{i1}^*, \ldots, x_{in}^o-x_{in}^*,M_i)$ of the ith-consumer, for i = 1,2,….,m, is a function of consumption that equals all of s-number of produced goods of various types denoted by the vector, but also including a quantity of money M_i in our specific case. This vector is denoted by $Q_i = \{q_{i1}, q_{i2},\ldots,q_{is}, M_i\}$. The ith-consumer owns n-types of total quantity of primary factors as endowments, with j = 1,2,…,n. Of these given productive endowments, the ith consumer uses x_{ij}^* for work. Hence he uses $(x_{ij}^o - x_{ij}^*)$ for leisure activity. We denote the net supply of productive factors by $x_i^* = \{x_{i1}^*, x_{i2}^*, \ldots, x_{in}^*\}$ and the net leisure activity vector is $(x_i^o - x_i^*) = \{((x_{i1}^o - x_{i1}^*), \ldots, (x_{in}^o - x_{in}^*)\}$.

To all of these we also specifically include the quantity of money that the ith individual owns, say M_i. Of this he supplies M_i* for productive activity (e.g. investment, and in general spending). Thus he saves $S_i = (M_i - M_i^*)$. The nature of savings as it so appears is unproductive activity in the dichotomy between productive and unproductive use of money and demand and supply of goods and factor endowments. Thereby, all the activities generated by savings, such as interest rate, bonds, banking operations based on paper-money, and the fractional reserve requirements monetary system that creates the interest-bearing idle stocks of money by way of bank savings, and future uncertain portfolios with speculative risk and return conjectures, are all unproductive activities linked with the unproductive nature of saving as opposed to the idea of resource mobilization. In the latter case, the full endowment of M_i would be used for productive activity in linkage with the production of Q and the offer of x_{ij}.

Consequent to these two kinds of uses of money, saving, which is delayed injection as investment over time into productive activity, always cause withdrawal from potential output (Ventelou, 2005) along the continuous path of savings and output. Thereby, the potential (full-employment) level of output, and factor utilization at the potential level of output (hence employment of various factor endowments) are never attained. As a result of such suboptimal output and factor utilization, the utility level too remains suboptimal.

While leisure is definitely beneficial for recycling factor productivity and efficiency, and likewise, regular recovery of capital is beneficial for productivity and efficiency of capital, etc, yet such kinds of recycling are not linked with saving as money held away from productive spending. Hence in the dichotomy between productive and unproductive utilization of factor endowments, the x_{ij} are not unproductive. The consumer utility function remains optimizable with x_{ij} as defined; but not so with savings, and thereby not with the withdrawal of money from generating potential output.

It is possible however, but this is a case of situational demand and supply of factors, that when potential output is generated by the continuous mobilization of M_i in production, then x_i* will increase and will ultimately limit itself to all of factor endowments in demand and supply required to generate the potential output. This kind of consequence of leisure tending to zero is situational rather than a necessary condition of production and factor use.

The result relating to x_{ij} and S_i in respect of production and consumer utility is this: All forms of spending, not simply mobilization of M_i into investment and production, will cause full mobilization of M_i (and thus saving) continuously along the path of growth of potential output. Besides, although the Walrasian form of general equilibrium modeling done by Henderson and Quandt does not include the effect of ethics in economic change, this chapter will include this aspect as well. Thus it is necessary that the spending ought to be in the *good things of life*, not simply in productive alternatives. The point of generating higher returns from spending in the *good things of life* is pointed out by Sen (1985) and Rawls (1971, also pointed out by Sen, 1989).

The next matter is to examine the theoretical underpinnings of money, saving, output, and factor utilization with stable price relationship. It is a theoretical conclusion that in a free market economy as depicted by Pareto optimality, a lower range of factor supply will yield lower levels of output. Also saving as financial withdrawal from potential output will reduce the supply of goods and services. Consequently, in these two cases the supply curve of goods and factors will shift backwards, while the demand curve for the same categories may remain unchanged or will also shift backwards according to the willingness of household members to take leisure in preference to work. The prices of all kinds will increase at such lower levels of output and quantity of factors. Furthermore, as savings increase, a root cause of this will be higher interest rates. This too will militate against potential output and factor utilization. Besides, as the price level increases, the real interest rate will decline. The effect then will be a lower rate of return on bonds and shares. Money will fly out of such financial instruments into bank savings.

The Great Depression was characterized by such an economic downturn. National savings were driven into bank-savings and remained unutilized in productive investment and all forms of productive spending. Governments had finally to intervene to satisfy Keynes' recommendation for increasing Government expenditure policy and incur debt financing. The cost of stabilizing the economy was a buildup of deficit financing, which turns out eventually in higher interest rates and taxes.

MATHEMATICAL DEDUCTIONS FROM THE PARETO-OPTIMAL GENERAL EQUILIBRIUM RESULT

Henderson and Quandt have given the following three results of their Lagrangian maximization of individual utility functions subject to the existence of competitive market clearance for goods and services (productive factors). That is, total consumption equals total production; total factor demand equals total factor supply. Note that in every case, the money variable, which denotes the ith individual spending of money in the jth good, M_{ij}, is included as per our requirement in this chapter. M_{ij} carries all the connotations as mentioned above.

Individual consumer utility function takes the form,

$$U_i = U_i(q_{i1}^*,\ldots,q_{is}^*, x_{i1}^{o} - x_{i1}^*, \ldots, x_{in}^{o} - x_{in}^*, M_{i1}, \ldots M_{in}); i = 1,2,\ldots,m \quad (1)$$

Likewise, individual firm-specific production function with money is,

$$F_h(q_{h1}, \ldots, q_{hs}, x_{h1}, \ldots, x_{hn}, M'_{h1} .. M'_{hs}) = 0;\ h = 1,2,\ldots, N \tag{2}$$

The money variable from the production side is included as M'_{lk},
Constraints on goods and services for optimization are,

$$\text{(services=factors) } \Sigma_{i=1}{}^{m}\, x_{ij}{}^{*}=\Sigma_{h=1}{}^{N}\, x_{hj}; \tag{3}$$

$$\text{(goods) } \Sigma_{i=1}{}^{m}\, q_{ij}{}^{*}=\Sigma_{h=1}{}^{N}\, q_{hs}; \tag{4}$$

$$\text{(money spent = money used) } \Sigma_{i=1}{}^{m}\, M_{ij}=\Sigma_{h=1}{}^{N}\, M'_{hj} \tag{5}$$

The Lagrangian optimization yields the following results:

Consumption and Production Relationship Including Money

$$\alpha = [\partial U_1/\partial q_{1j}{}^{*}]/[\partial U_1/\partial q_{1k}{}^{*}] = \ldots = [\partial U_m/\partial q_{mj}{}^{*}]/[\partial U_m/\partial q_{mk}{}^{*}]$$

$$= [\partial U_1/\partial M_{1j}]/[\partial U_1/\partial M_{1k}] = \ldots = [\partial U_m/\partial M_{mj}{}^{*}]/[\partial U_m/\partial M_{mk}{}^{*}]$$

$$= [\partial F_1/\partial q_{1j}]/[\partial F_1/\partial q_{1k}] = \ldots =[\partial F_N/\partial q_{1j}]/[\partial F_N/\partial q_{1k}]$$

$$= [\partial F_1/\partial M'_{1j}]/[\partial F_1/\partial M'_{1k}] = \ldots= [\partial F_N/\partial M'_{Nj}]/[\partial F_N/\partial M'_{Nk}]; \tag{6}$$

$j,k = 1,2,.., s$

From these equalities it can be shown that

$$-(dq_{lk}/dq_{lj}) = \alpha;$$

$$-(dM_{lk}/dM_{lj}) = -(dM'_{lk}/dM'_{lj}) = \alpha \tag{7}$$

The implications from these derivations is that both output and monetary flows are monotonic as long as there is full mobilization of money and bank-savings as withdrawal from economic resource run down to zero.

Consumption, Production, and Factor Relationship Including Money

$\beta = [\partial U_1/\partial(x_{1j}^o - x_{1j}^*)]/[\partial U_1/\partial(x_{1k}^o - x_{1k}^*)] = \ldots$

$= [\partial U_m/\partial(x_{mj}^o - x_{mj}^*)]/[\partial U_m/\partial(x_{mk}^o - x_{mk}^*)]$

$= [\partial U_1/\partial M_{1j}]/[\partial U_1/\partial M_{1k}] = \ldots = [\partial U_m/\partial M_{mj}]/[\partial F_m/\partial M_{mk}]$

$= [\partial F_1/\partial q_{1j}]/[\partial F_1/\partial q_{1k}] = \ldots = [\partial F_N/\partial q_{Nj}]/[\partial F_N/\partial q_{Nk}];$

$= [\partial F_1/\partial M'_{1j}]/[\partial F_1/\partial M'_{1k}] = \ldots = [\partial F_N/\partial M'_{Nj}]/[\partial F_N/\partial M'_{Nk}];$ (8)

$i = 1,2,\ldots,m;\ h = 1,2,\ldots,N;\ j = 1, 2, \ldots, n;\ k = 1, 2, \ldots, s$

The implications here are the following:

$- d(x_{lk}^o - x_{lk}^*)/d(x_{lj}^o - x_{lj}^*) = \beta;$

$- dM_{lk}/dM_{lj} = \beta,$

from consumers side of money in utility function;

$dM'_{lk}/dM'_{lj} = \beta,$ (9)

from production side of money in the production function.

Factor endowments, consumption, output and money demand and money supply move in tandem with each other. The more is money injected into the economy by its mobilization and thus drawing down the bank-savings, the more monotonic positive relationship is generated between money, output and factor endowments. But the direction of movement of the above variables between goods and services is driven by marginal rates of substitution. This postulate is the perennial neoclassical assumption of competition, scarcity of resources and steady-state equilibrium and utility and output optimization. The marginal rate of substitution between factor use, production of different commodities, and money in demand and supply between different goods in demand and supply *must* exist in order for relative prices to exist. The existence of the marginal rates of substitution is thereby the fundamental axiom in all of these neoclassical results to attain Pareto-optimality.

These relationships between consumption, production, factor endowments, and money are pointed out in Table 1.

THE MONEY, PRICE, AND OUTPUT RELATIONSHIP

Quantity Theory and the Exchange Equation from Microeconomic Foundations

To make the above general equilibrium Pareto-optimal treatment of money in relation to consumption, output and factor endowments comply with various monetary theories, we consider micro-type monetary flows, M_{ij}, M_{hj}', as defined above in the case of consumer utilities and firm productions, respectively. i = 1,2,.., m denotes numbered consumers; j = 1,2,…,s denotes consumptions; h = 1,2,…, N denotes numbered firms or projects; j,k = 1,2,…,s denote production outlets, outputs.

In the sense of micro-money, the quantity of money for each of the micro-spending outlets is given by,

$$M_{ij} = M'_{hj} = \text{accounts settlement} = \kappa_j.(p_G.x_{ij} + p_Q.q_{kj} + p_F.x_{ij} + p_F'.q_{kj} + r.q^f_{kj}) \quad (10)$$

The total stock of money is,

$$M_j = M'_j = \Sigma_{i=1}^{N} M_{ij} = \Sigma_{h=1}^{M} M_{hj} = \kappa_j.P_j.y_j,\ j = 1,2,\dots s \quad (11)$$

where, κ_j denotes the average of the inverse of velocities of money circulation across j-number of projects (firms). P_j is aggregate price level of the different categories of spending shown above. y_j denotes the real value of the aggregate spending as shown. The result is the project-specific equations of exchange.

In the resulting case for aggregation over all projects in the economy-wide sense, we have the exchange equation of quantity theory of money,

$$M = \Sigma_{j=1}^{s} \kappa_j.P_j.y_j = \kappa.P.y \quad (12)$$

Table 1. Consumption (C), production (Q), factor interrelationships between commodities (firms) under the influence of money

	ΔQ_l	ΔC_l	ΔF_l	ΔQ_k	ΔC_k	ΔF_k
ΔM_{dl} in utility of 'l'	+	+	+	-	-	-
ΔM_{sl} in production of 'l'	+	+	+	-	-	-
ΔM_{dk} in utility of 'k'	-	-	-	+	+	+
ΔM_{sk} in production of 'k'	-	-	-	+	+	+

A great deal of debate has raged over the appropriate values of the velocity of money circulation (v), and hence regarding its inverse, κ. Marquis (1996) considers the following equations for estimating the pricing relationship between real value of money and the real value of output:

We re-write the exchange equation as,

v = y/(M/P),

which can take the following values as shown in Figure 1:

= (y > M/P),

a mismatch between production and its monetary valuation. The result would be an inflationary situation in the business cycle with aggregate demand (spending) running in excess of aggregate supply corresponding to the potential level of output.

= (y < M/P),

a mismatch again. The result is a recessionary situation in the business cycle with aggregate demand remaining below aggregate supply corresponding to the potential level of output.

= (y=M/P),

matching between production, spending andquantity of money. Now money flow circulates perfectly in the economy across each optimally money-absorbing projects. This is the non-inflationary and non-recessionary situation of money, price, output and spending relationship. It is also the situation for all of real output (aggregate demand) to be mobilized into aggregate supply while carrying the economy towards

Figure 1. Various contours for v = y/(M/P)

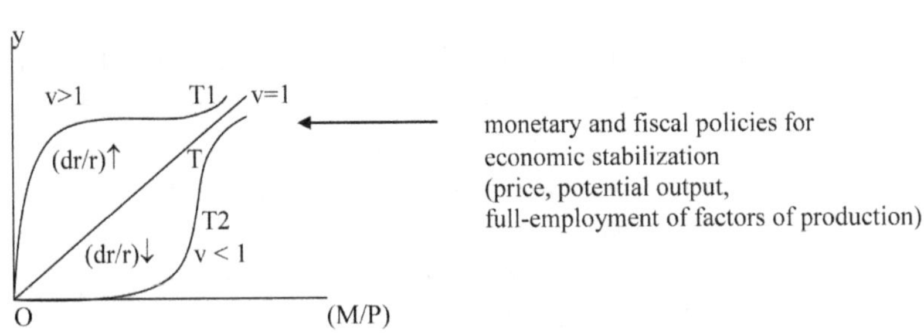

potential real output by distributing money in matching with specific projects across the economy.

MILTON FRIEDMAN'S VERSION OF QUANTITY THEORY AND EQUATION OF EXCHANGE

Lately, Friedman (1989) extended the equation of exchange to include financial securities in the following form of the equation of exchange. In our equation of exchange we included the financial variables with the price (r) and the financial securities (q^f_{kj}). Friedman's extended quantity theory equation of exchange is of the form (edited by author),

$$M_d = M_s = M = \kappa.P.L.f(y, w, r, p^\wedge,u); \text{ or } M/P = \kappa.L.f(y, w, r, p^\wedge,u) \qquad (13)$$

Here M denotes the quantity of money in circulation; P denotes the price level; L denotes the population size. L is needed because the exchange equation is constructed from the micro to the macro level aggregation. 'y' denotes real output; 'w' denotes a fraction of wealth based on the monetary base; 'r' is the vector of rates of interest in different financial papers; 'p^' is the rate of inflation, 'u' is a random residual variable.

In Friedman's equation $\kappa = 1$. That is $v = 1$. In the above form of the equation of exchange, the signs of coefficients related to y and w are positive. The signs related with the coefficients of r and p^ are negative. Thus in our case, developed independently, the sign of the term for the financial output with $r.q^f_{kj}$, is negative. Also the best scenario for effective monetary transmission is like Friedman's condition of the above-mentioned equation of exchange with $v = 1$.

The appearance of 'r' with the financial output term, if as a rate of interest, would mean withdrawal from monetary flow in the form of bank-saving. Consequently, the exchange equation will yield a quantity of money mobilized into the economy for generating potential output. This will yield a point of relationship between real income and real money, where $v < 1$ in Figure 1. In such a situation, a policy to restore economic stabilization would be to lower the rate of interest, and thus increase investment and spending, and release bank-savings towards financing the aggregate demand and aggregate supply. This brings the aggregate demand and aggregate supply into equilibrium at the potential output level, and thereby creating full-employment of factor endowments at non-inflationary prices.

To prove this kind of negative effect of interest rate on the flow of quantity of money to establish economic stabilization we note the following simple version of the quantity-of-money function *a la* Friedman:

$$M/P = f(r^{(-)},y^{(+)}) = a_0 + a_1.\log y - a_2.\log r; \tag{14}$$

a-coefficients are expected to be positive in their signs.
Thereby,

$$\log v = \log y - \log(M/P) = \log y - [a_0 + a_1.\log y - a_2.\log r] \tag{15}$$

$$dv/v = (1 - a_1).dy/y + a_2.dr/r \tag{16}$$

The result of putting into effect an economic stabilization policy will be a trend of,

$v \rightarrow 1$. Hence, $dv/v \rightarrow 0$.

Consequently,

$$dy/y = -[(a_2/(1-a_1)].(dr/r). \tag{17}$$

There are two ways of understanding the above equation. Firstly, if $[(a_2/(1-a_1)] > 0$, then an increase in interest rate decreases the growth of real income. The recessionary phase persists. A reversion to low rates of interest is needed for economic stabilization. Secondly, if $[(a_2/(1-a_1)] < 0$, then we write, $dr/r = -[(1-a_1)/a_2].(dy/y)$. Now as real income increases, then for price stabilization to take effect, the nominal output is stabilized by drawing it towards the potential output with an increase in the rate of change of 'r'. Thus a reversion to $v = 1$ is required for economic stabilization around the non-inflationary full-employment level of output. These relationships are pointed out in Figure 1.

KEYNESIAN MONETARY RELATIONS DERIVED FROM QUANTITY THEORY OF MONEY, OUTPUT, AND PRICES

Take the exchange equation, which mentions that the demand (M_d) equals supply (M_s) of money in defining the quantity of money, and then equates this quantity with the real value of output according to the circulation of money over number of transactions. Thereby,

$M_d/P = M_s/P = M/P = \{f(r^{(-)},y^{(+)})$ in the simple case;

$$\{f(B,r,y,P,\sigma) \text{ in a slightly more detailed form} \tag{18}$$

The Keynesian version of demand for money will include transaction demand, precautionary demand and speculative demand components. The money supply will remain exogenously set by the central bank. Otherwise, in a financial deregulated market, money can be generated by the commercial banks' multiple credit creation of new money, the money-multiplier formula. It can then be readily shown that the monetary equilibrium LM curve is a positively sloped curve in (r,y).

Besides, since $M = \kappa.Py = \kappa.(C+I+G+(X-M))$, with each of C, I, G, X, M being positive function of y and negative function of 'r', therefore, the expenditure sector IS curve is accordingly determined by the scalar of the inverse of the velocity of money circulation, κ. The IS-curve is still of the form, nominal output $Y = (A/B) - (C/B).r$.

The difference from the traditional interpretation of the IS-curve in this form is that either of the coefficients (A/B) or (C/B) may assume negative values. This will turn out the IS-relationship between Y and r to be a positive slope of different magnitudes. Such a case occurs when technological change involving cost embodied in the variable 'B' mentioned above causes shifts in the IS-curve to the extent of making the slope positive. It is a sign consistent with the inflationary condition when increasing income is drawn back from potential output level by the increase in the rate of interest (See explanation connected with Figure 1 for $v > 1$).

MONETARY DISEQUILIBRIUM

The result of IS-curve and LM-curve moving in the same direction may invoke disequilibrium condition of economic stabilization (Venieris & Sebold, 1977). Business cycles will reinforce explosively along the inflationary side of the (r,y) relationship, and will cause ratchet effects. This can be marked by conditions of hyperinflation, wherein the usual monetary and fiscal policies fail to stabilize the economy. Structural institutional and policy-theoretic changes are required.

During Keynes' time the revolution in theoretical intellection marked the advent of the coming of Keynes' General Theory. On the institutional side it was deficit financing but put in productive outlets (Hutt, 1979). In Friedman's monetarism (Bordo, 1989) and the Austrian paradigm of monetary *laissez faire* (Black, 1970; Fama, 1980; Hall, 1997, also mentioned by Yaeger, 1985; Greenfeld & Yaeger, 1963) market was judged as the ultimate arbiter of the correction of monetary disequilibrium. The correction could also result from automatic stabilization, which too is a combination of market economy and government regulations. Present days' Russia is such an example, with output increasing along with increasing rates of interest, but government staying with its regulations, however, had insufficient effectiveness in economic stabilization.

Heightened economic instability in the disequilibrium relations between IS and LM curves will cause volatility overall. This will reflect on higher values of σ. Consequently, the entire monetary function f(B,r,y,P,σ), and thereby, the quantity of money in circulation (demand = supply) will become unstable. The resulting forms of disequilibrium are marked by explosive forms of the Cobweb *tatonement* relations (La Salle & Lefschetz, 1961). These can be further combined with evolutionary disequilibria caused by excessive government regulations, wrong market choices of technology, and unproductive outlets. The international economy run by the animal spirit of competition in globalization can accentuate such disequilibrium conditions, as is now the case with financial market volatility and information asymmetry.

Disequilibrium conditions interrelating money, output, prices and productive spending can further compound when commercial banks are deregulated to create money, and interest-rate liberalization is invoked by the central bank to aid commercial banks become front runners in national privatization program following global trends. In such a case, government expenditure that plays a lever in fiscal policy will decline. Conversely, private sector adjustments to spending will increase. Consequently, deficit will increase. Upon this, the rate of interest will increase along with increases in the real and nominal income levels. Thus an increase in (r,y) takes place (Choudhury, 1999). This has been the perennial predicament with many frontline countries in economic growth in recent times – for example, the case of the Far East Asian financial crisis (Cheong, Nor & Isa, 2008).

The sudden flurry in higher prices accompanying higher (r,y) occurred at the time when the global economy went out of the Bretton Woods Arrangement. Marquis (op cit) points out the various phases of monetary history over a span of time. We show this in Figure 2 (adapted from Marquis, op cit).

The implication of the velocity v(M1) tending to unity in the sense of the quantity theory of money is that, total demand for money equals the quantity of money in circulation. But this constraint would not yield any of the Keynesian IS-curves (negative or positive). The presence of the rate of interest is essential. The rate of interest enters the M1-version of the IS-curve by introducing it with the wealth variable, w. This rate(s) of interest then becomes a candidate in the vector of interest rates, r, as shown above with Friedman's extended equation of exchange.

There is an unsolved puzzle here though. For as shown in Figure 2 and argued out above with $v \to 1$, business cycle will stabilize with Savings = Investment around the non-inflationary potential level of output. But for this to happen, the rate of interest must run down, most preferably to zero, or to the level consistent with the low level liquidity trap. The result will be non-existence of the Keynesian IS and LM curves.

This consequence points out the difference between the Fisher form (Fisher, 1911) of the exchange equation of quantity theory, and respectively the Friedman's extended form with interest. Financial papers in the latter case generate financial

Figure 2. Secular changes in the velocity of money circulation, M1

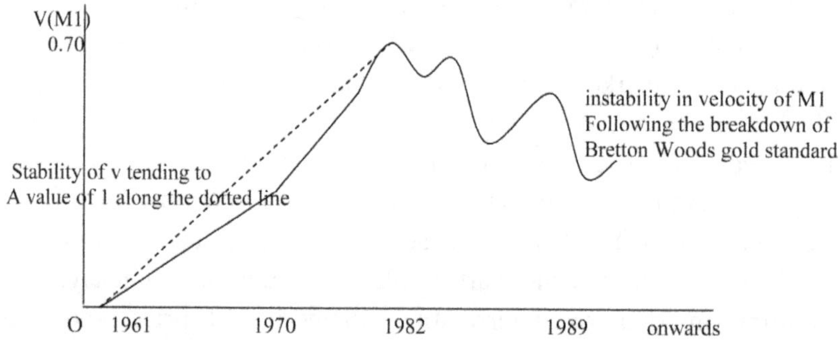

output to add to the GDP, and the Keynesian forms of the IS and LM curves. The Fisher version of the exchange equation is consistent with the M1 demand and supplies of money, but not with the Keynesian IS and LM curves and thus does not carry the implications so embodied in these.

MONEY-COMMODITY-MONEY: M-C-M THEORY AGAIN

The M-C-M theory is an evolution of the Marxist dialectical model of social change in the domain of money and resource distribution and ownership. In his prognosis of capitalism Marx denigrated money in terms of its commodification. The theory explained at length by Heilbroner (1985) explains how money accumulates as capital endowment over stages of economic change and development. The dialectical nature of development using the medium of money is shown to be like a capital stock whose growth rate depends upon two ways of accumulation.

Firstly, money as commodity-capital accumulates by means of the rate of interest over time. If money depreciates in value, as by the rate of inflation, then the real rate of interest marks the accumulative price of money according to the well-known formula of real rate being the nominal rate of interest net of the rate of inflation to yield a positive value for inflation compensation on monetary depreciation. Money thus accumulates in this framework as a capital stock by its growth rate, which is counted as the real rate of interest. Money breeds money through this process of its commodification like capital accumulation in terms of a capital good.

Secondly, money can be treated as a spending to generate goods and services. This process requires the transmission of money into economic activity to yield the new stock of money. The question remains: What acts as the lever to drive into and through the productive system? In the capitalist system that Marx's theory of M-C-M has denigrated, it is the rate of interest. But as it was noted above, the rate of interest remains a leakage and an impediment in effective monetary transmission into the real economy. The higher the rate of interest the higher the bank-saving and the lower is the mobilization of money into the real economy. That is, a robust theory of monetary transmission and growth cannot be expected on the basis of an M-C-M model with interest rate in it. In such a case, the net value of C by the nominal interest rate (i_N) compounded by the productive growth rate (g) is determined by,

$$C = C_0 e^{(g-i_N).t} = C_0 e^{(g-i_R-p^{\wedge}).t}, \text{ for } C = C_0 \text{ at } t = t_0. \tag{19}$$

By the M-C-M model, monetary transmission will mean,

$$M_0 = C_0 \rightarrow C = p.\, C_0 e^{(g-i_R-p^{\wedge}).t} \rightarrow M_1 \rightarrow C' \rightarrow M_2 \rightarrow \text{etc. in continuity.} \tag{20}$$

p denotes the real price of C_0, and M_0 denotes the stock of money at t_0. C and M_1 denote the formation of commodity yielding new money in the M-C-M.

This implies that the higher are the twin diseases of the economy, namely interest rates and inflation, the lower is the effectiveness of monetary transmission to yield productive increase in the quantity of money. This consequence is perpetual. Consequently, a potential level of output is never possible in the presence of a continuous stream of savings driven by interest rates. Savings remain a perpetual withdrawal from generating productivity, growth and GDP. Over and above this relationship, the inflation factor further causes a withdrawal from real productivity, growth and GDP. As long as interest rate and inflation abide, the intensity of business cycle will deepen monotonically. The more costly it now becomes to stabilize the economy and carry the output towards potential level and generate full-employment factor utilization. Such is the capitalist prognosis pointed out by Marx in his theory of commodification of money.

Carchedi (1991; the figure and explanation are adapted from Carchedi) explains the dynamics of the M-C-M model in an elegant way as follows. Consider Figure 3.

The notations are as follows: M denotes an initial stock of money ; C denotes commodity. This includes labor power (LPo) and capital (means of production, MP) in exchange value of the commodity denoted by Ce.

Thus in stage 1, a stock of money is used to buy productive factors without first putting them into the productive process. This is considered to be a capitalist attitude. The net result is firstly, defining a productive medium by means of labor and means of production (physical quantities such as capital, land, etc.) to produce commodities.

In stage 2, the productive process turns out commodities by means of the primary factors of production (LPo and MP). The productive medium CPP thus produces physical and abstract forms of commodities denoted by Ce'. Ce' has monetary value in terms of prices that measures total value as intrinsic value (that of the productive factor time put into production of Ce' at stage 1 (Ce) plus an extra value that the capitalist raises in market exchange, denoted by s > 0. This Marx's surplus-value that is raised by the capitalist through market exchange, that is use value Ce plus surplus value s, yields capitalist market exchange value. Prices are determined by the markets to yield this value as profits to the capitalist, according to Marx.

This last medium of market activity is determined in stage 3, where the capitalist accumulates more money through the medium of 's' as surplus value. The total process from stage to stage continues *ad infinitum*.

The M-C-M structure of dialectical relationship has been projected onto the social relationships by Sztompka (1991). The dialectical model showing M-C-M dynamics and social change are fundamental ways of constructing and explaining the historical process. They are interrelated, as money and social functions are integral parts of human experience.

Figure 4 (a modified version of Sztompka's figure, op cit) explains the process of social construction by the dialectical reference. Structure denotes the existing episteme of thought, according to which interactively, the Praxis as ontology of the constructed social world is established, but in interaction with Agency. Such interaction marks the discursive medium of social reconstruction. The interactive and evolutionary (dialectical) combination of any given stage of social reconstruction establishes the subsequent similar stages of future epochs of change. The progress of one stage of social reconstruction to the subsequent stages is through the transmission mechanism. It integrates Operation of the overall social perspective comprising Structure, which is mobilized together with Action of the individuals and institutions. Institutions comprise the agents who put the Agency into its social dynamics. The interaction between Operations and Action in this dialectical sense comprises overall Praxis. This fires the inner dialectics of the whole evolutionary system. History is then described as the continuity of the forgoing processes forming evolutionary social dialectics.

In our case, in respect of the money-economy interrelated capital accumulation and productive process, we treat M at the market and institutional levels. We endow the central bank exclusively or the commercial banks in conjunction with the central

Figure 3. M-C-M model of money, production, and value

$M \rightarrow Ce \{LPo \text{ and } MP\} \rightarrow CPP \rightarrow Ce' \{Ce + s\} \rightarrow M \{M + m\}$ (expression 21 of Chapter 10)

Stage 1 stage 2 stage 3 etc. in continuity

bank to produce a quantity of money. This quantity of money is required by the changing market conditions and preferences on holding money in liquidity contrary to productive assets. Ce then includes both productive and unproductive factors of production. The latter case is of generating savings by commercial banks and having statutory reserves at the central bank, and excess reserves at the commercial banks denoting withdrawal from potential resource mobilization. The productive sector is thereby affected adversely by such a withdrawal. A diminishing of financial resource mobilization adversely affects productive resource mobilization and vice-a-versa *ad infinitum* in continuity of the M-C-M relationships and stages of relations.

Figure 3 can be projected on to Figure 4 in the sense of the M-C-M model to yield Figure 5. This would explain the social construction of money in the entire world-system framework. Money would then cease to be a frozen entity among powerful artifacts. Consequently, money would empower most powerfully social change and vice-versa.

The inference drawn out of Figure 5 is that both the M-C-M monetary and economy relationship and the Marxist prognosis of capitalism monetary paradigm in connection with its impact on social change and social evolution remain permanent. Underlying such permanent social consequences is the nature of hegemony shown as the historical pattern of convergence to capitalism. This point was made by Fukuyama (1992). The convergence to the civilization supremacy of Occidentalism was claimed by Hegel (1956). In all of these social states, the M-C-M marks the monetary version of the historical social prognosis of capitalism by the arguments of Marxism. The prognosis though does not point out what the positivistic cure can be to the capitalistic malaise of the function of money in the economy and its consequences on wellbeing.

Likewise, in Figure 5 the combining of social dialectics with the M-C-M dynamics does not establish the other social and historical arrangement that remains permanent in social reconstruction. This is to observe the social wellbeing and economic efficiency as complements in social change rather than appearing as conflicting goals.

Figure 4. The dialectics of social change and evolution

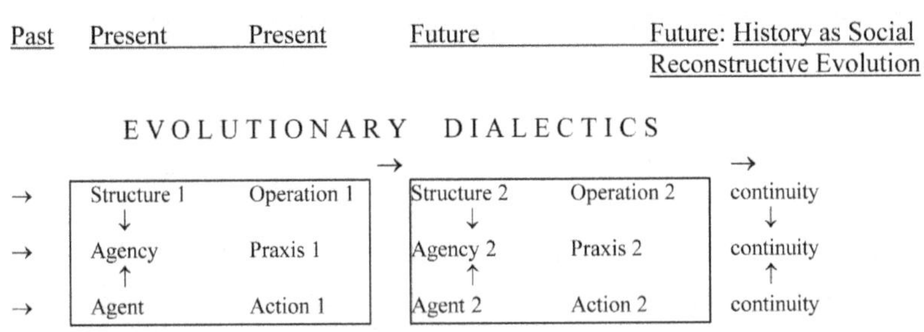

Figure 5. The social reconstructive dialectics using money

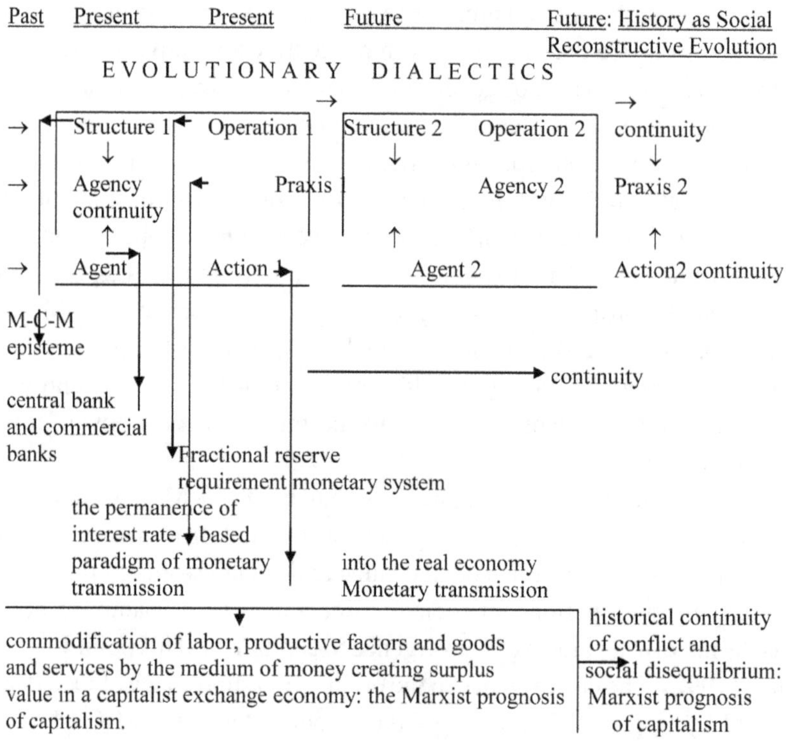

Marxism is premised on a conflict-ridden disequilibrium model of dialectics. On the other hand, capitalism is based on rent-seeking behavior. Thus none of these paradigms of social change with money in it can bestow the true future of an economy that can coexist with wellbeing. We therefore ask the question and address it: Is there a model of economic and social change that is intrinsically permanent in civilization dynamics as the human yearning for goodness and moral possibility (Choudhury, 2009)?

LAISSEZ FAIRE THEORY OF MONEY, PRICE, AND ECONOMY

The Austrian School of Economics (Schumpeter, 1961) and its fellowship found in the recent works on the economics of entrepreneurship (Kirzner, 1981) promote a return to an entrepreneurial form of free market exchange economy. The emergent change is not quite the same as the treatment of free market exchange economy like the one by Friedman. Entrepreneurship is of key importance in the creative destructive model of conflict, innovation and technological change as the properties of entrepreneurial spirit according to the Austrian School. Money plays a key role within the dialectics of the entrepreneurship economic school. That is because development is now led by technological innovation and choices by entrepreneurs. This combination is indispensably a microeconomic perspective. Money thereby chases micro-projects. Now all of these explanations return us to the Pareto-optimal model of money, prices, production, and factor payments. The formalism here then leads to the construction of the quantity theory of money and prices from the microeconomic level to its macroeconomic aggregation.

The dynamics of creative destruction underlie the random variation that Hayek (1999) refers to as intertemporal exchange ratios between different commodity prices. Resource mobilization will then be guided by such random exchange-ratios. The most uncertain of all commodities treated in the economic world is money in its transmission to the real economy. By the randomness of money and its financial price as the rate of interest, any predictable path of resource utilization including human resources and evolution of prices, output and monetary stock over time will be distorted. This kind of distortionary movement of price-ratios intertemporally, or even at a point in time due to random fields of environmental effects, will mean that the utility-basis of deriving demand prices, and the production-based determination of supply prices will defy exact equilibrium situations.

The Austrian School nonetheless promoted the *laissez faire* conception of money. Yaeger (1997 p. 367) writes in this regard by pointing to the Black-Fama-Hall (BFH) ideas on monetary reform: "The BFH system would get rid of any distinct money existing in a definite quantity. The government would be forbidden to issue obligations fixed in value in the unit of account and especially suitable as media of exchange.... No longer would there be any such thing as money whose purchasing power depended on limitation of its quantity. No longer, then, could there be too much of it, causing inflation, or too little, causing depression, or a sequence of imbalances, causing stagflation. A wrong quantity of money could no longer cause problems because money would not exist."

The idea behind the *laissez faire* theory of money will give a boost to the rise of the commercial banks as agents of accelerated money generators. The central bank will increasingly become inactive as the money creator in the first place. Central bank as government agency will simply enforce contracts and settlements of payments. But the fear will always hang. That is without the consciousness among borrowers and spenders on the proper use of money to be circulated in the proper kinds of choices the animal spirit to speculate will distort exchange-prices. This will cause a return to monetary disequilibrium. The monetary disequilibrium effect then would spread into production, prices and factor utilization along with its adverse effects on social wellbeing.

CONCLUSION: IS THERE A CONVERGENCE IN A THEORY OF MONEY, PRICE, OUTPUT, AND EMPLOYMENT?

Laidler (1989) pointed out that the quantity theory of money is in question everywhere in economics. That is, according to the equation of exchange, the causality between money and prices remains undefined. Consequently, also in the M-C-M model the direction of change between money and output remains indeterminate. It is circular in nature without an initial terminal point. According to Keynes in combination with a theory of micro-foundation of quantity theory and its equation of exchange, the IS and LM general equilibrium remains fuzzy, and thus, the potential level of output remains indeterminate. Fiscalist of the Keynesian persuasion argues in favor of non-inflationary full-employment level of output. Yet monetarism argues that there is never a non-inflationary possibility in the face of inflation sensitivity of spending and rational expectations in the Keynesian general equilibrium model.

In the neoclassical orientation of the theme, where we started out, the theory of micro-foundation of money, price, output and factor utilization together with wellbeing, has caused incongruence between the various approaches mentioned on this topic. This problem of incongruence now concludes this chapter as follows.

In this regard we note the linked diagrams of Figure 6. These show that there is no settled convergence in and between the contending theories on the matter of monetary equilibrium matching with economic equilibrium. Keynesian General Equilibrium of money, expenditure explained by the intersection of (IS, LM) is changed into a disequilibrium state in quantity theory of money and prices with random influence of i_R on output, price and money transmission. The result then is macroeconomic disequilibrium according to the monetarist school (quantity theory). Contrarily, the fiscalist school (Keynesian) maintains full-employment as the macroeconomic goal. At the end, interaction between the Keynesian School and the monetarist school on the theme of output, prices (spending), and money results in overall disequilibrium. This denies equilibrium to form 'anywhere', even around the general equilibrium points of the macro-economy (Grandmont, 1989).

The final states of these disequilibria are further confounded by the M-C-M interference on social and economic disequilibrium caused by the Marxist prognosis of capitalism. The presence of i_r in the utility function coming from the side of money, output, price and interest rate disturbs the properties of the utility function and utility-analysis that we started with to establish the micro-foundations of money, output, price, and rate of interest.

Monetary disequilibrium persists in the prevailing principal theories. This point is noted by Yaeger (1997, pp. 409-10) as well (bracketed version provided by this author): "Abolition of price stickiness (as in Keynesian liquidity trap), even if it were possible, contrary to fact, would hardly dispel the problem of monetary

Figure 6. Can the money, price, output, and productivity disequilibriums be avoided in mainstream economic theory?

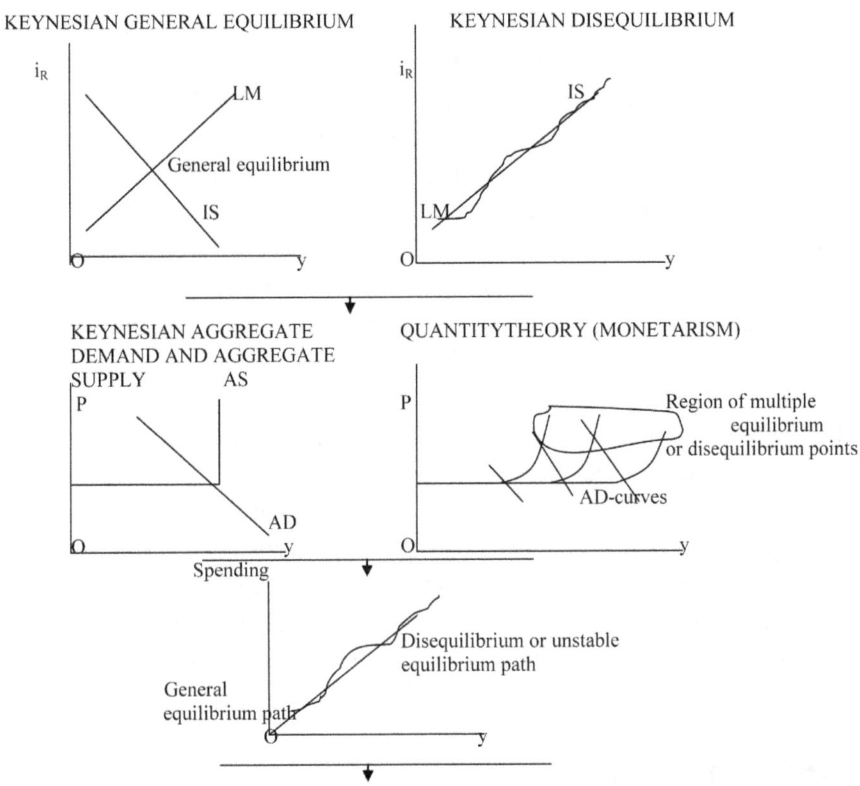

M-C-M IMPLICATIONS

Each of the curves shown above remains in disequilibrium or unstable equilibrium because of the perpetual Marxist capital versus labor conflict with surplus value causing a permanent less-than potential output and factor use.

NEOCLASSICAL IMPLICATIONS

In the Walrasian General Equilibrium model the utility function, $U = U(y,E,i_R,M/P)$, with E denoting employment, gives positive relationship between the variables and the utility function. This is a contradiction respecting the relationship concerning i_R. The same is true of the production relationships.

disturbances in a system of decentralized decision making. Great volatility of the price level would undercut the rationale of money itself and could even aggravate mis-coordination, as through expectations and debt burden. An economy beset by monetary disturbances faces a catch-22. It is damned whether or not it exhibits great flexibility of wages and prices (neoclassical case)."

The Main Points

The diagrams in Figure 6 point out the principal debilities of the mainstream monetary theories and systems between Keynesianism governed by fiscal economic stimulation and monetarism governed by the quantity theory of money. In contrast to the monetary and fiscal complementary theory emergent in the context of unity of knowledge as episteme, the other theories give an opposite picture. That is because of the role of interest as control variable to establish equilibrium level of output at the unstable point of full-employment level of output. Contrarily, the absence of interest rate and its replacement by trade-related real sector oriented financial instruments cause real output and spending to move together. Thereby also the quantity of money and spending complement causing IS and LM curves to coincide, But this is contrary to the case of perpetual trade-off between monetary and fiscal policies and effects on inflation and output.

The messages of the two systems are opposed to each other because of the epistemic difference between these two systems of thought. The episteme of unity of knowledge causes pervasive complementarities between the selected variables (e.g. money and spending). Kennesianism and monetarism cause tradeoff between all variables taken together or in pairs. Yet at the end we find that the episteme of unity of knowledge applies to the world-system uniformly and everywhere. It is this episteme that establishes the socio-cybernetic study of reality in unity of knowledge.

REFERENCES

Black, F. (1970, Autumn). Banking and interest rates in a world without money. *Journal of Banking Research*, 8-20.

Bordo, M. D. (1989). The contribution of a monetary history of the United States 1867-1960. In Bordo, M. D. (Ed.), *Money, History and International Finance: Essays in Honour of Anna J. Schwartz*. Chicago, IL: University of Chicago Press. doi:10.7208/chicago/9780226066899.001.0001.

Carchedi, G. (1991). *Frontiers of political economy*. New York, NY: Verso.

Cheong, C. W., Nor Abu Hasan, S. M., & Isa, Z. (2008). Market efficiency of the Malaysian stock exchange: Further evidence. *International Journal of Management Studies*, *15*(2), 41–68.

Choudhury, M. A. (1999). A critique of econometric modeling for development studies: A political economy approach with special reference to Malaysia. In Ghosh, B. N., & Salleh, M. S. (Eds.), *Political Economy of Development in Malaysia* (pp. 105–123). Kuala Lumpur, Malaysia: Utusan Publications.

Choudhury, M. A. (2007). *The universal paradigm and the Islamic world-system, economy, society, ethics and science*. Singapore: World Scientific Publications. doi:10.1142/6344.

Choudhury, M. A. (2009). Dialectics in socio-scientific inquiry: Islam contra occident. *The International Journal of Sociology and Social Policy*, *29*(9/10), 498–511. doi:10.1108/01443330910986289.

Fama, E. (1980). Banking in the theory of finance. *Journal of Monetary Economics*, *6*, 39–57. doi:10.1016/0304-3932(80)90017-3.

Fisher, I. (1911). *The purchasing power of money*. New York: Macmillan.

Friedman, M. (1989). Quantity theory of money. *New Palgrave: Money*.

Fukuyama, F. (1992). *The end of history and the last man*. New York: The Free Press.

Grandmont, G.-M. (1989). Temporary equilibrium. In Eatwell, J., Milgate, M., & Newman, P. (Eds.), *New Palgrave: General Equilibrium* (pp. 297–304). New York, NY: W.W. Norton.

Greenfeld, R. L., & Yaeger, L. B. (1963). A laissez-fare approach to monetary stability. *Journal of Money, Credit and Banking*, *15*, 302–315. doi:10.2307/1992481.

Hall, R. E. (1997). The government and the monetary unit. In Yaeger, L. B. (Ed.), *The Fluttering Veil, Essays on Monetary Disequilibrium* (pp. 383–391). Indianapolis, IN: Liberty Fund.

Hayek, F. A. (1999). Intertemporal price equilibrium and movements in the value of money. In *Good Money, Part One: The New World* (pp. 186–227). Chicago, IL: University of Chicago Press.

Hegel, G. W. F. (1986). *The philosophy of history* (Sibree, J., Trans.). New York, NY: Dover Books.

Heilbroner, R. (1985). The ideology of capital. In *The Nature and Logic of Capitalism* (pp. 107–140). New York, NY: W.W. Norton.

Henderson, J. M., & Quandt, R. E. (1971). *Microeconomic theory: A mathematical approach*. New York, NY: McGraw-Hill.

Hutt, W. H. (1979). The academic appeal of Keynesian doctrine & the nature of Keynesian thesis. In *The Keynesian Episode, a Reassessment*, (pp. 87-119). Indianapolis, IN: Liberty Fund.

Kirzner, I. (1981). Entrepreneurship, entitlement, and economic justice. In Paul, J. (Ed.), *Reading Nozick, Essays on Anarchy, State, and Utopia*. Totowa, NJ: Rowan & Allanheld.

La Salle, J., & Lefschetz, S. (1961). *Stability by Liapunov's direct method*. New York, NY: Academic Press.

Laidler, D. (1989). The quantity theory of money is always and everywhere controversial - Why?. *Atlantic Canada Economic Papers and Proceedings, 18*.

Marquis, M. H. (1996). Full employment and monetary policy neutrality. In *Monetary Theory and Policy* (pp. 170–198). St. Paul, MN: West Publishing Co..

Rawls, J. (1971). *A theory of justice*. Cambridge, MA: Harvard University Press.

Schumpeter, J. A. (1961). *The theory of economic development*. Cambridge, MA: Harvard University Press.

Sen, A. (1985). The moral standing of the market. In Paul, E. F., Paul, J., & Miller, F. D. (Eds.), *Ethics and Economics*. Oxford, UK: Basil and Blackwell.

Sen, A. (1989). Justice. In Eatwell, J., Milgate, M., & Newman, P. (Eds.), *New Palgrave, Social Economics* (pp. 181–189). New York: W.W. Norton.

Sztompka, P. (1991). The model of social becoming. In *Society in Action, the Theory of Social Becoming* (pp. 87–120). Chicago, IL: The University of Chicago Press.

Venieris, Y. P., & Sebold, F. D. (1977). The Keynesian revolution. In *Macroeconomics, Models & Policy* (pp. 336–353). New York, NY: John Wiley & Sons.

Ventelou, B. (2005). Keynesian economics and the American polity. In *Millennial Keynes* (pp. 3–37). Armonk, NY: M.E. Sharpe.

Yaeger, L. B. (1997). *The fluttering veil: Essays on monetary disequilibrium*. Indianapolis, IN: The Liberty Press.

Chapter 11

The Future of Monetary Reform and the Real Economy:

The Ethics of 100 Percent Reserve Requirement Monetary System[1]

ABSTRACT

The further analytical result derived from the previous chapters on the money and real economy relationship with financial bridging in a gold-standard system is now further extended to the requirement of the 100% Reserve Requirement Monetary System with the Gold-Standard. The formal model in this regard is developed in order to bring out the power of unity of the ethical worldview of avoiding interest rates and its replacement by trade instruments. The relationship between the Central Bank, commercial banks, and the real economy with the interest-replacing trade instruments is explained. The resulting configuration of the financial and banking system in this regard under the episteme of unity of knowledge is made to explain how stabilization is attained in this same kind of epistemic worldview and its monetary and real economy interrelationship. Thus, the socio-cybernetic worldview of pervasive complementarities, equivalently participation, representing unity of knowledge in the good things of life, is once again expounded.

DOI: 10.4018/978-1-4666-4643-8.ch011

Copyright ©2014, IGI Global. Copying or distributing in print or electronic forms without written permission of IGI Global is prohibited.

INTRODUCTION

The prologue is our starting premise.

The *Qur'an* (2: 275) declares, "As for those who devour interest, they behave as the one whom Satan has confounded with his touch. Seized in this state they say: 'Trade is but a kind of interest', even though Allah has made trade lawful, and interest unlawful."

Keynes (1930, p. 368) picked up such wisdom of the inverse relationship between trade and interest and wrote, "The strenuous purposeful money-makers may carry all of us along with them into the lap of economic abundance. But it will be those peoples, who can keep alive, and cultivate into a fuller perfection, the art of life itself and do not sell themselves for the means of life, who will be able to enjoy the abundance when it comes."

Such are the messages of moral highness and wisdom picked up in this chapter.

The fundamental point here is to establish the fact that the *only* way of phasing out interest rate from Islamic activities is to understand and implement the formalism of the inverse relationship that permanently exists between trade in the good things of life and the rate of interest as the impediment to the free flow of resources into such tradable activities.

The central bank and commercial banks and financial intermediaries as practitioners must understand this organic relational concept of intellection in relation to money and the real economy. The monetary system and the real economy with the financial instruments between would thus be shown to formalize the intellection paradigm – which indeed is a truly scientific revolution. The result is replacement of the fractional reserve requirement monetary system by the 100 percent reserve requirement monetary system backed by the gold standard. Likewise, the organic relationships of such a monetary arrangement including its monetary policy and transmission mechanism would structurally change the nature of markets and its institutional relations and individual preferences. The result at the end will be a phased down interest rate regime into a trade-related one by the rise of the tradable relationships that are generated. The change is a truly of the social cybernetic nature.

The foundational methodology that enters this kind of organically relational worldview with the episteme of unity of knowledge (the divine law in Islam) provides the functional ontology of the socially and morally constructed money, production and real economy circular causation relationship. It models the legitimacy of trade as the resource mobilization instrument, while rejecting interest as the permanent impediment of resource mobilization.

THE FUTURE OF MONETARY REFORM AND THE REAL ECONOMY: A PROBLEM OF TRADE VS. INTEREST

Often in recent economic and financial experience it has been proven that a low rate of interest by bank regulation, macroeconomic policy objectives, and market forces have ended in fiasco in stabilizing the economy. The low real rate of interest during the 1960s in the face of low nominal rate of interest fueled the subsequent increase in inflation; and this resulted in stagflationary economic periods (Siven, 1978). The recent macroeconomic policy to drive the nominal rate of interest to zero in Japan, as an example, resulted in non-performing loans that were abundantly provided to borrowers. Most starkly true, the sub-prime mortgage rates on real estate in southern United States resulted in an aggressive spirit of borrowing to fuel the housing boom that turned sour.[2] The inference drawn is that a low or zero rate of interest is a necessary but not a sufficient condition for the road to economic bliss. Structural changes in the relationships between money, finance, and market exchange must be established simultaneously with reduction in the rate of interest.

OBJECTIVE

Our objective in this chapter is to explain the necessary and sufficient conditions of economic and social bliss that is reached by the endogenous interaction between money, finance and the real economy. Such is a truly cybernetic nature of the social economy in the good things of life. The idea of endogenous relations is conveyed by the systemic interrelations between entities and variables of the socioeconomic problem under study. These internal dynamics generate causality and learning by interaction. The concept is similar to what Paul Krugman termed as 'self-governing equilibrium' resulting in self-organized behavior. The change occurs simultaneously with the phasing down of interest rates. This kind of total change is also tantamount to the pursuit of endogenous interrelationship between the central bank, the commercial banks, and the market economy exchanging in 'the good things of life'.

The explanation of these kinds of changes is carried out in reference to our phenomenological model of unity of knowledge, upon which stands the Islamic world-system governing 'everything' permanently and indispensably. Within this kind of learning and unified world-system we study the endogenous relationships of pairing in unity between the economic and financial domains as mentioned above in respect of money, finance and the real economy.

ZERO RATE OF INTEREST: A NECESSARY BUT NOT SUFFICIENT INSTRUMENT FOR AN ISLAMIC ECONOMY

In Malaysia for instance, a recent program towards zero-inflation rate (*cipher-inflasi*) resulted in a mismatch between the subsequently high rates of interest and zero rate of inflation (mid-nineties). When the Southeast Asia financial crisis hit Malaysia (mid-1990's) high interest rates were used as macroeconomic monetary policy to invite foreign capital to shore up the declining exchange rate. But the relationship between interest rates and exchange rates remained volatile (Choudhury, 1999), suggesting that there is no way of stabilizing the exchange rate and inflation rate relationship just by using the instrument of rates of interest. Evidence does not support this.

Malaysia's experience with Islamic funds has soured in regards to their performance. As for example there is the experience with the now diminishing *mudarabah* (profit-sharing) and *musharakah* (equity participation) forms of financing. Islamic banks and finance companies have withdrawn almost completely from these principal Islamic financial instruments. These instruments are replaced by secondary financial instruments, all of which are subject to *shar'iah* concerns (Choudhury, 2008a). Likewise, despite earnest efforts to promote Islamic financing and profitability in the face of interest-free financing of projects and investments, Islamic banks in Malaysia could not herald even a distinct prospect for the wellbeing of the *ummah*, the conscious world nation of Islam, in the field of Islamic networked flow and organization of institutions for common resource sharing (trade). The assertion is borne out by the fact that Islamic banks and development planning in Malaysia never accounted for a clear direction of Islamic financing there towards ameliorating either her own broader Islamic global picture or the momentum of trade, development, and related policy instrumentation for the Muslim World. The Islamic Development Bank Annual Reports for a long time now bring out these facts on the basis of poor levels of inter-communal trade flow statistics in the Muslim World.

The current lure with *sukuk,* bonds that revolve around the principal financing instruments of *mudarabah* and *musharakah* and the like, and the market of sale of *musharakah*-linked bonds in real assets to the private sector to finance mega projects, have ended up in deep *shar'iah* concerns (Usmani, see internet website). *Sukuk* financing problems arise from the sale of debt with interest to private outlets. The *sukuk* holders can then proportion this equity instrument between the government and private businesses through public shareholding. Consequently, such projects pass on the debt hangover as an intergenerational burden to debtor companies.

An alternative would be for such companies to engage in debt-equity swaps (Krugman, 1989; Blackwell & Nocera, 1989; Choudhury, 1989). Debt-equity swaps involve large investors to retire the debt or a part of it for an indebted country by paying it out in these proportions (i.e. investing to buy the debt). In exchange, the debt-ameliorated country treats such an investment as an equity swap for the retired debt. Debt-equity swaps can be managed effectively in the case of equity-participation (*musharakah*).

The debt overhang and the allowance for financing debt in the private sector are thus at best extended over time, rather than being a comprehensive financing mode that can be instituted for phasing out the interest rate regime caused by debt overhang. The goal of financing interest-bearing, debt-ridden projects by interest-free financing instruments therefore does not cure the interest-rate stigma. Thereby, the true impact of financing by Islamic participatory instruments is not reached, even when the interest-free goal is targeted to reach a given level of efficacy. Yet in the name of interest-free financing as the focus of Islamic finance, Islamic banks and finance companies, Muslim governments and large businesses and projects are raising the clamor of *sukuk* (Gassner, 2008; *Business Islamica*, 2008).

CAPITALIZATION OF INCOME FLOWS AND THE RATE OF INTEREST

From the history of western economic thought we learn about alternatives to interest-rates in asset-valuation. Sraffa and Keynes referred to one such alternative interest rate as 'the own rate of interest' (Sraffa, 1932; Donzelli, 2004).[3] Likewise, we note the arguments in support of the Austrian concept of money and interest rates (Wicksell, 1934).

The first of the above-mentioned issues indicates that traditional economic theory, like the ones claiming the concept of 'own rate of interest', equated the rate of interest with the marginal productivity of capital or the marginal efficiency of investment. Wicksell's problem points out how the rate of interest is equivalently treated as a discount factor to evaluate capital-flow over time. Such notions have been used by Islamic economics and finance to erect their so-called 'rate-of-return' concept according to the marginal productivity theory, and the use of asset valuation based on discount-rate formulas. Islamic banks have adopted these rules thoroughly; Islamic gurus support and preach them (Vogel & Hayes, 1998).

One can also refer to the continued practice of discounting by the mechanism of the time-value of money now being carried out in the Islamic Development Bank and all Islamic banks around the world. This is also the confirming evidence of a survey of research departments and directors of the Islamic banks in Indonesia that was carried out by Choudhury (2011).

The notion of a low interest rate or phased-down interest rate in economic and financial arrangements has prevailed in the literature. But the concept of how the rate of interest emerges in the economy, and how it can be phased down in this system by an endogenous economic process, has not matured either in the mainstream literature and practice or within the theory and practice of Islamic economics and finance. The latter area thus remains inextricably submerged in mainstream academic thinking relating to the money, interest rate, and real economy relations. The result of this intellectual debility is reflected in a flawed conception that is transmitted into the Islamic rules concerning worldly matters (*fiqh al-muamalat*), Islamic financial institutions, and the conceptions underlying the academe of Islamic economics and finance.

The net result of these developments in the history of economic thought in respect of the theory of interest and capital accumulation, and which Islamic economics and finance have emulated, is this: Capital accumulation embodies savings arising from abstemiousness in present consumption for attaining maximum intertemporal consumer utility. This idea is embodied in the classical theory of intertemporal savings and consumption contributed by Ramsey (1928). The capitalized value of all future yields from present abstemiousness in consumption is obtained by a discounting method that invariably imputes the discount rate as the shadow rate of interest for capitalizing future uncertain yields.

THE POSITION OF ISLAMIC ECONOMICS AND FINANCE IN RESPECT OF CAPITALIZATION OF ASSETS WITH INTEREST-FREE INSTRUMENTS

Islamic economic and finance gurus have adopted a discounting approach by the time-value of money in asset valuation. They thus failed to understand the interest-rate implications of the discounting approach. The result in asset-valuation is that a future market, which remains undetermined, many a times unknown, would be capitalized at a rate either less or greater than the expected rate of return on the stream of future income flows.

Especially, in such a case of discount-rate indeterminacy, micro-enterprises have difficulty in tying up commitment to a mark-up that determines the investors' and shareholders' dividends and profits. Microenterprises bear the burden of the excessive cost of capital. The problem arises when large shareholders aim at discounting their risk by taking a larger share of the profits in joint venture. This leaves smaller residual shares and dividends for the small borrowers and participants in Islamic funds. Microenterprises thus find it costly to refinance their assets by means of the lower share of total profits of joint ventures

The same result can swing in favor of microenterprises at the expense of shareholders when an under-valuation of the intergenerational flow of projected returns takes place. In such a case, the question is this: Can the investor be risk-avert and divert potential investments into risk-free alternatives, such as short-term trade using *murabaha* (mark-up asset pricing) financing instrument? None of these alternatives comes to the benefit of socioeconomic development of the community, and beyond of the *ummah*. Indeed, a prevalent problem of Islamic banks is either lack of investments or an over-subscription of shareholders' capital. These results are reflected in the variable, 'financing/deposit ratio', which is found to move away on either side from the expected value of numerical unity (Choudhury, 2009) in Islamic banks. Islamic banks in Indonesia show such financing problems in their annual reports (Bank Muamalat Annual Report 2007; Bank Mandiri Annual Report 2006).

Consequently, although interest-free financing has been promoted by Islamic banks, yet the method towards realizing this goal has not been well-defined in terms of investment-liquidity problem, and asset-valuation and socioeconomic development of the *ummah*. Besides, as it was pointed out above, secondary financing instruments have been used in place of the principal Islamic financing instruments to argue in favor of operations in interest-free financing. Yet there are looming *shar'iah* problems relating to interest rates in these secondary financing instruments.

Two of these problems are firstly, the absence of the idea of pooled funds made by combining individual types of financing modes. The *shar'iah* gurus have not looked into this possibility. The second one is the difference of the often used jargon of *shar'iah*-compliance from the great *objective and purpose* of the *shar'iah*, the *maqasid as-shar'iah* (Mufeedh Choudhury, 2009).

Both of these approaches in asset-valuation and financing run into the same kinds of methodological problems mentioned above. They generate ineffective socioeconomic development effects. A clear example is the almost negligible difference between Islamic banks and conventional banks in respect of such Islamic and conventional modes of financing. This situation is found to be empirically true of Islamic financing everywhere (Choudhury, 2008a).

THE MONEY, FINANCE, AND REAL ECONOMY RELATIONSHIPS IN AN INTEREST-FREE REGIME OF SOCIOECONOMIC CHANGE

Islamic economists argue on behalf of establishing an interest-free regime of socioeconomic change, yet by retaining the existing fractional monetary reserve system, despite introducing the compelling need for delivering social justice (Chapra, 1985). The arguments, prescriptions, and implementation of such an approach through interest-free targeting are untenable. We explain this problem below in terms of a general system – the cybernetic model -- of comprehensive socioeconomic transformation. Further details on the analytical version of the general equilibrium system are given by Choudhury (1997). The idea expressed in this reference and similar references is that, interaction leading to unifying relations (integration) between an expanding economic and financial system (evolutionary), cause systemic learning. That is evolutionary type equilibriums with complementarities (IIE-learning model) arise along the IIE-processes. The result is heightened participation causing empowerment for the participants; and complementarities between variables representing the good things of life.

If interest-based financing is accelerated by the rise of trade-based instruments in the Islamic case, then there is decreasing need and incentive for holding savings in banks and capital markets. Consequently, Islamic banks become outlets of mobilizing savings continuously into spending in the good and productive things of life. This process, which is continuous across continuums, generates participatory dynamics between spending possibilities (relations); and between their entities (representative variables denoting socioeconomic variables and financing instrumental variables). These variables define the relations and represent the agencies (agents, institutions, markets etc. underlying the relations and their constituent variables). Indeed, the Islamic world-system, within which are studied the complementary relations between money, finance, and the real economy, is fully participatory in nature in its normative model (Choudhury, Zaman and Harahap, 2008).

The result then is to interactively integrate the three domains – money, finance, and the real economy in participatory ways, so that they learn by circular causation between them. Such causation is the same as to generate endogenous relations between the representative pairing variables. Indeed, pairing is the *Qur'anic* cybernetic message of pervasive complementarities between entities and their representative variables. The circular causation phenomenon is termed equivalently as learning behavior in the midst of complementary relations. The pervasive principle of extensive complementarities is the clearest manifest sign of unity of knowledge, which denotes the epistemological premise of the money, finance, and real economy system of circular causation relations. The result is formalism on the basis of the episteme of unity of knowledge.

As pointed out in the Preface, this episteme of the monotheistic law remains 'universal' and 'unique' in conception and application in 'everything'. In the present case, we study the money, finance, and the real economy complementary circular causation relations according to the same epistemology of unity of knowledge as derived from the monotheistic law as functional ontology working in the experiential order.

The argument here is this. Phasing down the rate of interest in Islamic financing can neither be sustainable in the absence of a simultaneous overhaul of the monetary system in relation to the real economy, nor will the ruptured goal of unity between money, finance, and real economy lead to the realization of anything that is truly Islamic in the *ummah* sense.

Indeed alternatively, mainstream economic thought did vouch for development-financing regimes devoid of interest rate (Sauer, 2002), but with a failed conception. Likewise, at the present time of global financial and banking crisis, central banks in most countries are lowering their prime rates to zero to bring about lower bank lending rates and stimulate spending. Yet we cannot say that these economies and the banking system have been transformed into the Islamic banking and finance kinds.

The fact is that interest-rate reduction to zero cannot be attained independently of structural change. Such is the case with Islamic banks today. They follow the idea of '*shar'iah*-compliance' instead of focusing on and rising up from the foundation of *maqasid as-shar'iah* (the purpose and objective of the *shar'iah*). Consequently, no structural change has come about in a substantively foundational way for the *ummah*. Only a small segment of the financial sector (less than 2 percent of the global capital market) remains *relatively* free of interest-based transactions.

Then how can an Islamic capital market arise? The fundamental transformation into the money, finance, and real economy complementary linkages remains hampered by the blockage in the flow of resources in the mere presence of '*shar'iah*-compliance' idea. A better possibility for realizing the impact of interest-free financing in the real economy is to establish the wide range of linkages that money-finance-real economy interrelations generate and are sustained. Such is the cybernetic view of a participatory and complementary social economy.

Therefore, to base all transactions on interest-free instruments in the Islamic economic and financial system is only *a necessary condition* of Islamizing the financing and banking system. By itself the abolition of interest financing is *not a sufficient condition* in establishing the alternative of trade and participatory development in the Islamic *ummah*. It is therefore necessary to combine the interest-free transformation as a process that is linked with simultaneous change in monetary policies and money-finance-real economy circular causal *inter*-relations. Such relations are generated between the central bank, the commercial bank and the real economy by circular causation. The resulting new economic arrangement based on complementary circular causation between variables and their representative agents would cause the emergence of unified, synergetic interrelationships between the monetary system, the financial instrumentation, the real economy, and the banking and other institutions. We now turn to a formalism of the underlying dynamics in such a case.

THE CIRCULAR CAUSATION BETWEEN THE CENTRAL BANK, COMMERCIAL BANKS, AND THE REAL ECONOMY IN THE MIDST OF MONEY, FINANCE AND REAL ECONOMY RELATIONS

Consider the resource flows in Figure 1. The circular connections and two-way arrows explain the circular causation relations between the various entities as noted. Most importantly, in this kind of circular causation relationships there occurs the simultaneously complementary and participatory linkages between the central bank, the commercial banks (Islamic banks and other banks), and the resulting complementarities in the real economy between the good things of life as ordained by the *shar'iah.* Such unifying relationships bring out the nature of monetary policy and the complementary money, finance and market transformation in the Islamic economy.

The Islamic economy is essentially based on free-market orientation. But at the same time, it is guided by knowledge induction and appropriate *shar'iah* instruments and policies to realize resource mobilization into the good things of life. In this respect, the central bank generates a supply of money as is conventionally known. That is, the supply of money to banks in excess reserve pursues multiple credit creation backed by promissory notes. Also, the intent of the underlying monetary policy is to attain a stable and productive macroeconomic state of the general (circular) flows of goods and services in physical and monetary terms.

Figure 1. Central bank, commercial bank and real economy interrelations in money, finance, and real economy with resource mobilization and market transformation of the Islamic economy

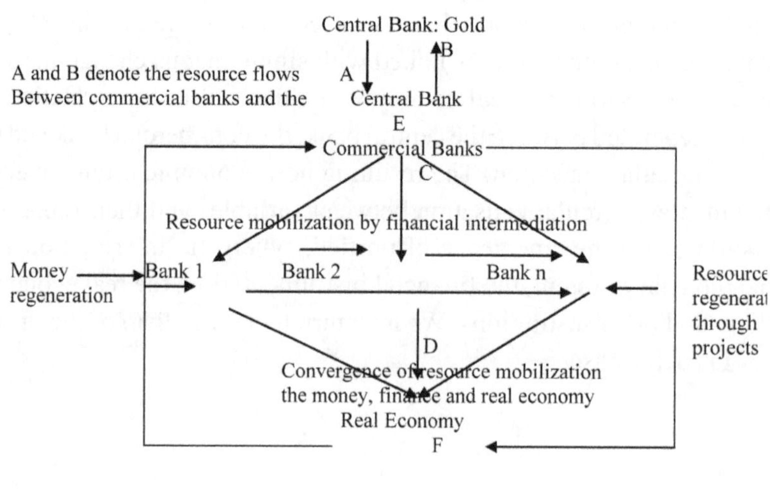

In the Islamic case, the concept of money supply is replaced by the concept of 'quantity of micro-money' pursuing the needs of specific projects that are based on the *maqasid as-shar'iah*. The concepts of demand and supply of money are now replaced by that of 'quantity of *micro-money specific* in circulation to approved projects'. In other words, such projects are financed by the full circulation of a quantity of micro-money in specific projects, as needed.

Explaining Figure 1: The Central Bank, Commercial Banks, and Real Economy Linkages

In Figure 1, the label 'A' denotes injection of funds as a quantity of currency (↓). Currency is thereby equivalent to money serving as a medium of satisfying the additional demand of commercial banks to finance real economy project-specific development in a situation where market demand for funds exceeds the available financial resources to fund the projects. The point here is that resource mobilization through the commercial banks (Islamic banks) will run its own course through the real economy.

Through such a currency flow, a quantity of micro-money is linked up with market exchange by the use of financial instruments. Real bills can be endogenously generated by commercial banks under the authority of the central bank (Green, 1989). Now there would be an automatic equilibrium circulation of currency through the commercial banks entering the real economy. This kind of an equilibrium process of money-finance-real resource linkage must however be governed by appropriate central bank regulations on sustaining a stable and growing economy.

We note in such a case, there is no excess creation of money by the central bank when an automatic equilibrium process is maintained between the monetary flows generated by linkages between the commercial banks and the real economy. The commercial banks under the authority of central bank guidance can generate the real bills for the increased resource mobilization as needed. Alternatively, it is possible that central banks create the extra quantity of money needed to finance a growing real economy. The cost underlying this additional flow of a quantity of money will be recovered from bank seigniorage. Seigniorage is revenue gained by the central bank to cover the cost of producing a quantity of money by gold-backing. The cost will be collected from the borrowing commercial banks that themselves earn participatory returns from the yields of the real economy funding of projects, also from market exchange in approved goods and services. The central bank and commercial bank interrelationship abides. The quantity of money required to finance additional projects in the real economy arises from the increased demand for goods and services that result in project development.

Such an automatic circulation of money into projects—hence the name micro-money (Choudhury & Hoque, 2004)—in relation to the real economy, is shown in Figure 1 by the circular direction of arrows (→). The direction of the arrow indicates mobilization of monetary and real resources between banks and the real economy.

On the one side, there is the quantity of goods and services in demand. On the other side, this real economy demand is satisfied by the monetary injection. This injection of money equals a quantity of currency in circulation. The carrier of this circularly regenerated monetary stock through the real economy in response to the demand for regenerated resources comprises the bundle of trade-related instruments. Trade and commerce thereby replace interest-based businesses of all kinds.[4] The principal meaning and objective of the quantity of money now becomes the equilibrium need (demand and supply) for currency to finance productive and appropriate projects in response to the increased demand for the corresponding kinds of goods and services connected with such approved projects in the light of the *shar'iah*. An effective transmission of money through financial instruments would thus take place to finance the real economy of goods, services, and projects in the light of the *shar'iah*.

The result thus is contrary to bank-savings. We mean by bank savings that part of the earned and national income that is withheld by banks to serve interest-bearing and speculative portfolio over time.[5] Contrarily, as trade increases the flow of resource into the real economy is enhanced. The quantity of micro-money increases in pursuit of real demand for goods and services in the good possibilities of life connected with projects. The diversion of income into bank-savings to earn interest rate is diminished. This kind of internal adjustment in the financing medium brings out the logical and formal basis of trade, which positively affects resource mobilization through market-oriented real economic transformation with linkage to monetary flows through financing instruments. The consequence of this kind of circular flow dynamics is a continuous liquidation of savings at every moment of time in the life of the economy by its financial resource mobilization into approved spending outlets.

However, when the total financing cannot be done by the available bank deposits by households (wherein savings = financial resource mobilization), the banks call for additional financing from shareholders and depositors and the expansion of a quantity of money by the central bank loaned out to the commercial banks. In such a case, the (financing/deposit)-ratio exceeds unity. The principal shareholder/stakeholder of the Islamic banks, in the sense of lender of last resort, is the central bank. Besides, other principal shareholders' share-capital can be secured in the central bank for the benefit of lending to commercial banks in the situation of excess demand for funds to finance approved projects. These parts of the monetary flow are included in the label 'A' in Figure 1.

There is yet another type of monetary flow between the commercial banks and the central bank: When the demand for money to finance projects declines due to lower market demand, the 'excess reserve' in commercial banks is liquidated. The resulting amount of un-mobilized financial resources cannot remain in the commercial banks. The commercial banks are not allowed to hold this saving as excess reserve, for fear of causing multiple credit creation. Excess reserves held in commercial banks will otherwise negate the above-mentioned dynamics of trade over saving in regenerating resources and the quantity of micro-money to meet real demand for goods, services and projects. The unutilized savings must thus be deposited fully as 'reserve' with the central bank. The fund remains with the central bank until it is called back by the commercial banks to finance subsequent rounds of enhanced demand in the real economy. This mechanism is shown at the point 'B' in Figure 1 (↑).

A SIMPLE VERSION OF FINANCIAL FLOWS BETWEEN THE CENTRAL BANK, COMMERCIAL BANKS, AND REAL ECONOMY

A simple form of the financial flows schema through the monetary and real economy linkage can be seen in Figure 2. The following symbols are defined: The important idea here is to convey the dynamics of circular links between money, finance, and real economy that generate cause and effect of sustained resource flow in monetary and physical terms by circularly interrelating them.

Figure 2. Circular flow of resource augmentation (and contraction) between central bank, commercial bank, and real economy

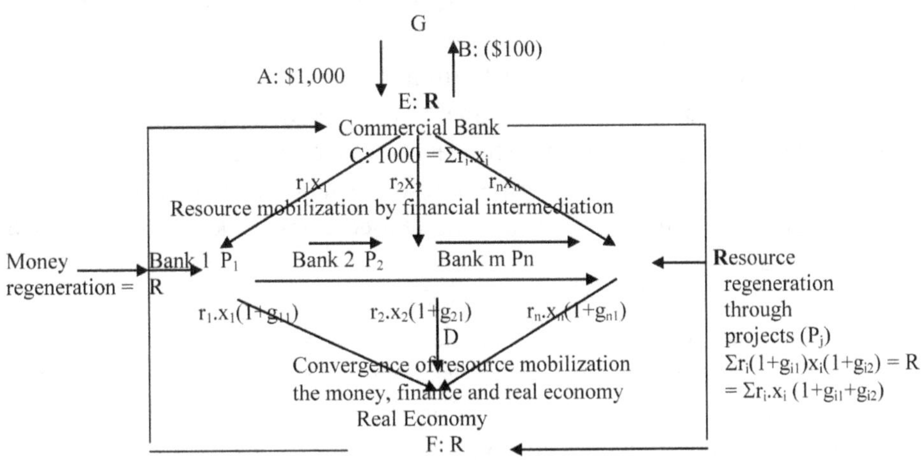

- r_i, i =1,2,..,n denotes the ith resource outlet, e.g. food, real estate, cultivation (micro-level).
- x_i, i = 1,2,..,n denotes unit investment on the ith resource outlet; i.e. per unit of the spending outlet.
- $r_i.x_i$ denotes the total investment on ith resource outlet.
- g_{i1} denotes growth obtained by developing $r_{i.}$
- g_{i2} denotes expansion by growth of $x_{i.}$
- R denotes the total regenerated resources following monetary circulation by financial intermediation across projects financed by the consortium of m-number of banks and shareholders in the real economy.
- P_i denotes the n-number of projects financed by banks.

As the circular flow of resources continues over time across several projects with their increasing product and risk diversifications, so also the resources get augmented by compounding of $(1+g_{i1}+g_{i2})$ over time.[6] Commercial banks can now supply real bills as currency to finance the augmented resource development. As long as the augmented financial resources following real economy growth denoted by $(1+g_{i1}+g_{i2})$ continues over time, there is no reason to go into fractional reserve requirement monetary system. All the generated resources remain with the commercial bank across specific projects. The central bank holds none of the statutory reserve. This though is the ideal case of 100 percent utilization of commercial bank real bills in the real economy in pursuit of approved possibilities.

The initial amount of $1,000 from the central bank is the case where the investment demand in the real economy is high and the commercial banks fall short of this amount to finance all projects. Consequently, the (financing/deposit)-ratio exceeds unity.

We next examine the possibility of resource leakage from the banking system. The important issue here is to note that the quantity of money exists in circularity between the demand of the real sector, the availability of loanable funds with the banks, and the additional requirements from the Central Bank. In the last case, certain amount of funds could fail to meet the optimal requirements of the real economy, thus causing leakages from the desired money, finance, and real economy interrelationship. Indeed, the usual case of resource mobilization must accept leakages through the commercial banks in the real economy linkages with financial instruments carrying money. Consequently, the resulting contraction of yields in the real economy allows for say, $900 resource mobilization. This would then cause $100 to remain as savings in the commercial banks to yield interest income on idle financial resources when fractional reserves return. Thereby, the inter-bank flows of such savings in speculative assets will trigger multiple credit creation and an accumulating amount of interest cost on debt capital.

To avoid such a situation when the resources are not fully mobilized into the real economy, the commercial banks hand over the \$100 unutilized financial resource to the central bank for safe-keeping. *This becomes the 100 percent potential reserve of the commercial bank with the central bank.* Note here this definition of the 100% reserve requirement monetary system (100%RRMS) with the gold standard (explained below), which is quite different from the 100 percent reserve requirement monetary idea explained in the literature (Rist, 1940; Friedman, 1968).

The commercial bank would use this 'saved' resource at a later date on the basis of its legitimate claim based on credit-worthiness due to increased possibility in financing diversified projects. At the time of such a future release of funds from the central bank, the 100 percent reserve converts to money in circulation in the form of a quantity of currency.

The central bank is entrusted with the protection of the value of underutilized financial resources through the commercial banks. This value protection cannot be done by paper and promissory notes or any such *numeraire* whose long-term stability is in question. The choice is gold as the required stable monetary *numeraire*. The long-term stability of gold has been proven historically (Choudhury & Hoque, op cit). Thus a stock of gold denoted by G is stored by the central bank to stabilize the value of the central bank reserve, which subsequently becomes currency in circulation.

Let the change of gold stock be denoted by ΔG (which in the special case equals the initial new stock G). Let ΔM denote the 100 percent reserve with the central bank. Let p_G denote the price of gold. For maintaining stability of the monetary stock, that is 100 percent reserve with the central bank, the condition is,

$$p_G \cdot \Delta G = \Delta M. \tag{1}$$

but ΔM would ultimately add to the currency stock (ΔC) when ΔM is re-injected into the real economy on demand. Thus,

$$p_G \cdot \Delta G = \Delta M = \Delta C. \tag{2}$$

Thereby,

$$\Delta C/\Delta G = p_G. \tag{3}$$

Now by 'mathematical integration' over the entire stock of currency, and thereby of the gold stock, with the condition that G = 0, when C = M = 0, M being the money held by the central bank under 100 percent reserve requirements monetary system, it is true that,

$$\Delta C/\Delta G = p_G, \tag{4}$$

so also,

$$C/G = p_G. \tag{5}$$

This proves that the value of gold that protects the marginal amount of money by a corresponding marginal amount of gold stock also simultaneously protects the entire currency as money in circulation in the real economy. Thus only effective pricing in the real economy values the currency value per unit of gold-backing of temporarily un-mobilized commercial bank reserve held with the central bank as 100%RRMS..

CENTRAL BANK FUNCTIONS IN 100% RRMS

The conclusion now is astounding: A small amount of gold is needed to protect the exchange value of the entire stock of currency in circulation. The regulatory condition though is this: The central bank must regulate stable price of gold over the long-run. Stability of gold price can be maintained by regulating the stock of gold in the economy/society. The Islamic state has the duty of moral suasion to attain such a goal of moderation on holding gold as precious metal. The same kind of regulation is extended to the mixed precious bi-metals, gold and silver.

In the 100%RRMS, the role of the central bank in monetary management is reduced to policy-making and regulation for supervising a sustainable market economy in approved goods, services and projects. This situation would involve supervising the management of a stable and growing economy in concert with the participation of commercial banks as the principal medium for mobilizing money and finance between banks, the financial sector, and the real economy.

The power of creating money by the central bank is reduced to managing a stock of gold to maintain the value of money as currency in circulation (see *Money Matters* on 100%RRMS, internet version). This function too is inversely related with the velocity and volume of the circularly mobilized money and finance through the real economy (Figures 1 and 2).

Gaining from the extensively participatory nature of the 100%RRMS and the real economy, the central bank also engages in a continuous activity of knowledge sharing with the central bank and the agents representing the real economy. This generates an overarching 'learning process' towards determining the general-system relations involving the central bank, the commercial banks, and the real economy. Thereby, *technical analysis*, the resulting *information sharing*, and *development of such learnt policies and endogenous learning experience* become the principle attributes in central bank function in the money, finance and real economy interrelationships with 100% RRMS.

All functions conventionally endowed on the central bank cease to have effect. Governance is replaced by the participatory decision-making analytical forums. The conventional functions on the other hand are money supply and monetary regulation, interest rate and exchange-rate setting by regulating the monetary reserve of the countries balance of payments. All these targets are converted into endogenous causality in our 100%RRMS. Inflation targeting too is left to market adjustment in the midst of the features of 100%RRMS with the gold standard and the micro-monetary perspective of project financing.

THE LAISSEZ FAIRE CONCEPT OF MONEY AND MEDIUM OF EXCHANGE IN THE LITERATURE

Our delineation of a predominantly commercial and banking role in financial resource mobilization in the real economy with the central bank being a lender of last resort and an overseer of the currency value in market exchange in terms of a quantity of gold-backing, has strong precedence in the literature (Saving, 1977; Klein, 1975; Tullock, 1976; Tobin, 1963). Hayek thought about such a kind of private monetary system in which private banks will play the role of money circulation (Hayek, 1976). In this case, private money would all be valued on the basis of a given standard, such as gold, but they would compete with each other. In other words, competing quantities of money would be held by private institutions, especially banks, and this would be like holding money in terms of financial and other assets.

Yeager (1997, pp. 412-413) writes in regards to privately supplied money. Commercial banks would supply such funds. The central bank's authority in such a monetary system would be minimal. This is his prescription of monetary reform, which Yeager expands upon the work of Black, Fama and Hall -- BFH (Yeager, 1983):

Government would be banished from any role in the monetary system other than that of defining a unit of account or numeraire. We envisage a unit defined by a bundle of goods and services comprehensive enough for the general level of prices quoted in it to be practically steady. Merely by conducting its own accounting and transactions in the Unit—we tentatively so name it, with a capital U—the government would give private parties a strong incentive to adopt the same Unit.

Yeager continues on (op cit, p. 413):

No longer would the size of the numeraire, one Unit, be determined by the supply and demand for any medium of exchange. The Unit would be defined by goods and services having supplies and demands of an almost entirely nonmonetary character.

THE PRAXIS OF THE ISLAMIC APPROACH TO TRADE AND INTEREST RELATIONSHIP

Our arguments establish the fact that interest-rate alleviation in the Islamic economy cannot be enforced by exogenous forces, policies and measures. If it is so done, as is presently practiced by Islamic venues everywhere in the world, the replacement of interest rate will not be sustained without simultaneously charting the constructive change that the trade and financing instruments must generate between money, finance, and the real economy. Presently, there is no such attempt by Islamic banks and Muslim countries in their economic Islamization experiment. Consequently, the program of Islamization of the financial sector has not proceeded to the extent of contributing to academia, to the rise of the *ummah* endowed by its own capital markets, in inter-communal international trade dynamics, and socioeconomic development programs. This is the continued import of our inference from earlier analysis in this work. That is, merely a construal of interest-free financing modes does not form adequate benchmark of the *shar'iah*. Islamization is not an adequate approach in such a partial view of Islamic change. The *ummah* view, in which money, finance, and real economy interrelationships play the crucial role of structural change and monetary reform must emanate from the cybernetic type general-system objective based on the epistemology of unity of knowledge.

We have argued and explained that the Islamic program to phase down interest rate, and replace it by trade instruments[7], must be carried out within a generalized system and cybernetic model of circular causal relations between money, finance, and the real economy. This simultaneously involves pervasively complementary interrelations between the central bank, the commercial banks, and the 100 percent reserve requirements monetary system with the gold numeraire. Such pervasively complementary relations generate organic relations in reference to the epistemology of systemic unity of knowledge.

Thus the question arises: Can the central principle of pervasive complementarities be derived from any other epistemological premise other than the monotheistic foundations? We note here the empirical and policy-directional role played by the principle of pervasive complementarities in explaining the epistemology of unity of knowledge by using the constructed *functional* ontology of unity in diversity of the world-system.[8] In this chapter we have narrowed down such a problem treatment to the unity of participatory relations between money, finance and the real economy.

The answer to our above question is in the negative. The dividing line between Islam and all other systems is the ultimate quintessence of epistemological reference to the oneness of God, or equivalently, the oneness of the monotheistic law, which projects the unity of knowledge in relation to the world-system. In all other systems the origin of knowledge is premised on the epistemology of rationalism. Rationalism and its entire constructed system operate on the basis of methodological individualism, conflict, competition and notions of scarcity of resources, and thereby, of substitution between contested entities. The rationalist mind is inextricably rooted in such behavior at the level of the individual, institution, society and human relations. Such a character remains globally at large in this rationalist world-system. Even socio-scientific theories and programs of the rationalist origin stand upon this nature of the world-system and 'everything' in it (Barrow, 1991; von Mises, 1978; Choudhury, 2008b).

EXTENDING THE ARGUMENTS TO THE OPEN ECONOMY CASE

Two cases need to be studied here. The first one is when a regional group together adopts a common currency. Such an arrangement is gaining momentum. It is voiced strongly by Mundell (2000) in respect of his prescription for a one world-currency. Likewise, there is the Euro, the American dollar, and a growing interest in a common Gulf Cooperation Council (GCC) currency following the inception of a future GCC common market and monetary union. In our case, the example is of an incomplete regional arrangement for 100 percent reserve requirements with the gold standard.

In the latter case, fractional reserve monetary system is treated as dual with the Islamic banking system. Segmented markets would be necessary to establish the desired money, finance, and real economy interrelations. This kind of an incomplete monetary transformation is presently practiced by some Islamic financial outlets, notably the Islamic Bank Bangladesh and the Islamic Society of North America Housing Co-operative. In general, the phasing out of interest rates in Islamic financial operations is embedded in a general system of simulated interrelations that must be realized with the simultaneous development of the emergent trade versus interest paradigm.

Following such recent development, a return to the 100 percent reserve requirement monetary system with the gold standard would be extended within the segmented region that would adopt this arrangement. The principle of resource mobilization is promoted in this regional grouping to establish a complementary and participatory trade and development regime. A regulatory and learning medium is enhanced by means of active networking between partners and Islamic banks.

A given stock of gold is parceled through the medium of an Islamic bank for settlement of payments. This is a significant global project that can be considered by the Islamic Development Bank. Since the stock of gold required for stabilizing currencies would not be great, and would be inversely proportional to the extent and speed of resource mobilization, therefore, large stock of gold and its minting cost would be avoided. Besides, the cost of the gold minting would be covered by the seigniorage that the central bank would collect from the commercial banks in terms of the cost of production of gold required to protect currency value and a legitimate mark-up (Black, 1989) of the reserve held. Seigniorage would also be collected by participatory arrangements that would exist in a cooperative agreement to share risk and returns between the central bank and commercial banks, and between the commercial banks and the clientele in the real economy. The latter case is well-known in the profit-loss (*mudarabah*) and equity participation (*musharakah*) arrangements of Islamic banks.

For the participatory sharing of risk and return between the central bank and commercial bank the resulting seigniorage arises in the case of partial financial resource mobilization by the commercial banks. Now the commercial banks share the services that the central bank renders by paying for these services in terms of the cost of procuring gold stock by the central bank plus a service charge on the commercial banks. The commercial banks can roll over this cost to their clientele in the real economy by way of service charges. This shows that both service charges and interest rates are inversely related to productivity and product and risk diversifications. These positive changes are causally related to resource mobilization through commercial banks. The principal cost that would exist is caused by leakages. This is where the full productivity of the use of money and finance in the real economy fails -- always, partially, but increasingly so in the interest-bearing system. In order to reduce such leakages and share in the full realization of profitability and cost-reduction, Islamic banks benefit from the joint consequences of risk and product diversifications. These conditions always exist effectively in a joint pursuit of resource mobilization, which is exemplified by the Islamic economic and financial system.

The paradigm of the participatory, thus endogenous relations between the central bank, commercial banks (Islamic banks) and real economy remains unchanged for the open economy, as is the case with the closed domestic economy. In the open economy case, national central bank, commercial banks, and real economy relations are further extended by the bank of international settlements of payments in the Islamic networked monetary arrangement. Figures 1 and 2 are now extended to incorporate the additional monetary institution of international monetary settlement.

PRODUCTIVITY DETERMINED EXCHANGE RATE IN 100% RRMS WITH THE GOLD STANDARD

The exchange rate (E) is defined on grounds of productivity, avoiding the monetary intervention except in exigency of under-mobilization of financial resources. The following formula reflects this:

Terms-of-trade, $t = p_X.X/p_M.M$. (6)

- X denotes volume of exports; p_X denotes price export.
- M denotes volume of imports; p_M denotes price of imports.

Rewrite equation (6) as,

$E = p_X/p_M = t.(M/X)$ is the nominal exchange rate. (7)

X and M are both determined by their similar dynamics, within the country-specific or region-specific 100%RRMS with the gold standard. Therefore, (M/X) assumes a stable value, say ‘a’. Thereby,

$E = a.t$ (8)

E defines the exchange rate. It is shown to have a stable relationship with the terms-of-trade variable.

As free trade expands between partners in the region with full or partial 100%RRMS with the gold standard, as explained above, then M/X tends to 1. Hence trade liberalization along with a phased in transformation into a 100%RRMS arrangement within and across the integrating region, result in stability of the exchange rate and the terms-of trade simultaneously.

It is implied from our continuing formalism below that with a greater speed of economic integration, institutional networking of every kind, technological diffusion, factor mobility, and production and risk diversifications in the midst of the 100%RRMS arrangement, expression (8) will cause an upward trend in t, and thereby, in E. The coefficient ‘a’ will be induced by the force of economic integration, which in our case of participatory trade and development, is based on learning and endogenous interrelations in the spirit of systemic unity of knowledge.

THE FUNCTIONS OF MONEY IN 100 PERCENT RESERVE REQUIREMENTS MONETARY SYSTEM (100%RRMS)

The resource mobilization issue in trade versus financial interest implies that increased complementarities in the system are required so as to simulate the wellbeing that is attained from such complementarities over learning processes. The function of money, finance, and Islamic banks is precisely to attain this wellbeing objective. So what are the functions of monetary aggregate in such a system?

Is money a *store of value*? The value of money arises from the real economy in terms of feasible exchange of goods, services, and project financing. The absence of store of value in money means that, there is no productive value in money as such. Rather, the stability of currency value in international exchange is attained by means of the gold standard in the way as we have explained for the 100%RRMS in money, finance, and real economy circular causation interrelationships.

Is money a *unit* of exchange? Yes, this is true; for money in 100%RRMS determines the true relationship between unit value of money and the price of goods and services in exchange. Currency is equivalent to money in circulation in this system. This amount of money in circulation is supported by the gold standard in order to be stable and sound money as currency (von Mises, 1981). Indeed, the Prophet informally denominated various values to monetary units called *danaq* and *mithqal*, in terms of physical units of basic needs (Allouche, 1994).

Is money a *medium* of exchange? This property of money is true only in the static case. In the intertemporal case of resource mobilization it is difficult to ascertain the state of demand and supply of goods and services at future time-periods. It is also difficult to ascertain the risk-contingencies that exist at future points of time. Also, consumer preferences, systemic risk, and costs of future flows of goods and services, and financial demand in projects, are all based on subjective factors, and are thus undeterminable. Consequently, it is impossible to ascertain the value of goods and services in exchange, and thereby, the value of money that would back up such a real economic value.

Therefore, money does not have any market of its own, which otherwise results in interest rate as the price of money and financial instruments. Islamic money being micro-money and specific to projects that need to be financed, the quantity of money (currency) in circulation in the economy is determined by full quantum flows into specific projects. We write the relations in this case between micro-money and project-specific financing as,

$$M^*V = P^*y, \text{ or } M = (P^*y)/V \quad (9)$$

When V = 1, or 100 percent circulation (full micro-money mobilization through banks), then,

$$M = Pxy \tag{10}$$

Expression (9) means that the value of a stock of micro-money equals the total spending value in terms of the prices and quantities of approved goods and services in exchange pertaining to specific projects (activity).

Note that 'y' denotes real output. Thus an alternative definition of money is the value of GDP, which in turn represents the value of all spending (expenditures). But all these implications are specified by projects, rather than by the economy as a whole. We therefore interpret that a quantity of money, M, is driven fully into financing a project(s). This is the meaning of full quantum financing of projects by *micro-money*.

Hence, V ≅ 1. This is equivalent to the consequence of 100%RRMS, in which, any saved (un-mobilized money as currency) is totally surrendered to the central bank. Otherwise, the micro-money as currency is totally mobilized as resource to fit into projects in the real economy.

We can write Equation 10 in the light of the project-specific condition of micro-money transmission (M*) through commercial bans as,

$$M^* = \Sigma_i M_i = \Sigma P.y_i = P.y \text{ for economy-wide case.} \tag{11}$$

These kinds of project-specific circulation of micro-monetary 'units' were considered by Yeager (1983) in his *laissez-faire* approach to monetary reform. Yeager's *Unit* of money and Hayek's (1976) *competitive currency units* are weighted against a bundle of goods and services whose prices remain stable by supply and demand in market exchange against the value of the currencies used as monetary units for denoting exchange value of real goods and services. This kind of currency valuation against the real goods and services in market exchange can be used both in the regional and international sense. For example, units of currency can be the Islamic Dinar. The common commodity base for valuation is gold and silver in the 100%RRMS with the gold standard.

Yet the currencies in circulation may not be strictly in these precious metals. Any government certified way of holding money as a means of settling payments nationally, regionally, and internationally can be protected by the minting of the 'residual' stock of gold, G, shown in Figure 2.

IN THE END: FUNCTIONS OF MONEY

We have debated against the notions of demand and supply of money, and replaced these by the concept of quantity of micro-money mobilized into projects through the banking sector through a system of complementary relations between money, finance and the real economy, using appropriate participatory financing instruments. This chapter has also rejected the unquestioned acceptance of the notions of the mainstream functions of money. Of these, only the function of unit of exchange as it is actually realized or intertemporally established with market transactions is acceptable. The function of store of value is untenable, for value is jointly claimed by money and market exchange of real goods and services as they are temporally realized and as payments are settled. The function of money as medium of exchange is rejected in the absence of well-determination of the exchange values of goods and services over time.

Ludwig Von-Mises (1981, p. 84) writes in regards to the notion of money as medium of exchange (slightly edited):

Its (state) task thus becomes that of determining, in accordance with the intent of the contracting parties, what is to be understood by money in commercial transactions. From the legal point of view, money is not the common medium of exchange, but the common medium of payment of debt settlement.

In this chapter, we have gone a step further by arguing that money is a convention to settle payment-contracts at every determined moment of a clearly realized market exchange in the real economy.

CONCLUSION: INFERENCES ON THE ISLAMIC ALTERNATIVE ON GLOBAL FINANCIAL CRISIS

Islamic banks are claimed to have remained safe from the financial crisis that is sweeping the world today (The Times, 16 April, 2013). Central banks of most countries have cut down their prime lending rates to near zero to stimulate consumer and investment lending. Yet the deepening crisis continues. Islamic banks although insulated from the global financial crisis due to their operations that do not involve the stock market and speculative financing, have yet not gained advantage of the situation to contribute to the *ummah* future, and thereby, to show the path out of the crisis for the rest of the world, except by pointing out the zero-interest agenda and the alternative trade financing instruments.

This chapter argued that reducing the interest towards zero is not a new recommendation of any economic system during financial crisis. Spending and innovation require venture capital to be freely mobilized by development-financing instruments through commercial banks. Yet such a central bank policy is not taking effect toward stabilizing the global financial system.

This chapter points out that simultaneously with the phasing out of interest rate to zero, it is necessary to reconstruct the general-system design of the relations between the central bank, the commercial bank, and the real economy. Within such general-system reconstruction must be taken up all such circular causation synergies that establish pervasive complementarities between the productive and good things of life that are not simply *shar'iah*-compliant but also meet the demands of the greater purpose of wellbeing that is embedded in the objective and purpose of the *shar'iah* (*maqasid as-shar'iah*). This is an economic, financial and social panacea for the Muslim and non-Muslim alike. Indeed to the contrary, unethical, unsocial, and thereby immoral things equally abhor all peoples and cultures.

Most fundamentally, underlying this common heritage of mankind upon which to build, renew, or reconstruct old and fallen systems, there is the epistemological shift away from rationalism. Rationalism breeds methodological individualism, which is at the core of the postulate and design of economic rationality. Contrarily, the epistemology of systemic unity of knowledge as of core of unity of the monotheistic law in relation to the world-systems, establishes the world-systems on the foothold of organic cooperation. Discourse as of participation and complementarities with convergence towards organic consensus remains the goal and the result universally.

Discourse leads to new patterns of monetary futures. The global financial crisis requires a change in the monetary arrangements along with fiscal stimulus through reduced interest rates to restore stability. Our above-mentioned recommendations can be extended for global institutional reform. In that case, the central banks of member states would be superseded by a regional bank of reconstruction and development. In the case of the Islamic *ummah* such a global monetary reform can be guided by the Islamic Development Bank or otherwise.

On this issue, the International Monetary Fund has a standing idea. The IMF-U.S. Treasury Secretary muses on such a direction of monetary reform in the following words:

This is an important moment for the IMF and its future. The IMF has a critical role to play in the global resolution of the financial crisis. The proposed modernizing reforms will begin the process of making the IMF more representative of the global economy. It is strongly in the U.S. interest that the Fund fulfills these responsibilities in order to retain its relevance and preeminent place in the international monetary system. The need for a strong and effective IMF is all the more pressing in the chal-

lenging global economic environment we find ourselves in today. (http://www.treas.gov/press/releases/hp1307.htm, U.S. Department of the Treasury, Deputy Assistant Secretary Sobel Remarks on the Global Financial Crisis and the IMF's Response, Dec. 2, 2008).

The above quote signifies the urgency of the time to launch the blueprint of a future reform of the monetary system in conjunction with the outlook of the real economy to restore global economic and financial stability. This chapter has pointed out what structure of reasoning and institutional change will be required inside such an alternative form of money, finance, and real economy interlinked system in the Islamic economic, financial, and social framework and for the global order. Such is the wide perspective of social cybernetic concerning the system studied.

The important point to note in this and earlier applied chapters is the universal character of the contextual application of the episteme of unity of knowledge to mundane issues of economics, finance, science, and society. In this chapter, as earlier, the highlight was placed on money, finance and the real economy symbiotic linkages as the sure sign of the socio-cybernetic perspective of the monotheistic world-system at work.

REFERENCES

Allouche, A. (1994). *Mamluk economics, a study and translation of Al-Maqrizi's Ighathah*. Salt Lake City, UT: University of Utah Press.

Bank Muamalat. (2007). *Annual report 2007*. Jakarta, Indonesia: Bank Muamalat.

Bank Syariah Mandiri. (2006). *Annual report 2006*. Jakarta, Indonesia: Bank Syariah Mandiri.

Barrow, J. D. (1991). *Theories of everything, the quest for ultimate explanation*. Oxford, UK: Oxford University Press.

Black, S. (1989). Seigniorage. In Eatwell, J., Milgate, M., & Newman, P. (Eds.), *New Palgrave: Money* (pp. 314–315). New York: W.W. Norton.

Blackwell, M., & Nocera, S. (1989). Debt-equity swaps. In Frenkel, J. A., Dooley, M. P., & Wickman, P. (Eds.), *Analytical Issues in Debt* (pp. 311–345). Washington, DC: International Monetary Fund.

Business Islamica. (2008, March). Gulf mega-sukuk issues: A 'rich man's club'. *Business Islamica,* pp. 18-19.

Chapra, M. U. (1985). *Towards a just monetary system*. Leicester, UK: The Islamic Foundation.

Choudhury, M. A. (1989). Privatisation of the Islamic dinar as an instrument for the development of an Islamic capital market. In *Islamic Economic Co-operation* (pp. 272–294). London, UK: Macmillan.

Choudhury, M. A. (1997). *Money in Islam*. London, UK: Routledge.

Choudhury, M. A. (1999). A critique of econometric modeling for development studies: A political economy approach with special reference to Malaysia. In Ghosh, B. N., & Salleh, M. S. (Eds.), *Political Economy of Development in Malaysia* (pp. 105–123). Kuala Lumpur, Malaysia: Utusan Publications.

Choudhury, M. A. (2006). The principle of complementarities in the shuratic process and the implications for the socio-scientific order. In *The Koranic Principle of Complementarities Applied to Social and Scientific Themes*. Lewiston, NY: The Edwin Mellen Press.

Choudhury, M.A., Zaman, & Harahap, S.S. (2008). An evolutionary topological theory of participatory socioeconomic development. *World Futures*, *63*, 584–598. doi:10.1080/02604020701681219.

Choudhury, M. A. (2008a). Islamic economics and finance – A fiasco. *The Middle East Business and Economic Review*, *20*(1), 38–51.

Choudhury, M. A. (2008b). Islam versus liberalism: Contrasting epistemological inquiries. *International Journal of Social Economics*, *35*(4), 239–268. doi:10.1108/03068290810854538.

Choudhury, M. A. (2009). *Money, finance and the real economy in Islamic banking and finance, perspectives from the maqasid as-shari'ah*. (M.SC. dissertation). Department of Economics, Banking and Finance Program, University of Stirling, Stirling, UK.

Choudhury, M. A. (2011). Pointwise application of circular causation in Islamic valuation model. In *Islamic Economics and Finance: An Epistemological Inquiry*. Bingley, UK: Emerald.

Choudhury, M. A. (2012). On the existence of evolutionary learning equilibriums. *Journal of Science*, *16*, 75–88.

Choudhury, M. A., & Hoque, M. Z. (2004). Micro-money and real economic relationships in the 100 percent reserve requirement and the gold standard. In *An Advanced Exposition of Islamic Economics and Finance* (pp. 199–220). Lewiston, NY: The Edwin Mellen Press.

Donzelli, F. (2004). *Rise and decline of the notion of own rate of interest in Sraffa* (Working Paper No. 32.2004). Milan, Italy: Universita degli Studi di Milano.

Friedman, M. (1968). Real and pseudo gold standards. In *Dollars and Deficits* (pp. 247–265). Englewood Cliffs, NJ: Prentice-Hall.

Gassner, M.S. (2008, March). Revisiting Islamic bonds, are 85% of sukuk haram?. *Business Islamica*, pp. 22-23.

Green, R. (1989). Real bills doctrine. In Eatwell, M. Milgate, & P. Newman (Eds.), New Palgrave: Money, (pp. 310-313). New York: W.W. Norton.

Hayek, F. (1976). *Choice in currency* (Occasional Paper 48). London, UK: Institute of Economic Affairs.

International Monetary Fund (IMF). (2008, December 2). Retrieved from http://www.treas.gov/press/releases/hp1307.htm

Keynes, J. M. (1963). Economic possibilities for our grandchildren. In *Essays in Persuasion* (p. 368). New York: W.W. Norton.

Klein, B. (1975). The competing supply of money. *Journal of Money, Credit and Banking*, 4.

Krugman, P. R. (1989). Market-based debt-reduction schemes. In Frenkel, J. A., Dooley, M. P., & Wickman, P. (Eds.), *Analytical Issues in Debt* (pp. 258–278). Washington, DC: International Monetary Fund.

Money Matters. (n.d.). Retrieved from http://www.themoneymasters.com/mra.htm

Mundell, R. A. (2000, November 8). *Presentation at the economic forum on one world, one currency: Destination or delusion?* Washington DC: International Monetary Fund. Retrieved from http://www.imf.org/external/np/tr/2000/tr001108.htm

Ramsey, F. P. (1928). A mathematical theory of savings. *The Economic Journal, 38*(152), 543–550. doi:10.2307/2224098.

Rist, C. (1940). *History of monetary and credit theory from john law to the present day*. London, UK: Allen Unwin.

Sauer, J. B. (2002). Meaning, method and social science, a realist account. *Humanomics: International Journal of Systems and Ethics, 18*(3/4), 101–113.

Saving, T. R. (1977). A theory of the money supply with competitive banking. *Journal of Monetary Economics, 3*, 289–303. doi:10.1016/0304-3932(77)90023-X.

Siven, C. (1978). The interaction between multiplier and inflationary processing. In Strom, S., & Werin, L. (Eds.), *Topics in Disequilibrium Economics*. London, UK: Macmillan Press Ltd..

Sraffa, P. (1932, March). Dr. Hayek on money and capital. *The Economic Journal*, 42. doi:10.2307/2223735.

The Times. (2013, April 16). Islamic finance. *The Times.*

Tobin, J. (1963). Commercial banks as creators of 'money. In Carson, D. (Ed.), *Banking and Monetary Studies* (pp. 408–419). Homewood, IL: Irwin.

Tullock, G. (1976). Competing moneys. *Journal of Money, Credit and Banking*, 7.

Usmani, M.T. (n.d.). Retrieved from http://www.failaka.com/downloads/Usmani_SukukApplications.pdf

Vogel, E. F., & Hayes, S. L. (1998). *Islamic law and finance: Religion, risk and return, Arab and Islamic law*. The Hague, The Netherlands: Kluwer Law International.

Von Mises, L. (1976). *The ultimate foundation of economic science*. Kansas City, KS: Sheed Andrews & McMeel.

Von Mises, L. (1981). The return to sound money. In *The Theory of Money and Credit*. Indianapolis, IN: Liberty Fund.

Wicksell, K. (1934). A mathematical analysis of Dr. Akerman's problem. In Newman, P. (Ed.), *Readings in Mathematical Economics: Capital and Growth II* (pp. 3–28). Baltimore, MD: The Johns Hopkins Press.

Yeager, L. B. (1983, Spring). Stable money and free-market currencies. *The Cato Journal*, 305–326.

Yeager, L. B. (1997). *The fluttering veil*. Indianapolis, IN: Liberty Fund.

ENDNOTES

1 This paper was written by Professor MasudulAlamChoudhury and (Late) Professor Sofyan S. Harahap, who was Professor of Accounting, Director of Postgraduate Program in Islamic Economics and Finance, and Dean of the Faculty of Economics, Trisakti University.

2 In the subprime mortgage market, purchase price of the housing asset remains lower than the Present Value of discounted future cash-flows (capitalization). This phenomenon is well known.

3 The 'own rate of interest = $\%\Delta(p_c/p_c^f)$; where p_c denotes current price of a commodity; p_c^f denotes future price of the commodity. The idea is that each commodity is intertemporally valued according to its own interest rates. But in static equilibrium model, these divergent interest rates converge to a given rate.

4 The *Qur'an* declares (2:275): "... *Allah* has permitted trading and forbidden riba (interest)...."

5 Savings = Personal Income – Spending – personal tax; whereas also the supply function is S = S(i,I), i: rate of interest. Hence, savings is that part of unspent income that is sensitively influenced by interest rate.

6 Assume $g_{i1} = 5\%$; $g_{i2} = 5\%$ for i=1,2,..,n number of financed projects. For ten rounds of resource mobilization and regeneration through the commercial banks, the amount of money that will be created as a result equals $1000x(1.10)^{10} = 2593.742$. For n = 10 projects, the total quantity of money in circulation equals 10x2593.74 = 25,937.42.

7 These are the participatory development-financing instruments of *mudarabah* (profit-sharing), *mushrakah* (equity-participation), *murabaha* (mark-up pricing), and questionably the secondary financing instruments and Islamic bonds called *sukuk*.

8 *Functional* ontology is the logical explanation of the being of a certain reality (e.g. mathematical model, logical formalism), as opposed to ontology taken in the metaphysical sense of the being of God or what Heidegger called Dasein. In Islamic belief we cannot work at the level of critical discourse of the latter. But functional ontology is accepted Islamic medium to unravel the unity of the divine laws at work in the world-systems. Functional ontology can be subjected to scientific discourse.

APPENDIX

Evolutionary Micro-Money Equilibriums with Unity of Knowledge in the System and Cybernetic Sense

According to the definition resulting in the expression of micro-money we can write, noting that every variable and the coefficients is induced endogenously by the learning variable, θ:

$$MV = \sqrt[\gamma=\Sigma\alpha i]{[\Pi_i MV_i]^{\alpha i}} \quad (12)$$

$$= [\Pi P_i]^{\gamma}.[\Pi Y_i]^{\gamma};\ \gamma = 1/\Sigma\alpha_i$$

$$=F(p_1,p_2,\ldots p_n,\ y_1,y_2,\ldots,y_n)$$

$$dMV/d\theta = (dMV/dp_i).(dp_i/d\theta) > 0 \quad (13)$$

>0, stable=+constant by virtue of the endogenous effect.

$$dMV/d\theta = (dMV/dy_i).(dy_i/d\theta)> 0 \quad (14)$$

>0, stable=+constant by virtue of the endogenous effect.

Expressions (13) and (14) represent the direction of ethico-economic reconstruction.

The combination of learning effect and stabilizing result signified by expressions (12)-(14) yields the Figure 3. The arrows indicate the stabilizing results at punctuated points of learning equilibriums (encircled like the region A). At these points 'M.V' evolves along the stable path of the interactive and integrative (simplified by '(j,k)') experience given by $A(\theta) = \cup_j \cap_k[\{(M.V_{i(j,k)})\}[\theta] = \cup_j \cap_k[F_{(j,k)}(p_1,p_2,\ldots p_n, y_1,y_2,\ldots,y_n)][\theta]$.

The points like A's are stable points of evolutionary learning equilibriums. The detailed mathematical proof can be seen in Choudhury (2012). Here we explain this as follows: In reference to the learning process Figure 1 of Chapter 1 governed by the episteme of unity of knowledge, there are evolutionary processes that each establish a circular causation estimation followed by simulation to attain a wellbeing target.

There are thus two kinds of learning processes occurring. Firstly, the implication of Figure 1 (Chapter 1) works within intra-processes. The attained simulated results of intra-processes are then evolved inter-processes by the same kind of interactive,

Figure 3. Intra- and inter-systemic evolutionary learning equilibriums of micro-money

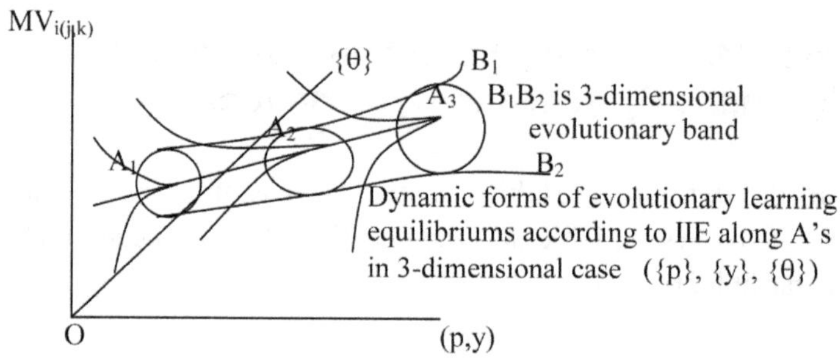

integrative, and evolutionary learning dynamics. Such intra- and inter- systemic dynamics resulting in simulacra of attained wellbeing results by circular causation to test out the degrees of complementarities (organic unification) existing, and that can be reconstructed between the micro-monies in circulation in the absence of interest, and being totally driven by trade is the manifestation of system and cybernetic forces at work in reference to the episteme of unity of knowledge.

Consider now,

$$p = [\Pi_i P_i]^{\gamma};\ y = [\Pi Y_i]^{\gamma} \quad (15)$$

For evolutionary stability condition *intra-system* we take an element say,

$$x_i \in A_i;\ x_i{}^* = \text{limiting } \{x_i\} \in A_i, \text{ for } \{\theta\} \in (\Omega, S). \quad (16)$$

Therefore, $|x_i - x_i{}^*| < \varepsilon_i$, an indefinitely small but positive value.

For evolutionary stability condition *inter-system* we take an element say,

$$Y_s \in A_s;\ x_i{}^* = \text{limiting } \{x_i\} \in A_i, \text{ for } \{\theta\} \in (\Omega, S);\ y_s{}^* = \text{limiting } \{y_s\} \in A_s, \text{ for } \{\theta\} \in (\Omega, S) \quad (17)$$

Therefore, $|(x_i - x_i{}^*) + (y_s - y_s{}^*)| < \varepsilon_i + \varepsilon_s = \varepsilon_{is}$, an indefinitely small but positive value.

Thereby, $\varepsilon_{is}/d\theta < 0$, but $(\theta, \varepsilon_{is})$ is strictly non-zero in evolutionary learning phases of the interactive and integrative (j,k), and evolutionary processes intra-system and inter-systems. All the variables mentioned are knowledge induced intra-system and inter-systems. Such dynamics reflect the system and cybernetic phenomenology in reference to the episteme of unity of knowledge.

Chapter 12
Conclusion

ABSTRACT

This is a concluding chapter. It summarizes the system and cybernetic power of unity of knowledge as the episteme and carrier of morality and ethics from the monotheistic law to the world-system. The point with which this book started, the universality and uniqueness of the monotheistic law in the socio-cybernetic understanding of God and the world-system, is further summarized. There is no other way, the conclusion challenges.

INTRODUCTION

The moral-social intellection in this book has taken us in the direction of questioning many of the existing theories and practices of economic, financial, and social reasoning, both in mainstream and Islamic perspectives. Thereby, the prospect of bringing God into the extended design of the cybernetic nature of the world-system as an integral whole, in the light of the worldview of epistemic unity of knowledge, proved to be a missing project in the existing mainstream and Islamic economic, finance and social models. To reintroduce God in the world-system in terms of the monotheistic law that functions on the basis of its 'universal' and 'unique' epistemology of unity of knowledge in 'everything' is to reconstruct the world-system according to the emergent moral and ethical precepts arising there from. Such a project requires a new epistemological scholarship and its application to the details of the world-system. The result is a distinct phenomenological model in the field of heterodox socio-scientific theory.

This book has cast its deepening study in this direction of inquiry. It is a rare work in the face of the forgotten field considering the dynamics of the monotheistic law in the holism of the socio-scientific worldview. The emergence is the law of

DOI: 10.4018/978-1-4666-4643-8.ch012

Copyright ©2014, IGI Global. Copying or distributing in print or electronic forms without written permission of IGI Global is prohibited.

monotheistic oneness that is extensively, and hence 'universally' and 'uniquely' analytically, grounded and applied, in the scheme of 'everything'. The overarching cybernetic model unravels the grand design of the learning multiverse over the dimensions of knowledge, space and time. The argument made is that, by missing out God in the intellection and concrescence of the universal design a great portion of the human order is left out from scientific explanation (Choudhury, 2011). The fact is that the humankind of every genre over historical time and civilizations never abandoned God from his understanding of total reality.

Therefore, the question remains: How can the great world-systems, such as economics, finance, and society be left out of the equation of the monotheistic entirety? This book therefore questioned the incompleteness of the existing socio-scientific inquiry without God in it; that is without the monotheistic law in the explanatory grand design of the learning universe from beginning to the end. God appears in such a socio-scientific universe in terms of the epistemology of unity of knowledge as a substantive field of socio-scientific inquiry as a cybernetic connectivity. Upon this is constructed a phenomenological model of scientific analysis, intellection, discourse, and advancement together with application in a broad field of worldly reality.

This book formalized the general model of the emergent epistemic unity of knowledge and the consequential unified world-system. It then applied the emergent learning model to the particular study of economics, finance, and society and their further subsets. Examples of such subsets that were studied are banking, money-finance-real economy, and the theoretical reconstruction of several prevailing thinking in economics, finance, and social order.

SUMMARY OF CONTRIBUTIONS

Phenomenological Formalism of Epistemic Unity of Knowledge and the World-System

In the direction of the moral-social reconstruction of prevalent positivism, initiated by this project of epistemic unity of knowledge at its foundation, we have crossed a vast territory of socio-scientific inquiry. The organic learning design of the universe we studied was a truly cybernetic and systemic worldview of unity of knowledge. We supported such conceptual thought by the applied case studies with empirical contributions.

To summarize, the theme studied in this book comprises the following issues: The construction of the phenomenological model of unity of knowledge premised on the law of monotheistic oneness and its ontological functioning in the real world of diverse issues and problems. This model was then uniformly applied to a spectrum of topics. The book showed that the same model can be improvised and applied to both the social and scientific fields and their varied issues and problems. Yet the issues and problems remain distinct by symbiotic interrelations in the grand moral-social design of the world-system.

In the holism of systems, neither science nor society with its economics, financial, social and congruent sub-systems remain symbiotically embedded, interacting, integrating and learning by repetitive evolutionary epistemology of organic unity in relationship with the diversity of details the world-system. In the end, neither science nor society with its economics, finance, and the sub-systems remains insulated and independent of the episteme of unity of knowledge. Yet this kind of unification of the embedded diversity of interdependent, and thus learning systems in epistemic unity of knowledge, is not a numinous monotheistic conception of reality. Contrarily, the emergent epistemology and its phenomenological worldview, model, and applied formalism applies to both the generalized design and to particulars.

The human and non-human worlds are therefore particulars in themselves, but embedded in their unified interrelationships, and hence are members of the learning entirety. The conclusion we reach in this sense of evolutionary epistemology is that, through the interrelationship between the human and non-human embedded world—although worldly knowledge commences in human volition—the intellectual interface with the artefacts of the real world causes change, and hence learning as simulated possibilities in the interacting and integrative (unifying) world-systems.

The book refers to this kind of universally interdependent learning phenomenon functioning in unity of knowledge as the interactive, integrative and evolutionary model. This is the IIE-learning model; it explains the IIE-learning process. The driving factor underlying the evolutionary learning model is knowledge. Knowledge-flows emanating from the monotheistic origin address particular problems in the light of its epistemological origin. The epistemological origin of knowledge is mathematically identified as a super-cardinal topology of the monotheistic law of unity of knowledge and its induced world-system that encompasses both the generality and the particular issues. The IIE-learning model in epistemic unity of knowledge is applied to the theory of 'everything' in the dimensions of knowledge, time and space.

INTRA-SYSTEM AND INTER-SYSTEMS EVOLUTIONARY EPISTEMOLOGY (RADNITZKY, ET AL., 1988)

In the domain of diversified world-systems addressed by and within the learning worldview of unity of knowledge we have studied events as they appear and are explained in the dimensions of knowledge, space, and time, as opposed to the contemporary way of understanding reality, which is bounded simply by the space-time universe (Wallerstein, 1998). Several mainstream topics have been studied in good depth in the emergent fresh epistemological and phenomenological worldview. These are the integral relationship between science and the moral law. Systemic unification between money, finance, and banking as unified world-systems with institutions, has been studied in good depth. New perspectives of the monetary integration with finance and the real economy leading to the moral-social possibility of a new financial architecture; monetary transmission within the 100 percent reserve requirements monetary system has been formalized. The central configurative principle of pervasive complementarities that logically replaces the traditional postulates of marginal rate of substitution, resource scarcity, competition, and methodological individualism has been developed and applied.

The emergent moral-social reconstruction in thought and application is studied as a complementary pairing between markets and institutions. Both are transformed by the new worldview as endogenous systems that interact, integrate, and evolve together along IIE-learning processes. Within the pertinent moral and ethical sensitivity to the market-institutional interrelated issues and questions that arise, the investigations on the macroeconomics of monetary and fiscal relations turn out to be studied in the light of their microeconomic foundations. Thereby, the social choice structure of decision-making comes to be studied in terms of the micro-foundations of preference formation.

Consequently, the book studied the extensive meaning and application of simulation of the socio-scientific criterion of wellbeing with circular causation relations between variables that represent their candidacy in the expanding set of 'the good things of life'. New dimensions of monetary and fiscal policies in relevance to the moral-social transformation are thereby examined. The possibility of morality and ethics in socio-scientific formalism, explanation and application is thus shown to be a micro-foundational academic enterprise. Upon this the micro-foundation of macroeconomic cybernetic worldview is formalized.

The study of the micro-foundational epistemological question on formalism in epistemic unity of knowledge led the book to a critical examination of various mainstream ideas. Also such ideas bear on a critical examination of the mainstream theories that have been emulated by Islamic economics, finance, and social ideas. The book pointed out the scientific problems caused by such questionable imitations. These results pointed proved to be an unwanted innovation of the *shari'ah* (the Islamic law).

In the midst, the great purpose and objective of the *shari'ah* based on the monotheistic law, termed as the *maqasid as-shari'ah*, has been forgotten. Thereby, the ambivalence of *maqasid as-shari'ah* against the concocted idea of *shari'ah*-compliance in Islamic finance is thoroughly critiqued and abandoned. The critical prognosis of

Islamic economics and finance on methodological grounds re-established the study of moral-social reconstruction of Islamic economics, finance, science, and society on the fundamental epistemological premise of the Islamic worldview. This comprises the three elements of the *Qur'anic* epistemology: the *Qur'an*, the Prophetic guidance (*sunnah*), and the epistemologically legitimate discourse (*shura*) with consciousness (*tasbih*) of those in authority. The result of these fundamental elements of true Islamic epistemology is the deriving of laws and rules from the fundamental sources (*ijtihad*) through a participatory medium of discursive determination.

As opposed to this primal premise of Islamic epistemology there have appeared innovations in the interpretations of *ijtihad*. Ever since Islamic thought took the petrified road of traditional *fiqh* (legal interpretations) for the convenience of limiting intellectual inquiry to space and time agencies. This led to a traditional interpretation the *shari'ah*. *Fiqh*, found in such a field of self-interest, has become a vastly problematic field of legal, and thereby often proved contrary to the analytical knowledge of the socio-scientific thought. This widest field of socio-scientific knowledge is afforded by the purpose and objective of the *shari'ah* – the *maqasid as-shari'ah*. The *maqasid* ought to rule over every particular issues derived from the general theory of epistemic monotheistic unity of knowledge and its induction of the world-system. The book has thereby argued for a return to the epistemological foundation for every new inquiry emerging out of discourse (*shura*) and new rules derived in direct reference to the epistemic sources (*ijtihad*).

This book has thereby used a double-edged sword. It applied it equally to the mainstream socio-scientific intellection on the one side; and to Islamic thought on the other side, as these prevail presently in economics, finance, society, and in their further disaggregate sub-systems. Examples of the latter kinds of sub-systems studied in this book are ethicized perspectives of banking, monetary and fiscal policies, money and real economy, institutional structure, and the behavioural basis of micro-foundation of macroeconomic theory. The macroeconomic aggregation is seen as the complex compounding of micro-foundational preferences in regards to the variables characterizing 'everything' in general and in particular.

Further institutional matters and policy issues, such as corporate governance, Corporate Social Consciousness and Responsibility (CSCR), productivity and efficiency in the light of moral-social reconstruction are studied with their policy-theoretic meanings. Empirical perspectives are undertaken in the simulation problems of wellbeing criterion subject to a system of circular causation relations between the variables.

ADDRESSING SOCIAL ISSUES IN SYSTEMS AND CYBERNETICS

Among the specific topics studied in depth in the light of moral-social reconstruction using the episteme of unity of knowledge are poverty and its underlying causes; and the ameliorative measures for attaining levels of poverty alleviation. The key factor for poverty of the abject type is explained to be the presence of interest rate and its related financing instruments. Interest rate mechanism is explained to disable social participation and cause obstruction to the free flow of financial resources into the real economy.

Contrary to the presence of interest rates, the micro-foundational perspective of complex aggregation to the economy-wide level is shown to be attainable by the knowledge induction of preferences, and by the choice of proper development paradigm. The book presents such a development choice, within which 'the good things of life' are identified as the basic-needs. It is argued that any social system that is touched by interest rate and its various instruments are incapable of achieving basic-needs regime of development. Consequently, poverty prevails; and poverty alleviation as the great focus of wellbeing and social policy is thwarted.

The social factors affecting poverty and poverty alleviation are accordingly discussed within development regimes with and without interest rates. The influence of interest rates on resource mobilization is contrasted by its opposite social arrangement. This is the social order of participation and ownership, empowerment and sustainability of life-sustaining productive activities between the rich and poor in their unified social bond. Development-financing instruments of trade in 'the good things of life' are thus shown to be the sure way of establishing the above-mentioned attributes for poverty alleviation, contrary to the regime of interest rates.

Contrary to the regime based on interest rate as a financing instrument, this book goes at length to present the theory and functioning of participatory financing instruments. Such development-financing instruments through their active function in promoting trade in 'the good things of life' are brought out as the result of the epistemological origin of thought and action in the phenomenological model of unity of knowledge and the world-system. This formulation essentially presents the system and cybernetic worldview of social issues.

Yet in the way that these classical and more recently secondary financing instruments are studied in the light of the IIE-learning model in this book is quite different from their treatment in the so-called shari'ah-compliant doctrinaire. The latter does not address the primal epistemological premise of unity of knowledge. A thorough criticism is raised on this ground of inadequacy of the prevalent understanding of participatory financing instruments in the Islamic economics and finance literature.

Participation and complementarities within and between critical variables and the nature of their specific systems comprising 'the good things of life' are treated as substantive concepts in the epistemological sense, thus leading into a rigorous study of the IIE-learning model. The result is discovery of several concepts showing their applications in economics, finance, and society and their sub-systems. Among these substantive new contributions in this book is the wellbeing function. Its simulation is carried out by circular causation relations in unity of knowledge between the selected variables. There are also the concepts of epistemic knowledge and its derived knowledge-flows, the world-system, and ethical endogeneity arising from the moral-social consequences of unity of knowledge.

Yet another contribution is in the area of learning equilibriums and Fixed Point Theorem in the evolutionary epistemological model of IIE-processes. The end result is formalism of the generalized model of ethical endogeneity relating to money, finance, real economy, and monetary and fiscal policies with new approaches to monetary transmission. A model of complementarities is formalized by unifying the monetary and fiscal policies with price stability, employment and development sustainability in the light of the IIE-learning model of epistemic unity of knowledge.

CONCLUSION

The most significant contribution of this book is in the area of extending and completing the model of socio-scientific explanation in the universal sense of including monotheism in the law and reasoning concerning the world-system. The model and analytics underlying this substantive and indispensable unification of knowledge with the world-system is premised on a socio-scientific and cybernetic possibility. This is attained by the phenomenology and application of the monotheistic law of oneness as opposed to the numinous idea of oneness of the universe in the light of the unity of God as metaphysical ontology. The numinous metaphysical methodology of addressing God and the universe is dysfunctional except by personal belief only. Contrarily, the concept, 'functional' or 'engineering' ontology that the book has conceptualized and used means the formalism arising from the epistemological praxis. The functional ontological formalism then establishes the design, explanation, functioning, and application of the law of unity of knowledge. This book discovered such an epistemology in the monotheistic law of unity of knowledge. This thereby created unification of the world-system with its generality and particulars.

Here then is the substantive meaning of the theme of *God and the world-system* for realizing the moral-social foundation of a good society for 'everything' and for all. This is true for the generalized systemic formalism in terms of fresh grounds of intellection, which is a social cybernetic worldview, and for the particular cases erected on the moral basis of Islamic economics, finance, and society.

In final conclusion, the spectre of non-sustainability of a social order in the face of a materialist society on the one hand; and on the other hand of an ethical order of sustainability can be read off the case of the American economy today. Here is what Steve Slavin wrote in his blog (http://findarticles.com/p/articles/mi_m1272/is_n2586_v122/ai_14995070/) on such an issue. It puts into context the rise and fall of the American dream based on ethical issues.

America is being transformed from an industrial colossus to a tired, down-at-the-heels, post-industrial society. It is becoming a nation of the rich and super-rich at the top, a mass of poor people on the bottom, and a powerless middle class squeezed in between.

More and more, the U.S. is taking on the trappings of Third-World poverty. The streets are filled with homeless people and beggars. Crime is rampant, and the drug epidemic continues to rage out of control. The contrast between poverty and affluence never has been sharper, except that now there seems to be a lot poorer.

Figure 1 asserts the opposite movements: On the one side, the sustainable social order is based on a true call to *God-consciousness* within the material order. This is the model of God (monotheism) and the world-system. Against this is the non-sustainable social order that is based on the calling of *gold-consciousness* within the material order.

Conclusion

Figure 1. Visages of the American economy: God and gold consciousness

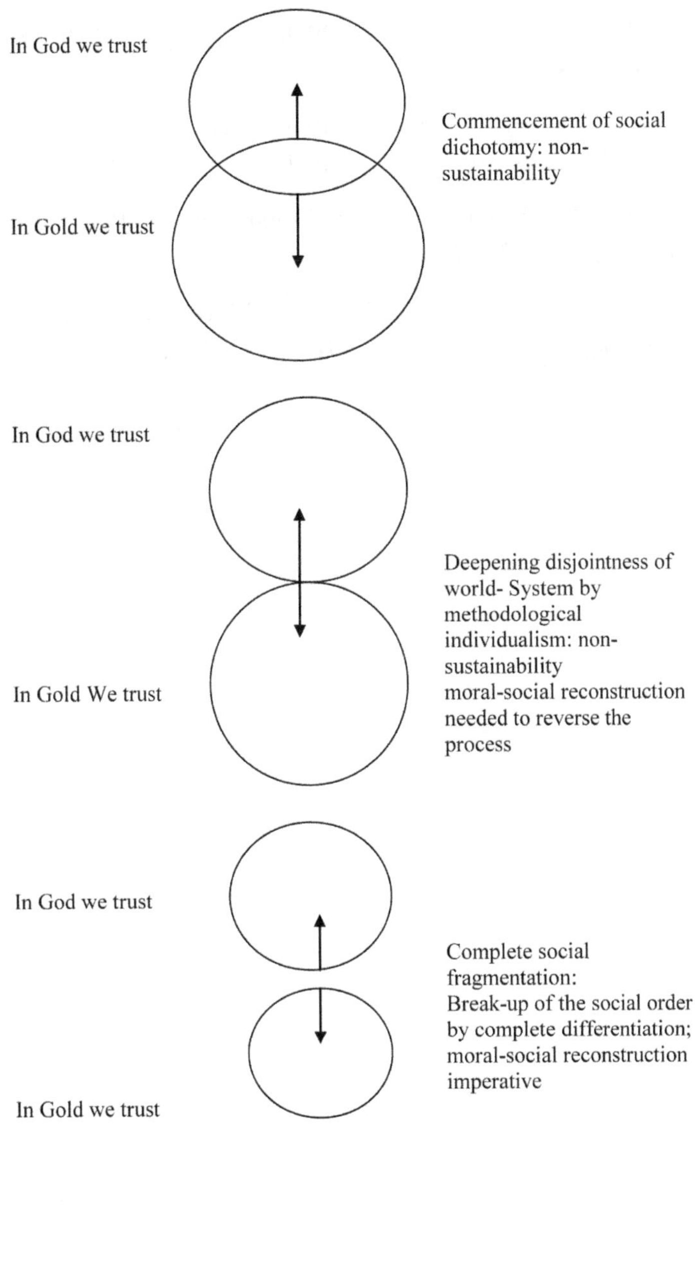

REFERENCES

Choudhury, M. A. (2011). *Islamic economics and finance: An epistemological inquiry*. Bingley, UK: Emerald.

Radnitzky, G., & Bartley, W. W. III, (Eds.). (1988). *Evolutionary epistemology, rationality and the sociology of knowledge*. La Salle, IL: Open Court.

Slavin, S. (n.d.). Retrieved from http://findarticles.com/p/articles/mi_m1272/is_n2586_v122/ai_14995070/

Wallerstein, I. (1998). Spacetime as the basis of knowledge. In Borda, O. F. (Ed.), *People's Participation, Challenges Ahead* (pp. 43–62). New York: The APEX Press.

Glossary

ARABIC TERMS

Athman: Price.
Bay' Muajjal: Deferred payments on asset-holding.
Dhat: Theology of God.
Fiqh: Interpretation of the rulings from the Qur'an and the Sunnah (see below).
Hablum-Min-Allah: Duties to God.
Hablum-Min-Annas: Duties to man (society).
Ijtihad: Deriving rules from the epistemological courses of the Qur'an and the sunnah (see below).
MAQADIR Al-Amwal: Quantity of objects of value.
Maqasid As-Shari'ah: Purpose and objective of the Islamic Law.
Maslaha (Wal-Ihtisan): Wellbeing by the public purpose.
Miyar Al-Amwal: Measurement of object of value.
Muamalat: Worldly affairs.
Mudarabah: Profit-sharing by participatory means in the absence of interest rates.
Mujtahid: The learned in Islamic scholarship based on the shari'ah.
Murabaha: Mark-up pricing.
Musharakah: Equity-financing in joint venture in the absence of interest rates.
Shari'ah: Islamic Law.
Qard e-Hassana: Interest-free loan.
Qur'an: The divinely revealed book of Islam as guidance to Mankind.
Riba: Financial interest of all kinds.
Riba Al-Fadl: Excess in value in exchange.
Riba Al-Nasiah: Intertemporal interest rate.
Shara'ee: Learned participants of the shura.
Shura: Institution and process of consultation in Islam.
Sufi: Mystic scholar.
Sukuk: Islamic participatory bond.
Sunnah: Guidance of the Prophet Muhammad.
Tariqa: Practices and fellowship of sufis.
Tasbih: Worshipping world-system on the basis of monotheistic consciousness.
Tasbih-Shura: Integrating shura with tasbih for gaining monotheistic consciousness.
Tawarruq: Financial murabaha.
Tawhid: Monotheism, oneness of God.
Ummah: The world nation of Islam.
Zakah: Wealth tax for meeting social equality by means of redistribution of wealth according to the shari'ah.

Compilation of References

Abdul-Majid, M., Saal, D. S., & Battisti, G. (2010). Efficiency in Islamic and conventional banking: An international comparison. *Journal of Productivity Analysis*, *34*, 25–43. doi:10.1007/s11123-009-0165-3.

Acquier, A., Gond, J.-P., & Pasquero, J. (2011). Rediscovering Howard R. Bowen's legacy: The unachieved agenda and continuing relevance of social responsibilities of the businessmen. *Business & Society*, *50*(4), 607–646. doi:10.1177/0007650311419251.

Adorno, T. W. (2007). *Negative dialectics (introduction)*. New York, NY: Continuum International Publishing Group.

Agius, I. (1990). Towards a relational theory of intergenerational ethics. In S. Busuttil, E. Agius, P.S. Inglott, & T. Macelli (Eds.), Our Responsibilities Towards Future Generations. Malta: The Foundation for International Studies in cooperation with UNESCO.

Allen, C., Smit, I., & Wallach, W. (2005). Artificial morality: Top-down, bottom-up, and hybrid approaches. *Journal of Ethics and Information Technology*, *7*(3), 149–155. doi:10.1007/s10676-006-0004-4.

Allouche, A. (1994). *Mamluk economics: A study and translation of Al-Maqrizi's Ighatah*. Salt Lake City, UT: University of Utah Press.

Al-Qaradawi, Y. (1999). *The lawful and prohibited in Islam*. Indianapolis, IN: American Trust Publications.

Amin, R. (2004). *The celestial management*. Jakarta, Indonesia: Bening Publishing.

Amin, S. (1977). *Imperialism and unequal development*. New York, NY: Monthly Review Press.

Ansari, M., & Choudhury, M. A. (1991). The idea of sustainable development in Islam. *The Journal of Development Studies*, *9*, 1–21.

Anwar, S., Romansyah, D., Sigit, P., & Watanabe, K. (2011). Treating return of mudharabah time deposit as investment instrument: a utilization of artificial neural networks (ANNS). *Humanomics: International Journal of Systems and Ethics, 27*(2).

Arrow, K. J. (1951). *Social choice and individual values*. New York, NY: John Wiley & Sons.

Arrow, K. J. (1974). *The limits of organization*. New York, NY: W.W. Norton.

Ashford, R. (1994). The binary economics of Louis Kelso: A democratic private property system for growth and justice. In Miller, J. H. (Ed.), *Curing World Poverty, the New Role of Property* (pp. 99–132). New Hope, KY: Saint Martin de Porres Press.

Bank Indonesia. (2002). *The blueprint of Islamic banking development in Indonesia.* Jakarta, Indonesia: Bank Indonesia.

Bank Muamalat. (2007). *Annual report 2007.* Jakarta, Indonesia: Bank Muamalat.

Bank Muamalat. (2009). *Reinforcing our business foundation.* Jakarta, Indonesia: Bank Muamalat.

Bank Syariah Mandiri. (2006). *Annual report 2006.* Jakarta, Indonesia: Bank Syariah Mandiri.

Barrow, J. D. (1991). *Theories of everything, the quest for ultimate explanation.* Oxford, UK: Oxford University Press.

Batbeck, S., & Blackburn, K. (2008). *On the macroeconomics of microfinance* (Discussion Paper No. 106). Manchester, UK: Centre for Growth and Business Cycle Research, University of Manchester.

Bator, F. M. (1957). The simple analytics of welfare maximization. *The American Economic Review*, 47.

Bavinck, H. (2013). *Essays on religion, science, and society* (Bolt, J., Ed.). Grand Rapids, MI: Baker Academic.

Becker, G. S. (1989). Family. In Eatwell, J., Milgate, M., & Newman, P. (Eds.), *The New Palgrave: Social Economics* (pp. 64–76). New York, NY: W.W. Norton.

Berman, H. J. (1989). Beyond Marx, beyond Weber. In McCullough, H. B. (Ed.), *Political Ideologies and Political Philosophies.* Toronto, Canada: Wall & Thompson.

Billington, M. O. (2002, November 15). Gold dinar: An economic and strategic response to chaos. *Executive Intelligence Review.*

Black, F. (1970, Autumn). Banking and interest rates in a world without money. *Journal of Banking Research*, 8-20.

Black, S. (1989). Seigniorage. In Eatwell, J., Milgate, M., & Newman, P. (Eds.), *New Palgrave: Money* (pp. 314–315). New York: W.W. Norton.

Blackwell, M., & Nocera, S. (1989). Debt-equity swaps. In Frenkel, J. A., Dooley, M. P., & Wickman, P. (Eds.), *Analytical Issues in Debt* (pp. 311–345). Washington, DC: International Monetary Fund.

Blaug, M. (1968). *Economic theory in retrospect.* Homewood, IL: Richard D. Irwin.

Blaug, M. (1970). *An introduction to the economics of education.* London, UK: Penguin Press.

Blaug, M. (1980). *The methodology of economics.* Cambridge, UK: Cambridge University Press.

Blaug, M. (1993). *The methodology of economics.* Cambridge, UK: Cambridge University Press.

Bohr, N. (1985). Discussions with Einstein on epistemological issues. In Folse, H. (Ed.), *The Philosophy of Niels Bohr: The Framework of Complementarity.* Amsterdam, The Netherlands: North Holland Physics Publishing.

Boland, L. A. (1989). On the methodology of economic model building. In *The Methodology of Economic Model Building* (pp. 39–63). London, UK: Routledge.

Bordo, M. D. (1989). The contribution of a monetary history of the United States, 1867-1960 to monetary history. In *Money, History, and International Finance: Essays in Honor of Anna J. Schwartz* (pp. 15–78). Chicago, IL: The University of Chicago Press. doi:10.7208/chicago/9780226066899.001.0001.

Boulding, K. E. (1971). Economics as a moral science. In Glass, J. F., & Staude, J. R. (Eds.), *Humanistic Society*. Pacific Palisades, CA: Goodyear Publishing Co. Inc..

Bowen, H. R. (1953). *Social responsibilities of the businessman*. New York, NY: Harper.

Breuer, R. (1991). *The anthropic principle: Man as the focal point of the universe*. Boston, MA: Birkhauser.

Brown, W. B., & Hogendorn, J. S. (2000). *International economics in the age of globalization*. Toronto, Canada: Broadview Press.

Bruteau, B. (1997). *God's ecstasy*. New York, NY: The Crossroad Publishing Co..

Buchanan, J. M. (1999). The domain of constitutional economics. In *The Logical Foundations of Constitutional Liberty*. Indianapolis, IN: Liberty Fund.

Buchanan, J. M., & Tullock, G. (1990). Individual rationality in social choice. In *The Calculus of Consent, Logical Foundations of Constitutional Democracy*. Indianapolis, IN: Liberty Fund.

Business Islamica. (2008, March). Gulf mega-sukuk issues: A 'rich man's club'. *Business Islamica,* pp. 18-19.

Cagan, P. (1989). Monetarism. In Eatwell, J., Milgate, M., & Newman, P. (Eds.), *Money, the New Palgrave* (pp. 195–205). New York, NY: W.W. Norton.

Campbell, D. T. (1988). *Evolutionary epistemology*. Evolutionary Epistemology.

Capra, F. (1982). The systems view of life. In *The Turning Point*. London, UK: Flamingo.

Capra, F. (1983). The systems view of life. In *The Turning Point*. London, UK: Flamingo.

Carchedi, G. (1991). *Frontiers of political economy*. New York, NY: Verso.

Carnap, R. (1966). Kant's synthetic a priori. In Gardner, M. (Ed.), *Philosophical Foundations of Physics*. New York: Basic Books, Inc..

Chapra, M. U. (1985). *Towards a just monetary system*. Leicester, UK: The Islamic Foundation.

Cheong, C. W., Nor Abu Hasan, S. M., & Isa, Z. (2008). Market efficiency of the Malaysian stock exchange: Further evidence. *International Journal of Management Studies, 15*(2), 41–68.

Choucri, N. (1995). Introduction: Theoretical, empirical, and policy perspectives. In *Global Accord* (pp. 1–40). Cambridge, MA: The MIT Press.

Choudhury, M. A. (2009). *Money, finance, and the real economy in Islamic banking and finance: perspectives from the maqasid as-shari'ah*. (Unpublished Masters Dissertation). Department of Economics, University of Stirling, Stirling, UK.

Choudhury, M.A. (2011a). The dynamics of the Shari'ah and the world-system. *King Abdulaziz University Journal: Islamic Economics, 23*(2).

Choudhury, M.A., & Hossain, M.S. (2010). Neuro-cybernetics of socio-scientific systems. *Mind and Society, 9*.

Choudhury, M.A., & Zaman, S.I. (2009). Self-referencing as socio-scientific methodology in contrasting paradigms. *Kybernetes: International Journal of Cybernetics, Systems and Management Studies, 38*(6).

Choudhury, M. A. (1989). Privatisation of the Islamic dinar as an instrument for the development of an Islamic capital market. In *Islamic Economic Co-operation* (pp. 272–294). London, UK: Macmillan.

Choudhury, M. A. (1993). *Comparative development study: In search of the world view*. New York: Macmillan Press Ltd., & St. Martin's Press.

Choudhury, M. A. (1996). A theory of social systems: Family and ecology as examples. *Kybernetes. The International Journal of Systems and Cybernetics, 25*(3).

Choudhury, M. A. (1997). *Money in Islam*. London, UK: Routledge.

Choudhury, M. A. (1998). *Studies in Islamic science and polity*. London, UK: Macmillan Press Ltd. doi:10.1057/9780230378032.

Choudhury, M. A. (1999). A critique of econometric modeling for development studies: A political economy approach with special reference to Malaysia. In Ghosh, B. N., & Salleh, M. S. (Eds.), *Political Economy of Development in Malaysia* (pp. 105–123). Kuala Lumpur, Malaysia: Utusan Publications.

Choudhury, M. A. (2000a). *The Islamic worldview: Socio-scientific perspectives*. London, UK: Kegan Paul International.

Choudhury, M. A. (2000b). A social contractarian theory of markets: Rawls, Gauthier, neoclassicism and the alternative. *International Journal of Social Economics, 27*(3). doi:10.1108/03068290010384268.

Choudhury, M. A. (2001). On the existence of evolutionary learning equilibriums. *Journal of Science, 16*, 1–13.

Choudhury, M. A. (2003). *Dynamic analysis of trade and development in the Islamic world: Selected case studies*. Dhaka, Bangladesh: Bangladesh Institute of Islamic Thought.

Choudhury, M. A. (2006). *Circular causation model in the Koran*. Lewiston, NY: The Edwin Mellen Press.

Choudhury, M. A. (2006). Development of Islamic economic and social thought. In Kabir Hassan, M., & Lewis, M. (Eds.), *Handbook of Islamic Banking*. London, UK: Edward Elgar Publishing Company.

Choudhury, M. A. (2006). Islamic macroeconomics? *International Journal of Social Economics, 33*(2). doi:10.1108/03068290610642238.

Choudhury, M. A. (2006). The principle of complementarities in the shuratic process and the implications for the socio-scientific order. In *The Koranic Principle of Complementarities Applied to Social and Scientific Themes*. Lewiston, NY: The Edwin Mellen Press.

Choudhury, M. A. (2007). *The universal paradigm and the Islamic world-system, economy, society, ethics and science*. Singapore: World Scientific Publications. doi:10.1142/6344.

Choudhury, M. A. (2008a). Islamic economics and finance – A fiasco. *The Middle East Business and Economic Review, 20*(1), 38–51.

Choudhury, M. A. (2008b). Islam versus liberalism: Contrasting epistemological inquiries. *International Journal of Social Economics, 35*(4), 239–268. doi:10.1108/03068290810854538.

Choudhury, M. A. (2009). Dialectics in socio-scientific inquiry: Islam contra occident. *The International Journal of Sociology and Social Policy*, *29*(9/10), 498–511. doi:10.1108/01443330910986289.

Choudhury, M. A. (2010). A neurocybernetic theory of management system. In Gunasekaran, A., & Sandhu, M. (Eds.), *Handbook on Business Information Systems*. Singapore: World Scientific Publications. doi:10.1142/9789812836069_0010.

Choudhury, M. A. (2010). The Islamic panacea to global financial predicament: A new financial architecture. *Journal Hadari*, *2*(2), 41–72.

Choudhury, M. A. (2011). A probabilistic model of learning fields. *The Journal of Muamalat and Islamic Finance Research*, *7*(1).

Choudhury, M. A. (2011). *Islamic economics and finance: An epistemological inquiry*. Bingley, UK: Emerald Publishers.

Choudhury, M. A. (2011). Overlapping generation model for Islamic asset valuation: A phenomenological application. In *Islamic Economics and Finance: an Epistemological Inquiry* (pp. 173–188). Bingley, UK: Emerald Publications.

Choudhury, M. A. (2011). Pointwise application of circular causation in Islamic valuation model. In *Islamic Economics and Finance: An Epistemological Inquiry*. Bingley, UK: Emerald.

Choudhury, M. A. (2011a). The future models of Arab political economy. *World Futures: The Journal of General Evolution*, *67*(6), 437–448.

Choudhury, M. A. (2011b). Family as socio-economic management system. *International Journal of Management Systems*, *18*(1).

Choudhury, M. A. (2011b). *Islamic economics and finance: An epistemological inquiry*. Bingley, UK: Emerald.

Choudhury, M. A. (2011c). A probabilistic model of learning fields. *The Journal of Muamalat and Islamic Finance Research*, *7*(1).

Choudhury, M. A. (2012). On the existence of evolutionary learning equilibriums. *Journal of Science*, *16*, 75–88.

Choudhury, M. A., & Hoque, M. Z. (2004). *An advanced exposition of Islamic economics and finance*. Lewiston, NY: The Edwin Mellen Press.

Choudhury, M. A., & Hoque, M. Z. (2004). Micro-money and real economic relationships in the 100 percent reserve requirement and the gold standard. In *An Advanced Exposition of Islamic Economics and Finance* (pp. 199–220). Lewiston, NY: The Edwin Mellen Press.

Choudhury, M. A., & Hossain, M. Z. (2010). A socio-statistical study of a composite index of human wellbeing. In Priya, A. (Ed.), *Handbook of Human Development and Management*. Serials Publication.

Choudhury, M. A., & Korvin, G. (2002). Simulation versus optimization. *Kybernetes: International Journal of Cybernetics. Systems and Management Studies*, *31*(1), 44–60.

Choudhury, M. A., & Malik, U. A. (1992). *Foundations of Islamic political economy*. London, UK: Macmillan Press Ltd..

Choudhury, M. A., & Zaman, S. I. (2009). Self-referencing as socio-scientific methodology in contrasting paradigms. *Kybernetes: The International Journal of Systems & Cybernetics*, *38*(6), 994–1008.

Choudhury, M.A., Zaman, & Harahap, S.S. (2008). An evolutionary topological theory of participatory socioeconomic development. *World Futures*, *63*, 584–598. doi:10.1080/02604020701681219.

Colander, D. (2003). Integrating ethics and altruism with economics, or altruism, economics, and Hume's dictum – A response to Morris Altman. *Journal of Economic Psychology*, *26*, 758–761. doi:10.1016/j.joep.2005.06.003.

Collard, D. (1978). *Altruism and economy: A study in non-selfish economics*. New York: Oxford University Press.

Commission on Global Governance. (1995). Global civic ethic. In *Our Global Neighbourhood: A Report of the Commission on Global Governance*. New York, NY: Oxford University Press.

Condorcet, M. J. A. N. (1785). *Essai sur l'application de l'analyse a la probabilite des decisions rendues a la pluralite des voix*. Paris, France: Imprimerie Royale.

Coombs, H. C. (1990). *The return of scarcity: Strategies for an economic future*. Cambridge, UK: Cambridge University Press. doi:10.1017/CBO9780511552281.

Crane, R. D. (2011). Foreword. In Choudhury, M. A. (Ed.), *Islamic Economics and Finance: An Epistemological Inquiry*. Bingley, UK: Emerald.

Daly, H. (1992). From empty-world to full-world economics: Recognizing an historical turning point in economic development. In Goodland, R., Daly, H., El-Serafy, S., & von Drost, B. (Eds.), *Environmentally Sustainable Economic Development: Building on Brundtland*. Malta: Center for Development Studies.

Dampier, W. C. (1961). Scientific philosophy and its outlook. In *A History of Science and Its relations with Philosophy and Religion*. Cambridge, UK: Cambridge at the University Press.

Dampier, W. S. (1961). *A history of science and its relations with philosophy and religion*. Cambridge, UK: Cambridge University Press.

Darwin, C. (1936). *Descent of man*. New York, NY: Modern Library.

Dasupta, A. K. (1987). Marginalist challenge. In *Epochs of Economic Theory*. Oxford, UK: Basil Blackwell.

Davies, G. (2002). *A history of money*. Cardiff, UK: University of Wales Press.

Davis, K. (1960). Can business afford to ignore social responsibilities? *California Management Review*, *2*(3), 70–77. doi:10.2307/41166246.

Dawkins, R. (1976). *The selfish gene*. New York: Oxford University Press.

Dawkins, R. (2006). *The god delusion*. London, UK: Transworld Publishers.

Dawkins, R. (2006). The roots of morality: why are we good? In *The God Delusion*. London, UK: Transworld Publishers.

Debreu, G. (1959). *A theory of value*. New York: John Wiley & Sons.

Denison, E. F. (1962). *The sources of economic growth in the U.S., & the alternatives before us*. Washington, DC: Committee for Economic Development.

Dilworth, D. (2008). *Scientific progress: A study concerning the nature of the relation between successive scientific theories, studies in epistemology, logic, methodology, and philosophy of science*. Berlin: Springer Science.

Donzelli, F. (2004). *Rise and decline of the notion of own rate of interest in Sraffa* (Working Paper No. 32.2004). Milan, Italy: Universita degli Studi di Milano.

Edel, A. (1970). Science and the structure of ethics. In Neurath, O., Carnap, R., & Morris, C. (Eds.), *Foundations of the Unity of Science*. Chicago, IL: University of Chicago Press.

Einstein, A. (1954). *Relativity, the special and the general theory* (Lawson, R. W., Trans.). London, UK: Methuen University Paperbacks.

Einstein, A. (1954a). The problem of space, ether, and the field in physics. In Commins, C., & Linscott, R. N. (Eds.), *Man and the Universe: The Philosophers of Science*. New York: The Pocket Books, Inc..

Einstein, A. (1954b). Considerations on the universe as a whole. In *Relativity, the Special and the General Theory* (Lawson, R. W., Trans.). London: Methuen.

Einstein, A. (n.d.). The laws of science and the laws of ethics. In *Lectures in Physics*. New York, NY: Philosophical Library.

Ekelund, Jr., & Hebert. (1990). *A history of economic theory and method*. New York, NY: McGraw-Hill Publishing Co.

Ekins, P. (1992). *A new world order, grassroots movements for global change*. London, UK: Routledge.

Epstein, R. (1992). Justice across the generations. In Laslett, P., & Fishkin, J. (Eds.), *Justice between Age Groups and Generations, Philosophy, Politics, and Society*. New Haven, CT: Yale University Press.

Etzioni, A. (1988). What is rational? In *The Moral Dimension: Towards a New Economics*. New York, NY: The Free Press.

Fama, E. (1980). Banking in the theory of finance. *Journal of Monetary Economics*, *6*, 39–57. doi:10.1016/0304-3932(80)90017-3.

Farmer, R. E. A. (2010). *How the economy works*. Oxford, UK: Oxford University Press.

Fisher, I. (1911). *The purchasing power of money*. New York: Macmillan.

Fitzpatrick, T. (2003). Postmodernism and new directions. In Alcock, P., Erskine, A., & May, M. (Eds.), *Social Policy* (pp. 125–133). Oxford, UK: Blackwell.

Foucault, M. (1972). *The archeology of knowledge and the discourse on language* (Sheridan, A. M., Trans.). New York: Harper Torchbooks.

Foucault, M. (1983). *Beyond structuralism and hermeneutics: The archeology of the human sciences* (Dreyfus, H. L., & Rabinow, P., Trans.). Chicago, IL: University of Chicago Press.

Friedman, M. (1989). Quantity theory of money. *New Palgrave: Money*.

Friedman, M. (1953a). The methodology of positive economics. In *Essays in Positive Economics* (pp. 3–46). Chicago, IL: University of Chicago Press.

Friedman, M. (1953b). Monetary and fiscal framework for economic stability. In *Essays in Positive Economics* (pp. 133–156). Chicago, IL: University of Chicago Press.

Friedman, M. (1956). The quantity theory of money – A restatement. In Friedman, M. (Ed.), *Studies in the Quantity Theory of Money* (pp. 3–24). Chicago, IL: The University of Chicago Press.

Friedman, M. (1960). *A program for monetary stability*. New York, NY: Fordham University Press.

Friedman, M. (1962). *Capitalism and freedom*. Chicago, IL: The University of Chicago Press.

Friedman, M. (1968). Real and pseudo gold standards. In *Dollars and Deficits* (pp. 247–265). Englewood Cliffs, NJ: Prentice-Hall.

Friedman, M. (1989). The quantity theory of money. In Eatwell, J., Milgate, M., & Newman, P. (Eds.), *New Palgrave: Money* (pp. 1–40). New York, NY: W.W. Norton.

Fukuyama, F. (1992). *The end of history and the last man*. New York: The Free Press.

Gassner, M.S. (2008, March). Revisiting Islamic bonds, are 85% of sukuk haram?. *Business Islamica*, pp. 22-23.

Gauthier, D. (1986). *Morals by agreement*. Oxford, UK: Oxford University Press.

Gel'fand, I. M., & Shenitzer, A. (1961). Introduction to tensors. In *Lectures on Linear Algebra* (pp. 164–185). New York, NY: Interscience Publishers, Inc..

Ghazzali. (n.d.). *Ihya ulum-id-din*. (M.F. Karim, Trans.). Lahore, Pakistan: Sh. Muhammad Ashraf.

Gleick, J. (1987). *Chaos, making a new science*. New York, NY: Viking Penguin.

Glock, H.-J. (2001). The development of Wittgenstein's philosophy. In *Wittgenstein: A Critical Reader*. Oxford, UK: Blackwell.

Goodland, R., Daly, H., El-Serafy, S., & von Drost, B. (Eds.). (1992). *Environmentally sustainable economic development: Building on brundtland*. Malta: Center for Development Studies.

Grandmont, J.-M. (1989). Temporary equilibrium. In Eatwell, J., Milgate, M., & Newman, P. (Eds.), *New Palgrave: General Equilibrium*. New York: W.W. Norton.

Green, R. (1989). Real bills doctrine. In Eatwell, M. Milgate, & P. Newman (Eds.), New Palgrave: Money, (pp. 310-313). New York: W.W. Norton.

Greenfeld, R. L., & Yaeger, L. B. (1963). A laissez-fare approach to monetary stability. *Journal of Money, Credit and Banking*, *15*, 302–315. doi:10.2307/1992481.

Green, R. (1989). Real bills doctrine. In Eatwell, M., & Newman, P. (Eds.), *New Palgrave: Money* (pp. 310–313). New York: W.W. Norton.

Greenspan, A. (2010, August 2). *Alan Greenspan: US 'risks double-dip recession'*. Retrieved from http://www.bbc.co.uk/news/business-10835176

Grilichez, J. (1970). Notes on the role of education in production function and growth accounting. In Hansen, L. W. (Ed.), *Education, Income and Human Capital*. Washington, DC: National Bureau of Economic Research.

Gruber, T. R. (1993). A translation approach to portable ontologies. *Knowledge Acquisition*, *5*(2), 199–200. doi:10.1006/knac.1993.1008.

Guessoum, N. (2011). *Islam's quantum question*. London, UK: I.B. Tauris.

Gulen, M. F. (2006). *Toward global civilization of love & tolerance*. Somerset, NJ: The Light, Inc..

Hahne, J. (2012). Science and religion: Reality toolkit, *Yale Scientific*. Retrieved from http://www.yalescientific.org/2012/05/science-and-religion-realitys-toolkit/

Hall, R. E. (1997). The Government and the monetary unit. In Yaeger, L. B. (Ed.), *The Fluttering Veil, Essays on Monetary Disequilibrium* (pp. 383–391). Indianapolis, IN: Liberty Fund.

Hammond, P. J. (1987). On reconciling Arrow's theory of social choice with Harsanyi's fundamental utilitarianism. In Feiwel, G. R. (Ed.), *Arrow and the Foundations of the Theory of Economic Policy*. London, UK: Macmillan Press.

Hammond, P. J. (1989). On reconciling Arrow's theory of social choice with Harsanyi's fundamental utilitarianism. In Feiwel, G. R. (Ed.), *Arrow and the Foundation of the Theory of Economic Policy* (pp. 179–221). London, UK: Macmillan.

Haniffa, R., & Hudaib, M. (2007). Exploring the ethical identity of Islamic financial institutions via communications in the annual reports. *Journal of Business Ethics*, *76*(1), 103–122. doi:10.1007/s10551-006-9272-5.

Harsanyi, J. C. (1955). Cardinal welfare, individualistic ethics, and interpersonal comparisons of utility. *The Journal of Political Economy*, 63.

Hart, H. L. A. (1997). Justice and morality. In *The Concept of Law*. Oxford, UK: Oxford University Press.

Hawking, S. W. (1988). *A brief history of time: From the big bang to black holes*. New York: Bantam Books, Inc..

Hawking, S. W., & Mlodinow, L. (2010). *The grand design*. London, UK: Transworld Publishers.

Hawley, A. H. (1986). *Human ecology*. Chicago, IL: The University of Chicago Press.

Hayek, F. (1976). *Choice in currency* (Occasional Paper 48). London, UK: Institute of Economic Affairs.

Hayek, F. (1979). *The counter-revolution of science*. Indianapolis, IN: Liberty Fund Inc..

Hayek, F. A. (1999). Intertemporal price equilibrium and movements in the value of money. In *Good Money, Part One: The New World* (pp. 186–227). Chicago, IL: University of Chicago Press.

Hegel, G. W. F. (1986). *The philosophy of history* (Sibree, J., Trans.). New York, NY: Dover Books.

Heidegger, M. (1988). The thesis of modern ontology: the basic ways of being are the being of nature (res extensa) and the being of mind (res cogitans). (A. Hofstadter, Trans.). In *The Basic Problems of Phenomenology*, (pp. 122-224). Bloomington, IN: Indiana University Press.

Heilbroner, R. (1985). The ideology of capital. In *The Nature and Logic of Capitalism* (pp. 107–140). New York, NY: W.W. Norton.

Heilbroner, R. L. (1986). The ideology of capital. In *The Nature and Logic of Capitalism*. New York, NY: W.W. Norton.

Heilbroner, R., & Milberg, W. (1995). The crisis of vision. In *The Crisis of Vision in Modern Economic Thought*. Cambridge, UK: Cambridge University Press.

Heiskala, R. (2003). *Society as semiosis*. New York, NY: Peter Lang.

Henderson, H. (1999). *Beyond globalization: Shaping a sustainable global economy*. West Hartcourt, CT: Kumarian Press.

Henderson, J. M., & Quandt, R. E. (1971). *Microeconomic theory: A mathematical approach*. New York, NY: McGraw-Hill.

Holton, R. (1992). Economic sociology: An evaluation of a culture-inclusive theory of economy and society. In *Economy and Society*. London, UK: Routledge.

Hubner, K. Dixon, P.R., Jr., & Dixon, H.M. (1985). Foundations of a universal historistic theory of the empirical sciences. In Critique of Scientific Reason, (pp.105-122). Chicago, IL: The University of Chicago Press.

Hull, D. L. (1988). *Science as a process: An evolutionary account of the social and conceptual development of science*. Chicago, IL: University of Chicago Press. doi:10.7208/chicago/9780226360492.001.0001.

Hume, D. (2007). *Writings on economics* (Rotwein, E., Ed.). New Brunswick, NJ: Transaction Publishers.

Husserl, E. (1965). *Phenomenology and the crisis of philosophy* (Lauer, Q., Trans.). New York: Harper & Row Publishers.

Hutt, W. H. (1979). The academic appeal of Keynesian doctrine & the nature of Keynesian thesis. In *The Keynesian Episode, a Reassessment*, (pp. 87-119). Indianapolis, IN: Liberty Fund.

Infeld, L. (1951). General relativity and the structure of our universe. In Schilpp, P. A. (Ed.), *Albert Einstein: Philosopher-Scientist*. New York, NY: Tudor Publications.

Inglott, P. S. (1990). The rights of future generations: Some socio-philosophical considerations. In Busuttil, S., Agius, E., Inglott, P. S., & Macelli, T. (Eds.), *Our Responsibilities Towards Future Generations* (pp. 17–27). Malta: Foundation for International Studies & UNESCO.

International Monetary Fund (IMF). (2008, December 2). Retrieved from http://www.treas.gov/press/releases/hp1307.htm

Islahi, A. A. (1988). Ibn Taimiyah's concept of money and monetary policy. In *Economic Concepts of Ibn Taimiyah* (pp. 139–143). Leicester, UK: The Islamic Foundation.

Islam Policy. (2011, January 7). *Use gold dinar for trade urges Dr. Mahathir bin Muhammad*. Retrieved from http://www.islampolicy.com/2011/01/use-gold-dinar-for-trade-urges-dr.html

Ismail, S. M. (1989). *Critical analysis of capitalism, socialism and Islamic economic order*. Lahore, Pakistan: Oriental Publications.

Jackson, E. T., & Kassam, Y. (Eds.). (1998). *Knowledge shared, participatory evaluation in development cooperation*. West Hartford, CT: Kumarian Press.

Johannessen, J.-A. (2006). Organizations as social systems: The search for a systemic theory of organizational innovation processes. *Kybernetes: International Journal of Systems and Cybernetics*, 27(4), 359–387. doi:10.1108/03684929810219404.

Kandalvi, M. Z. (n.d.). *Faza'il-e-a'amal*. Karachi, Pakistan. *Urdu Bazar.*.

Kant, I. (1949). *The philosophy of Kant* (Friedrich, C. J., Trans.). New York, NY: Modern Library.

Karim, F. (n.d.). *Imam Ghazali's ihya ulum-id-din*. Lahore, Pakistan: Sh. *Muhammad Ashraf.*.

Kellert, S. H. (1993). *The wake of chaos, unpredictable order in dynamical systems*. Chicago, IL: The University of Chicago Press. doi:10.7208/chicago/9780226429823.001.0001.

Kelso, L., & Patricia, H. (1965). *Two-factor theory: The economics of reality*. New York: Random House.

Kenen, P. (1985). *The international economy*. Englewood Cliffs, NJ: Prentice-Hall, Inc..

Keynes, J. M. (1963). Economic possibilities for our grandchildren. In *John Maynard Keynes Essays in Persuasion* (pp. 358–373). New York: W.W. Norton.

Kim, W. C., & Mauborgne, R. (2005). *Blue ocean strategy*. Boston, MA: Harvard University Press.

Kim, W. C., & Mauborgne, R. (2005). Creating blue oceans. In *Blue Ocean Strategy* (pp. 3–22). Boston, MA: Harvard Business School Press.

Kirkpayrick, T. (2012, September 23). God, money, and you. *Good News: A Magazine of Understanding*. Retrieved from http://www.ucg.org/marriage-and-family/god-money-and-you/

Kirzner, I. (1981). Entrepreneurship, entitlement, and economic justice. In Paul, J. (Ed.), *Reading Nozick, Essays on Anarchy, State, and Utopia*. Totowa, NJ: Rowan & Allanheld.

Klein, B. (1975). The competing supply of money. *Journal of Money, Credit and Banking*, 4.

Klein, L. R. (1946). Remarks on the theory of aggregation. *Econometrica*, 14.

Kobayashi, Y. (1988). An economic analysis of Japanese beauracracy. In Choudhury, M. A. (Ed.), *Political Economy of Development in Atlantic Canada* (pp. 25–47). Sydney, Canada: University College of Cape Breton.

Korten, D. C. (1995). Restore money's role as a medium of exchange. In *The Post-Corporate World* (pp. 195–197). San Francisco, CA: Berrett-Koehler Publishers, Inc..

Korten, D. C. (1995). The ecological revolution. In *When Corporations Rule the World* (pp. 261–276). London, UK: Earthscan.

Korten, D. C. (1995). *When corporations rule the world*. London, UK: Earthscan.

Krugman, P. (1996). *The self-organizing economy*. Cambridge, MA: Blackwell Publishers.

Krugman, P. R. (1989). Market-based debt-reduction schemes. In Frenkel, J. A., Dooley, M. P., & Wickman, P. (Eds.), *Analytical Issues in Debt* (pp. 258–278). Washington, DC: International Monetary Fund.

Kuhn, T. S. (1970). *The structure of scientific revolution*. Chicago, IL: University of Chicago Press.

Kumbhakar, S. C., & Lovell, C. A. K. (2000). *Stochastic frontier analysis*. Cambridge, UK: Cambridge University Press. doi:10.1017/CBO9781139174411.

Kupka, I. A. K., & Peixoto, M. M. (1993). On the enumerative geometry of geodesics. In M.W. Hirsch, J.E. Marsden, & M. Shub (Eds.), *From Topology to Computation: Proceedings of the Smalefest*, (pp. 243-253). New York, NY: Springer-Verlag.

Kuran, T. (2004). *Islam and mammon: The economic predicaments of Islamism*. Princeton, NJ: Princeton University Press.

La Salle, J., & Lefschetz, S. (1961). *Stability by Liapunov's direct method*. New York, NY: Academic Press.

Laidler, D. (1989). The quantity theory of money is always and everywhere controversial - Why?. *Atlantic Canada Economic Papers and Proceedings, 18*.

Ledger, C., & Pickard, S. (Eds.). (2004). *Creation and complexity: Interdisciplinary issues in science and religion*. Adelaide, Australia: ATF Press.

Levine, D. (1988). *Needs, rights, and the market*. Boulder, CO: Lynne Reinner.

Lucas, R. E. Jr. (1975). An equilibrium model of the business cycle. *The Journal of Political Economy*, *83*, 1113–1144. doi:10.1086/260386.

Maddox, I. J. (1970). *Elements of functional analysis*. Cambridge, UK: Cambridge University Press.

Mahdi, M. (1964). *Ibn Khaldun's philosophy of history*. Chicago, IL: The University of Chicago Press.

Mankiw, G. (2003). *Macroeconomics* (5th ed.). New York, NY: Worth Publishers.

Mariani, A.-M., Saal, D. S., & Battisti, G. (2009). The impact of Islamic banking on the cost efficiency and productivity change of Malaysian commercial banks. *Applied Economics*.

Marquis, M. H. (1996). Full employment and monetary policy neutrality. In *Monetary Theory and Policy* (pp. 170–198). St. Paul, MN: West Publishing Co..

Martinez-Alier, J. (1987). Methodological individualism and inter-generational allocation. In *Ecological Economics, Energy, Environment and Society*. Oxford, UK: Basil Blackwell.

Marx, K. (1892). Capital, a critique of political economy vol. II: The process of circulation of capital. (F. Engels, Ed.). Moscow, Russia: Progress Publishers.

Masson, P. R., Krueger, T. H., & Turtleboom, B. G. (Eds.). (1997). *EMU and the international monetary system*. Washington, DC: International Monetary Fund.

Masud, M. K. (1995). Shatibi's life and works. In *Shatibi's Philosophy of Islamic law*. Kuala Lumpur, Malaysia: Islamic Book Trust.

Maturana, H. R., & Varela, F. J. (1980). *Autopoiesis and cognition: The realization of the living*. Dordrecht, The Netherlands: Reider. doi:10.1007/978-94-009-8947-4.

McGrath & Barney. D. (2012). Capital as money. New York: Kindle Books.

Mehmet, O. (1997). Al-Ghazali on social justice: Guidelines for a new world order from an early medieval scholar. *International Journal of Social Economics*, *24*(11), 1203–1218. doi:10.1108/03068299710193570.

Millennium Development Goals. (n.d.). Retrieved from http://www.undp.org/mdg/basics.shtml

Minford, P., & Peel, D. (1983). Rational expectations models: The basic method. In *Rational Expectations and the New Macroeconomics*. Oxford, UK: Martin Robertson.

Mittelman, J. H. (1988). What works in the third world? In Out From Underdevelopment, (pp. 159-186). Baskingstroke, UK: Houndmills.

Money Matters. (n.d.). Retrieved from http://www.themoneymasters.com/mra.htm

Moore, G. E. (1962). *Principia ethica*. Cambridge, UK: Cambridge University Press.

Mundell, R. A. (2000, November 8). *Presentation at the economic forum on one world, one currency: Destination or delusion?* Washington DC: International Monetary Fund. Retrieved from http://www.imf.org/external/np/tr/2000/tr001108.htm

Mydin, A. K., & Larbani, M. (2004). The gold dinar: The next component in Islamic economics, banking and finance. *Review of Islamic Economics*, *8*(1), 5–34.

Myrdal, G. (1957). An unexplained general traits of social reality. In *Rich Lands and Poor, the Road to World Prosperity*. New York, NY: Harper & Row.

Myrdal, G. (1958a). Ends and means in political economy. In Streeten, P. (Ed.), *Value in Social Theory, a Selection of Essays on Methodology by Gunnar Myrdal* (pp. 206–230). New York, NY: Harper & Brothers Publishers.

Myrdal, G. (1958b). The logical crux of all science. In Streeten, P. (Ed.), *Value in Social Theory, a Selection of Essays on Methodology by Gunnar Myrdal* (pp. 231–236). New York, NY: Harper & Brothers Publishers.

Myrdal, G. (1958c). The principle of cumulation. In Streeten, P. (Ed.), *Value in Social Theory, a Selection of Essays on Methodology by Gunnar Myrdal* (pp. 198–205). New York, NY: Harper & Brothers Publishers.

Myrdal, G. (1958d). *Value in social theory: A selection of essays on methodology by Gunnar Myrdal* (Streeten, P., Ed.). New York, NY: Harper & Brothers Publishers.

Myrdal, G. (1987). Utilitarianism and modern economics. In Feiwel, G. R. (Ed.), *Arrow and the Foundations of the Theory of Economic Policy* (pp. 273–278). London, UK: Macmillan.

Nasr, S. H. (1992). The Gnostic tradition. In *Science and Civilization in Islam*. New York, NY: Barnes & Noble.

Nightingale, D. V. (1982). *Workplace democracy: An inquiry into employee participation in Canadian work organizations* (pp. 165–169). Toronto, Canada: University of Toronto Press.

Nikaido, H. (1968). *Convex structure and economic theory*. New York: Academic Press, Inc..

Noreha, H., Ahmed, M. S., & Choudhury, M. A. (2011). Circular causation relations using Malaysian data on money and real GDP. In Choudhury, M. A. (Ed.), *Islamic Economics and Finance, an Epistemological Inquiry*. London: Emerald Publishing.

Nozick, R. (1974). Distributive justice. *Philosophy & Public Affairs*, 3.

Nozick, R. (2001). *Invariances: The structure of the objective world*. Cambridge, MA: The Belknap Press of the Harvard University Press.

O'Donnell, R. M. (1989). Types of probabilities and their measurement. In *Keynes: Philosophy, Economics & Politics* (pp. 81–105). London, UK: Macmillan Press Ltd..

Overman, E. S. (1988). *Methodology and epistemology for social science: Selected papers of Donald T. Campbell*. Chicago, IL: The University of Chicago Press.

Palan, R. (2000). New trends in global political economy. In Palan, R. (Ed.), *Global Political Economy, Contemporary Theories* (pp. 1–18). London, UK: Routledge.

Parsons, T., & Smelser, N. (1956). *Economy and society*. London: Routledge & Kegan Paul.

Patterson, S. (2010). *The quants*. London, UK: Random House Business Books.

Paul, E. F., Miller, F. D. Jr, & Paul, J. (Eds.). (1995). *The just society*. Cambridge, UK: Cambridge University Press.

Pham, H. (2009). *Continuous-time stochastic control and optimization with financial applications*. Berlin, Germany: Springer. doi:10.1007/978-3-540-89500-8.

Phelps, E. S. (1989). Distributive justice. In Eatwell, J., Milgate, M., & Newman, P. (Eds.), *The New Palgrave: Social Economics*. New York, NY: WW. Norton.

Pindyck, R. S., & Rubinfeld, D. L. (2001). *Microeconomics*. Upper Saddle River, NJ: Prentice-Hall, Inc..

Pogge, T. W. (1995). Three problems with contractarian-consequentialist ways of assessing social institutions. In Paul, E. F., Miller, F. D. Jr, & Paul, J. (Eds.), *The Just Society* (pp. 221–242). Cambridge, UK: Cambridge University Press.

Polanyi, K. (1957). *The great transformation*. Boston, MA: Beacon Press.

Popkin, R. H., & Stroll, A. (2003). Hume's analysis of causation. In *Philosophy* (pp. 265–275). Oxford, UK: Made Simple Books.

Popper, K. (1978). Natural selection and the emergence of mind. *Dialectica*, *22*(3), 339–355. doi:10.1111/j.1746-8361.1978.tb01321.x.

Popper, K. (1998). *Conjectures and refutations: The growth of scientific knowledge*. London, UK: Routledge & Kegan Paul.

Popper, K. (2004). *The logic of scientific discovery*. London, UK: Routledge.

Prigogine, I. (1980). *From being to becoming*. San Francisco, CA: W.H. Freeman.

Primavesi, A. (2000). *Sacred gaia*. London, UK: Routledge. doi:10.4324/9780203451786.

Quinton, A. (1989). *Utilitarian ethics*. La Salle, IL: Open Court.

Radnitzky, G., & Bartley, W. W. III, (Eds.). (1988). *Evolutionary epistemology, rationality and the sociology of knowledge*. La Salle, IL: Open Court.

Ramsey, F. P. (1928). A mathematical theory of savings. *The Economic Journal*, *38*(152), 543–550. doi:10.2307/2224098.

Rawls, J. (1971). *A theory of justice*. Cambridge, MA: Harvard University Press.

Resnick, S. A., & Wolff, R. D. (1987). A Marxian theory. In *Knowledge and Class*. Chicago, IL: University of Chicago Press.

Resnick, S. A., & Wolff, R. D. (1987). *Knowledge and class: A Marxian critique of political economy*. Chicago, IL: The University of Chicago Press.

Rist, C. (1940). *History of monetary and credit theory from john law to the present day*. London, UK: Allen Unwin.

Romer, P. M. (1986). Increasing returns and long-run growth. *The Journal of Political Economy*, *94*, 1002–1037. doi:10.1086/261420.

Rosenlicht, M. (1968). *Introduction to analysis*. New York, NY: Dover Publications, Inc..

Rucker, R. (1982). Large cardinals. In *Infinity and the Mind* (pp. 273–286). New York, NY: Bantam Books.

Rucker, R. (1983). *Infinity and the mind*. New York, NY: Bantam New Books.

Russell, B. (1903). Relations. In *Principles of Mathematics* (pp. 95–100). New York, NY: W.W. Norton.

Russell, B. (2001). *The problems of philosophy*. Oxford, UK: Oxford University Press.

Said, E. (1978). *Orientalism*. New York, NY: Random House.

Saif & Dadang. (2011). Treating return of mudharabah time deposit as investment instrument: A utilization of artificial neural networks (ANNS). *Humanomics: International Journal of Systems and Ethics, 27*(2).

Samuelson, P. A. (1949). International factor-price equalization once again. *The Economic Journal*, 59.

Sauer, J. B. (2002). Meaning, method and social science, a realist account. *Humanomics: International Journal of Systems and Ethics, 18*(3/4), 101–113.

Saving, T. R. (1977). A theory of the money supply with competitive banking. *Journal of Monetary Economics, 3*, 289–303. doi:10.1016/0304-3932(77)90023-X.

Schiller, R. J. (2000). *Irrational exuberance*. New York, NY: Broadway Books.

Schumacher, E. F. (1973). *Small is beautiful, economics as if people mattered*. London, UK: ABACUS.

Schumpeter, J. A. (1961). *The theory of economic development*. Cambridge, MA: Harvard University Press.

Schumpeter, J. S. (1968). The scholastic doctors and the philosophers of natural law. In *History of Economic Analysis*. New York: Oxford University Press.

Seidel, V. J. (1986). *Kant, respect and injustice: The limits of liberal moral theory*. London, UK: Routledge & Kegan Paul.

Sen, A. (1977). Rational fools: A critique of the behavioural foundations of economic theory. *Philosophy & Public Affairs*, 6.

Sen, A. (1985). The moral standing of the market. In Paul, E. F., Paul, J., & Miller, F. D. (Eds.), *Ethics and Economics*. Oxford, UK: Basil and Blackwell.

Sen, A. (1986). Exchange entitlement. In *Poverty and Famines, an Essay on Entitlement and Deprivation* (pp. 167–173). Oxford, UK: Clarendon Press.

Sen, A. (1989). Justice. In Eatwell, J., Milgate, M., & Newman, P. (Eds.), *New Palgrave: Social Economics*. New York, NY: W.W. Norton.

Sen, A. (1990). Freedom and consequences. In *On Ethics and Economics* (pp. 58–89). London, UK: Basil Blackwell.

Sen, A. (1999). Functioning and well-being. In *Commodities and Capabilities* (pp. 17–21). New Delhi, India: Oxford University Press.

Shackle, G. L. S. (1971). *Epistemics & economics*. Cambridge, UK: Cambridge University Press.

Shackle, G. L. S. (1972). *Epistemics & economics: A critique of economic theory*. Cambridge, UK: Cambridge University Press.

Shipler, D. (1986). *Arabs and Jews*. New York, NY: Times Books.

Simon, H. (1957). *Models of man*. New York, NY: John Wiley & Sons.

Simon, H. A. (1960). Decision making and organizational design. In Pugh, D. S. (Ed.), *Organization Theory* (pp. 202–223). Hammondsworth, UK: Penguin Books.

Simon, H. A. (1952-53). A behavioural model of rational choice. In *Models of Man*. New York, NY: John Wiley & Sons, Inc..

Singe, H. W., & Ansari, J. A. (1988). Forty years of changing thought on development problems. In *Rich and Poor Countries*. London, UK: Unwin Hyman Inc..

Siven, C. (1978). The interaction between multiplier and inflationary processing. In Strom, S., & Werin, L. (Eds.), *Topics in Disequilibrium Economics*. London, UK: Macmillan Press Ltd..

Slavin, S. (n.d.). Retrieved from http://findarticles.com/p/articles/mi_m1272/is_n2586_v122/ai_14995070/

Smullyan, R. M. (1992). *Godel's incompleteness theorems*. New York: Oxford University Press.

Solow, R. (1980). *Growth theory, an exposition*. Oxford, UK: Oxford University Press.

Soros, G. (2000). Reflexivity in financial markets, reflexivity in history. In *Open Society* (pp. 59–90). New York: Public Affairs.

South Commission. (1990). *The challenge to the south*. Oxford, UK: Oxford University Press.

Sraffa, P. (1932, March). Dr. Hayek on money and capital. *The Economic Journal*, 42. doi:10.2307/2223735.

Stigler, G. J. (1970). The influence of events and policies on economic theory. In Rima, I. H. (Ed.), *Readings in the History of Economic Theory*. New York: Holt, Rinehart & Winston, Inc..

Stiglitz, J. E. (2003). *Globalization and its discontents*. New York, NY: W.W. Norton.

Streeten, P. (1981). From growth to basic needs. In Streeten, P. (Ed.), *Development Perspectives*. New York: St. Martin's Press.

Streeten, P. (1994). Positive and normative political economy and normative political economy. In *Strategies for Human Development, Global Poverty and Unemployment*. Copenhagen, Denmark: Handelshojskolens Forlag.

Streeten, P. A. (1981). *Development perspectives*. London, UK: Macmillan.

Sztompka, P. (1974). Functional-subsystemic analysis. In *System and Functions, Towards a Theory of Society* (pp. 124–134). New York, NY: Academic Press.

Sztompka, P. (1974). *System and function, towards a theory of society*. New York, NY: Academic Press.

Sztompka, P. (1974). Systemic models in functional analysis. In *System and Functions, Towards a Theory of Society* (pp. 47–57). New York, NY: Academic Press.

Sztompka, P. (1991). *Society in action: The theory of social becoming*. Chicago, IL: The University of Chicago Press.

Sztompka, P. (1991). The model of social becoming. In *Society in Action, the Theory of Social Becoming* (pp. 87–120). Chicago, IL: The University of Chicago Press.

Taleb, N. N. (2007). *The black swan: The impact of the highly improbable*. New York: Random House.

Taylor, O. H. (1967). *Economics and liberalism*. Cambridge, MA: Harvard University Press.

Temkin, L. S. (1995). Justice and equality: Some questions about scope. In Paul, E. F., Miller, F. D. Jr, & Paul, J. (Eds.), *The Just Society* (pp. 72–104). Cambridge, UK: Cambridge University Press. doi:10.1017/S0265052500004684.

The Times. (2013, April 16). Islamic finance. *The Times.*

Thurow, L. (1983). *Dangerous currents: The state of economics*. New York, NY: Random House.

Tisdell, C. (1989). Imperialism, economic dependence and development: A brief review of aspects of economic thought and theory. *Humanomics*, *5*(2). doi:10.1108/eb006093.

Tobin, J. (1958). Liquidity preference as behavior towards risk. *The Review of Economic Studies*, *26*(1), 65–86. doi:10.2307/2296205.

Tobin, J. (1963). Commercial banks as creators of 'money. In Carson, D. (Ed.), *Banking and Monetary Studies* (pp. 408–419). Homewood, IL: Irwin.

Tullock, G. (1976). Competing moneys. *Journal of Money, Credit and Banking*, 7.

Uittenbogaard, A. (n.d.). *A brief history of monotheism, from the desert to the grand unification*. Retrieved from http://www.abarim publications.com/Book_Review/index.html#.UWpA1rWmh30

United Nations Development Program (UNDP). (1999). *Human development report*. New York, NY: Oxford University Press.

Usmani, M. T. (2004). *An introduction to Islamic finance*. Karachi, Pakistan: Maktaba Ma'Ariful Qur'an.

Usmani, M.T. (n.d.). Retrieved from http://www.failaka.com/downloads/Usmani_SukukApplications.pdf

Vadilo, U. T. (2002). The architecture of the gold dinar economy: An academic perspective. In *Viability of the Islamic Dinar* (pp. 335–360). Kuala Lumpur, Malaysia: International Islamic University Malaysia, Research Center.

Vanek, J. (1971). The participatory economy in a theory of social evolution. In *The Participatory Economy: an Evolutionary and a Strategy for Development* (pp. 51–89). Ithaca, NY: Cornell University Press.

Venieris, Y. P., & Sebold, F. D. (1977). The Keynesian revolution. In *Macroeconomics, Models & Policy* (pp. 336–353). New York, NY: John Wiley & Sons.

Ventelou, B. (2005). Keynesian economics and the American polity. In *Millennial Keynes* (pp. 3–37). Armonk, NY: M.E. Sharpe.

Vickery, W. S. (1960). Utility, strategy, and social decision rules. *The Quarterly Journal of Economics*, *74*, 507–535. doi:10.2307/1884349.

Vogel, E. F., & Hayes, S. L. (1998). *Islamic law and finance: Religion, risk and return, Arab and Islamic law*. The Hague, The Netherlands: Kluwer Law International.

von Bohm-Bawerk, E. (1890). *Capital and interest*. London, UK: William Smart.

Von Mises, L. (1976). *The ultimate foundation of economic science*. Kansas City, KS: Sheed Andrews & McMeel.

Von Mises, L. (1981). The return to sound money. In *The Theory of Money and Credit*. Indianapolis, IN: Liberty Fund.

Waliullah, S. (n.d.). *Hujjat allah al-baligah*. Beirut, Lebanon. *Dar Al-Marifat.*.

Walker, M., & Unterhalter, E. (2010). The capability approach: Its potential for work in education. In Walker, M., & Unterhalter, E. (Eds.), *Amartya Sen's Capability Approach and Social Justice in Education*. London, UK: Palgrave Macmillan.

Wallerstein, I. (1974). *The modern world systems theory: Capitalist agriculture and the origins of the European world-economy in the sixteenth century*. New York, NY: Academic Press.

Wallerstein, I. (1998). Spacetime as the basis of knowledge. In Bordo, O. F. (Ed.), *People's Participation, Challenges Ahead* (pp. 43–62). New York, NY: Apex Press.

Whittaker, J. K. (1987). The limits of organization revisited. In Feiwel, G. R. (Ed.), *Arrow and the Foundations of the Theory of Economic Policy*. London, UK: Macmillan.

Wicksell, K. (1934). A mathematical analysis of Dr. Akerman's problem. In Newman, P. (Ed.), *Readings in Mathematical Economics: Capital and Growth II* (pp. 3–28). Baltimore, MD: The Johns Hopkins Press.

Wiener, N. (1966). *God & golem, Inc.: A comment on certain points where cybernetics impinges on religion*. Boston, MA: The MIT Press.

Witham, L. (2010). *Marketplace of the gods: How economics explains religion*. Oxford, UK: Oxford University Press. doi:10.1093/acprof:oso/9780195394757.001.0001.

Wood, G. (Ed.). (1998). *Money, prices and the real economy*. Cheltenham, UK: Edward Elgar.

World Bank. (2000). *World development report 2000-2001*. New York: Oxford University Press.

Wunsch, G. (1988a). Theories of causation. In *Causal Theory and Causal Modeling, Beyond Description in the Social Sciences* (pp. 21–66). Leuven, Belgium: Leuven University Press.

Wunsch, G. (1988b). Causal modeling in the social sciences. In *Causal Theory and Causal Modeling, Beyond Description in the Social Sciences* (pp. 169–196). Leuven, Belgium: Leuven University Press.

Xuemoue, W., & Dinghe, G. (1999). Pansystemic cybernetics: Framework, methodology and development. *Kybernetes: International Journal of Cybernetics. Systems and Management Studies*, *28*(6/7), 679–694.

Yaeger, L. B. (1997). *The fluttering veil: Essays on monetary disequilibrium*. Indianapolis, IN: The Liberty Press.

Yeager, L. B. (1983, Spring). Stable money and free-market currencies. *The Cato Journal*, 305–326.

Zohar, D., & Marshall, I. (2004). *Spiritual capital*. San Francisco, CA: Berrett-Koehler Publishers, Inc..

Zsolnai. (2002). New agenda for business ethics. In L. Zsolnai (Ed.), *Ethics in the Economy, Handbook of Business Ethics*. New York, NY: Peter Lang.

About the Author

Masudul Alam Choudhury is Professor of Economics in the Department of Economics and Finance, College of Economics and Political Science (CEPS), Sultan Qaboos University, Muscat, Sultanate of Oman. He is also the International Chair and a founder member of the Postgraduate Program in Islamic Economics and Finance, Trisakti University, Indonesia. Professor Choudhury taught economics for twenty-two years in Cape Breton University, Sydney, Nova Scotia, Canada before taking his retirement. He now continues on to conduct advanced research and teaches at all levels of pedagogy. His research area of focus and teaching at the doctoral level is economics and epistemology of unity of knowledge, and its functional ontological conceptualization and application to the world-system in diverse areas. In this domain are included political economy, economic theory, financial issues, and integral relations between science and society. His methodological approach is system-oriented and mathematical while invoking philosophy of science and empirical application. Professor Choudhury has published profusely in refereed journals and many book with leading scholarly publishers. His above-mentioned focus has prevailed in all such academic outlets.

Index

D

E

F

G

H

J

K

L

M

N

R

S

T

U

V

W

Z

www.ingramcontent.com/pod-product-compliance
Lightning Source LLC
LaVergne TN
LVHW062110200926
848484LV00007B/1633

* 9 7 8 1 4 6 6 6 4 6 4 3 8 *